The
Supreme Court
Yearbook
1997–1998

The justices of the Supreme Court. From left are Justices Clarence Thomas, Antonin Scalia, Sandra Day O'Connor, Anthony M. Kennedy, David H. Souter, Stephen G. Breyer, and John Paul Stevens; Chief Justice William H. Rehnquist; and Justice Ruth Bader Ginsburg.

The
Supreme Court
Yearbook

1997–1998

Kenneth Jost

Congressional Quarterly Inc.
Washington, D.C.

FEB 1 8 1999

Photo credits: cover, 286, R. Michael Jenkins; frontispiece, 267, Ken Heinen; 3, 30,
44, 64, AP/Wide World Photos; 33, Court TV; 37, *Baton Rouge Advocate;* 44, *Bangor
Daily News;* 48, 52, Reuters; 56, *Los Angeles Times;* 60, United Mine Workers of America;
138, William Spain; 270, 281, 284, Collection, the Supreme Court Historical Society;
273, Joseph McCary; 277, Supreme Court; 282, White House.

Printed in the United States of America

ISBN   1-56802-410-X (pbk)
ISBN   1-56802-411-8
ISSN   1054-2701

Contents

Preface

The Supreme Court's 1997–1998 term got off to a slow start, but it ended with memorable decisions on sexual harassment, discrimination against people with the AIDS virus, and separation of powers between Congress and the president. The Court made it easier to hold employers responsible for sexual misconduct in the workplace, extended legal protections to people with HIV infection, and nullified a law giving the president the power to veto individual items in congressional money bills.

The reporters who cover the Court had a busy few weeks digesting and analyzing those decisions before settling into a quiet summer and awaiting the start of a new term. But as the term was set to begin, the Supreme Court press corps suffered a great loss: the death of the Court's longtime public information officer, Toni House.

Toni worked as a reporter for the *Washington Star,* covering everything from embassy parties to police and local courts, for fifteen years before the newspaper's demise in 1981. A year later, Chief Justice Warren E. Burger improbably chose this somewhat brash, somewhat flashy journalist to head the office responsible for the care and feeding of the press.

The office itself is improbable. The Court issues almost nothing by way of information except its written opinions. The justices themselves rarely talk to the media and have resisted all proposals to televise Court sessions. Nonetheless, within the constraints of her position, Toni was helpful, knowledgeable, efficient, and ever enthusiastic.

Toni died of lung cancer at the age of fifty-five on September 29, 1998. Chief Justice William H. Rehnquist called her "a popular presence around the Court." All nine justices attended a memorial service held in St. Matthew's Cathedral in Washington the day after the new term began.

In each of the previous editions, we have thanked Toni and her staff for their help in covering the Court. Now, Toni, thanks one last time for all that you did in sixteen years in helping the press and public understand the Court. You will be missed.

This ninth edition of *The Supreme Court Yearbook* again includes an overview of the term (Chapter 1), detailed accounts of some of the major decisions (Chapter 2), summaries of each of the Court's decisions (Chapter 3), a preview of the coming term (Chapter 4), and excerpts from the major decisions (Appendix). As before, I want to thank the many lawyers, reporters, and experts whose comments and coverage help inform my work. At Congressional Quarterly Books, thanks to Talia Greenberg for her attentive editing and diligent production work. And, as always, thanks to Katie and to Nicole and Andrew for their love and support.

1 An Interesting Term

Beth Ann Faragher, Kimberly Ellerth, and Joseph Oncale came from different parts of the country and different backgrounds. They had never met, but they shared a common experience. All three said they were victims of sexual harassment in their jobs.

Faragher, a former lifeguard, said she and her female coworkers were constantly leered at, propositioned, and groped by male supervisors. Ellerth, a former sales representative for a clothing manufacturer, claimed she had to endure clumsy come-ons from a company vice president. And Oncale said he was taunted, threatened, and assaulted by male supervisors on an offshore oil rig.

After leaving their jobs, all three decided to go to court, suing their former employers under the federal civil rights law that prohibits discrimination because of sex. But each faced difficult legal hurdles. Faragher had never complained to city officials about the supervisors' behavior. Ellerth's supervisor had gotten Ellerth her scheduled raise despite her spurning his alleged advances. And Oncale faced judicial disagreement about whether sexual harassment applied to behavior between people of the same sex.

All three cases reached the Supreme Court in its 1997–1998 term. Twelve years earlier the Court had opened the door to sexual harassment suits against employers in federal court, but the justices had said little about the issue since then. Lower courts were divided and employers and employees uncertain about the legal rules on the subject. All turned toward the Court for answers.

The Court's answers, when they came, drew remarkably widespread approval. Yes, the Court ruled unanimously, federal law prohibits same-sex sexual harassment. Yes, the Court said in a 7–2 decision on the last day of the term, employers may have to pay damages for sexual harassment even if they did not know about the behavior. Yes, the Court said in another 7–2 ruling on the same day, an employee may sue for sexual harassment even for unfulfilled threats to deny a raise or promotion.

Women's groups and civil rights organizations applauded the rulings. Employers said they were glad to have some clear rules. Legal commentators noted the remarkable degree of agreement among the justices.

The Court had one other sexual harassment case before it during the 1997–1998 term. The victim was a former high school student, Alida Star Gebser, in the small Texas town of Lago Vista. Gebser was seduced by her social studies teacher. The fifteen-month affair was undisputed, and the legal rules against the teacher's behavior unmistakable. When the girl and her mother sued the school district, however, lower courts said no. The school district could not be held responsible, they said, because no one in an official position knew about the affair.

Surprisingly, perhaps, the Court said that Gebser in fact had no claim against the school district. By a 5–4 vote, the justices said that the law Gebser used to get into court did not allow her to hold the school district liable for the teacher's offense unless a ranking official knew about it and did nothing to stop it.

Many people found the results paradoxical at the least: an underaged high school student had less legal protection from sexual harassment than adults in the workplace. Whatever one thought of the rulings, the decisions exemplified the pattern—or lack of one—in the Court's rulings in the 1997–1998 term.

Ideological lines were often blurred and voting alliances shuffled in the term's ninety decisions. Conservative justices provided critical votes for expanding civil rights protections and sometimes found themselves speaking up for the rights of criminal defendants. Meanwhile, liberal justices cast significant votes in some cases to narrow constitutional rights or expand presidential power.

"The standard ideological boundaries broke down," Eugene Volokh, a conservative constitutional law expert at UCLA Law School, commented afterward. Burt Neuborne, a professor at New York University Law School and former national legal director of the American Civil Liberties Union, agreed: "You got some strange bedfellows this term."

Still, the Court's predominantly conservative orientation was reflected in the justices' voting pattern, which showed a continuing alignment among the five conservatives on one side and the four liberal-leaning justices on the other. *(See Table 1-1.)* The conservative domination could also be seen in many of the decisions, such as the 5–4 split in Gebser's sexual harassment suit. That was one of six one-vote decisions where the Court's conservatives formed the majority: Chief Justice William H. Rehnquist and Justices Sandra Day O'Connor, Antonin Scalia, Anthony M. Kennedy, and Clarence Thomas. "The voting patterns indicate that there's still a 5–4 operating majority for the conservative justices," Neuborne observed.

The Court's left-of-center justices—John Paul Stevens, David H. Souter, Ruth Bader Ginsburg, and Stephen G. Breyer—prevailed in closely divided cases only by pulling over one of the conservatives. As in years past, Kennedy and O'Connor provided the critical fifth vote for some of the term's liberal decisions. But, in the year's most surprising division, the Court's most conservative justice, Thomas, led a five-vote majority that for the first time ever struck down a government forfeiture as a violation of the Eighth Amendment's prohibition against "excessive fines."

Court watchers on all sides agreed that the rulings buttressed the justices' frequent insistence that the ideological labels put on them are often

All nine Supreme Court justices and retired justice Byron R. White leave Grace Covenant Presbyterian Church in Richmond, Virginia, after the funeral of retired justice Lewis F. Powell Jr. Powell, who served on the Court from 1972 to 1987, died August 24, 1998, at the age of ninety.

Table 1-1   Justices' Alignment, 1997–1998 Term

This table shows the percentage of decisions in which each justice agreed with each of the other members of the Court. Of the ninety signed opinions on the merits for the 1997–1998 term, forty-three (or 47.8 percent) were unanimous.

The voting pattern shows the Court's continuing division into a predominantly conservative wing consisting of Chief Justice Rehnquist and Justices O'Connor, Scalia, Kennedy, and Thomas and a left-of-center bloc consisting of Justices Stevens, Souter, Ginsburg, and Breyer. The voting blocs were somewhat less cohesive, however, than in the 1996–1997 term.

On the conservative side, for example, each of the justices voted with each of the other four at least 84 percent of the time except for Scalia and Kennedy. Their alignment dropped to 78 percent from 82 percent in the previous term. On the liberal side, each justice voted with each of the other three at least 81 percent of the time, but the alignments were not quite so close as in the previous term. Stevens and Ginsburg, for example, voted together 81 percent of the time this term, compared with 84 percent in the 1996–1997 term.

Two pairs of justices—Rehnquist-Kennedy and Scalia-Thomas—tied for the most closely aligned, voting together in 92 percent of the cases. But Scalia and Thomas separated more often than in the previous term, when they voted together in all but one case. Among the liberals, Ginsburg and Breyer continued their close alignment, voting together in 87 percent of the cases.

Stevens and Scalia voted together the least often, agreeing in only one-fifth of the nonunanimous decisions; Stevens and Thomas voted together somewhat more often, in 27 percent of the divided rulings. In the previous term, they had agreed in many fewer— only one-tenth—of the divided rulings.

	Rehnquist	Stevens	O'Connor	Scalia	Kennedy	Souter	Thomas	Ginsburg	Breyer
Rehnquist		31.9	76.1	63.8	85.1	42.6	70.2	59.6	42.6
		64.4	87.6	85.6	92.2	70.0	84.4	78.9	70.0
Stevens	31.9		34.8	21.3	42.6	63.8	27.7	63.8	72.3
	64.4		66.3	58.9	70.0	81.1	62.2	81.1	85.6
O'Connor	76.1	34.8		69.6	74.0	47.8	71.8	45.7	47.8
	87.6	66.3		84.3	86.6	73.0	85.4	68.5	73.0
Scalia	63.8	21.3	69.6		58.7	37.0	85.1	61.7	32.0
	85.6	58.9	84.3		77.8	66.7	92.2	64.4	64.4
Kennedy	85.1	42.6	74.0	58.7		55.3	63.8	63.0	53.2
	92.2	70.0	86.6	77.8		76.7	81.1	80.0	75.6
Souter	42.6	63.8	47.8	37.0	55.3		36.2	68.1	76.6
	70.0	81.1	73.0	66.7	76.7		66.7	83.3	85.6
Thomas	70.2	27.7	71.8	85.1	63.8	36.2		38.3	29.8
	84.4	62.2	85.4	92.2	81.1	66.7		67.8	63.3
Ginsburg	59.6	63.8	45.7	61.7	63.0	68.1	38.3		74.5
	78.9	81.1	68.5	64.4	80.0	83.3	67.8		86.7
Breyer	42.6	72.3	47.8	32.0	53.2	76.6	29.8	74.5	
	70.0	85.6	73.0	64.4	75.6	85.6	63.3	86.7	

Note: The first number in each cell represents the percentage of agreement in divided decisions. The second number represents the percentage of agreement in all signed opinions.

misleading. "This Court has a core group that self-consciously see themselves as not bound by ideological motive," said Chai Feldblum, a professor at Georgetown University Law Center and liberal advocate in gay and disability rights cases. John Roberts, a lawyer with the Washington firm Covington & Burling and former law clerk to Rehnquist, agreed. "This Court approaches cases like judges," he said. "They move very cautiously, very incrementally. They don't move in sudden lurches, and you tend to get very precise, carefully reasoned opinions."

The blurring of the Court's ideological divisions stemmed in part from the relative lack of sharply drawn legal disputes during the term. Conservative justices had flexed their muscles over the past few years by limiting affirmative action and racially motivated redistricting, curbing Congress's power to intrude on the states, and easing the restrictions on government support for religious activities. But the Court had no full-blown decisions on any of those issues during the term. And, in the term's most significant constitutional confrontation, the justices divided across their normal ideological lines to strike down the Line Item Veto Act, which gave the president the power to disapprove individual items in spending bills passed by Congress.

Instead, as several Supreme Court reporters emphasized in their end-of-term wrap-ups, the justices confronted disputes where ideology mattered less and practicalities more. The Court consciously laid down rules aimed at discouraging sexual harassment in the workplace by giving employers incentives to adopt antiharassment policies and employees incentives to use any complaint procedures provided. It ruled that people who have the AIDS virus are entitled to legal protections against discrimination even if they have no visible symptoms. And it said people are entitled to the protections of the attorney-client privilege even after they die.

On those and other issues, the Court "captured a societal consensus," the *Washington Post*'s Joan Biskupic wrote at the end of the term. "It was as if they looked at the range of American beliefs and drew a circle around the center."

Overall, though, the Court continued to wield its power to move in a conservative direction—favoring law enforcement in criminal cases, narrowing access to the courts, and somewhat expanding protection for private property. "The close decisions are continuing to move to the right," said David Cole, a professor at Georgetown University Law Center and frequent advocate before the Court on First Amendment issues. "They are disputes over whether to do something very conservative or to maintain the status quo. They are rarely disputes over whether to do something progressive or maintain the status quo."

The Conservative Justices

Chief Justice Rehnquist himself took note of the Court's somewhat sleepy nine months when he spoke to a meeting of federal judges the day after the term ended. "It's been an interesting term," Rehnquist told the judges, "if not quite so full of highly charged cases as last term."

Indeed, the justices had ended the previous term in June 1997 with a bang. In their final days, they threw out a major provision of a popular gun control law, emphatically rejected any constitutional right to physician-assisted suicide, and eased the ban on using tax funds for educational services at parochial schools. Each of those cases had reflected conservative positions long favored by Rehnquist: supporting states' rights, curbing expansions of individual rights, and relaxing the rules on separation of church and state.

The Court steered a more moderate course in the 1997–1998 term, with the help of some uncustomarily centrist opinions and votes from Rehnquist. Most tellingly, he joined in the end-of-term decisions that tightened the rules on sexual harassment in the workplace, leaving his conservative colleagues Scalia and Thomas in dissent. Earlier, he voted out of character to help produce rulings that gave voters the right to sue the Federal Election Commission for failing to enforce campaign finance disclosure laws and that eased restrictions on habeas corpus petitions by convicted inmates.

One statistic—the number of dissenting votes—helped document Rehnquist's seeming shift. Kennedy was once again the justice who cast the smallest number of dissenting votes, but Rehnquist cast the second lowest number—one less than O'Connor, who normally followed behind Kennedy in that position. *(See Table 1-2.)* In years past, Kennedy and O'Connor most often cast the "swing votes" on the Court; this term, Rehnquist did too.

The pattern induced some speculation that Rehnquist, in his eleventh term as chief justice, was acting more as an institutional leader than a conservative crusader. "He's a little less ideological than he used to be," Neuborne said. Others, however, thought it was not Rehnquist but the Court itself that had moved. "He has remained consistent in his views," Roberts said. "The Court has moved toward him."

Rehnquist's opinions could support either view. A longtime critic of habeas corpus, he wrote the 7–2 decision that allowed an Arizona death row inmate to get a new hearing on his effort to block his execution on grounds of mental incompetency—in the face of the 1996 law Congress passed to try to curb successive habeas corpus petitions. But he also wrote the main opinion in an Ohio case that blocked a death row inmate's due process challenge to the state's executive clemency procedures. And he wrote the unanimous opinion in a California case that barred a bid by death row inmates to block the state from using expedited procedures to dispose of their federal habeas corpus challenges.

Rehnquist wrote for the Court in two other significant pro–law enforcement criminal law decisions. In one unanimous ruling, Rehnquist rejected any requirement that police officers show some special need before executing a no-knock search warrant that results in damage to property. In the

Table 1-2   Justices in Dissent, 1997–1998 Term

Justice	8–1/7–1	7–2	6–3	5–4	Total	Percentage
	Division on Court					
Rehnquist	—	—	3	6	9	10.0
Stevens	6	3	5	9	23	25.6
O'Connor	—	1	4	5	10	11.2
Scalia	—	5	8	8	21	23.3
Kennedy	1	—	1	2	4	4.4
Souter	1	1	3	9	14	15.6
Thomas	—	5	7	4	16	17.8
Ginsburg	—	2	7	10	19	21.1
Breyer	—	3	4	7	14	15.6

Note: The totals reflect cases where justices dissented in whole or in part from the major legal holding or effect of a decision. There were ninety signed opinions in cases decided on the merits during the 1997–1998 term. Because of a recusal, Justice O'Connor participated in eighty-nine cases.

other, he wrote the majority opinion in a decision that permitted the government to prosecute someone who had already been fined in a civil proceeding for the same conduct; the decision scrapped a 1989 precedent that had barred such a prosecution under the Double Jeopardy Clause.

Among the rest of his eleven majority opinions, Rehnquist wrote for the conservative bloc in a 5–4 decision sustaining part of a property rights challenge to a program, operating in all fifty states and the District of Columbia, to help pay for legal aid to the poor. But he also wrote the opinion in the closely watched case upholding the attorney-client privilege after someone's death; three of the Court's conservatives dissented from the ruling, which rejected an effort by Independent Counsel Kenneth Starr to get notes from the lawyer for the late White House deputy counsel Vincent Foster.

Rehnquist's most noteworthy dissenting opinion came in the final week's ruling that extended the protections of the Americans with Disabilities Act to people infected with HIV, the human immunodeficiency virus that causes AIDS. In contrast to the majority, Rehnquist found no basis for treating a person with HIV as disabled just because he or she might spread the disease to a sexual partner or, for a woman, to a fetus if she became pregnant. Those are "voluntary choices," Rehnquist said, not the kinds of physical limits that are properly treated as disabilities under the law.

It was Kennedy who spoke for the majority in the HIV case, and the substance and tone of his opinion differed markedly from Rehnquist's legalistic approach. In a portion of his opinion that he summarized at length from the bench, Kennedy traced in medical detail what he termed "the pervasive, and invariably fatal, course of the disease." HIV disease, he wrote, "must be regarded as a physiological disorder . . . from the moment of infection." And, he continued, there was "little difficulty" in concluding that it impaired a person's reproductive ability as well as any number of what the disabilities rights law called "major life activities."

Kennedy's ten majority opinions included two others that expanded civil rights protections: the ruling in the Ellerth sexual harassment case and an earlier decision tightening protections for older workers under federal age-discrimination laws. In both of those decisions, Kennedy rejected pleas by businesses to limit their obligations to workers under federal civil rights law. In the age discrimination case the Court enforced, 6–3, a law protecting older workers' rights to bring suit after being fired even if they signed a waiver of any legal claims. The law set up "strict" rules governing such waivers, Kennedy wrote, "and we are bound to take Congress at its word."

Among his other majority opinions were two in habeas corpus cases. The rulings differed in result and tone. In one Kennedy led a 5–4 liberal majority that protected the right of convicted inmates to bring habeas corpus pleas to the Court itself—again in the face of the 1996 law limiting habeas corpus procedures. In the other he led a 5–4 conservative majority that sharply upbraided the federal appeals court in California for a last-minute decision to grant a new trial to a death row inmate. He closed the opinion with a strongly worded call for "finality" in criminal cases. "[T]he State's interest in actual finality outweigh the prisoner's interest in obtaining yet another opportunity for review," Kennedy wrote.

Kennedy's most important other majority opinion came in a First Amendment case. He had a record of viewing First Amendment rights expansively, but this one posed a conflict between the rights of a government-owned broadcast network and those of a political candidate who sought access to a campaign debate being sponsored by the broadcaster. Kennedy rejected the candidate's claim in a 6–3 decision that warned that government-owned broadcasters would be less likely to hold such debates if they had to invite all qualified candidates.

As in years past, the centrist Kennedy felt obliged in some important cases to qualify his stance. In the line-item veto case, for example, he acknowledged the importance of controlling what he called "improvident spending" but voted nonetheless to strike down the law. In contrast, he joined the Court's conservatives in rejecting a constitutional rule to allow criminal defendants to introduce polygraph tests as evidence but wrote a separate opinion saying their ban in most states and federal courts was probably unwise.

Kennedy dissented in only four cases, marking at least his seventh straight year of casting the fewest dissenting votes of any of the justices. In two, he joined with three other conservatives in opposing expansions of defendants' rights. The first ruling made it harder for prosecutors to use a confession made by one defendant against a codefendant. The second was the forfeiture ruling, which barred the government from confiscating more than $350,000 in cash from a Los Angeles man who failed to report the currency as required when he was about to leave the country. Writing for the four dissenters, Kennedy sharply criticized the decision. "Money launderers will rejoice" in the implications of the ruling, he said.

In contrast to Rehnquist and Kennedy, O'Connor's opinions and votes showed if anything a modest shift to the right. Her nine majority opinions, along with one opinion for a four-justice plurality, took mostly conservative stances, and she wrote dissenting opinions from conservative perspectives in two of the term's most important cases: the HIV and attorney-client privilege cases. But she also wrote middle-ground opinions in other cases and parted with some of the conservatives in other rulings generally depicted as liberal in effect.

The final week showed both sides of O'Connor. Without writing opinions herself, she joined in the workplace sexual harassment rulings. Earlier in the week, though, she led the conservative majority in the 5–4 decision that all but closed the door on federal court suits by students against school districts for sexual harassment by teachers. O'Connor acknowledged that sexual harassment of students was "an all too common aspect of the educational experience," but she said that school districts could be liable only if guilty of "deliberate indifference" toward the conduct.

In the same week O'Connor wrote the main opinion in a ruling that struck down on property rights grounds a law aimed at protecting health benefits for retired coal miners. The law required financial contributions to the insurance fund from some companies no longer in the coal business. O'Connor agreed with the companies that what she termed the "severe, disproportionate, and extremely retroactive burden" on the companies amounted to an unconstitutional "taking" of the company's property without compensation. She wrote for four justices; Kennedy provided the fifth vote on a different ground—due process.

Critics have faulted O'Connor for what they view as a too frequent resort to split-the-difference opinions—most notably in affirmative action cases. This term she split the difference in a First Amendment challenge to a law requiring the National Endowment for the Arts to consider "decency" in awarding grants. O'Connor's opinion upheld the provision, but only after stripping it of much of its force by calling it largely advisory. The ruling prompted separate opinions from both sides. Conservatives Scalia and Thomas said she had "gutted" the law, while Souter determined it should be struck down as a violation of free speech.

O'Connor showed the same approach in other cases. She dissented in the HIV case but wrote a separate opinion distancing herself from much of Rehnquist's dissent. She similarly separated herself from Rehnquist's opinion rejecting the due process claim in the executive clemency case. In a separate concurrence, O'Connor said due process might impose requirements on the procedures used; three liberal justices—Souter, Ginsburg, and Breyer—joined her opinion.

In another fractured ruling, O'Connor wrote a pivotal opinion to reject a sex discrimination attack on the law governing citizenship for out-of-wedlock children with one citizen and one foreign parent. The law required a citizen father but not a citizen mother to take a special step for the child to become a citizen. When a Texas man and his Filipina-born daughter challenged the law, O'Connor said she doubted the constitutionality of the provision but—along with Kennedy—cast the critical vote to dismiss the suit on legal standing grounds.

In criminal law cases, O'Connor generally took pro–law enforcement positions. For example, she wrote the 5–4 decision on the last day of the term that rejected a double jeopardy challenge to the implementation of so-called "three-strikes" laws imposing longer sentences on defendants with two or more prior convictions. But she also cast the pivotal vote in the codefendant's confession case and joined two of the rulings easing restrictions on habeas corpus pleas.

O'Connor wrote the term's earliest major decision in a closely watched antitrust case. The unanimous ruling—issued in early November—made it easier for manufacturers or suppliers to set maximum prices to be charged by dealers. Maximum-price agreements, O'Connor wrote, were unlikely to harm "consumers or competition."

As in years past, Scalia and Thomas positioned themselves at the conservative end of the Court's ideological spectrum. They also continued their pattern of fairly close alignment with each other, voting together in 92 percent of the cases. As a result, they wrote majority opinions in fewer of the term's major decisions. They also wrote more separate or dissenting opinions than their conservative colleagues and often found themselves dissenting from 7–2 or 6–3 decisions that two or three of their conservative colleagues joined. For example, they were the lone dissenters in five of the ten cases decided by 7–2 votes.

Scalia's conservatism was apparent even in the one seemingly liberal ruling that he wrote during the term. He wrote the majority opinion in the Oncale case, recognizing same-sex sexual harassment on the job as a federal civil rights violation. The opinion was fairly short—only seven pages—and concluded with a cautionary passage. In same-sex cases, Scalia stressed, judges and juries should use "common sense" and "an appropriate sensitivity to social context" to distinguish between "simple teasing or roughhousing among members of the same sex" and conduct that a reasonable person would find "severely hostile or abusive."

In another short and unanimous opinion, Scalia wrote in a Pennsylvania case that the federal disabilities rights law applied to state prisons. The ruling was limited, though, to interpreting the statute. Scalia explained that the state had not properly raised a constitutional challenge to the law on the ground of states' rights.

Among the other of his ten majority opinions were two that reflected Scalia's efforts to narrow rules on access to federal courts. In one he wrote for a unanimous Court in rejecting a labor union's suit under federal labor law seeking damages from a company for alleged fraud in entering into a collective bargaining agreement. In the other he threw out an environmental group's suit against a Chicago-area steel company for violating a "right-to-know" law requiring disclosure of toxic chemicals used on site. The environmental group had no "redressable" injury, Scalia said, because the company had remedied the violation and the law did not provide for monetary damages.

In his only 5–4 opinion of the term Scalia straddled the fence between the Court's conservative and liberal blocs. The case involved a National Labor Relations Board (NLRB) rule severely limiting an employer's right to poll unionized workers to determine whether the union had lost majority support. Scalia's opinion upheld the policy but concluded the NLRB had applied it too strictly. There were two partial dissents. Rehnquist and three other conservatives dissented from the decision to uphold the policy, while Breyer and three other liberal justices said Scalia's opinion had "rewritten the rule . . . without adequate justification."

Scalia was far more prolific during the term in writing separate or dissenting opinions. Many of them were sharply written. He accused O'Connor of "gutting" the "decency clause" in the arts funding case. In habeas corpus cases, he charged the majority—as he put it in one of the dissents—with "judicial willfulness" by ignoring Congress's "obvious intent" to limit the procedures for ruling on pleas by convicted inmates. And, in his most extended dissent, Scalia argued for upholding the Line Item Veto Act on the ground that it did nothing more than recognize the president's long-standing discretion over spending money appropriated by Congress. The title of the bill, Scalia said, "has succeeded in faking out the Supreme Court."

While those dissenting opinions all reflected Scalia's judicial conservatism, he joined with liberals in dissenting from a pair of rulings on a recurrent criminal law issue. The question was how far lawmakers can go in establishing new sentencing factors without creating a new offense that must be proved as part of a defendant's trial. In two unrelated cases, Scalia led four dissenters in insisting that provisions to impose substantially higher sentences on the basis of prior convictions added new "elements" to the offense that had to be included in an indictment and proved at trial. The majority said the penalty enhancements simply added new sentencing factors for a judge to consider after a conviction.

Thomas made his biggest mark on the term with his opinion in the forfeiture case. The decision also marked the first time in his seven years on the Court that he had joined with four liberal justices in a 5–4 decision. The opinion was carefully reasoned and strongly written. The defendant's currency reporting violation had caused the government only "minimal" harm, Thomas said, and the money seized—$357,144 altogether—was "unrelated to any illegal activities." On that basis, the forfeiture was "grossly disproportional" to the offense.

On the surface, Thomas's opinion—backing a criminal defendant by a precedent-setting application of a Bill of Rights provision—seemed out of character. On a second look, though, his vote appeared to follow from his skeptical view of government power to affect property rights. "You can see why someone with his views would be offended by what happened in that case and would have voted the way he did," Roberts remarked.

In other cases Thomas did take pro–law enforcement positions. He wrote the majority opinion in a 5–4 decision in the final week rejecting a Pennsylvania parolee's effort to use the exclusionary rule to bar illegally obtained evidence in a parole revocation hearing. Earlier, he wrote the opinion upholding the military courts' ban on the use of lie detector evidence in criminal trials. "There is simply no consensus that polygraph evidence is reliable," Thomas wrote.

Among the rest of his ten majority opinions, Thomas wrote the 5–4 decision in one closely watched business dispute—a clash between banks and federally chartered credit unions. Thomas's opinion backed the banking industry in strictly interpreting the federal law to limit the expansion of credit unions. The ruling provided an unusual split on the preliminary question of whether the banks had standing to bring the suit. Thomas led a mostly conservative majority in recognizing standing, while O'Connor and three of the more liberal justices said they would have dismissed the suit.

Thomas's dissenting opinions were less frequent and less pointed than Scalia's. In the most important of his dissents, Thomas disagreed along with Scalia in the two sexual harassment cases. Thomas called the majority's rule imposing "vicarious liability" on employers for a supervisor's misconduct "a whole-cloth creation." And he complained that the decision gave employers little guidance on how to defend such suits—"thus ensuring a continuing reign of confusion" in the law. Instead, Thomas argued, employers should be liable for a supervisor's sexual harassment "only if the employer is truly at fault." And in those cases—as in Oncale's—Thomas emphasized that sexual harassment should be narrowly construed. "Popular misconceptions notwithstanding," he wrote, "sexual harassment is not a freestanding federal tort."

Thomas had been closely aligned with Scalia ever since he joined the Court in 1991. Their agreement peaked in the 1996–1998 term, when they disagreed only once in eighty signed decisions. This term they disagreed more often—in six out of ninety signed decisions. The forfeiture ruling was one of five criminal cases in which Scalia and Thomas voted differently. They also disagreed in the line-item veto case; Thomas voted to strike down the law, while Scalia voted to uphold it.

The common voting pattern prompted insinuations from some of Thomas's critics that he was simply following the more senior Scalia. Thomas responded to those comments in a speech to the National Bar Association, an organization of African American lawyers, a month after the term ended. Thomas's invitation stirred criticism within the organization, which had opposed his confirmation and disagreed with his opposition to affirmative action. In the July 29 speech, Thomas said it was "silly, but expected" for "some" people to think that he was "being led by other members of the Court." As for the criticism of his views on racial issues, Thomas said he was pained "to be perceived by many members of my race as doing them harm." But he ended with a defiant declaration of independence: "I come to state that I am a man, free to think for myself and do as I please."

The Left-of-Center Justices

Despite the seeming moderation in the Court's decisions, the four left-of-center justices were less visible in the 1997–1998 term than in some years in the recent past. Stevens had written two of the most important rulings in 1997: the decision clearing the way for a trial of the sexual harassment lawsuit against President Bill Clinton and the ruling striking down the federal law aimed at curbing children's access to sexually explicit material on the Internet. One year earlier, Ginsburg had written the ruling requiring the admission of women to the previously all-male Virginia Military Institute, while Breyer wrote the main opinions in two important First Amendment disputes.

This term, Stevens wrote the majority opinion in the line-item veto case, and Souter shared with Kennedy the assignments in two of the workplace sexual harassment decisions. But Stevens's and Souter's other majority opinions came in lesser cases, and Ginsburg and Breyer simply wrote no majority opinions in what could be termed major cases.

Stevens's opinion in the line-item veto case vindicated his position from the previous year, when the Court refused a plea by members of Congress to rule on the constitutionality of the law. He devoted nearly half of his opinion to ruling that the private parties challenging the law did have legal standing to bring these cases. In the remaining fourteen pages, Stevens readily concluded that the law was unconstitutional because it gave the president the power to repeal a portion of a statute approved by Congress. "There is no provision in the Constitution," Stevens wrote, "that authorizes the President to enact, to amend, or to repeal statutes."

Stevens wrote only five other majority opinions—and only one in a 5–4 decision. In that case, Stevens led the other liberal justices in overturning a federal appeals court decision that would have created a more difficult standard for citizen suits claiming that state or local officials retaliated against them for exercising their freedom of speech. In another divided ruling, Stevens wrote the 6–3 decision that made it easier for the federal government to prosecute someone for dealing in firearms without a federal license. And in one closely watched business case, Stevens wrote the unanimous opinion that backed discount retailers' right to import so-called "gray market" products—goods manufactured in the United States, sold abroad, and then brought back into the U.S. for resale, usually at lower prices than at authorized dealers. The ruling was based on a close reading of federal copyright law, but it also reflected Stevens's long-standing skepticism of efforts by businesses to use the law to limit competition.

Stevens also wrote the pivotal opinion in the immigration law case involving citizenship rights of out-of-wedlock children. Stevens accepted the government's justifications for the challenged provision, which gave children of citizen mothers automatic citizenship while denying citizenship to children of citizen fathers unless the father established paternity by the time the child reached the age of eighteen. The case found Stevens in uncustomary alliance with Rehnquist and at odds with his three liberal colleagues, who complained that the law reflected an outdated sexual stereotype.

As in years past, Stevens was the Court's most frequent dissenter, casting negative votes in twenty-three cases. At six cases, he also led the justices again in lone dissents. Four of these came in criminal cases; in each Stevens was the only justice to support an extension of constitutional rights to criminal defendants or inmates. In the lie detector case, for example, he argued in an opinion longer than the majority decision itself that a defendant had a constitutional right under the Sixth Amendment to try to prove the reliability of a favorable polygraph result.

Stevens's major dissent came in the high school sexual harassment case. Writing for the liberal bloc, he complained that the majority decision made it too difficult for plaintiffs and thwarted Congress's intent in prohibiting sex discrimination in federally funded programs. The ruling, he said, "is not faithful . . . to our duty to interpret, rather than to revise, congressional commands." In another important dissent, Stevens called for more demanding review of a government-owned broadcaster's decision to exclude a fringe political candidate from a campaign debate; Ginsburg and Breyer joined his dissent.

Souter, whose unexpectedly liberal record on the Court had disappointed his earlier conservative supporters, showed both his liberal views and conservative background in his opinions and votes during the term. He generally sided with the liberal bloc, but the former New Hampshire attorney general continued to separate from the liberals and ally with the conservatives in some criminal law rulings.

In his most important opinion for the term, Souter wrote the 7–2 decision in the Faragher sexual harassment case. His opinion dissected complex legal principles at greater length than Kennedy's companion ruling the same day in the Ellerth case. But, like Kennedy, Souter ended by justifying the liability rules for employers on the ground that it would "recognize the employer's affirmative obligation to prevent violations and give credit . . . to employers who make reasonable efforts to discharge their duty."

The rest of Souter's eleven majority opinions included two noteworthy decisions backing law enforcement. In one, he wrote for a 7–2 majority to deny an effort by a suspected Nazi war criminal to invoke the Fifth Amendment privilege against self-incrimination in an immigration proceeding on the ground that his answers might expose him to criminal prosecution in another country. The thirty-three page opinion significantly narrowed an expansive Warren Court precedent on the reasons for the privilege. In another, he wrote the unanimous opinion in a California case that all but blocked any damage suits against officers by people injured in high-speed police chases.

Souter also wrote a unanimous opinion in a closely watched business case involving financial responsibility for toxic waste cleanup under the federal "Superfund" law. The decision, based on principles of corporation law, blocked the government from automatically holding a parent company liable for cleanup costs at a site operated by a subsidiary company.

Souter's liberal views came across more cleanly in his dissenting opinions and votes. He led the liberal bloc in dissenting from the decision to bar the use of the exclusionary rule in parole revocation proceedings. He was the only justice to vote to strike down the decency clause on federal arts funding. And he wrote one of two dissenting opinions in the property rights challenge to the legal aid–funding programs.

President Clinton's two appointees to the Court, Ginsburg and Breyer, had a mostly low-key term. "It was striking how few majority opinions Ginsburg and Breyer wrote" in major cases, said Erwin Chemerinsky, a professor at the University of Southern California Law Center. In fact, Ginsburg and Breyer both had a lot of work: Ginsburg wrote eleven majority opinions and Breyer ten. But only one generated any front-page news coverage.

In that ruling, Ginsburg wrote the decision to overturn a court order obtained by General Motors to block a former GM engineer from testifying against the company in a product liability suit. GM had gotten an injunction from a Michigan state court judge to prevent the engineer from testifying in a trial in Missouri. Ginsburg, who had developed something of a specialty in procedural and jurisdictional issues in her five years on the Court, said the Michigan court "lacks authority to control courts" in another state. The decision was unanimous, but in a separate opinion three justices said Ginsburg's opinion had undermined the constitutional provision requiring courts in one state to give "full faith and credit" to orders issued by courts in other states.

Ginsburg's other majority opinions included several that dealt with similar procedural issues in relatively arcane disputes. But she did write one of the Court's decisions that held a law passed by Congress to be unconstitutional. The case involved a 1986 tax on shippers to help pay for maintaining and developing harbors. Ginsburg wrote the unanimous opinion holding that imposing the levy on exporters violated the constitutional prohibition on taxing exports.

A former women's rights litigator, Ginsburg wrote her strongest dissent for the term on a familiar issue: sexual stereotypes. In the immigration law case, Ginsburg said the decision to treat citizen mothers and fathers differently for purposes of qualifying their out-of-wedlock children for citizenship amounted to unconstitutional sex discrimination. The law, she said, had the effect of "shaping government policy to fit and reinforce" an outmoded sex-based generalization. In oral arguments in the case, Ginsburg had sharply questioned the Clinton administration's lawyer for backing away from the government's position two years earlier opposing sex discrimination in the Virginia Military Institute case; Ginsburg had written the opinion in that case, striking down the state school's all-male admissions policy.

Interestingly, Breyer wrote an even more forceful dissent than Ginsburg in the immigration law case, and he emphasized his disagreement by reading portions from the bench. "What sense does it make" to impose conditions on fathers but not mothers, he asked, when "paternity can readily be proved" and "women and men both are likely to earn a living in the workplace?" Souter joined both of the opinions.

Ginsburg and Breyer had the closest alignment among the liberal justices; they voted together in 87 percent of the cases, including almost all of the term's most important decisions. Their votes reflected liberal stands in favor of broadly applying civil rights protections and—often in dissent—in favor of expanding rights for criminal defendants and prison inmates. They dissented together, for example, in the decision refusing to extend Fifth Amendment privilege in potential foreign prosecutions. The ruling had the effect, Breyer wrote, of diminishing "the basic values which . . . underlie the Fifth Amendment's protections. . . ."

The two Clinton appointees differed, however, in the term's most important constitutional law ruling: the decision to strike down the line-item veto law. Ginsburg joined the majority opinion invalidating the law. Breyer wrote a long and meticulous dissent that concluded the law was constitutional. Breyer's stance surprised Court watchers; he had appeared to voice strong doubts about the measure in oral arguments. In his opinion, however, the former congressional staffer said that the law did not improperly give the president legislative powers or shift the balance of power between Congress and the president. The law "skirts a constitutional edge," he wrote at the end of his opinion, but the Constitution "authorizes Congress and the President to try novel methods in this way."

Breyer's majority opinions, like Ginsburg's, came in cases involving relatively technical issues. In perhaps his most important ruling, Breyer wrote the 6–3 decision that gave voters the right to sue the Federal Election Commission to enforce federal campaign finance laws. His other majority opinions included three 5–4 rulings in criminal cases—a reflection of Breyer's pivotal position between the conservative and liberal blocs on many criminal law issues. In two of the opinions, Breyer wrote decisions making it easier for federal prosecutors to seek longer sentences in certain cases; in the third, he led the liberal bloc plus O'Connor in somewhat tightening the rules for using a defendant's confession against a codefendant at trial.

In a term that saw relatively few sharply joined ideological disputes, the Court's left-of-center justices did not have many opportunities for sharpened rhetoric, either in majority opinions or in dissents. Even so, the liberal justices' general quiet seemed striking. "There is not that much of a hard left," commented UCLA professor Volokh. "The liberals are not terribly liberal. There is not a firm liberal bloc."

Looking Ahead

As the justices left Washington for their summer recess at the end of June, reporters and Court watchers were left to make sense of the term's ninety decisions. Overall patterns or trends seemed hard to discern. "Decisions don't give court clear identity," the *Washington Times* said in an end-of-term headline. The year was "short on big issues," the *Chicago Tribune* said in a headline.

Some observers speculated the term's relative quiet was deliberate. At the least, they suggested, the justices wanted to take a breath after the momentous rulings one year earlier, in May and June 1997. Others saw a broader purpose. "This may be the way that Rehnquist expresses the view that the Court should be 'the least dangerous branch,' to borrow the phrase from Alexander Hamilton, and the least heard from," said Douglas Kmiec, a constitutional law expert at Notre Dame Law School and former Justice Department official under President Ronald Reagan. "Take the least number of cases and confine those decisions to what people might call lawyers' work."

The coming term, set to open on the traditional first Monday of October (October 5), seemed to offer more of the same. Out of thirty-three cases accepted for review before summer, none seemed likely to produce banner headlines. Early attention was focused most on a constitutional challenge to a Chicago ordinance aimed at keeping criminal gangs off the streets. *(See "Preview of the 1998–1999 Term," pp. 134–148.)*

The composition of the Court also seemed likely to be unchanged when the new term opened. Some political observers and reporters speculated in the spring that Stevens might be planning to retire, but the justice hired a full complement of law clerks for the new term and gave no public sign that he was thinking of stepping down.

Even in a low-key term, the Court flexed its judicial muscles in a number of ways. It was hardly being timid or passive when it adopted new rules to curb sexual harassment in the workplace, acted to protect people with HIV from discrimination, or struck down the line-item veto and four other recently enacted federal statutes. "This was a pretty interesting term," said A. E. (Dick) Howard, a professor at the University of Virginia Law School, echoing Rehnquist's description. Perhaps the justices generated fewer headlines, he said, "but they clearly matter in terms of shaping the Constitution and other areas of the law."

2 | *The 1997–1998 Term*

The opposing forces in the fierce war over affirmative action were bracing for another battle before the Supreme Court as the justices opened their new term in October 1997. The case was a so-called "reverse discrimination" suit brought and won by a white high school teacher, Sharon Taxman, against the Piscataway, New Jersey, school board. When budget cuts forced a layoff in 1989, the school board let Taxman go while keeping a black teacher deemed to be equally qualified. The board specifically said the choice was aimed at promoting racial diversity in the school's faculty.

Taxman, suing under the federal law prohibiting racial discrimination in employment, won a $144,000 back pay award at trial. The verdict was upheld by the federal appeals court in Philadelphia. Opponents of affirmative action were delighted when the suburban school board asked the justices to review the case; they thought the dispute presented a perfect opportunity for the Court's conservative majority to further limit the use of racial preferences in the workplace. But supporters of affirmative action saw the case as nothing but bad news.

Less than two months before the scheduled Supreme Court argument, however, Taxman and the school board unexpectedly agreed to settle the case. The settlement called for Taxman to be paid $186,000, plus $247,500 in fees for her attorneys. The board acceded to the settlement in a late-night meeting on November 21 after a coalition of civil rights groups agreed to pay about 70 percent of the total.

"Tactical Retreat" the *New York Times* said of the settlement in its next-day headline. "Rights Groups Ducked a Fight, Opponents Say."

The civil rights organizations' decision to pay around $300,000 was, in fact, exactly that: a desperate move to get the case off the Supreme Court's docket and avoid an all but certain defeat. "A lot of people felt this was a lousy case to bring to the Supreme Court," William T. Coleman Jr., chairman of the board of the NAACP Legal Defense and Educational Fund, told the *Times* in an interview. The group's longtime general counsel, Elaine Jones, was reported to have been instrumental in pushing the idea.

Opponents of affirmative action, surprised and disappointed to see the case dissolve, made the best they could of the development: they gloated. "This settlement demonstrates the panic within the civil rights establishment," said Clint Bolick, litigation director of the conservative Institute for Justice. "The defenders of racial preferences are running for the hills."

For the Court, the settlement removed the term's biggest case from the calendar. Indeed, without it, the justices had no sharply joined disputes set for argument on the kinds of hot-button issues that the Rehnquist Court's core conservatives seemed to favor: abortion, race, religion, and states' rights. Nor did any of those issues surface in the remaining cases the justices agreed to review before the mid-January cutoff for the 1997–1998 term. By the end of the term, a few Court-watchers were visibly disappointed. "The *Seinfeld* term," one television legal commentator called it, referring to the popular situation comedy proclaimed by its creators to be "about nothing."

The description had a kernel of truth, but no more. Even without any major rulings in race-related disputes, the Court stayed busy with civil rights cases throughout the term—and civil rights groups counted some significant victories. Business groups had to sort out the implications of the civil rights decisions as well as a number of other rulings affecting employers, manufacturers, and businesses that served the public. The Court ruled on an unusually large number of criminal cases, most of them won by police and prosecutors. And Congress watched as its supposedly coequal branch of government struck down five federal statutes—the highest number in a term in recent memory. *(See Table 2-1.)*

Civil rights groups won their victories in areas that had generated increasing public controversy but received little attention from the Court: sexual harassment and disability rights. The rulings interpreted federal statutes—Title VII of the Civil Rights Act of 1964 and the Americans with Disabilities Act (ADA)—to give employees a better chance of winning damage awards from their employers for sexual harassment on the job and to extend to people with HIV the legal protections against discrimination accorded to other people with disabilities.

In two of the rulings, the Court held that an employer is liable for any sexual harassment by a supervisor that has a concrete effect on an employee's pay, position, or assignment, and it can also be held liable for a supervisor's misconduct even if it has no concrete effect. In the latter situation, however, the employer could avoid liability by showing that it had an effective policy against sexual harassment and that the employee failed to complain about the misconduct.

The rulings, civil rights advocates said, would do more than help workers who took their complaints to federal court. "Plaintiffs are going to win more lawsuits, but the more important thing is that employers are going to do more to stop the harassment," said Eric Schnapper, a professor at the University of Washington Law School who was one of the attorneys representing the plaintiffs in the separate cases.

In a third decision, the Court held that sexual harassment applies to conduct between people of the same sex. That ruling too was cheered by civil rights groups, including gay rights advocates. The message of the ruling, said Matt Coles, director of the American Civil Liberties Union's gay

Table 2-1   Laws Held Unconstitutional

The Supreme Court issued six decisions during the 1997–1998 term that held unconstitutional federal laws or state laws or constitutional provisions.

Decisions (in chronological order)	Law Held Invalid
Federal Laws	
Feltner v. Columbia Pictures Television, Inc. [p. 77]	Copyright Act of 1976 provision for non-jury trial in "statutory damage" cases
United States v. United States Shoe Corp. [p. 79]	Harbor Maintenance Tax Act of 1986
United States v. Bajakajian [p. 95]	Money laundering forfeiture provision
Eastern Enterprises v. Apfel [p. 127]	Coal Industry Retiree Health Benefit Act
Clinton v. City of New York [p. 113]	Line Item Veto Act
State Laws	
Lunding v. New York Tax Appeals Tribunal [p. 131]	No state income tax deduction for alimony paid by nonresidents

rights project, was that "male or female, gay or straight, nobody should have to face sexual harassment when they go to work in the morning."

The disability rights ruling established that people with HIV are protected against discrimination even if they have no visible symptoms of the disease. The ruling largely supported a claim by a Maine woman against a local dentist who refused to treat her in his office. The Court, however, gave the dentist another chance to prove to a lower court that treating her could have created a health or safety risk for himself or his staff. In a second case, the Court held that the disability rights laws applied to state prisons.

Disability rights advocates applauded the rulings, the Court's first interpretations of the 1990 law. "These two cases could not have been better in reinforcing the broad coverage of the ADA," said Georgetown law professor Chai Feldblum. "That is an essential and important message from the Supreme Court to the lower courts: this is a broad law, and it is intended to be interpreted as a broad law."

Other civil rights advocates noted the contrast with some earlier Rehnquist Court decisions that had adopted more restrictive readings of federal civil rights statutes. "We have a Court that is prepared to effectuate congressional intent rather than frustrate congressional intent, which is what the Court was doing in the 1980s," said Steven Shapiro, the ACLU's national legal director.

The Court also gave a protective reading to another federal antidiscrimination law, this one affecting older workers. The case involved a 1990 law that amended the Age Discrimination in Employment Act to make it harder for employers to get employees to waive any legal claims they might have under the law. By a 6–3 vote, the Court rejected a company's effort to enforce a waiver that did not comply with the terms of the law; the company argued that the former employee "ratified" the agreement by accepting $6,000 in severance pay.

Civil rights groups suffered one high-profile defeat in a sexual harassment suit brought under a different federal statute: Title IX of the Education Amendments of 1972. That law prohibited sex discrimination by schools that received federal funds and had previously been interpreted by the Court to allow private damage suits for sexual harassment by teachers. By a 5–4 vote, however, the Court set a difficult standard for students to meet in recovering damages from school districts. Plaintiffs were required to show that high-ranking officials knew about the misconduct and failed to take steps to prevent it.

Women's rights advocates contrasted the decision with the more favorable rulings about sexual harassment on the job. "We've got an unfortunate situation where students have less protection than employees in the workplace," said Marcia Greenberger, a lawyer with the NOW Legal Defense Fund.

Civil rights groups also suffered some setbacks among an unusually large number of Court rulings in civil rights damage suits brought against state or local government officials. In the most significant, the Court rejected a suit by the parents of a Sacramento, California, teenager killed in a high-speed police chase. The Court unanimously held that police cannot be held liable for a chase-related injury or death unless they intended to cause harm to the victim. It also ruled that local lawmakers are absolutely immune from liability in federal civil rights suits for their official actions. But the Court did rule that prosecutors are subject to suit for making false statements in court papers. And the justices rejected, by a 5–4 vote, a heightened standard for plaintiffs to meet in damage suits requiring proof of improper motives by government officials.

The Court kept busy with business law cases almost from the start of the term until its final day. "There were a lot more meat and potato cases for business than in prior years," said Stephen Bokat of the U.S. Chamber of Commerce. The results were mixed: some significant victories, some significant defeats, and no overall pattern.

The sexual harassment and HIV cases concerned employers as much as they did civil rights advocates. Business advocates had mixed reactions to the new rules on liability for sexual harassment. Some welcomed the Court's efforts to clarify the rules, while others said the decisions still left businesses without clear guidelines on how to avoid liability. The ruling in the HIV case also caused concern that the Court was creating new problems for businesses by expanding coverage of the ADA, which bars companies from discriminating against persons with disabilities either as customers or as employees.

The Chamber of Commerce had urged the Court to adopt a more relaxed negligence standard for employer liability in sexual harassment cases. Although the Court rejected the argument, Bokat later called the decisions "a partial defeat and a partial victory." The positive result, he said, was that "businesses have a way to defend themselves. The Court made it clear that if you have these complaint procedures and utilize them properly, you have a defense."

But William Kilberg, a Washington lawyer who filed a brief in the case on behalf of the National Association of Manufacturers, was less positive. "We'll have to have more cases to try to clarify what this round of clarification has meant," he said. Among other unsettled issues, Kilberg said, was the question whether an employer would have a good defense in a court suit if it rejected an employee's complaint after conducting a good-faith investigation.

Bokat was less equivocal about the potential effects of the HIV decision for employers. "They're leading down a slippery slope," he said. "People who have been disadvantaged in the workplace will take advantage of every possible cause of action they have, and businesses will settle. . . . That's the reality of the workplace."

Business interests suffered some other setbacks in workplace-related cases. The age discrimination case made it harder for employers to protect against liability after laying off older workers. In another case based on a federal statute, the Court ruled that employers are required to offer a former worker continued health benefits even if the employee has separate coverage under a spouse's insurance. The Court also backed labor interests by somewhat expanding the time period for filing suit against an employer for failing to make legally required contributions to an industrywide pension plan.

Other labor-related rulings were mixed for business. In the most significant, the Court issued a split decision on employers' efforts to overturn a National Labor Relations Board (NLRB) policy that made it difficult to poll workers to determine whether a union had lost majority support among employees—a possible first step toward deunionization. The Court voted 5–4 to uphold the rule but then turned around to decide, by a different 5–4 vote, that it had been applied too strictly in the case under review. In another labor law case, the Court blocked a union's suit against an employer for alleged fraud by misleading the union during bargaining about its plans to subcontract much of its work after a contract was reached.

Business scored some important victories in other areas. A ruling in a toxic tort case cheered business groups by strengthening the authority of

Table 2-2   Reversals of Earlier Rulings

The Supreme Court issued three decisions during the 1997–1998 term that explicitly reversed a previous ruling by the Court. The ruling brought the number of such reversals in the Court's history to at least 215.

New Decision	Old Decision	New Holding
State Oil Company v. Khan (1997)	*Albrecht v. Herald Co.* (1968)	Maximum price agreements between suppliers and dealers not *per se* illegal
Hudson v. United States (1997)	*Halper v. United States* (1989)	No double jeopardy violation in prosecuting someone after civil fine for same conduct
Hohn v. United States (1998)	*House v. Mayo* (1945)	Supreme Court may review appeals court's denial of "certificate of appealability" in habeas corpus cases

trial judges to keep out scientific evidence challenged as unreliable. Two rulings in separate cases made it more difficult for environmental groups to bring disputes into federal court. And in the first significant ruling of the term, the Court eased the antitrust rules against price ceilings imposed by manufacturers or suppliers on their dealers. The decision overruled a 1968 precedent, one of three times during the term that the Court explicitly rejected its prior rulings. *(See Table 2-2.)*

In addition, two of the Court's rulings overturning federal statutes favored industry challenges to congressional enactments. One ruling struck down a law requiring financial contributions to a coal miners' health benefits fund from companies that had since left the industry. Another exempted exporters from a 1986 tax on shippers imposed to help pay for harbor improvements. Major business interests seemed likely to be the losers from a third ruling striking down a federal statute. In that case, the Court strengthened the guarantee for jury trials in copyright infringement cases—a ruling likely to make it harder for entertainment companies, publishers, and other copyright holders to collect damage awards.

The Court, as usual, also had before it a number of disputes between different industries. In one of those cases, the Court upheld, 5–4, an effort by the banking industry to control the growth of federally chartered credit unions. Congress moved quickly to reverse the ruling, however, by amending the federal law governing credit unions. In another business versus business dispute, the Court backed discount retailers over manufacturers in a case over efforts to block the so-called "gray market"—goods manufactured in the United States, sold abroad, and then imported back to the United States for sale at discounted prices.

The Court's criminal law rulings reflected its impatience with death penalty challenges and its disinclination to establish new constitutional rules protecting suspects or defendants. "Overall it's still a favorable environment" for law enforcement, said Kent Scheidegger, legal director of the Criminal Justice Legal Foundation, which filed friend-of-the-court briefs in several cases. But the Court did invoke the Eighth Amendment's previously unused Excessive Fines Clause to limit forfeiture of defendants' property in criminal cases. And it slightly limited the impact of the law Congress passed in 1996 to speed up death penalty challenges in federal habeas corpus cases.

The Court's frustration with protracted death penalty appeals surfaced most forcefully in a case from California, where a federal appeals court issued an eleventh-hour stay of execution to a state inmate convicted of murder fifteen years earlier. In 1996 the appeals court had turned down the inmate's claim that his trial lawyer mishandled the case, but nearly two years later the court withdrew the decision and blocked the scheduled execution. In a blistering 5–4 ruling, the Court said the appeals judges had committed a "grave abuse of discretion." Dissenting justices also faulted the procedure but said the ruling was an unnecessary overreaction to an isolated case.

Some of the Court's other death penalty decisions also seemed likely to have limited impact. In a Virginia case, the Court refused by a 6–3 vote to require that juries be instructed to consider mitigating evidence offered by a defendant against imposing the death sentence. However, Virginia had changed its jury instructions before the ruling. In another case, from Nebraska, the Court held that capital juries did not have to be given instructions on lesser degrees of homicide such as manslaughter if state law did not recognize them as "included offenses" for first-degree murder. Laws in most states, however, were different. In a case with broader implications, though, the Court refused to mandate specific procedures for states to use in considering executive clemency requests from death row inmates.

The Court's most dramatic death penalty ruling came in a case where the justices rejected pleas from the International Court of Justice and the U.S. State Department to halt the execution of a Paraguayan national in Virginia. Angel Francisco Breard sought to block his execution for a 1992 murder on the ground that he had confessed before being allowed to confer with a representative of the Paraguayan Embassy, as provided in a treaty between the United States and the South American country. The Paraguayan government filed legal actions on Breard's behalf both in U.S. courts and before the international tribunal, also known as the World Court. Lower federal courts rejected Paraguay's suit, but the World Court issued a ruling ordering the United States to halt the execution. Despite the State Department's plea to heed the World Court's order, on April 14 the justices voted, 6–3, not to hear the case. In a dissenting opinion, Breyer, joined by Stevens and Ginsburg, said the issues in the case deserved "less speedy consideration." Breard was executed later that night.

Somewhat unexpectedly, the Court issued two rulings that relaxed restrictive habeas corpus provisions in the 1996 Antiterrorism and Effective Death Penalty Act. One of the rulings, softening the law's ban on "successive" habeas corpus petitions, allowed an Arizona death row inmate to get a new hearing in his effort to block his execution on mental incompetency grounds. The other decision, in a Nebraska drug case, eased the act's limits on appealing lower-court denials of habeas corpus petitions. In a third ruling, however, the Court threw out an effort by California death row inmates to block the state from taking advantage of the law's expedited procedures for handling death row appeals.

The Court turned aside pleas to expand constitutional rights in two closely watched cases. In one, the justices said the Sixth Amendment did not guarantee a criminal defendant a right to introduce evidence of a favorable lie detector test at trial. In another, they said the Fifth Amendment could not be used to block questioning that might subject a person to prosecution in a foreign country. In a third, the Court overruled a nine-year-old precedent to cut back the protections under the Constitution's Double Jeopardy Clause. The ruling held that the government ordinarily can prosecute a defendant for a crime even if he or she has already been fined or disciplined in a civil proceeding.

In search-and-seizure cases, the Court refused to establish a special rule for cases where police destroy property—for example, breaking down a door—when executing a no-knock search warrant. The justices also refused, by a 5–4 vote, to apply the exclusionary rule to bar the use of illegally obtained evidence in parole revocation hearings. But in another 5–4 decision, the Court did make it harder for prosecutors to use a defendant's confession against a codefendant at trial.

The forfeiture case was also decided by a 5–4 vote, with Thomas joining the liberal justices in opposition to his customary conservative allies. The ruling required the government to return more than $300,000 in cash seized from a Los Angeles man for failing to report the currency when he was about to leave the country. Thomas said the forfeiture violated the Excessive Fines Clause because it was "grossly disproportional to the gravity of the offense." Four dissenters said the decision would weaken the government's prosecution of money-laundering cases.

The justices split, 5–4, in two other decisions that made it easier for lawmakers to provide for longer sentences for defendants based on conduct not related to the specific crime being prosecuted. The rulings held that lawmakers have broad discretion to define such conduct as a "sentencing factor" for a judge's consideration rather than a new offense that would have to be proven beyond a reasonable doubt. The first of the decisions came in a little-noticed ruling in March on a federal immigration law; the justices then applied that ruling on the last day of the term in a decision that eased the enforcement of so-called "three-strikes" laws enacted by a number of states to give longer prison terms to defendants with two or more prior convictions. In an unusual split, the conservative Scalia joined with three liberals—Stevens, Ginsburg, and Breyer—in dissenting from the rulings.

The Rehnquist Court's activist streak had emerged most often in the past few years in its constitutional rulings on federalism, separation of powers, and the First Amendment. This term the Court again used its power to police the power arrangements between the executive and legislative branches by striking down the Line Item Veto Act. But the term ended with no major rulings on the powers of the states vis-à-vis the federal government. And the Court's only First Amendment decisions turned aside claims by individuals attacking government policies on free speech grounds.

The ruling to strike down the 1996 law giving the president power to "cancel" individual spending items or some special tax breaks from laws passed by Congress provoked sharp disagreements not only among politicians in Washington but also among legal experts. Critics viewed the decision as an overly formalistic approach to separation of powers principles, but others hailed the ruling as a way to force Congress to exercise more discipline itself over spending issues.

Louis Fisher, a constitutional law scholar at the Library of Congress, noted that the case did not present the typical problem in separation of powers cases: Congress or the president trying to intrude on the powers of the other. "There's no interference here," he said. "It was something that bothered the justices," Fisher added. "They wanted to kill it, and they figured out a way to do it."

But New York University law professor Burt Neuborne viewed the decision more positively. "The justices were right in approaching this as a major change," he said. "It shifts power in a very dramatic way." He was equally sanguine about the long-term impact of the ruling. "The Court appears to be insisting that Congress take responsibility for its decisions," he said. "If that's what they're saying, I think it can only be healthy for democracy in this country."

President Clinton had used the power given him by the 1996 law to disapprove eighty-two separate line items for an estimated one-year savings of $355 million. But Congress in March overrode the president's decision to remove thirty-eight projects from a military construction bill; that action reduced the projected five-year savings from Clinton's vetoes to less than $600 million.

Supporters of states' rights ended the term disappointed by the Court's failure to add to its recent pronouncements favoring the states in federalism issues. The Court in 1997 had given states' rights advocates a dramatic victory by striking down a law requiring local law enforcement officers to conduct background checks on prospective gun purchasers. Two years earlier, the Court had ruled, in *United States v. Lopez,* that Congress had also improperly intruded on the states by passing a law to make it a federal crime to possess a firearm near a school.

The Lopez decision, in particular, seemed to open up new questions about the scope of Congress's power to enact criminal laws tied to tenuous theories of regulating interstate commerce. But the Court had nothing new to say on the subject this term, and critics of expansive federal power were disappointed. "Several terms past *Lopez,* we still have no flesh on the bones," said Notre Dame Law School professor Douglas Kmiec.

The most closely watched ruling affecting the states, in fact, had nothing to do with momentous constitutional issues. It was instead a border dispute between New Jersey and New York over a tiny but culturally significant piece of real estate: Ellis Island, the historic gateway in New York Harbor for millions of immigrants. The Court, dissecting an 1834 compact between the two states, ruled that New York could keep the land that originally formed the island but that New Jersey had sovereignty over the larger part added by landfill over the years.

The Court struck down only one state law on constitutional grounds during the term. By a 6–3 vote, it invalidated a New York law that denied to nonresidents a deduction on their state income tax for alimony payments. The law, Justice O'Connor said, "smacks of an effort to penalize the citizens of another state." The Court also struck down Louisiana's unique "open primary" system for electing members of Congress, which permitted a candidate to win election by getting a majority of the vote in an early primary open to candidates of all parties. The unanimous decision held that the system violated a federal law—enacted under the Constitution's Elections Clause—that required a uniform date for congressional balloting.

States were losers in one important ruling regarding American Indians during the term. The 6–3 decision reaffirmed the rule that Indian tribes cannot be sued in state courts. In his opinion for the Court, however, Justice Kennedy suggested that Congress might want to reconsider the doctrine. Indian tribes lost four other cases during the term. The most important of the rulings, in a case from Alaska, overturned a federal appeals court decision that state officials said could have led to the designation of vast stretches of land as semisovereign "Indian country."

The Court had little to say about the First Amendment during the term, and its rulings showed more deference to government officials than many of its rulings in recent years. In one case, the Court refused to strike down a law passed by Congress requiring the National Endowment for the Arts to consider "general standards of decency" in awarding grants to artists. In the other, it upheld a decision by the state-owned public broadcasting network in Arkansas to bar Ralph Forbes, a fringe candidate for Congress, from a campaign debate that it sponsored.

Free speech advocates voiced disappointment with the rulings but noted that the Court had taken a cautious approach in both. In the arts case, the Court said the so-called "decency" clause did not impose any flat prohibitions on the kind of art that the Endowment could fund. "There's an implicit warning there to the government that it ought not, cannot go too far in using its funding power to suppress speech," commented the ACLU's Steven Shapiro.

In the campaign debate case, the Court refused to apply a strict constitutional test to a government-owned broadcaster's decisions on inviting or not inviting candidates. But it did hold that a station's decision to exclude a particular candidate had to be "reasonable" and that a candidate could not be excluded "based on [the candidate's] viewpoint."

The ruling did not apply to public broadcast stations not owned by governmental bodies or to debates—like the then-recent presidential debates—sponsored by private organizations. And Shapiro, who filed a brief with the Court supporting Forbes's claim, noted that public broadcasters were still free to invite all comers for campaign debates. "I would like to think that these debates will become more inclusive, rather than more exclusive," he said. "But certainly this decision does not require that."

Sexual Harassment

Employers' Liability for Supervisors' Misconduct Broadened

Faragher v. City of Boca Raton, decided by a 7–2 vote, June 26, 1998; Souter wrote the opinion; Thomas and Scalia dissented. *(See excerpts, pp. 240–250.)*

Burlington Industries, Inc. v. Ellerth, decided by a 7–2 vote, June 26, 1998; Kennedy wrote the opinion; Thomas and Scalia dissented. *(See excerpts, pp. 250–261.)*

When Beth Ann Faragher and Kimberly Ellerth thought their bosses were making improper sexual advances, they did what most women do when they confront sexual harassment in the workplace: they put up with it. After leaving their jobs, however, the two women went to court and charged their employers with illegal sex discrimination under Title VII of the Civil Rights Act of 1964.

Faragher, a former lifeguard for the city of Boca Raton, Florida, lost her case before the federal appeals court in Atlanta. Ellerth, a former sales associate for the clothing company Burlington Industries, lost at the trial level,

Beth Ann Faragher

but the federal appeals court in Chicago reinstated her suit. Both cases reached the Supreme Court, which this term issued parallel rulings in the two cases, making it easier for victims of sexual harassment to recover monetary damages from their employers for misconduct by supervisors.

Many, perhaps most, of the growing number of women in the workplace could easily relate to the allegations that Faragher and Ellerth made in their complaints.

Faragher worked as a lifeguard in Boca Raton part time and summers from September 1985 to May 1990 while attending college. Throughout her tenure, Faragher said, she and other female lifeguards were subjected to lewd comments, sexual come-ons, and physical gropes. She accused two supervisors of misconduct: Bill Terry, chief of the marine safety section of the city's parks and recreation department, and David Silverman, a lieutenant and later captain in the section.

Ellerth began working for Burlington in March 1993; she was based in a two-person office in Chicago and reported to Theodore Slowik, a mid-level vice president in New York. In her suit, Ellerth said Slowik repeatedly made sexually suggestive remarks to her and made unmistakable sexual propositions to her at least twice: during a business trip in the summer and a promotion interview in March 1994.

The allegations—proven in court in Faragher's case and denied by Burlington and Slowik in Ellerth's suit—were crude in the extreme. Faragher claimed that both Terry and Silverman repeatedly made comments about the physical appearance of the female lifeguards and talked about having sex with them. Terry once placed his hand on her buttocks, she said, and Silverman had pantomimed an act of oral sex in front of her.

In her suit, Ellerth claimed that Slowik had invited her to the hotel lounge during the summer 1993 business trip, made remarks about her breasts, and—when she gave him no encouragement—bluntly warned her: "You know, Kim, I could make your life very hard or very easy at Burlington." In the promotion interview, she alleged, Slowik told her she was not "loose enough" and then reached over and rubbed her knee.

Neither Faragher nor Ellerth made a formal complaint against their supervisors before quitting their jobs, however, even though both the city and Burlington had written policies prohibiting sexual harassment on the job. Faragher and other women lifeguards did informally talk about the problem with another supervisory-level male lifeguard, but he never raised the issue with higher-level managers in the department. Ellerth said she knew about Burlington's sexual harassment policy but never told her immediate supervisor about Slowik's behavior because he would have been obliged to report it to higher-ups. Later, it came out that her husband had counseled against reporting Slowik's behavior for fear she could lose her job just as the couple were buying their first house.

When the cases reached court, both Boca Raton and Burlington insisted that whatever the supervisors may have done, they as employers could not be held liable for conduct about which they had never known. In addition, Burlington argued that Ellerth had not been hurt at all, since she had successfully rebuffed Slowik's advances and had never been passed over for a promotion or raise during her fourteen months with the company.

Employers had been grappling with sexual harassment since the Supreme Court's first ruling on the issue in 1986. In that case, *Meritor Savings Bank v. Vinson,* the Court unanimously held that "severe and pervasive" sexual harassment that created an "abusive working environment" amounted to discrimination on the basis of sex in violation of Title VII. The opinion was written by Rehnquist, then an associate justice; one week later, he was nominated to be elevated to chief justice.

The ruling encouraged more employees, mostly women, to file sexual harassment complaints with the federal Equal Employment Opportunity Commission or the courts. The allegations ran the gamut of intersexual behavior from forced sex and in-office groping to nude pin-ups and off-color jokes. Inevitably, the lower court rulings did not yield completely clear answers about how bad behavior had to be to be ruled sexual harassment.

To try to make some sense of the various factual situations, courts differentiated between two categories of sexual harassment complaints. *Quid pro quo* harassment occurred when a supervisor conditioned some tangible job benefit—like a raise, promotion, or favorable assignment—on an employee's submitting to a sexual demand. A more general complaint about an offensive sexual climate in the workplace was termed a "hostile environment" claim.

The distinction guided courts in determining when to hold the employer itself liable for sexual harassment. Generally, courts held that employers were automatically liable in a *quid pro quo* case but that plaintiffs had to show some measure of fault on the employer's part to prevail in a hostile environment case. For plaintiffs, holding an employer liable was critical, since courts generally held that individual supervisors were not subject to Title VII claims.

The Supreme Court gave only limited guidance on the issue in its 1986 ruling. It admonished lower courts that had held employers automatically liable for their supervisors' misconduct. But it also said that an employer was not insulated from liability simply because it had not been aware of the problem or because it had a grievance procedure for dealing with sexual harassment complaints.

The confusion over the liability issue increased through the 1990s as the number of sexual harassment cases was also rising. The increase in litigation stemmed in part from the dramatic accusations of sexual harassment brought against Clarence Thomas during his Supreme Court confirmation hearings in 1990. Even though Thomas steadfastly denied the allegations, the hearings helped to raise awareness of the issue and to fortify many women to complain about offensive behavior on the job, either to their employers or in the courts. In addition, Congress gave new incentives to sexual harassment claims in 1991 by revising the federal job discrimination law to allow plaintiffs to recover compensatory and punitive damages, not just back pay and attorneys' fees.

The legal confusion was reflected in the various court rulings in Faragher's and Ellerth's cases. The federal judge who heard Faragher's case found three possible rationales for holding the city liable, all of which were rejected by the federal appeals court in Atlanta by a vote of 7–5. In Ellerth's case, the lower court judge said Burlington could not be held liable, but the federal appeals court in Chicago reinstated the suit in a decision that produced eight opinions among the twelve judges as well as an unsigned plea on behalf of the full court asking the Supreme Court to "bring order to the chaotic case law in this important field of practice."

The judge in Faragher's case had no problem finding that Terry and Silverman—both of whom had been fired after another female lifeguard finally filed a complaint against them—had created a hostile working environment for the women employees. There were three bases for holding the city liable, he said. First, he ruled the city had "constructive knowledge" of the sexual harassment because it was so pervasive. Second, the city was liable under a doctrine known as *respondeat superior* that treats a supervisor as an employer's agent in some situations. Finally, the judge found the city had "imputed knowledge" of the misconduct based on the complaint to Robert Gordon, the third supervisor.

The Eleventh U.S. Circuit Court of Appeals rejected each of those grounds. It said that the misconduct was not so pervasive as to create constructive knowledge. The doctrine of *respondeat superior* did not apply, the appeals court said, because Terry and Silverman were not acting within their normal duties. And Gordon was not a sufficiently high-ranking official to impute his knowledge to the city itself.

In Ellerth's case, the trial judge ruled Burlington could not be held liable under a hostile environment theory because it had no knowledge of Slowik's misconduct. The company also could not be held liable under a *quid pro quo* theory, the judge said, because Ellerth had not suffered any tangible injury. The Seventh U.S. Circuit Court of Appeals disagreed. It held that an employer could automatically be held liable in a *quid pro quo* case even if the employee rebuffed the sexual advance and did not suffer any adverse consequence.

The Court's decisions to hear the two cases in separate arguments in March and April prompted a flood of briefs from interest groups. Civil rights and women's rights organizations, along with the Clinton administration, urged a stricter standard for liability. Business groups argued that employers should not be held liable for sexual harassment unless they actually knew of the misconduct.

Faragher's case was argued on March 29 along with a separate case, *Gebser v. Lago Vista Independent School District*, testing the liability of school districts for sexual harassment of students by teachers. *(See pp. 39–42.)* In both cases, the justices appeared to be tilting against expansive theories of liability.

Kimberly Ellerth

Faragher's lawyer, William Amlong of Fort Lauderdale, faced particularly tough questioning as he staked out a position that seemingly would hold employers liable in most instances of supervisors' misconduct. "That sounds like strict liability," Rehnquist and Kennedy exclaimed in virtual unison at one point.

The Clinton administration lawyer supporting Faragher, Assistant Solicitor General Irving Gornstein, faced a similar challenge when he outlined a three-part test that ended by asking whether the employer "should have known" about the misconduct. The "practical effect," Souter said, would be "an absolute rule." Rehnquist had a different objection. "We're looking for something that's simple and fairly easy to administer," he told Gornstein.

But Washington attorney Harry Rissetto, representing Boca Raton, also had some difficult moments. Souter noted that employers were held liable for racial discrimination by supervisors and asked why the same rule should not apply to sexual harassment. When Rissetto hesitated, Souter suggested that one reason might be that sexual harassment is more difficult to detect. "That's part of it," Rissetto said. But Souter returned to the question later and caught Rissetto with nothing to add. "I'm embarrassed to give you the same answer, Your Honor," the lawyer said.

The justices heard arguments in Ellerth's case only three weeks later, on April 22, but they appeared less inclined than in the previous argument toward limiting employer liability. They also were openly baffled by the distinction between *quid pro quo* and hostile environment cases.

"How did we come to this distinction?" Ginsburg asked Burlington's lawyer, James Casey. "The statute doesn't say a word about *quid pro quo.*" Later, when Ellerth's lawyer, Ernest Rossiello, said the Court itself had cited the distinction in its first ruling on the issue, Scalia objected. "Don't put it all on us," he said.

Relying on the distinction anyway, Casey insisted that an employer could not be automatically liable in a *quid pro quo* case for what he called a supervisor's "unfulfilled threat." But O'Connor put him on the spot by asking whether a company would be liable if a supervisor "repeatedly" took an employee to an isolated location "for sexual gratification" even if nothing happened. When Casey meekly acknowledged yes, Souter jumped in: "Then why not in one instance alone?"

But Rossiello and Deputy Solicitor General Barbara Underwood were challenged in turn when they argued for holding Burlington liable when Ellerth had not suffered any job-related injury. "When there's been no employer action," Scalia said, "I find it much more difficult to leap to a theory of employer responsibility."

Despite the muddled arguments, the Court's decisions in the two cases, issued on the last day of the term, reflected a surprising measure of unity and clarity. Going in reverse order of seniority, Souter announced his opinion in the Faragher case, followed by Kennedy with the Ellerth decision. The announcements from the bench made clear what was even clearer from the written opinions: the two justices had coordinated their drafting to produce a single rule for determining employers' liability for sexual harassment by supervisors.

The rule, moreover, was tough on employers, imposing indirect or "vicarious" liability for sexual harassment by a supervisor whenever any "tangible employment action" resulted. An employer could also be held liable if the employee did not suffer any visible consequence. In those cases, the employer had a defense—but a demanding one. The employer had to show that it "exercised reasonable care to prevent and correct promptly any sexually harassing behavior" *and* that the employee "unreasonably failed to take advantage of any preventive or corrective opportunities provided by the employer or to avoid harm otherwise."

The rulings stopped short of requiring employers to establish antiharassment policies, but the message to do so was nonetheless clear. "[T]he need for a stated policy" could be "appropriately addressed . . . when litigating the first element of the defense," the Court declared. And an employee's failure to use a complaint procedure "will normally suffice to satisfy the employer's burden of the defense." Then, by way of emphasis, the opinions continued: "No affirmative defense is available, however, when the supervisor's harassment culminates in a tangible employment action, such as discharge, demotion, or undesirable reassignment."

Applying that test to the Faragher case, Souter said the appeals court was wrong to throw out the lower court judgment in Faragher's favor. The evidence of sexual harassment was "clear" and "undisputed," Souter said, and the city had no "serious prospect" of presenting an affirmative defense. The evidence showed that the city had failed to tell employees about its sexual harassment policy and, in any event, did not provide a way to bypass supervisors in registering complaints. And Faragher had asked for and been awarded only a nominal $1 in damages, so there was no need for further proceedings to determine whether she had failed to try to mitigate her injuries.

In Ellerth's case, the Court confronted the additional issue of the distinction between hostile environment and *quid pro quo* claims. The solution was all but to discard it. The two terms, Kennedy wrote, "are helpful, perhaps, in making a rough demarcation" between two types of cases, but "beyond this are of limited utility." If a threat is carried out, Kennedy said, the employee has established a violation of Title VII. If not, the plaintiff must show that the unfulfilled threats were sufficiently severe or pervasive to create a hostile work environment.

With that background, Kennedy concluded that Ellerth had made out a possible claim against Burlington and was entitled to proceed to trial. On remand, he said, Ellerth would have a chance to add to her allegations, and Burlington would have an opportunity to present an affirmative defense.

The vote in the two cases was identical, 7–2. The majority included the Court's left-of-center bloc—Stevens, Souter, Ginsburg, and Breyer; the two centrist conservatives, O'Connor and Kennedy; and Rehnquist, author of the original *Meritor* opinion. As if to avoid any risk of further confusion, none of the majority justices wrote a separate opinion in *Faragher,* and only Ginsburg wrote separately in *Burlington Industries.* In a one-paragraph opinion concurring in the judgment, she said she agreed that the *quid pro quo* and hostile work environment labels were not "controlling" in determining liability and also agreed with the rule, which she noted was "substantively identical" to that in Faragher's case.

The dissenting justices were Scalia and Thomas. Surprisingly, perhaps—given his personal experience with the issue—it was Thomas who wrote the dissenting opinion. Employers should be liable for sexual harassment, he wrote in a nine-page opinion in the *Burlington Industries* case, only if the employer "knew, or in the exercise of reasonable care should have known, about the hostile work environment and failed to take remedial action."

"Sexual harassment is simply not something that employers can wholly prevent without taking extraordinary measures—constant video and audio surveillance, for example—that would revolutionize the workplace in a manner incompatible with a free society," Thomas continued. "The most that employers can be reasonably charged with, therefore, is a duty to act reasonably under the circumstances."

Civil rights and women's groups cheered the rulings. "It's a tremendous victory for women," said Kathy Rodgers, executive director of the NOW Legal Defense Fund. But leading business groups also were pleased with getting a clear rule for determining employer liability: "They gave us a bright-line test that makes it clear to employers what they must do to protect themselves from being sued," said Stephen Bokat, vice president and general counsel of the U.S. Chamber of Commerce.

For Faragher, who had gone on to law school and gotten a job as a public defender in Denver, Colorado, the ruling meant the end of a long lawsuit in which she had sought nothing more than $1 in damages. "I think it's a great victory for women in the workplace, for any employee who's sexually harassed in the workplace," she told *ABC News.*

For Ellerth, who had moved to downstate Illinois and was staying at home with two young children, the Court's ruling only cleared the way for her to try to prove her allegations in court. Casey, Burlington's lawyer, said the company would have "a two-pronged defense: It didn't happen, and, even if you believe it did, there was a system in place to redress her grievances." But Rossiello dismissed his adversary's comments as "rhetoric." "There's a strong likelihood that she will get a verdict," he said.

Sexual Harassment

"Same-Sex" Misconduct Covered by Federal Job Bias Law

Oncale v. Sundowner Offshore Services, Inc., decided by a 9–0 vote, March 4, 1998; Scalia wrote the opinion. *(See excerpts, pp. 151–154.)*

An offshore oil rig is a quintessentially male workplace: an isolated job site where tough guys work "seven days on, seven days off," operating grimy machinery by day and sleeping in cramped quarters at night. Joseph Oncale—known as "Jody"—did not fit this stereotype. He was young, in his twenties, and slight of build. Apart from his appearance, however, there was no obvious explanation for what Oncale claimed happened to him in October 1991 while working as a roustabout on an oil rig off the coast of Louisiana.

Oncale claimed in a federal civil rights suit that he was "sexually assaulted, battered, touched, and threatened with homosexual rape" by two supervisors. He said the alleged taunts and threats—which the supervisors and their company denied—forced him to quit after barely three months on the job. Then, in 1994, he filed suit under Title VII of the Civil Rights Act of 1964, claiming that the conduct constituted sexual harassment in violation of federal law.

Joseph Oncale

The federal appeals court for Louisiana rejected Oncale's suit, saying the law did not apply to misconduct between employees of the same sex. But this term the Supreme Court disagreed. The justices ruled unanimously that Title VII's prohibition against sexual harassment applies equally to conduct between men and women, men and men, or women and women. But the Court also took the opportunity to stress that the law prohibited only seriously offensive behavior, not what the Court termed "male-on-male horseplay or intersexual flirtation."

Oncale, married and the father of two young children, depicted the behavior of the two supervisors—crane operator John Lyons and driller Danny Pippen—as far worse than horseplay. Twice, according to Oncale's complaint, Lyons pulled his penis from his pants and put it against Oncale's body—once on his head and once on his arm. Each time, Oncale claimed, Lyons threatened to rape him. On a third occasion, while in the shower, Lyons allegedly placed a bar in Oncale's anus while Pippen held him. The two men, according to Oncale's suit, "repeatedly" told him that they wanted to have sexual intercourse with him and intended to continue their assaults as long as Oncale worked on the rig.

Lyons and Pippen both denied the allegations, as did Sundowner Offshore Services Corp., which operated the platform for Chevron Corp. But attorneys for the defendants also argued, in a motion for summary judgment, that even if the allegations were true, sexual behavior between people of the same sex could not constitute sexual harassment under federal law.

Federal courts had been having difficulty with the issue. One federal appeals court—the Eighth Circuit—had allowed an Iowa factory worker to pursue a sexual harassment claim based on allegations that male coworkers had intentionally grabbed and squeezed his testicles. Other federal appeals courts had also endorsed in passing the validity of same-sex sexual harassment. But the Fifth Circuit, which covered Louisiana and Texas, had flatly held in 1994 that behavior between people of the same sex could never be sexual harassment.

Following the Fifth Circuit's precedent, the trial judge in Oncale's case granted summary judgment to the defendants. A three-judge Fifth Circuit panel followed suit, and the full appeals court turned aside Oncale's bid to have the decision reconsidered. Oncale—backed by the Justice Department—asked the Court to review the case, arguing that the Fifth Circuit's ruling was contradicted by the plain language of the statute and by all other administrative and judicial constructions of the law.

The Court's decision in June 1997 to review the case prompted a flurry of briefs from civil rights organizations, including gay rights groups, in support of Oncale's position and two briefs from employers' groups in opposition. In their briefs, the business groups claimed that recognizing same-sex sexual harassment would turn civil rights law into an unmanageable code of workplace behavior and ultimately force employers defending such suits to breach employees' privacy by asking about their sexual orientation.

The justices appeared to give the employers' position little credence when the case was argued on December 3. "There's not the slightest indication that [Congress] intended to federalize the regulation of conduct between men and men," Harry Reasoner, the Houston attorney representing Sundowner, told the justices.

"Why isn't it possible that a homosexual man or a nonhomosexual man could discriminate against another man, or a woman?" Breyer shot back.

"We have to reverse the Fifth Circuit," agreed Rehnquist. Under its ruling, he said, "a man or a woman who discriminates against a man or a woman is immune, and that seems hard to justify."

For Oncale's lawyer, Baton Rouge attorney Nicholas Canaday III, the major problem appeared to be reassuring the justices that a favorable ruling would not flood federal courts with minor workplace disputes. "Joseph Oncale was the victim of unwanted, unsolicited, and obnoxious sexual advances," Canaday said. "That is sexual harassment."

But Scalia said it was not clear that Oncale had been singled out because of his sex. "Is this a dirty word law?" he asked. "It wasn't enacted to establish politeness."

When Canaday struggled for an answer, Souter rescued him by suggesting that the sexual nature of the alleged conduct made "a stronger case of sexual discrimination than if it was nonsexual in nature."

The Court's decision three months later was both short and decisive. Its previous rulings, Scalia wrote in the unanimous opinion on March 7, had indicated that someone could be found guilty of discriminating against a person of the same race or of the same sex. On that basis, he concluded, "We see no justification in the statutory language or our precedents for a categorical rule excluding same-sex harassment claims from the coverage of Title VII."

Scalia stressed, however, that courts had to require plaintiffs to prove behavior "so objectively offensive as to alter the 'conditions' of the victim's employment." In looking at that issue, courts should consider both common sense and social context, he said. "A professional football player's working environment is not severely or pervasively abusive, for example, if the coach smacks him on the buttocks as he heads onto the field—even if the same behavior would reasonably be experienced as abusive by the coach's secretary (male or female) back at the office," he said.

All eight justices joined Scalia's opinion. Thomas added a one-sentence concurrence to stress that the decision required plaintiffs to prove, in the words of the statute, discrimination "because of . . . sex."

On the day of the ruling, gay rights groups hailed the decision as a victory. It "will benefit all Americans, not just gays," said Elizabeth Burke, a lawyer with the Human Rights Fund. Business groups, however, minimized the likely impact. "I don't think it happens that often," Stephen Bokat of the U.S. Chamber of Commerce said.

A few months later, a prominent lesbian rights' lawyer complained that the ruling appeared to be encouraging some heterosexual workers to charge homosexual coworkers with sexual harassment when they talked about their social lives or displayed pictures of their partners at the workplace. "It's being used a little bit as a sword against gay people by people who would like to see us closeted or intimidated," said Beatrice Dohrn, legal director of the Lambda Legal Defense and Education Fund.

By the time of the Court's ruling, the two employees named as defendants in Oncale's suit had left Sundowner for reasons unrelated to the litigation. With a trial scheduled in early fall 1998, a lawyer for the company said both the company and the individuals would continue to contest Oncale's allegations. "Whatever may have happened," Houston lawyer John Smither said, "was nothing more than on-the-job horseplay that occurs from time to time."

Oncale was working as a welder on another offshore oil rig at the time of the decision. Canaday said Oncale felt "vindicated," but realized that the case still had to go to trial. "He certainly recognized that nothing has been won yet," Canaday said.

Sexual Harassment

Schools' Liability for Teachers' Misconduct Limited

Gebser v. Lago Vista Independent School District, decided by a 5–4 vote, June 22, 1998; O'Connor wrote the opinion; Stevens, Souter, Ginsburg, and Breyer dissented. *(See excerpts, pp. 164–176.)*

When the principal of Lago Vista High School outside San Antonio, Texas, received complaints in October 1992 that teacher Frank Waldrop was making sexually suggestive comments in class, he assembled the teacher and parents together to talk about the problem. Waldrop denied saying anything offensive in class but offered an apology anyway. The principal counseled him to be more careful in the future, and the matter was closed.

Unbeknownst to the principal or other school officials, however, Waldrop had been having a sexual affair for months with a teenaged student in his class, Alida Star Gebser. The affair came to light only four months later, in January 1993, when a policeman discovered Waldrop and Gebser having sex outside Waldrop's car off a remote country road.

Waldrop was arrested and immediately fired; later, he pleaded guilty to having sex with Gebser and was given a form of suspended sentence. Meanwhile, Gebser and her mother, Alida Jean McCollough, also filed civil suits against both Waldrop and the Lago Vista school board in both Texas and federal courts. Texas law protected the school district from liability in state court. But Gebser appeared to have a good chance of recovering damages in the federal suit because of Title IX of the Education Amendments of 1972, which the Supreme Court had interpreted as prohibiting sexual harassment of students in any school system receiving federal funds.

In a closely divided ruling this term, however, the Court sharply limited the ability of victims of sexual harassment to use Title IX to hold school boards or colleges and universities liable for misconduct by teachers. By a 5–4 vote, the Court held that school systems could be forced to pay damages for sexual harassment only if ranking officials knew of the misconduct and failed—to the point of deliberate indifference—to do anything to stop it.

Gebser first met Waldrop in spring 1991 when, as an eighth-grader, she enrolled in a high school book discussion group that he led. Once in high school, she was assigned to other classes Waldrop taught. Gebser liked Waldrop as a teacher—but, as later evidence showed, Waldrop often made sexually suggestive remarks in the book group and in class. And one day in spring 1992, while visiting Gebser's house on the pretense of giving his student a book, he kissed and fondled her. "I was terrified," Gebser said later. But she told no one.

The two began having sexual intercourse later that spring and continued through the summer and fall. Still, Gebser did not report what was going on. "If I was to blow the whistle on that, I couldn't have this person as a teacher anymore," she said later. Besides, she said, Waldrop was "the one person in Lago administration . . . who I most trusted."

Sexual affairs between students and teachers have occurred, of course, throughout history. But in recent years educators, parents, and policy makers in the United States have strongly condemned such liaisons as immoral, unprofessional, and illegal. In February 1992—a few months before Waldrop's affair with Gebser began—the Supreme Court gave students and their families an additional legal tool to deal with the problem. It held that the federal law prohibiting sex discrimination in federally financed school systems, Title IX, allowed students to sue and recover money damages from a teacher or school system for sexual harassment. Even though Congress had not mentioned private lawsuits in the law, the Court said that recognizing an "implied right of action" would further Congress's intent of eliminating sexual discrimination in federally funded educational institutions. The unanimous ruling in *Franklin v. Gwinnett County Public Schools* reinstated a suit brought by a Georgia high school student who had charged that a teacher had forced her to have sex with him; she said that school district officials discouraged her from pressing charges with him and then dropped their investigation after firing him.

After the Court recognized a right to sue for damages under Title IX, lower courts had to decide the rules governing liability. Most federal appeals courts to address the issue held that, unless a school district or college had a procedure for dealing with sexual harassment complaints, it could not claim lack of knowledge of any misconduct as a defense. But other courts—including the Fifth Circuit in Texas in a pair of decisions in 1997—interpreted *Franklin* to mean that schools could not be held liable unless they knew of the sexual harassment and failed to do anything about it.

When Gebser's case reached the Fifth Circuit later that year, the appeals court, applying that principle, upheld a lower court's decision to reject the suit. Gebser then asked the Supreme Court to review the case. The Clinton administration and an array of women's rights groups urged the Court to adopt the broader standard of liability adopted by the majority of federal appeals courts to consider the question.

In presenting that position, Gebser's attorney, Terry Weldon of Austin, and Assistant Solicitor General Beth Brinkmann argued March 25 that the school district had been negligent by failing to provide students with information about what to do in the event of sexual misconduct by a teacher. "She did not know to whom she should turn," Weldon said.

But several of the justices were skeptical of applying the same broad liability rules governing workplace suits under Title VII to suits under Title IX. "The question we need to answer is whether a suit under Title IX should be governed by the principles of Title VII," O'Connor said as Weldon opened his argument.

Scalia added another reason for having a different liability standard under the two statutes: Congress's failure to specify a right to sue under Title IX. "The statute on its face doesn't even spell out that there's a private cause of action," Scalia said.

In her turn, Brinkmann drew a sharp response from Kennedy when she suggested that a school district should not be able to use its lack of knowledge of sexual harassment to protect itself from damages. "You're saying that the school district can be held liable for something it knew nothing about," Kennedy said.

The school district's lawyer, Wallace Jefferson of San Antonio, picked up on the point, stressing that Waldrop had not engaged in any misconduct toward Gebser on school grounds. "There is no way that anyone [in the school system] could have known about" the affair, Jefferson said. He also warned that a damage award could represent a significant chunk of the school district's $1.6 million annual budget—all because it received less than $100,000 in federal funds during the year.

The Court's decision three months later reflected Jefferson's defense of the school district's actions as well as the justices' doubts about an expansive standard of liability. Writing for the majority in the June 22 ruling, O'Connor reasoned that, in the absence of any directions from Congress, the Court had "a measure of latitude to shape a sensible remedial scheme." But she said the law contained "clues" that Congress would not have wanted a broad liability standard—notably, the requirement that the government give a school district notice of a violation of the law and an opportunity to correct the problem before cutting off federal funds.

In addition, O'Connor repeated the contrast she made during arguments between the two sex discrimination laws. "[W]hereas Title VII aims centrally to compensate victims of discrimination," she wrote, "Title IX focuses more on 'protecting' individuals from discriminatory practices carried out by recipients of federal funds."

For those reasons, O'Connor concluded, a broad liability standard "would frustrate the purposes of Title IX." Instead, she said, a school district could be liable for sexual harassment of a student only if an official "with authority to institute corrective action" had "actual notice" of the problem and was guilty of "deliberate indifference" in failing to correct it. Rehnquist, Scalia, Kennedy, and Thomas concurred in the opinion.

Dissenting justices countered that the ruling would actually "thwart" Title IX's purposes of preventing the use of federal funds to support discriminatory practices and to protect individuals from such practices. "It seems quite obvious," Stevens wrote, "that both of those purposes would be served— not frustrated—by providing a damages remedy in a case of this kind." Stevens warned that "few Title IX plaintiffs who have been victims of intentional discrimination will be able to recover damages under this exceedingly high standard."

Souter, Ginsburg, and Breyer joined the dissent. Separately, Ginsburg suggested that under the stricter liability standard a school district should be allowed to cite the existence of an effective anti–sexual harassment policy as a defense. Souter and Breyer joined her opinion; Stevens said the issue did not have to be decided.

Reaction to the ruling was predictably divided, both in Washington and in Texas. Jefferson, the school board's lawyer, said the decision would protect school systems from potentially ruinous damage awards. But Gebser's lawyer, Weldon, told the *Washington Post* that the ruling "basically allows the school districts to put on a blindfold and to benefit from their ignorance."

Gebser herself, who had graduated from high school and gone on to college by the time of the ruling, took the decision stoically, Weldon said. "We had steadily lost all through the process," the lawyer said. "She's sort of inured to that, I suppose."

Disability Rights

Anti-Bias Law Protects People with HIV

Bragdon v. Abbott, decided by a 5–4 vote, June 25, 1998; Kennedy wrote the opinion; Rehnquist, O'Connor, Scalia, and Thomas dissented. *(See excerpts, pp. 177–191.)*

When Randon Bragdon did a routine dental exam on Sidney Abbott on September 16, 1994, he discovered a small, gum-line cavity in a back tooth. Filling the cavity would also have been a routine procedure for the Bangor, Maine, dentist, except for one thing: Abbott was infected with the human immunodeficiency virus, HIV—the virus that causes the deadly disease AIDS.

Bragdon told Abbott that filling the cavity in his office would be dangerous but offered to perform the procedure in a local hospital. Abbott, however, insisted she was entitled to be treated in the office because of the federal law that prohibits discrimination against persons with disabilities—the Americans with Disabilities Act, or ADA.

The dispute set up an important legal test of the scope of the landmark 1990 law. Bragdon, after losing in two lower federal courts, took the case to the Supreme Court, which ruled this term that the disability rights law protected people with HIV from discrimination even if they had no outward symptoms. The ruling cheered AIDS activists and other disability rights groups, even though the justices left open the question whether treating a person with HIV in a medical office posed an unacceptable risk to the health or safety of medical workers.

The passage of the ADA in 1990 capped years of lobbying by disability rights groups. The law generally followed the model of other civil rights laws in prohibiting discrimination in the workplace, in government programs or services, or in public accommodations against anyone with a mental or physical disability. In one section, the law even went beyond previous civil rights laws: "public accommodations" were defined broadly to include virtually all retail and service establishments, including as one example "the professional office of a health care provider."

Other parts of the law, however, contained definitions and qualifications that differed from other, simpler civil rights statutes. First, the law contained a three-part definition of disability to mean "a physical or mental impairment that substantially limits one or more of [an individual's] major life activities." Second, the law allowed a business to deny service to someone with a disability if the individual "poses a direct threat to the health or safety of others." In addition, the law said that employers need not make special accommodations for disabled workers if the changes would result in "undue hardship."

Sidney Abbott, left, filed a discrimination complaint after dentist Randon Bragdon refused to treat her in his office because she had the virus that causes AIDS. The Supreme Court said federal law protects persons with HIV disease even if they have no visible symptoms.

The law helped people with disabilities enter the mainstream of American life in countless ways, most visibly in the creation of barrier-free access to public buildings and private businesses. It also generated some difficult legal issues, such as whether alcoholics or drug addicts were "disabled" and protected from discrimination in hiring or promotion. And it produced some grumbling from businesses as well as local and state governments about the costs of compliance.

Health care services for people with HIV or AIDS was one of the more contentious compliance questions arising under the law. AIDS was a deadly disease with no known cure or preventive treatment, and the virus had a long latency period before symptoms appeared. In addition, the virus could conceivably be spread through exposure to body fluids, such as blood or saliva, with which a health care worker could easily come into contact while treating someone with the disease.

Even so, both the American Medical Association and the American Dental Association issued guidelines saying that health care workers could safely treat persons with HIV/AIDS if they took safety precautions such as wearing masks and rubber gloves. In addition, despite the theoretical risks, as of mid-1998 the federal Centers for Disease Control and Prevention had not documented a single case in which a health care worker had contracted the virus from a patient.

Bragdon, however, was known in dental circles as an outspoken advocate of taking extra precautions for treating people with HIV/AIDS. He was not alone: polls of doctors indicated that as many as one-third of physicians said they would refuse to treat someone with the disease. For her part, Abbott was part of a nationwide movement challenging health care providers who refused to provide normal treatment to people with HIV.

Since Abbott had no visible symptoms, however, her lawyers had to struggle to meet the ADA's definition of disability. They contended that she was "substantially limited" in her ability to bear children, because of the risk of spreading the virus to a sexual partner or to a fetus, and that reproduction amounted to a "major life activity" under the law. The argument persuaded a federal judge in Maine and the First U.S. Circuit Court of Appeals in Boston. Both courts also rejected Bragdon's argument that he was justified in believing he could not treat Abbott safely in his office.

The Court's decision to hear the case marked its first opportunity to interpret the ADA as well as its first encounter with the legal issues created by the AIDS epidemic. In one earlier ruling, however, it had given a broad reading to the antidiscrimination provision of an earlier disability rights law that prohibited discrimination against persons with disabilities in any federally funded program or service. In that case, *School Board of Nassau County, Florida v. Arline* (1987), the Court ruled that a local school board could not fire a teacher with tuberculosis just because she had a contagious disease.

The new case drew an outpouring of briefs supporting Abbott from civil rights organizations, gay rights and other AIDS groups, and some medical associations, including the AMA. The Clinton administration also urged the Court to uphold the lower court decisions in Abbott's favor. For its part, the American Dental Association sided with Bragdon, contending—despite the association's guidelines for treating patients with HIV—that Abbott was not disabled under the law because reproduction was not a major life activity as the law used the term.

In presenting Bragdon's case to the Court on March 30, Bangor attorney John McCarthy faced skeptical questions from justices on both his major points. He opened by emphasizing what he described as the "risk of death" from treating patients with HIV or AIDS. But Breyer emphasized the lack of any cases of transmittal of the disease from patient to health care workers. "If that's so, how can we say that your client exercised reasonable judgment?" Later, Breyer challenged McCarthy again when the lawyer argued that Abbott was not limited in her reproductive abilities but merely making a "moral choice" not to bear children. "Are you disabled if you don't go out of the house because you know that you can give the whole town bubonic plague?" Breyer asked. When McCarthy meekly answered yes, Breyer declared: "I would think so."

In his turn, Bennett Klein, an attorney with the Boston-based organization Gay and Lesbian Advocates and Defenders representing Abbott, also emphasized that HIV was a "fatal, incurable, contagious disease," but for the purpose of showing that people with HIV needed strong legal protections against discrimination. Without such protection, Klein told the justices, "people with HIV would simply hide their conditions." But some of the justices indicated doubts that Abbott's condition met the legal definition of disability. "I have a problem," Scalia said, "with saying that affecting the ability to reproduce is a disability."

The division among the justices reemerged in the Court's decision on June 25. By a 5–4 vote, the Court forcefully declared that HIV disease met the ADA's definition of physical impairment "from the moment of infection and throughout every stage of the disease." After graphically describing the progression of the disease, Kennedy said that Abbott could have argued that it affected any of a number of life activities. At the least, he said, reproduction—"central to the life process"—amounted to a major life activity for purposes of the law. HIV infection "substantially limited" Abbott's reproductive ability, he continued, because of the "significant risk" of infecting the man during conception or the risk of infecting her child "during gestation or childbirth."

Kennedy stopped short, however, of giving Abbott a complete victory. The evidence in the courts below, he said, was inadequate to rule whether her condition posed a risk to the health or safety of Bragdon or his office staff. Instead, that issue had to be sent back to lower courts for further consideration. Still, Kennedy heartened AIDS advocacy groups by stressing that any risk assessment "must be based on medical or other objective evidence," not on any subjective belief on Bragdon's part—"even if maintained in good faith."

Four justices—Stevens, Souter, Ginsburg, and Breyer—concurred in Kennedy's opinion. But Stevens and Breyer said they would have gone ahead and rejected Bragdon's argument about the risks of treating HIV patients; they concurred in the remand only to create a majority position. Ginsburg added a brief concurrence, saying it was "wise to remand" in view of the importance of the risk issue to health care workers.

In the main dissenting opinion, Rehnquist contended that reproduction was not a major life activity under the ADA's definition, which he said applied only to activities "essential in the day-to-day existence of a normally functioning individual." In addition, he said that Abbott's "voluntary" choice not to engage in sex or bear children because of her condition did not amount to a "substantial limit" on her activities. Scalia and Thomas joined his opinion; O'Connor wrote a somewhat narrower dissent also concluding that reproduction did not amount to a major life activity under the law. All four concurred in remanding the case, and Rehnquist predicted that Bragdon would be able to show that it was "objectively reasonable" for him to conclude that treating Abbott in his office would pose a safety risk.

The tentative result did not dampen the enthusiastic reaction to the decision from disability rights and AIDS advocacy groups. Klein told reporters he was "elated" with the decision. Daniel Zingale, executive director of AIDS Action, called the ruling "a victory of reason and responsibility over irrationality and illogic." Several disability rights experts suggested the ruling could also protect other people with manageable diseases, such as cancer or diabetes, from discrimination. But Bragdon's attorney made clear his client would continue to argue that he was not obligated to treat Abbott in his office. "The point is," McCarthy told National Public Radio, "it's going to be done again."

Separation of Powers

Line Item Veto Act Held Unconstitutional

Clinton, President of the United States v. City of New York, decided by a 6–3 vote, June 25, 1998; Stevens wrote the opinion; Scalia, O'Connor, and Breyer dissented. *(See excerpts, pp. 219–233.)*

Deep inside in the massive 1996 Balanced Budget Act lay an obscure provision aimed at helping the state of New York settle a $2 billion dispute with the federal government over the costs of medical care for the poor. A similarly abstruse section in a 1996 tax act was meant to make it easier for farmer cooperatives to buy processing facilities from for-profit corporations.

To members of Congress, these provisions were routine legislative maneuvers to help out constituents. But to critics, they exemplified the kind of special-interest measures often passed by Congress that cost the federal treasury billions of dollars and would never win approval if exposed to full debate and consideration.

For more than a century, presidents of both parties had asked for the power to pencil such items out of omnibus bills passed by Congress. Finally, in 1996, President Clinton got the authority when a Republican-controlled Congress passed the Line Item Veto Act. The measure gave the Democratic chief executive the power—after signing a spending or tax bill into law—to "cancel" individual spending items or certain limited tax breaks contained in the measures.

The measure had popular support, but many members of Congress contended that it violated the procedures set out in the Constitution for enacting laws. This term, the Supreme Court agreed, in a 6–3 ruling that reaffirmed an age-old congressional practice and left critics of Congress scrambling for alternatives to curb so-called "pork-barrel" spending.

Ulysess S. Grant was the first president to ask for what later came to be called a "line-item veto" when he called on Congress in 1873 to approve a constitutional amendment to authorize the procedure. Congress refused. Sixty years later, a popular Democratic president, Franklin D. Roosevelt, asked for a line-item veto amendment. The House approved the proposal, but it died in the Senate.

Then in the 1980s a popular Republican president, Ronald Reagan, repeatedly called for a line-item veto. Reagan, who had served as governor

President Bill Clinton uses new power under the Line Item Veto Act to cancel two spending provisions and a special tax break on August 11, 1997. Groups challenging the law won a Supreme Court ruling declaring the act unconstitutional.

of California for eight years, noted that more than forty of the states' chief executives had the power to delete individual items from spending bills. But leaders of the Democratic majority in Congress denounced the idea, saying it would give presidents too much power and would not reduce spending very much anyway.

The partisan stalemate remained until Clinton's election as president in 1992 and the Republican victory in the 1994 congressional elections. A former Arkansas governor, Clinton endorsed the line-item veto in his presidential campaign and again after taking office. Two years later, the Republicans made the proposal part of the ten-point "Contract With America" that they used as a campaign platform in winning control of the House and the Senate.

Still, the proposal could not command the two-thirds majority needed for a constitutional amendment. So line-item veto supporters instead crafted a statute that they hoped would pass constitutional muster. As finally enacted in April 1996, the Line Item Veto Act authorized the president to "cancel" a spending item or a targeted tax break benefiting 100 or fewer taxpayers within five days after signing a bill into law. Congress could "disapprove" the president's cancellation by passing a new law containing the canceled item within the next thirty days—subject to a normal veto that Congress could override only by a two-thirds vote.

In exercising this new power, the law required the president to determine that each cancellation would "reduce the federal budget," "not impair any essential Government functions," and "not harm the national interest." A so-called "lockbox" provision required that any savings be used only for deficit reduction. The law was to take effect after the 1997 presidential inauguration and was to lapse if the federal government ever had a budget surplus—a seemingly remote possibility.

Before the law even went into effect, six members of Congress—five Democrats and one Republican—filed a federal court suit on January 2, 1997, challenging the measure as unconstitutional. They claimed the law violated the Constitution's Presentment Clause, which required that a bill be passed by both houses of Congress and signed by the president in identical form before becoming law. The lead plaintiff in the case was Robert C. Byrd, a veteran Democratic senator from West Virginia who was known for zealously guarding congressional power and skillfully funneling federal dollars to his home state. A federal judge agreed the law violated the Constitution, but the Court—voting 7–2 in *Raines v. Byrd*—decided in June 1997 that the lawmakers had no legal standing to bring the suit. *(See* Supreme Court Yearbook, 1996–1997, *p. 108.)*

With the legal cloud temporarily lifted, Clinton used the law in August 1997 to cancel two items from the budget act passed by Congress and one provision in the Taxpayer Relief Act. In canceling the items, Clinton said the law was a "powerful new tool" to control wasteful spending. But the savings projected by the administration totaled a mere $600 million over five years. And congressional supporters of the provisions insisted that each was justifiable on public policy grounds.

New York's powerful congressional delegation was particularly incensed at Clinton's deletion of the provision to resolve a dispute over federal reimbursement of the state's cost under the Medicaid program. The dispute involved a state tax on health care providers that federal regulators said could not be counted in calculating the amount of federal matching funds. With the issue still pending before the federal agency that administered the Medicaid program, New York's Democratic senator, Daniel Patrick Moynihan, inserted a provision into the budget act—section 4722—that effectively enacted New York's position in the dispute.

Supporters said the farmer cooperative provision—section 958 of the Taxpayer Relief Act—was aimed merely at equalizing the treatment of farmer co-ops with other agricultural concerns. The provision allowed a for-profit corporation to defer capital gains taxes on the sale of an agricultural processing facility to a farmer co-op just as it could do if the sale was to a for-profit company. An Idaho cooperative, the Snake River Potato Growers, Inc., had been pushing for the provision in the hope that it would help ease its purchase of a processing plant from a local company.

The groups affected by the two vetoes promptly filed suits challenging

Clinton's action: the city of New York, along with two hospitals, a hospital association, and two unions representing health care workers in one case; the Snake River co-op and one individual member in the other. As in the previous challenge, a federal judge in Washington ruled in March 1998 that the measure violated the Constitution. The administration asked the Supreme Court to hear the case on an expedited basis, as provided in the law, and the justices agreed.

When Solicitor General Seth Waxman presented his defense of the law to the Court on April 27, he faced sharply skeptical questions from justices across the ideological spectrum. Waxman argued that the president's "cancellations" did not amount to a true veto, but Ginsburg quickly cut him short. "You can call it a different word, but it's the same thing," she retorted. "It's gone."

Waxman tried again, insisting that the president was not "repealing" the law but only carrying out a cancellation power that Congress had delegated to him. "What's the difference between law-repealing and lawmaking?" Souter interjected.

Later, when Waxman tried to minimize the impact of the law, Rehnquist jumped in. "If we uphold it here," the chief justice said, "it could then be applied to a vast amount of spending."

In their turns, attorneys Louis Cohen and Charles Cooper—representing the Idaho farmers and the New York City plaintiffs respectively—faced fewer sharp questions on the merits of the case. But Scalia did question their standing to bring the suits since New York City had not yet suffered a cut in Medicaid assistance and the tax provision in the farmers' case would actually benefit the company selling the processing plant rather than the co-op. But Scalia nearly apologized for raising the issue—"I hate to bring this up," he said—and the other justices showed little interest in pursuing the questions.

The Court's ruling on June 25 began by recognizing the plaintiffs' standing in both cases and then, in a relatively brief fourteen pages, striking down the law as inconsistent with the Constitution. "This Act gives the President the unilateral power to change the text of duly enacted statutes," Stevens wrote for the majority. The laws left on the books after Clinton's "cancellations," Stevens said, were "truncated versions" of the bills passed by Congress. Whatever the policy arguments for the procedure, he concluded, "Congress cannot alter the procedures set out in Article I, section 7, without amending the Constitution."

Five justices—Rehnquist, Kennedy, Souter, Ginsburg, and Breyer—joined Stevens's opinion. In a five-page concurrence, Kennedy indicated sympathy with the act's goal of restraining "persistent excessive spending." But, he said, the measure "enhances the President's powers beyond what the Framers would have endorsed."

Scalia and Breyer wrote separate dissents, both adopting Waxman's argument that the act was a proper—almost unexceptional—delegation of power over federal spending from Congress to the president. "[T]here is not a dime's worth of difference between Congress's authorizing the President to *cancel* a spending item, and Congress's authorizing money to be spent on a particular item at the President's discretion," Scalia wrote. "And the latter has been done since the Founding of the Nation." Scalia, joined by O'Connor, also rejected the Snake River co-op's standing to bring the case.

In his dissent, Breyer insisted that the act did not allow the president to repeal a duly enacted law. "[H]e did not *repeal* any law, nor did he *amend* any law," Breyer said, referring to Clinton's cancellations. "He simply *followed* the law, leaving the statute[s], as they are literally written, intact." Unlike Scalia, however, Breyer recognized standing for both sets of plaintiffs; Breyer joined the rest of Scalia's opinion, and Scalia and O'Connor joined the main part of Breyer's.

Opponents of the line-item veto exulted in the decision. "A great ruling," exclaimed Moynihan, who had been one of the plaintiffs in the earlier challenge. "The Constitution is intact." Clinton, however, voiced regret. "The decision is a defeat for all Americans," the president said.

On Capitol Hill, some lawmakers talked of alternative ways to force votes on individual spending projects, such as breaking up omnibus appropriation bills, but the odds seemed against any such change. Meanwhile, the Office of Management and Budget announced on July 17 that it would release all the funds for items that the president had vetoed and no longer try to overturn New York's system of hospital taxes used to help pay for health care for the poor.

Attorney-Client Privilege

Confidences Protected after Death in Vincent Foster Case

Swidler & Berlin v. United States, decided by a 6–3 vote, June 25, 1998; Rehnquist wrote the opinion; O'Connor, Scalia, and Thomas dissented. *(See excerpts, pp. 233–240.)*

Vincent Foster was under a lot of stress when he went to the home of Washington attorney James Hamilton on Sunday morning, July 11, 1993. The deputy White House counsel and one-time law partner of first lady Hillary Rodham Clinton had been under intense public and media scrutiny since coming to Washington six months earlier because of his connections to two controversial investigations touching on President Clinton and his wife.

Foster, then forty-eight, began by asking Hamilton whether their conversation would be protected by the attorney-client privilege. "Without hesitation, I said that it was," Hamilton later related. Hamilton took three pages

Independent Counsel Kenneth Starr, left, subpoenaed notes from a lawyer's interview with White House deputy counsel Vincent Foster after Foster's suicide. The Supreme Court held the notes were protected by attorney-client privilege.

of handwritten notes during the two-hour conversation and then put them away in a file.

Nine days later, Foster committed suicide. The death stunned the Clintons and Foster's other friends. It also stirred suspicions among Clinton's critics that Foster had gone to the grave with damaging information about the Clintons.

Two-and-a-half years later, in December 1995, an independent counsel investigating the president subpoenaed Hamilton for the notes of his conversation with Foster. When Hamilton refused, Independent Counsel Kenneth Starr fought the issue to the Supreme Court, arguing that the notes would provide essential information that could not be obtained in any other way. But this term the Court rebuffed Starr's effort in a ruling that left Starr's inquiry incomplete but reinforced one of the oldest protections of confidentiality recognized in the law.

Foster had been entangled in two investigations: an examination of the failed Whitewater real estate deal from the Clintons' days in Arkansas and the firings of seven career White House travel office employees in May 1993. Foster had done some of the legal work on the Whitewater matter, a complex story with insinuations of possible political influence to help finance the deal or minimize the Clintons' eventual losses in the scheme. As a White

House lawyer, Foster had been involved in the so-called "Travelgate" affair. Critics said the sudden firings appeared aimed at benefiting the travel business of a friend of the Clintons, Hollywood producer Harry Thomason, and they suspected that the first lady was behind the move.

In public comments, Hillary Clinton minimized her role in the travel office episode. But in January 1996 a memo surfaced from a former White House aide, David Watkins, quoting Foster as telling him "regularly" that "the First Lady was concerned and desired action . . . the firing of the Travel Office." In seeking Hamilton's notes of his talk with Foster, Starr argued that the information would help determine whether White House officials had committed perjury, obstruction of justice, or other federal crimes in their accounts of the firings.

Hamilton, a partner in Washington law firm Swidler & Berlin, which had a substantial white-collar crime practice, had met and worked with Foster on the Clinton transition after the November 1992 election. In opposing the effort to subpoena the notes, he contended that without his promise of confidentiality to Foster, "we would not have had that conversation, and there would have been no notes" to argue about later.

In December 1996 U.S. district court judge John Garrett Penn agreed with Hamilton that the notes were protected from subpoena by the attorney-client privilege as well as by the attorney work-product doctrine, which generally protects legal memoranda and the like prepared by lawyers while representing clients. On appeal, however, a divided three-judge panel in August 1997 backed Starr's contention that the attorney-client privilege did not apply after the client's death.

The judges in the majority said that the costs of protecting communications after the client's death were "high" compared to what they depicted as a minimal risk of any chilling effect on client communications. The appeals court also rejected Hamilton's work-product argument, saying that the notes—which the judges examined *in camera*—included some "factual material" not protected by the doctrine.

The Court's decision to hear the case, and to hear it on an expedited basis after the end of the normal argument calendar, heightened the drama surrounding Starr's protracted investigations. Starr was simultaneously fighting separate privilege claims from the White House and Secret Service in connection with his investigation of allegations that Clinton had had a sexual relationship with a former White House intern, Monica Lewinsky.

Most legal commentators viewed the privilege claims in the Lewinsky case as tenuous. In contrast, however, the attorney-client privilege was well established and regarded by most lawyers as sacrosanct. Lawyers' groups rushed to file briefs with the Court urging support for Hamilton's position in refusing to turn over the notes. Overriding the attorney-client privilege after the client's death, the American Bar Association warned, could "confound many thousands of persons" who seek a lawyer's advice before their deaths.

Starr countered by noting that many legal commentators supported cutting off the privilege after a client's death. He also said that courts often disregarded the privilege in will contests—so-called "testamentary" cases. Lawyers' groups replied that the testamentary exception was a limited one, recognized only because it was thought to help make sure that a deceased client's property was distributed according to his or her true intentions.

When the Court heard arguments on June 8, most of the justices appeared skeptical of the independent counsel's position. A client "must feel free to tell a lawyer the truth, the whole truth, and all that," Rehnquist told associate independent counsel Brett Kavanaugh. Breyer said that lawyers and laypersons alike had long thought the privilege was virtually absolute. "They all think that's the rule," Breyer said, "so they think they're safe."

Only two justices—Scalia and Kennedy—appeared to voice support for enforcing Starr's subpoena. "Courts like to get to the truth," Scalia told Hamilton at one point. For his part, Kennedy said that with so many exceptions to the attorney-client privilege already extant, one more limit would not be a "sweeping change." To the contrary, Hamilton answered: "If the Supreme Court says that the privilege expires when the client dies, you will find many, many more cases raising this issue."

The Court ruled only seventeen days later, voting 6–3 to reject Starr's subpoena for the notes. Rehnquist said that recognizing the privilege after a client's death was supported by "the great body" of caselaw and by "weighty" policy reasons. "Knowing that communications will remain confidential even after death encourages the client to communicate freely and frankly with counsel," Rehnquist wrote. Even if clients have no reason to fear criminal prosecution after death, the chief justice continued, they still might be concerned about "reputation, civil liability, or possible harm to friends or family."

On that basis, Rehnquist concluded, the independent counsel had failed to make a "sufficient showing" to overturn the long-established privilege in the face of a grand jury subpoena in a criminal case. In a footnote, however, Rehnquist left open the question whether a criminal defendant could override the privilege if necessary to protect his or her constitutional rights. Those joining his opinion included Kennedy, despite his doubts during oral arguments, along with liberal-leaning justices Stevens, Souter, Ginsburg, and Breyer.

In a six-page dissenting opinion, O'Connor argued that the risks of harming someone's interests by disclosing conversations with his or her lawyer were "greatly diminished" after death, while the costs of recognizing an absolute privilege were "inordinately high." She argued the case should be returned to the trial judge for reconsideration. Scalia and Thomas joined her opinion.

Starr's office issued a bland reaction, voicing disappointment but promising to continue to pursue its investigation "as thoroughly and expeditiously as possible." By late summer, no indictments had been issued in the Travelgate affair. For his part, Hamilton told a news conference that the ruling was "a victory for the legal profession." Asked whether historians would eventually see the notes of his conversation with Foster, he said, "I will not answer that question."

Excessive Fines Clause

Forfeiture Struck Down for Currency Reporting Violation

United States v. Bajakajian, decided by a 5–4 vote, June 22, 1998; Thomas wrote the opinion; Kennedy, Rehnquist, O'Connor, and Scalia dissented. *(See excerpts, pp. 154–164.)*

When a federal customs inspector at Los Angeles International Airport asked Hosep Bajakajian whether he was taking more than $10,000 in cash out of the country on June 9, 1994, he lied and said no. In fact, other inspectors, using dogs specially trained to sniff out currency, had already determined that Bajakajian had hidden $230,000 in cash in his checked baggage. A search of his carry-on bag, his wallet, and his wife's purse uncovered more cash: all told, $357,144.

Bajakajian, a Syrian immigrant who owned two service stations in Los Angeles, tried to explain that he was en route to Cyprus to repay a debt to a friend who had helped him get started in the United States. Unmoved, the inspectors charged him with violating the federal anti–money laundering law that requires anyone leaving the country with more than $10,000 in cash to report the transaction.

As part of the indictment, the government asked for the forfeiture of all of the cash—as the currency-reporting law mandated for any "willful" violation. The federal judge who convicted Bajakajian, however, ordered only $15,000 turned over to the government. When a federal appeals court upheld the decision, the government took the case to the Supreme Court.

This term, the Court likewise refused to order all of Bajakajian's money confiscated. By a 5–4 vote, the Court held that the "grossly disproportional" penalty violated the Eighth Amendment's prohibition against "excessive fines." The ruling continued the Court's recent trend of closely scrutinizing the government's use of forfeiture to confiscate money or property used in committing crimes. But dissenting justices harshly criticized the decision, saying it flouted the will of Congress and gave money launderers cause to "rejoice."

When Congress first enacted a mandatory forfeiture proviso in 1970, it was aiming at organized crime kingpins and drug traffickers who dealt in large sums of cash. Congress provided for mandatory forfeiture for willful

Hosep Bajakajian

violations of the currency reporting law in 1992 after deciding that the previous penalties—short prison terms and small fines—were inadequate to deter money laundering violations.

Through the 1980s and 1990s, the federal government as well as state and local law enforcement agencies made aggressive use of forfeiture provisions not only to go after high-rolling criminals but also to seize money or property from offenders in less serious cases. The growing use of forfeitures prompted a backlash in Congress, where some normally pro–law enforcement conservatives joined with more liberal lawmakers to call for restricting the practice.

Congress failed to act on the issue, but the Court did. In a pair of decisions in 1993, the Court ruled unanimously that forfeitures—whether imposed in connection with a criminal prosecution or in a separate civil proceeding—were subject to the Eighth Amendment's Excessive Fines Clause. But the rulings in *Austin v. United States* and *Alexander v. United States* set no specific guidelines on how to determine when a forfeiture was "excessive" and therefore unconstitutional. *(See* Supreme Court Yearbook, 1992–1993, *p. 33.)*

Whatever the appearances in his case, Bajakajian insisted he was not the type of person Congress had in mind when it required forfeiture for violating the currency-reporting law. He was a legitimate businessman, repaying a legitimate debt, Bajakajian told authorities. As for his deception, Bajakajian explained that as a minority Armenian in his native Syria, he had always been leery about taking money in and out of the country. The customs inspector's interrogation had triggered the same reaction—a fear that he might be hurt or that the money might be taken from him. So he lied.

The federal judge hearing the case accepted Bajakajian's explanation. The money was not being laundered, the judge said, and Bajakajian's failure to tell the inspectors about the cash resulted from "cultural differences." On that basis, the judge ruled that forfeiture of the entire amount would be "extraordinarily harsh" and "grossly disproportionate to the offense." Instead, the judge fined Bajakajian the maximum $5,000 permitted under the Sentencing Guidelines and ordered $15,000 forfeited—an amount designed to "make up for what I think a reasonable fine should be."

The government appealed, arguing that all the money could be confiscated under a traditional doctrine permitting forfeiture of any property that is an "instrumentality" of a crime. But the Ninth U.S. Circuit Court of Appeals said that the money was not an instrumentality because the crime was "the withholding of information . . . not the possession or the transportation of the money." In fact, the appeals court said, none of the money was subject to forfeiture. Since Bajakajian had not filed a cross appeal, however, the appeals judges said they could not set aside the limited forfeiture.

The government again appealed, and the case came before the Court for argument early in the new term, on November 4. Assistant Solicitor General Irving Gornstein again pressed the government's dual arguments that Bajakajian's money was subject to forfeiture as an instrumentality of a crime or that the forfeiture in any event was, as he put it, "a permissible punishment for . . . a serious criminal offense."

Justices were skeptical of both. Could the Taj Mahal be forfeited if it was being used to sell a teaspoonful of marijuana? Breyer asked. Gornstein demurred but later said yes after changing the hypothetical. "If you're running a business out of the Taj Mahal," the government lawyer said, "yes, that certainly could be forfeited."

O'Connor then shifted the subject. "Suppose we don't share your enthusiasm for the instrumentality approach," she said. What about proportionality, she continued. The maximum fine was $250,000, and $350,000 was seized. "And you're saying that was proportional?" she concluded, with seeming incredulity. Gornstein did not flinch. "It certainly was proportional," he said, noting the stiff prison term—five to ten years—that Congress provided. "From that, you know Congress regarded this as a very serious offense," Gornstein said.

In his turn, Bajakajian's lawyer, James Blatt of Encino, California, emphasized the trial judge's finding that his client was carrying "lawful money for a lawful purpose." Rehnquist, however, appeared dubious that Bajakajian's crime resulted from "cultural differences." Scalia followed by voicing doubts that courts could enforce the Excessive Fines Clause on a case-by-case basis. "It's a lot of trouble," Scalia said. "I don't know if courts can handle that kind of a burden."

Still, Blatt later said that he felt encouraged at the end of his half-hour argument. And, even though Thomas asked no questions—as usual—Blatt said he thought he had the justice's attention. Thomas "was very aware of the discussions," Blatt recalled. "He seemed to be smiling a lot."

The justices deliberated over the case for more than seven months, an indication of a close vote or difficult issues or both. The ruling came on June 22, announced by Thomas. He began with a joke about the currency-sniffing dogs, saying they gave "new meaning to the phrase, 'Follow the money.' " Then he became serious.

Whether or not Bajakajian's money amounted to an "instrumentality" of his crime, Thomas said, the forfeiture amounted to punishment. It "serves no remedial purpose," he said, and was "designed to punish the offender." The forfeiture therefore was subject to the Excessive Fines Clause, he said, and the test to be applied "involves solely a proportionality determination."

Thomas acknowledged that the Court had never determined what would constitute an "excessive" fine, and he found no guide in the text of the clause or its history. Instead, he turned to a standard that the Court had used in applying the Eighth Amendment's prohibition against cruel and unusual punishment. "If the amount of the forfeiture is grossly disproportional to the gravity of the defendant's offense," Thomas said, "it is unconstitutional."

Applying that standard, Thomas said forfeiture of all of Bajakajian's money would violate the Excessive Fines Clause. The crime, he said, "was solely a reporting offense" and was "unrelated to any other illegal activities." Bajakajian was "not a money launderer, a drug trafficker, or a tax evader," he continued, and the crime had caused only "minimal" harm to the government.

The vote in the case was 5–4. Thomas, normally the Court's most conservative member, was joined by left-of-center justices Stevens, Souter, Ginsburg, and Breyer. Kennedy led four dissenters in a sharply written opinion that criticized the majority both on the law and on the facts of the case.

"The crime of smuggling or failing to report cash is more serious than the Court is willing to acknowledge," Kennedy wrote. The ruling "accords no deference, let alone substantial deference, to the judgment of Congress," he said, and gave "only a cursory explanation" for holding the forfeiture to be grossly disproportional.

As for Bajakajian's offense, Kennedy insisted that it too was more serious than the majority recognized. He lied about having the money and also about where it came from, Kennedy said, and hid most of it in a false-bottomed suitcase. And Kennedy was particularly incensed by the use of Bajakajian's background to explain his failure to obey the law. "This patronizing excuse demeans millions of law-abiding Americans," he wrote.

Finally, Kennedy said that some passages in Thomas's opinion suggested that, unlike criminal forfeitures, civil forfeiture was not subject to the Excessive Fines Clause at all. That result, he said, would actually weaken legal protections for property owners, since fewer procedural protections are given in civil than in criminal forfeitures.

The effect of the ruling on the government's use of forfeitures remained to be seen. Government lawyers emphasized that it would not affect the seizure of drugs or other illegal contraband. As for Bajakajian, Blatt said his client was "ecstatic" and "gratified" after the ruling. "He's an immigrant," the lawyer said a month after the decision. "For him to be able to use the justice system as he did, it's something he's still in awe of."

Pensions and Benefits

Act to Bolster Miners' Health Benefits Struck Down

Eastern Enterprises v. Apfel, Commissioner of Social Security, decided by a 5–4 vote, June 25, 1998; O'Connor wrote the plurality opinion; Breyer, Stevens, Souter, and Ginsburg dissented. *(See excerpts, pp. 191–206.)*

In the long and troubled history of labor-management relations in the coal industry, the creation of a health benefits fund for miners and their families after a nationwide strike in 1946 was a major milestone. Miners in remote areas who had often paid high fees for middling service from poorly trained company doctors finally felt somewhat assured of proper medical care for themselves and their families while they worked and after they retired.

By the 1980s, however, the industrywide health insurance program for retired miners was moving toward financial collapse. Rising health care costs were part of the problem. But the major cause was the shift in the industry away from unionization and the exodus of hundreds of many formerly unionized companies from the program. Courts allowed the departing companies to stop paying into the program even though the United Mine Workers (UMW) contended the miners had been led all along to expect guaranteed lifetime health benefits.

Congress, acting at the behest of the UMW and the unionized companies still paying into the industry plan, passed legislation in 1992 that required payments totaling millions of dollars from many of the companies no longer contributing to the program. The companies immediately challenged the law in court. Federal courts around the country upheld the act, but the Supreme Court this term struck it down. The narrowly divided ruling cast a cloud not only over the health benefits of retired miners and their widows but also over Congress's ability to fashion regulatory legislation imposing new obligations on businesses to deal with newly recognized consequences of their past activities.

The Coal Industry Retiree Health Benefit Act, sponsored by Sen. John D. Rockefeller IV, a Democrat from the coal-mining state of West Virginia, adopted one of the options for remedying the fund's financial crisis proposed by a special commission appointed by President George Bush's secretary of labor, Elizabeth Dole. The commission called either for an industrywide tax or a so-called "reachback" provision to impose liability for retirees' benefits on companies that no longer contributed to the fund—or a combination of both. Rockefeller inserted the coal levy into an omnibus tax measure in 1992, but Bush—who had prominently vowed not to increase taxes—vetoed the bill.

At the suggestion of administration budget officials, Rockefeller then opted for the "reachback" provision. The heart of the bill directed the com-

United Mine Workers members demonstrate outside the U.S. Capitol in favor of legislation to preserve benefits for retired miners and their families. The Supreme Court ruled a key part of the measure unconstitutional.

missioner of Social Security to assign the financial responsibility for so-called "orphaned" miners—miners who had worked for companies that had left the industry benefits plan—to one of those companies. The allocation scheme called for the retirees to be assigned to companies that had signed any of the industrywide agreements since 1978 that included specific provisions for lifetime health benefits. But a so-called "super reachback" provision allowed retired miners to be assigned to companies that had employed them earlier even if the company had never explicitly promised to pay for lifetime health care.

Out of about 100,000 beneficiaries eligible under the plan—more than two-thirds of them widows or children—only about 7,000 were assigned to super reachback operators. One of the businesses affected was Eastern Enterprises, a diversified company that owned Boston Gas Co. and that had been in the coal industry up to 1965, when it spun off its coal operations to a subsidiary. Eastern sold the subsidiary to another coal company in 1987.

With that background, Eastern decided to go to court when it was assigned financial responsibility for about 1,500 beneficiaries. The company's bill was substantial: $16 million through September 1997 and an estimated $100 million over the beneficiaries' projected lifetimes. It claimed that, in imposing that liability, Congress had "taken" its property without compensation in violation of the Fifth Amendment's so-called "Takings Clause." Alternatively, the company argued that the act violated its rights under the Due Process Clause, which prohibits depriving anyone of life, liberty, or property "without due process of law."

A trial court and the First U.S. Circuit Court of Appeals in Boston rejected Eastern's arguments and upheld the law. The Supreme Court agreed to hear Eastern's appeal, even though the justices had rejected similar constitutional attacks on laws imposing retroactive liability in pensions or benefits schemes. In one of those rulings, the Court in 1976 upheld provisions of the Black Lung Benefits Act of 1972 that required coal companies to compensate miners or their survivors for black lung disease even if the miners were no longer employed in the industry. In three other rulings in 1984, 1986, and 1993, the Court had upheld a 1980 law that sometimes required companies to make contributions to an industrywide pension plan after they left the industry.

When Eastern's case was argued March 4, justices sharply challenged the company's lawyer, John Montgomery of Boston, on both of the arguments for striking down the law. O'Connor began by asking whether Montgomery was arguing "substantive due process" or "procedural due process." The distinction was critical: the Due Process Clause had long been recognized to mandate procedural rights, but its use to justify substantive legal rights was highly controversial. When Montgomery hesitated, Scalia jumped in. "Substantive due process is not in good odor with regard to economic rights," he said.

Later, Kennedy was equally emphatic in questioning Eastern's "takings" argument. "Here the government doesn't take property and use it for a firehouse or school," he told the lawyer. "This is simply an adjustment of liability between two private parties."

But the justices also sharply questioned Deputy Solicitor General Edwin Kneedler as he defended the law. O'Connor and Scalia both emphasized that Eastern had never signed a collective bargaining agreement that called explicitly for lifetime health benefits for retirees. Kneedler insisted that Eastern, along with other coal companies, had led miners to believe all along that they were getting lifetime benefits. But Scalia suggested the UMW could have put such a provision in the contract if it was so important. "This was a sophisticated labor union," he said.

O'Connor closed by sharply questioning the law's long reach. The question, she told Kneedler, was "whether it's reasonable to think that [lawmakers] are going to look back thirty-some years to impose the liability. I mean, that's the shocker."

It was O'Connor who announced the Court's decision on June 25 to rule the law unconstitutional, and her opinion reflected both her distaste for the law and her preference for the company's Takings Clause argument against it. But she spoke for only four justices. Kennedy provided the critical fifth vote, and he firmly rejected the idea that the law could be viewed as a "taking" of Eastern's property. Instead, he said the law violated substantive due process because of what he called its "severe retroactive effect."

O'Connor began by acknowledging that the case did not present a "classic" takings claim. Nonetheless, she said, the law "permanently deprived" Eastern of the "assets" needed to satisfy its obligation not to the government but to the pension fund. Reciting the previous rulings in the pension cases, O'Connor said the precedents "have left open" the possibility that a law could be unconstitutional "if it imposes severe retroactive liability on a limited class of parties that could not have anticipated the liability, and the extent of that liability is substantially disproportionate to the parties' experience."

The Coal Act's allocation scheme, O'Connor continued, "presents such a case." It imposed upon Eastern what she called "a considerable financial burden" of $50 to $100 million. It interfered with the company's "reasonable investment-backed expectations" by reaching back "30 to 50 years"—"long after" the company believed its liabilities under the 1950 agreement had been settled. Moreover, Eastern's liability was "not calibrated" to any past actions or past agreements—"implicit or otherwise"—by Eastern. On that basis, O'Connor concluded, the law amounted to "an unconstitutional taking" as applied to Eastern.

With the takings issue settled, O'Connor said there was no need to address the substantive due process claim. Three justices—Rehnquist, Scalia, and Thomas—concurred. Thomas added a brief concurring opinion, suggesting that the Constitution's Ex Post Facto Clause could be used to invalidate the law. But he acknowledged that his approach would require overruling a 200-year-old precedent that the provision applied only to retroactive criminal laws.

In his opinion, Kennedy agreed that the law imposed "a staggering financial burden" on Eastern but disagreed that it could be viewed as a taking of the company's property. The law, he said, "neither targets a specific property interest nor depends upon any particular property" for its operation. Applying the Takings Clause, he said, "would expand an already difficult and uncertain rule to a vast category of cases." Instead, he said the law should be ruled a violation of Eastern's due process rights. "[D]ue process protection of property," he said, "must be understood to incorporate our settled tradition against retroactive laws of great severity."

Writing for the four dissenters, Breyer agreed with Kennedy that the Takings Clause did not apply, but he rejected Kennedy's conclusion that the law violated due process principles. He stressed that Eastern was being forced to contribute to benefits for miners that it had employed and contended that the company had "contributed" to the miners' expectation of receiving lifetime benefits. Most important, he said, Eastern "continued to obtain profits from the coal mining industry" through its subsidiary well after 1965.

"Taken together," Breyer concluded, "these circumstances explain why it is not fundamentally unfair for Congress to impose upon Eastern liability for the future health care costs of miners whom it long ago employed—rather than imposing that liability, for example, upon the present industry, coal consumers, or taxpayers."

Stevens, Souter, and Ginsburg joined Breyer's opinion. Stevens added a brief opinion—joined by the other three—disagreeing with O'Connor's reading of the history of the case.

Property-rights advocates cheered the ruling. The decision "shows that the majority of the Court is taking seriously the cases involving economic rights and liberties," said Paul Kamenar, legal director of the conservative Washington Legal Foundation. But the divided reasoning of the majority justices left constitutional law experts uncertain about its long-term impact. "It may be that the five justices in the majority were simply offended by the statute and that it won't go anywhere," said Johnny Killian, senior constitutional law scholar with the Library of Congress.

In the short term, the ruling promised more litigation by coal companies opposed to the funding scheme to try to limit their financial obligations and some efforts in Congress to try to craft a new solution. Meanwhile, Peter Buscemi, the attorney for the benefits fund, warned that if new money was not found somewhere, health benefits might have to be cut.

Freedom of Speech

"Decency" Clause for Arts Funding Upheld but Narrowed

National Endowment for the Arts v. Finley, decided by an 8–1 vote, June 25, 1998; O'Connor wrote the opinion; Souter dissented. *(See excerpts, pp. 206–218.)*

Karen Finley, a performance artist based in New York City, covered her nude body in chocolate in order to dramatize the sexual oppression of women. But when she sought a federal grant from the National Endowment for the Arts (NEA), she also helped dramatize a sharp cultural conflict in the United States over the government's role in subsidizing the arts.

Finley came into conflict with a congressional proviso passed in 1990 that required the NEA to consider "general standards of decency" in awarding grants. In passing the so-called "decency clause," Congress rejected tougher amendments that would have imposed an outright prohibition on some kinds of controversial art. But many people in the nation's arts community viewed even the softened restriction as an unconstitutional limitation on freedom of expression and challenged the provision in federal court.

The issue reached the Supreme Court this term, but the NEA blunted the dispute by depicting the decency clause as largely advisory. The Court,

Performance artist Karen Finley covers her body partly in chocolate to dramatize sexual oppression of women. Finley contested a federal law that "decency" be used in evaluating grants to artists, but the Supreme Court upheld the measure.

accepting the NEA's interpretation, upheld the provision. The ruling drew a sharp protest from two of the justices, who insisted the Court had gutted the provision and ignored Congress's intent. Nonetheless, Finley and other artists complained that leaving the decency clause on the books would inhibit free artistic expression.

The NEA's supporters often pointed out that the great bulk of its funding went to noncontroversial programs and projects like symphony orchestras and traveling theatrical presentations. But two small grants to support the work of provocative artists in 1989 generated a firestorm of criticism from conservative lawmakers and interest groups. One $30,000 grant went to the Institute of Contemporary Art at the University of Pennsylvania for a retrospective of the work of photographer Robert Mapplethorpe, a gay artist whose compositions included several starkly homoerotic photographs. A second artist, Andres Serrano, who had received a $15,000 grant from the NEA-funded Southeast Center for Contemporary Artists, drew harsh criticism for his photograph *Piss Christ,* which showed a crucifix immersed in urine.

Congress responded immediately with a provision in the NEA's appropriation bill for fiscal 1990 prohibiting funding of any obscene artistic works and setting up a commission to review the agency's procedures. The commission's report opposed any additional content restrictions on NEA grantees. Despite the recommendation, lawmakers introduced a new batch of restrictive proposals in 1990. One that failed would have prohibited funding any project that would have the effect of "denigrating" the beliefs of any religion or "any individual on the basis of race, sex, handicap, or national origin." Instead, a compromise version emerged that stipulated that grants were to be awarded based on "artistic excellence and merit . . . taking into consideration general standards of decency and respect for the diverse beliefs and values of the American public."

Finley and three other performance artists whose works all dealt with homosexual themes—John Fleck, Holly Hughes, and Tim Miller—had each filed applications for NEA grants while Congress was considering the legislation. Review panels approved the grants, but the NEA's chairman, John Frohmeyer, rejected them in June 1990. The four artists then filed a federal court suit contesting the denials; later, after the decency consideration provision went into effect, the National Association of Artists' Organizations joined the suit, and the case was expanded to include a constitutional attack on the clause.

Ultimately, all four artists submitted revised applications, which were approved. They pressed on with their suit, however, and a federal judge in California ruled the decency clause unconstitutionally vague in 1992 and barred the NEA from putting it into effect. The government settled with the artists by paying them roughly a quarter-million dollars. Despite the settlement, the Justice Department decided to appeal the district court ruling. In 1996 the federal appeals court for California, in a 2–1 decision, agreed with the artists that the decency clause was unconstitutional both because it was vague and because it amounted to viewpoint discrimination in violation of the First Amendment.

In asking the Court to reinstate the decency clause, Solicitor General Seth Waxman argued on March 31 that the provision was actually "rather innocuous." All the NEA had done to implement the proposal before the lower court injunction, he said, was to expand the grant review panels to create more diversity among the people acting on applications.

Several of the justices, however, were skeptical. "You're having a hard time convincing me the statute is essentially meaningless," Stevens said. "The whole message here," Ginsburg said, "is don't fund Serrano or Mapplethorpe."

When Waxman acknowledged that there would be constitutional difficulties in rejecting an application from a particular artist because of his viewpoint, however, Scalia jumped in to object. "The government doesn't have to buy Mapplethorpe," Scalia said, "so it doesn't have to fund Mapplethorpe."

In contrast to Waxman, the artists' lawyer—David Cole, a professor at Georgetown law school and frequent litigator on First Amendment issues—insisted that the decency clause did in fact have teeth. He told the justices it was "unconstitutional for the government to set up a funding program to fund private speech broadly and to exclude particular speech because of disapproval of the viewpoint." But O'Connor suggested that, with limited funding, the NEA had to use some criteria in awarding grants. And Breyer challenged Cole by asking whether the government was constitutionally required to fund racist speech.

It was O'Connor who announced the Court's decision on June 25, and she began by emphasizing the limited force of the decency clause compared to other legislative proposals Congress rejected. The provision "imposes no categorical requirement," she said, "in sharp contrast to congressional efforts to prohibit the funding of certain classes of speech." The decency clause was subject to so many different interpretations, O'Connor said, that it could not "in practice . . . effectively preclude or punish the expression of particular views." On that basis, she concluded, there was no "realistic danger that [the clause] will compromise First Amendment values."

In a briefer section, O'Connor also rejected the artists' argument that the decency clause was unconstitutionally vague. The provision, she said, "merely adds some imprecise considerations to an already subjective process." Four justices joined all of O'Connor's opinion: Rehnquist, Stevens, Kennedy, and Breyer. Ginsburg joined most of the opinion, but not O'Connor's one-paragraph passage that said Congress enjoyed "wide latitude" in deciding how to award subsidies in a competitive grantmaking program.

In a sharply worded opinion concurring only in the judgment, Scalia said that the ruling "sustains the constitutionality of [the law] by gutting it." In a section entitled "The Statute Means What It Says," Scalia described the NEA's interpretation of the clause as "so obviously inadequate that it insults the intelligence." Even if it imposed no "categorical" requirement, Scalia said, the clause meant that in awarding grants the NEA was required to exercise "viewpoint discrimination"—to "favor applications that display decency and respect, and disfavor applications that do not." And, in a section entitled "What the Statute Says Is Constitutional," Scalia concluded, "[S]uch favoritism does not 'abridge' anyone's freedom of speech." Thomas joined the opinion.

Souter, the lone dissenter, agreed with Scalia's interpretation but insisted the measure was unconstitutional. The provision, he said, "mandates viewpoint-based decisions in the disbursement of government subsidies," in violation of what he called "the fundamental rule . . . that viewpoint discrimination in the exercise of public authority over expressive activity is unconstitutional."

Reaction to the ruling was as mixed as the justices' opinions. House Speaker Newt Gingrich said the decision "vindicated the right of the American people not to pay for art that offends their sensibilities." But Cole had a different take. "The Supreme Court upheld [the decency clause] essentially by holding it to be meaningless," he told National Public Radio. Still, Cole said he feared the provision would have a "chilling effect" on artists seeking NEA grants.

Conservative groups clearly hoped that would be the result. "This is a positive ruling," Pat Trueman, director of government affairs for the conservative American Family Association, told the *Washington Post*. "But it doesn't work if you don't have people at the NEA who recognize the difference between decency and indecency."

For their part, Finley and other artists voiced sharp disappointment. "Who's going to be the decider of what's decent and what isn't?" Finley told the *New York Times* as she prepared for a New York run of her new show *The Return of the Chocolate-Smeared Woman*. "The witch hunt can happen anywhere."

3 | *Case Summaries*

Antiabortion groups seized on a new issue in the mid-1990s: a late-term procedure for terminating a pregnancy that they labeled a "partial-birth abortion." The procedure—formally called a dilation and extraction—involved the partial, feet-first delivery of a fetus from twenty to twenty-four weeks of pregnancy. At that stage, the fetus's head is too big to pass through a woman's cervix, even if the cervix is dilated. Therefore, a doctor makes a hole in the fetal skull, suctions the contents out with a catheter, and then collapses the skull to finish removing the fetus.

Abortion opponents, describing the operation in graphic terms, lobbied state legislatures and Congress to ban the procedure outright. Abortion rights advocates insisted that the procedure was rare and used almost exclusively in cases of life-threatening pregnancies or severely deformed fetuses. But they were clearly on the defensive. More than two dozen states passed laws prohibiting the procedure, as did Congress. President Bill Clinton vetoed the federal measure but indicated he might sign a bill if it allowed the procedure when needed to protect a woman's health.

The story was different, however, when abortion rights groups took the issue into the courts. Lower federal courts struck down several of the state laws, including one of the first—an Ohio law enacted in 1995. Then in November 1997, the Sixth U.S. Circuit Court of Appeals became the first federal appeals court to rule on the issue, striking down the Ohio law by a 2–1 vote. As one reason, the appeals court said the law left doctors guessing at its meaning. The ban covered any procedure that used a "suction device" to "remove the brain" of a fetus. That definition, the court said, also applied to the more common abortion technique of dilation and evacuation.

Antiabortion groups had expected a hard time in the lower courts but thought they had a better chance to sustain the new laws in the Supreme Court. When the dispute reached the Court, however, the justices declined to hear the case. (*Voinovich v. Women's Medical Professional Corp.*)

Ordinarily, the Court gives no explanation why it decides to review or not to review a lower court decision. In the Ohio case, however, three justices issued a rare dissenting statement explaining why they thought the Court should have agreed to review the case. Interestingly, the five-page statement never even mentioned the so-called "partial-birth" abortion issue.

Instead, Justice Thomas focused on a different issue in the law: whether laws banning abortions after a fetus becomes viable must contain an exception permitting the procedure in order to protect the mother's mental health.

Thomas noted that thirty-eight states had laws restricting postviability abortions and that most did not contain a maternal health exception. The appeals court had based its ruling on one of the Court's earlier abortion decisions, but Thomas said the appellate judges misread the precedent. The earlier decision, he said, "in no way supports the proposition that, after viability, a mental health exception is required as a matter of federal constitutional law." Chief Justice Rehnquist and Justice Scalia joined his opinion.

Antiabortion groups said there were other cases, with better-written laws, to try to uphold the partial-birth abortion bans. Still, they were disappointed that the justices had declined to take up the Ohio case—not only because they had failed to revive the Ohio law, but also because the Court held the key to upholding other abortion restrictions in the future. "The challenge for the prolife movement is whether they are willing to consider any further restrictions," said James Bopp, general counsel of the National Right to Life Committee. "So far, one has to say they're not."

For their part, though, abortion rights groups were also frustrated with the way the Court had been handling abortion cases. The Court had gone six years since its last extended decision on the issue. In that case—*Planned Parenthood of Southeastern Pa. v. Casey* (1992)—the Court had reaffirmed the "essential holding" of *Roe v. Wade* but had also indicated that states could regulate abortion procedures as long as the laws did not impose an "undue burden" on a woman's right to terminate a pregnancy. *(See* Supreme Court Yearbook, 1991–1992, *p. 30.)* Abortion rights groups had hoped the Court would fill in the definition of "undue burden" in a way that would curb the proliferation of restrictive laws. Instead, the justices turned aside most abortion disputes or, occasionally, issued summary rulings that did little to clarify the broader issues. "The Court is definitely doing all sorts of tortured decisionmaking to try to avoid some of the hard issues," said Janet Benshoof, president of the New York–based Center for Reproductive Law and Policy.

Except for Thomas's dissenting statement, there was nothing unusual, however, about the Court's decision not to hear the Ohio abortion case. Out of the thousands of cases on the Court's docket each year, the justices agree to review only a tiny percentage—in recent years, fewer than 100 cases. For the 1997–1998 term, the total number of cases on the Court's docket was 7,692; but the justices issued signed opinions on the merits in only ninety cases. *(See Figure 3-1.)*

Case selection is a vitally important part of the Court's work, but it is also the Court's least visible and least understood process. The terminology itself is arcane. Someone who appeals a case to the Court files a petition for a writ of "certiorari"—a Latin term ("to be more fully informed") for an order to a lower court to send the record of the case so that the Court can decide whether the ruling was correct. The other side can file, if it wants to, a statement in opposition to issuing the writ—in the Court's parlance, an "op-cert." The Court's rules admonish both sides to address not the merits

Figure 3-1   Supreme Court Caseload, 1960 Term–1997 Term

Total cases on docket

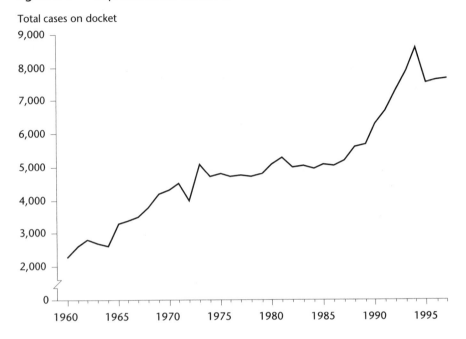

Number of signed opinions of the Court

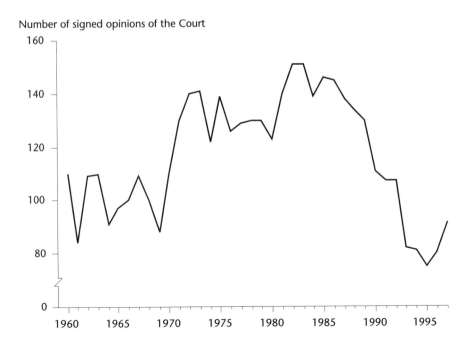

of the dispute but the reasons why the Court should or should not accept the case for review.

Lawyers rarely issue press releases or hold news conferences to announce that they have filed a "cert petition." The justices' work itself is also all behind the scenes. The vast majority of petitions are read not by the justices themselves but by their law clerks. Eight of the justices (all but Stevens) assign their clerks to work in a "cert pool" and prepare memoranda summarizing each case for the justices to consider. The justices then meet in a secret conference to decide whether to grant or deny certiorari. Most cases are rejected without discussion; only one-fourth or so of the cases are put on a "discuss list" for actual discussion in the conference.

The justices have almost complete discretion to decide which cases to accept and which to turn away. The Court's Rule 10 specifies that one reason for taking a case is a conflict between federal appeals courts or between state supreme courts. But the rule also says that the justices will consider whether a lower court "has decided an important question of federal law that has not been, but should be, settled by this Court." In other words, whatever the justices want to hear, they can.

The justices often point out that a decision not to review a case does not indicate that the Court agrees with the ruling and should not be interpreted as an endorsement of the lower court. Certainly, among the thousands of cases turned away every year there are many rulings that the Court would decide differently if the justices had the time. But the Court considers itself too busy merely to correct errors in lower court decisions.

On the other hand, the decision to review a case does ordinarily indicate that the justices have doubts about the lower court's ruling. Chief Justice Rehnquist himself acknowledged as much in a speech to federal judges this year. "One of the factors" in deciding whether to grant review, Rehnquist told the meeting of Fourth Circuit judges on June 27, 1998, is "a sense of disagreement with the lower court." Statistics bear him out. In most years, the Court reverses around two-thirds of the lower court decisions it reviews; this year, the figure was a little lower: a little over half.

In that light, the Court's case selection this year gave further evidence of its conservative tilt. The cases that the justices turned away provided further evidence of the Court's pro–law enforcement orientation on criminal law issues and reflected no interest in stretching First Amendment protections or privacy rights. The Court also encouraged conservatives by refusing to entertain a challenge to term limits for state legislators. But it turned aside conservative challenges to a number of liberal-backed federal laws.

In criminal law cases, the Court gave a green light to states passing laws requiring authorities to notify communities of convicted sex offenders in their neighborhoods. Some thirty-six states and the District of Columbia had passed so-called "Megan's laws"—modeled after a 1995 New Jersey statute named for a seven-year-old girl who was raped and murdered by a convicted child molester. A group of sex offenders in the state argued the law violated the Double Jeopardy Clause by imposing a new punishment after their convictions and sentences, but the justices declined to hear the case.

The Court also signaled no immediate interest in blocking states from using child endangerment statutes to prosecute women who use drugs while pregnant. The justices declined to hear an appeal by two South Carolina women who were convicted and jailed for giving birth to babies who tested positive for cocaine. Prosecutors had tried bringing similar charges in thirty other states but had generally been rebuffed by state courts.

The justices turned aside three closely watched First Amendment disputes. The Court refused to hear a challenge by the magazine *Penthouse* to a federal law that prohibited the sale of sexually explicit material on military property. It rejected a free-speech challenge to a federal ban on the sale of T-shirts on the national Mall and at the Vietnam Veterans Memorial in Washington, D.C. It also turned down an appeal by the publisher of a manual for "hit men" to block a civil lawsuit brought by the family of a woman and her disabled son murdered by a hired killer who used the book to plot the slayings.

On privacy issues, the Court refused to hear an appeal by two economists in the Office of Management and Budget who objected to being subjected to random drug testing because of their access to the Old Executive Office Building within the White House grounds. The justices also turned aside an effort by a political activist to require the Federal Bureau of Investigation to purge files containing information about him if there was no current law-enforcement investigation of him.

The justices acted on term limits for state legislators in a case from California. A federal appeals court panel had thrown out a measure limiting California representatives to six years in office and state senators to eight years. The full appeals court reinstated the measure, however, and the justices declined to hear the appeal. More than twenty states had passed tenure limits for state lawmakers. The Court in 1995 had ruled that states had no power to limit terms for members of Congress except through a constitutional amendment.

As the term neared an end, the justices rejected two other cases from California that invoked states' rights in challenging the reach of federal statutes. In one, the National Association of Home Builders contended, on Commerce Clause grounds, that the Endangered Species Act should not be used to protect the habitat of a endangered fly that was found only in two California counties. In the other, the state of California argued that the Tenth Amendment barred the enforcement of the Americans with Disabilities Act against state and local governments.

The number of cases that the Court decided on the merits during the year—ninety—represented a substantial increase over the previous year's total of eighty. It was the second consecutive yearly increase after a decade-long decline. There was one other signed opinion during the term. In that

Figure 3-2   Vote Divisions on Cases Decided in 1997–1998 Supreme Court Term

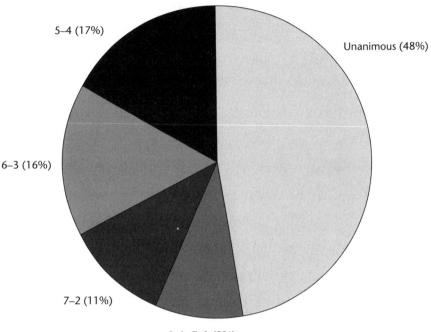

5–4 (17%)

Unanimous (48%)

6–3 (16%)

7–2 (11%)

8–1, 7–1 (9%)

Note: Figures do not add to 100% because of rounding.

case, the justices decided after hearing arguments that the case was not appropriate to settle the legal issue. (In legal terms, the Court "dismissed the writ of certiorari as improvidently granted.") Normally, those opinions are brief, unsigned, and unanimous; in this case, though, the justices disagreed, and there were signed opinions for the majority and the dissenters.

The Court also issued four *per curiam* or unsigned opinions on the merits without hearing arguments in the cases. Three were unanimous; a fourth—in a voting rights case from Georgia—was decided on a 7–2 vote. The most significant of the four reinforced one state's ability to extradite a fugitive from another state; the ruling limited the issues that the fugitive could raise in the state where he was found to try to block his return to the state trying to extradite him.

Overall, the Court was unanimous in nearly half of its signed decisions: forty-three out of ninety, or 47.8 percent, continuing an upward trend of the past several terms. The Court divided 5–4 in fifteen—one-sixth—of its cases, a somewhat lower proportion than the previous term. There were eight decisions with a single dissenter, ten with two dissenters, and fourteen decided by 6–3 votes. *(See Figure 3-2.)*

Following are summaries of the ninety signed opinions and four *per curiam* opinions issued by the Court during the 1997–1998 term. They are organized by subject matter: business law, courts and procedure, criminal law and procedure, election law, environmental law, federal government, First Amendment, immigration law, individual rights, labor law, property law, states, and torts.

Business Law

Antitrust

State Oil Company v. Khan, decided by a 9–0 vote, November 4, 1997; O'Connor wrote the opinion.

A manufacturer or supplier may set a maximum price to be charged by dealers without necessarily violating federal antitrust law.

The unanimous decision overruled a twenty-nine-year-old precedent, *Albrecht v. Herald Co.* (1968), that such agreements were per se illegal. Instead, the Court held that maximum price agreements between suppliers and dealers—vertical as opposed to horizontal price-fixing—were subject to the so-called "rule of reason": illegal only if they actually resulted in reduced competition.

Writing for the Court, O'Connor said, "We find it difficult to maintain that vertically-imposed maximum prices could harm consumers or competition to the extent necessary to justify their *per se* invalidation." In fact, O'Connor said, the ban on maximum price agreements could harm consumers and manufacturers by permitting "the unrestrained exercise of market power by monopolist-dealers." As for overruling the precedent, O'Connor said it was justifiable because the ruling had been "widely criticized since its inception" and "eroded" by subsequent decisions.

The decision came in a suit brought by a former service station operator who said he went out of business because his supplier effectively set a maximum price for the gasoline he sold. The Seventh U.S. Circuit Court of Appeals had allowed the suit to go forward, but—in an opinion by Judge Richard Posner, a noted authority on antitrust law—had urged the Court to use the case to overrule *Albrecht.* The decision was issued only four weeks after argument.

Banking

Beach v. Ocwen Federal Bank, decided by a 9–0 vote, April 21, 1998; Souter wrote the opinion.

The Court set a three-year time limit on a homeowner's ability to use the federal Truth in Lending Act to rescind a mortgage for a bank's failure to disclose financing charges accurately.

The ruling rejected an effort by a Florida couple to use the right of rescission established in the law as a defense in a foreclosure proceeding brought after they defaulted on their home mortgage. The couple claimed the bank's miscalculation of interest and financing charges allowed them to rescind the loan, but the bank said the law's three-year time limit for a rescission action also cut off a borrower's ability to use the provision as a defense. The Florida Supreme Court agreed with the bank, in conflict with rulings by several other state courts on the issue.

In a unanimous decision, the Court agreed that the law's three-year time limit applied to use of the provision in a foreclosure. After reviewing what he called the statute's "uncompromising language," Souter concluded, "[T]he Act permits no federal right to rescind, defensively or otherwise, after the 3-year period . . . has run."

National Credit Union Administration v. First National Bank & Trust Co., decided by a 5–4 vote, February 25, 1998; Thomas wrote the opinion; O'Connor, Stevens, Souter, and Breyer dissented.

The Court blocked federally chartered credit unions from expanding to include members from different employers.

The ruling—a victory for the banking industry—invalidated an interpretation of the 1934 Federal Credit Union Act by the National Credit Union Administration. The law limited credit union membership to "groups having a common bond of occupation or association" or "groups within a well-defined neighborhood, community, or rural district." Beginning in 1982, the agency interpreted the provision to allow credit unions to include employees of different employers, on the theory that each "group" of workers had its own "common bond." The North Carolina–based First National Bank & Trust Co. challenged the interpretation by filing separate suits against the agency and against the AT&T Family Federal Credit Union, which had used the liberalized interpretation to expand to include 110,000 members—only one-third of whom were AT&T employees. The federal appeals court for the District of Columbia held the agency had misinterpreted the law.

The Court agreed after first voting 5–4 to uphold the bank's legal standing to bring the suits. Writing for the majority, Thomas said the bank fell within "the zone of interests" protected by the act's limit on credit union expansion even though Congress "did not specifically intend to protect commercial banks." On the merits, Thomas held that Congress had "made it clear that the *same* common bond of occupation must unite each member of an occupationally defined federal credit union." The agency's interpretation, he said, "has the potential to read [the limitation] out of the statute entirely."

The dissenting justices did not reach the merits of the case. Instead, they argued that the bank had no standing to bring the suits. "The terms of the statute do not suggest a concern with protecting the business interests of competitors," O'Connor wrote.

The case produced an unusual split on the standing issue. O'Connor was joined in dissent by three liberal-leaning justices who normally took a broad view of standing: Stevens, Souter, and Breyer. The majority included four justices who more typically took a narrow view of standing: Rehnquist, Scalia, Kennedy, and Thomas.

Bankruptcy

Cohen v. De La Cruz, decided by a 9–0 vote, March 24, 1998; O'Connor wrote the opinion.

Federal bankruptcy law does not protect someone from being required to pay a court judgment for fraud.

The ruling favored tenants of a Hoboken, New Jersey, landlord, Edward S. Cohen, who won a treble damages award of $94,147 plus attorney's fees because he charged excessive rents under the city's rent control law. Ruling in Cohen's bankruptcy proceeding, two lower federal courts agreed with the tenants that their judgment was protected under a Bankruptcy Code provision prohibiting the discharge of a debt "to the extent . . . obtained by actual fraud."

In a brief and unanimous decision, the Court agreed. The fraud exception, O'Connor said, "encompasses any liability arising from money, property, etc., that is fraudulently obtained," including treble damages, attorney's fees, or other relief.

Fidelity Financial Services, Inc. v. Fink, decided by a 9–0 vote, January 13, 1998; Souter wrote the opinion.

The Court strictly interpreted the twenty-day deadline for lenders to file liens on a borrower's property in order to have a preferential right to repayment in a federal bankruptcy proceeding.

The ruling—a setback for lenders—came in a dispute between a Missouri woman and a Missouri bank that lent her money to buy an automobile. The bank "perfected," or publicly recorded, its lien on the car twenty-one days after the purchase. When the woman filed for bankruptcy, the bank claimed it met the thirty-day deadline set by state law for perfecting the lien. But lower federal courts ruled the bank had to meet the twenty-day deadline set in the federal Bankruptcy Code to be a secured rather than unsecured creditor.

Souter's opinion for the Court was densely statutory, but he summarized the holding succinctly in announcing the decision from the bench. "In short," Souter said, "twenty days means twenty days."

Kawaauhau v. Geiger, decided by a 9–0 vote, March 3, 1998; Ginsburg wrote the opinion.

Federal bankruptcy law allows someone to wipe out a debt for a medical malpractice judgment.

The ruling resolved a conflict between federal courts of appeals on how to interpret a Bankruptcy Code provision that barred a debtor from discharging any debt "for willful and malicious injury." The Eighth U.S. Circuit Court of Appeals, ruling in a case between a Missouri doctor and his former patient, held that the patient could not enforce his malpractice award in federal bankruptcy court.

In a brief and unanimous opinion, the Court agreed that the statutory exception did not apply to medical negligence. Ginsburg said the word "willful" in the statute applied to "a deliberate or intentional injury, not merely a deliberate or intentional act that leads to injury."

Copyright

Feltner v. Columbia Pictures Television, Inc., decided by a 9–0 vote, March 31, 1998; Thomas wrote the opinion.

A jury trial is constitutionally required in a copyright infringement suit brought under a provision for specified "statutory damages" if either party requests one.

The unanimous decision set aside an $8.8 million award by a judge in a copyright infringement suit brought by Columbia Pictures' television syndication unit against the former owner of three TV stations, C. Elvin Feltner. Columbia claimed that Feltner continued to air several of its programs after it had canceled a licensing agreement because of unpaid royalties. The studio brought an infringement suit under a provision added to the Copyright Act in 1976, section 504(c), that gave a plaintiff in an infringement suit the option to seek "statutory damages" of not less than $500 or more than $20,000 per infringement rather than having to prove the actual damages. Feltner asked for a jury trial, but the judge refused. He then awarded Columbia $20,000 for each of the 440 episodes of programs aired by Feltner after the cancellation of the licensing agreement—a total of $8.8 million. The Ninth U.S. Circuit Court of Appeals upheld the award, rejecting Feltner's claim that a jury trial was required by the statute or by the Seventh Amendment, which states that the right to a jury trial "shall be preserved" in "suits at common law."

The Court held that the statute did not provide for a jury trial, but the Seventh Amendment required one. Writing for eight justices, Thomas said historical practice in England and the American colonies established the right to a jury trial in copyright infringement cases and that federal copyright statutes had not changed that practice. "[A] jury must determine the actual amount of statutory damages under section 504(c) in order to preserve the substance of the common-law right of trial by jury," Thomas wrote.

In a separate concurring opinion, Scalia said he would interpret the statutory provision that damages be determined by "the court" to refer to a jury trial. On that basis, he said he would uphold the statute and avoid the need to rule on the constitutional issue.

Quality King Distributors, Inc. v. L'anza Research International, Inc., decided by a 9–0 vote, March 9, 1998; Stevens wrote the opinion.

The Court rejected an effort to use federal copyright law to control so-called "gray market" imports of goods manufactured in the United States, sold abroad, and then brought back into the U.S. for resale.

The ruling—a victory for discount retailers—barred a copyright infringement claim by a California-based hair-care products manufacturer, L'anza Research International, Inc. The company marketed its products domestically exclusively through professional salons but also sold them abroad, at reduced prices, through foreign distributors. L'anza sued Quality King Distributors, Inc., after discovering that the New York–based company had bought L'anza products from a foreign distributor for resale in the U.S. through discount stores. Claiming an infringement of its copyrighted labels, L'anza sought damages and an injunction against further imports. A district court judge barred the claim, but the Ninth U.S. Circuit Court of Appeals held the unauthorized importation constituted copyright infringement.

In a densely statutory decision, the Court unanimously held that the infringement claim was barred by the "first sale doctrine," which generally prevents a copyright holder from controlling distribution of a particular copy after selling it. "[O]nce the copyright owner places a copyrighted item in the stream of commerce by selling it," Stevens wrote, "he has exhausted his exclusive statutory right to control its distribution."

Stevens noted that the ruling could also apply to efforts to control distribution of "more familiar copyrighted materials such as sound recordings or books." The music and film industries and the Clinton administration had urged the Court to allow copyright claims against gray-market imports. Stevens said that the policy considerations for protecting what he termed "price discrimination" were "not relevant" to interpreting the text of the Copyright Act.

Taxation

Atlantic Mutual Insurance Co. v. Commissioner of Internal Revenue, decided by a 9–0 vote, April 21, 1998; Scalia wrote the opinion.

The Court sided with the Internal Revenue Service (IRS) in narrowing the ability of property and casualty insurers to avoid the effect of a 1986 provision limiting the deductibility of funds set aside for unpaid claims.

The Tax Reform Act of 1986 provided that insurers could not deduct the full amount of claims reserves for a given year but had to discount the amount over time. A transition provision softened the law's impact for the first year, but insurers were still barred from taking a full deduction for net additions to reserves during the year—so-called "reserve strengthening." The IRS and the industry took different positions on how to define reserve strengthening under the law.

In a unanimous opinion, the Court upheld the IRS regulation, which defined the term as any net additions to reserves. Scalia called the regulation "a reasonable accommodation . . . of the competing interests of fairness, administrability, and avoidance of abuse."

United States v. Estate of Romani, decided by a 9–0 vote, April 29, 1998; Stevens wrote the opinion.

The Court limited the federal government's ability to go ahead of other creditors in collecting debts from the estate of someone who has died.

The ruling resolved a seeming conflict between a 200-year-old law that gave the government priority in collecting debts from a decedent's estate and a more recent law, the Tax Lien Act of 1966. The so-called "priority" statute—first passed in 1797—provided that the government "shall be paid first" whenever a decedent's estate is inadequate to cover all its debts. The 1966 law set specific conditions for the government to follow in imposing a lien—legal notice of a debt—on property for the collection of unpaid taxes. Specifically, it provided that a tax lien "shall not be valid" unless proper notice is given.

Unanimously, the Court held that the Tax Lien Act took precedence over the priority statute. The 1966 law, Stevens wrote, was "the later statute, the more specific statute, and its provisions are comprehensive, reflecting an obvious attempt to accommodate the strong policy objections to the enforcement of secret liens."

The ruling rejected the Internal Revenue Service's effort to block the transfer of property from a Pennsylvania man's estate valued at $53,000 to a company that had a $400,000 judgment lien against the property. The IRS sought to use the 1797 statute because its tax liens could not be enforced against the earlier lien.

United States v. United States Shoe Corp., decided by a 9–0 vote, March 31, 1998; Ginsburg wrote the opinion.

The Court exempted exporters from a 1986 tax on shippers enacted to pay for maintaining and developing harbors, saying the levy violated the constitutional prohibition on taxing exports.

The Harbor Maintenance Tax Act of 1986 imposed a charge on all commercial cargo shipped through the nation's ports, including imports and exports; at the time of the Court's ruling, the levy was set at .125 percent of the value of the cargo. The act was challenged by exporters in some 4,000 cases as a violation of the Export Clause, which states: "No Tax or Duty shall be laid on Articles exported from any State" (Art. I, §9, cl. 5). The Court of International Trade and the U.S. Court of Appeals for the Federal Circuit, ruling in a case brought by United States Shoe Corp., agreed.

In a unanimous decision, the Court also held the levy violated the Export Clause, rejecting the government's argument that it amounted to a user fee. The tax, Ginsburg said, "is not a fair approximation of services, facilities, or benefits furnished to the exporters, and therefore does not qualify as a permissible user fee." The ruling left the tax in place for importers. Ginsburg also said exporters would not necessarily be exempted from a user fee. But, she added, "such a fee must fairly match the exporters' use of port services and facilities."

Courts and Procedure

Attorneys

Swidler & Berlin v. United States, decided by a 6–3 vote, June 25, 1998; Rehnquist wrote the opinion; O'Connor, Scalia, and Thomas dissented.

The attorney-client privilege ordinarily survives the death of the client and protects a lawyer from being compelled to disclose a client's confidences in response to a grand jury subpoena.

The ruling rejected an effort by Independent Counsel Kenneth Starr to subpoena notes taken by attorney James Hamilton of a conversation Hamilton had with then–White House deputy counsel Vincent Foster nine days before Foster's suicide in July 1993. Starr sought the notes for his investigation of possible obstruction of justice or other offenses in connection with the dismissal of employees in the White House Travel Office in May 1993. A federal district court ruled the notes were protected by the attorney-client privilege, but the federal appeals court in Washington said the privilege could be overridden after a client's death if necessary to obtain information of "substantial importance" to a criminal investigation.

By a 6–3 vote, the Court disagreed. Rehnquist said "the great body" of caselaw indicated that the attorney-client privilege ordinarily continues after a client's death. He then rejected the independent counsel's arguments to create an exception for criminal investigations. "[A] posthumous exception in criminal cases appears at odds with the goals of encouraging full and frank communication and of protecting the client's interests," Rehnquist wrote.

Writing for the dissenters, O'Connor argued that the privilege could be overridden for "a compelling law enforcement need" if the information sought was "not available from other sources." She also contended that a criminal defendant could overcome the privilege if necessary to obtain "exculpatory evidence." Rehnquist said the Court did not need to decide that issue. *(See story, pp. 51–55; excerpts, pp. 154–164.)*

Evidence

General Electric Co. v. Joiner, decided by 9–0 and 8–1 votes, December 15, 1997; Rehnquist wrote the opinion; Stevens dissented in part.

Federal trial judges were given strengthened authority to rule on the admissibility of scientific evidence.

The ruling—a setback for plaintiffs' groups—came in a toxic tort suit filed by a Georgia electrician, Robert Joiner, who blamed his cancer on exposure to chemicals used in electrical transformers. The trial judge excluded much of the scientific evidence offered by Joiner's attorneys and granted summary judgment to the three companies named as defendants. But the Eleventh U.S. Circuit of Appeals applied what it called a "particularly stringent standard of review" in overturning the decision to exclude the evidence.

Unanimously, the Court held that the appeals court should have applied a more deferential "abuse of discretion" standard. Rehnquist said that appeals courts "may not categorically distinguish between rulings allowing expert testimony and rulings which disallow it." The Court went on, by an 8–1 vote, to hold that the trial judge had not abused its discretion in excluding the challenged evidence.

In a concurring opinion, Breyer said trial judges should consider the appointment of independent experts and other judicial management techniques to help evaluate scientific testimony. Stevens joined most of the Court's opinion but in a partial dissent said he would remand the case to the appeals court to apply the standard laid down by the Court.

Federal Courts

City of Chicago v. International College of Surgeons, decided by a 7–2 vote, December 15, 1997; O'Connor wrote the opinion; Ginsburg and Stevens dissented.

Federal courts can exercise jurisdiction over state court appeals from local administrative agencies if the case also raises federal law claims.

The ruling set aside a decision by the Seventh U.S. Circuit Court of Appeals that a lower court had been wrong to exercise jurisdiction over a landmark preservation dispute in Chicago. The International College of Surgeons had contested the city's landmarks commission's refusal to permit it to demolish two historic lakeside mansions in order to build a high-rise luxury condominium. The surgeons' group challenged the action in Illinois state court on both state law and federal constitutional grounds. The city then invoked the procedure that permits a defendant to remove a dispute to federal district court if the suit is a "civil action" that would fall within the federal court's "original jurisdiction." The trial judge ruled for the city, but the appeals court held that the removal statute could not be used in a case involving a limited, so-called "on-the-record" review of a local administrative agency's decision.

In a 7–2 decision, the Court held that federal courts have discretion to hear such cases. O'Connor said the district court had "properly exercised federal question jurisdiction over the federal claim" in the suit and "properly recognized that it could thus also exercise supplemental jurisdiction over [the group's] state law claims." O'Connor added, however, that the district court could decline to hear such cases on several grounds—for example, if the state law issues were "novel" or "complex" or the state law claim "substantially predominates" over the federal claim.

In a dissenting opinion, Ginsburg, joined by Stevens, warned that the ruling would invite litigants to "routinely" bring to federal court direct appeals from the actions of "all manner" of local agencies, boards, and commissions. "Federal courts may now directly superintend local agencies by affirming, reversing, or modifying their administrative rulings," Ginsburg wrote.

Lexecon Inc. v. Milberg Weiss Bershad Hynes & Lerach, decided by a 9–0 vote, March 3, 1998; Souter wrote the opinion.

The Court made it harder to consolidate related cases for trial in a single federal court.

The ruling upset a common practice for handling so-called "multidistrict" lawsuits in federal courts. A federal statute allows a special panel, the Judicial Panel on Multidistrict Litigation, to combine pretrial proceedings in such cases. Over the years, judges handling such pretrial proceedings also began to assign to themselves the trial of such cases.

In a unanimous opinion, however, the Court said the statute on multidistrict litigation requires the judge handling pretrial proceedings to return the case to the district where it was filed. " . . . [W]e have to give effect to this plain command," Souter wrote, "even if doing that will reverse the longstanding practice under this statute. . . ."

The issue reached the Court in a defamation suit filed by Lexecon Inc., a Chicago-based consulting firm, against Milberg Weiss Bershad Hynes & Lerach, a prominent New York–based plaintiffs' law firm. The suit grew out of litigation over the highly publicized failure of an Arizona-based thrift, Lincoln Savings and Loan. The law firm wanted the case tried in Arizona, where other Lincoln-related litigation was being tried; the ruling sent the case back to Chicago, where Lexecon originally filed it.

Rivet v. Regions Bank of Louisiana, decided by a 9–0 vote, February 24, 1998; Ginsburg wrote the opinion.

A defendant in a state court suit cannot remove a case to federal court by claiming that the suit is barred by an earlier judgment in a federal case.

The ruling involved overlapping jurisdiction between a Louisiana court and a federal bankruptcy court in a dispute between first- and second-mortgage holders on a parcel of property. A partnership that held a lease on the property secured a first mortgage from Regions Bank and a second mortgage from a group of individual investors, but it then went bankrupt. The federal bankruptcy court allowed the bank to sell the leasehold. The individual investors then sued in state court, claiming that the property was transferred without satisfying their rights under the second mortgage. The bank removed the case to federal court, arguing that the bankruptcy court's ruling "precluded" the state court claim. Two lower federal courts agreed.

In a unanimous decision, the Court held that the case should not have been removed to federal court. Ginsburg explained that "preclusion" is "a defensive plea" that is "not a proper basis for removal." "[A] defendant cannot remove [a case] on the basis of a federal defense," she wrote.

Wisconsin Department of Corrections v. Schacht, decided by a 9–0 vote, June 22, 1998; Breyer wrote the opinion.

A federal court can hear part of a case that has been removed from state court even if it cannot hear other claims because of the Eleventh Amendment's prohibition of suits against states in federal court.

The complex ruling came in a suit filed in state court under federal civil rights law by a former Wisconsin prison guard, Keith Schacht, against the state's Department of Corrections and some individual officials. The state and the individual defendants had the case transferred to federal court, where a lower court judge granted summary judgment in favor of the individual defendants and dismissed the claims against the state because of the Eleventh Amendment. On Schacht's appeal, the Seventh U.S. Circuit Court of Appeals held that the case should not have been removed to federal court because it had no power to consider the claim against the state; on that basis, the appeals court set aside the judgment in favor of the individual defendants.

In a unanimous decision, the Court held that the presence of the claim barred by the Eleventh Amendment did not prevent the removal of the rest of the case to federal court. "[T]he federal court cannot hear the barred claim," Breyer wrote. "But that circumstance does not destroy removal jurisdiction over the remaining claims."

Jury Trials

Hetzel v. Prince William County, Virginia, decided by a 9–0 vote, March 23, 1998; *per curiam* (unsigned) opinion.

Federal courts are barred by the Seventh Amendment's jury trial guarantee from reducing a jury's damage award without offering the plaintiff the option of a new trial.

The ruling stemmed from a $750,000 jury award won by a Virginia woman, Janice Hetzel, in a federal job discrimination suit against a county government. The Fourth U.S. Circuit Court of Appeals ruled the damage award excessive and ordered the district court to recalculate the damages. The district court reduced damages to $50,000 but also held that Hetzel was entitled to a new trial. In a second ruling, however, the appeals court said the district court should have decided the correct damage amount and barred a new trial.

In a unanimous decision issued without hearing argument, the Court said the appeals court's ruling violated Hetzel's right to a jury trial. Citing an 1889 precedent, the Court said the order requiring a lower damage award without the option of a new trial "cannot be squared with the Seventh Amendment."

Quiet Title Actions

United States v. Beggerly, decided by a 9–0 vote, June 8, 1998; Rehnquist wrote the opinion.

A Mississippi family failed in its effort to use belatedly discovered historical evidence to reopen a property ownership dispute with the federal government over land on a barrier island off the state's coast.

The ruling turned aside a plea by Clark Beggerly and other family members to set aside their agreement in 1982 to relinquish their claims to the land on Horn Island in return for a payment of $208,175.87 from the federal government. The payment settled a so-called "quiet title" action brought by the government to establish legal ownership over the land, which the government wanted to acquire to establish a national seashore on the island. The Beggerly family bought the land at a tax sale in 1951, but the government later contended that the island had actually been public land ever since before the Louisiana Purchase. Years after the 1982 settlement, a genealogist hired by the Beggerlys discovered evidence refuting the government's position. The family filed a new suit in 1994 seeking to set aside the settlement. The Fifth U.S. Circuit Court of Appeals sustained their right to bring the suit and then ruled in favor of the Beggerlys' claim to the land.

In a unanimous decision, the Court held that neither of the two legal rules cited by the appeals court could be used to set aside the settlement. Rehnquist said that the family's suit could not be brought as an "independent action" under a provision of the Federal Rules of Civil Procedure, Rule 60(b); that rule, Rehnquist said, could be used only to correct a "manifest injustice." In addition, Rehnquist said the appeals court was wrong to invoke a doctrine called "equitable tolling" to extend the time period for the Beggerlys to bring their suit. The twelve-year statute of limitations was "generous" enough, Rehnquist said.

State Courts

Baker v. General Motors Corp., decided by a 9–0 vote, January 13, 1998; Ginsburg wrote the opinion.

A state court cannot enter an injunction preventing a person from testifying in a proceeding involving different parties in a court in another state.

The ruling cleared the way for a former General Motors engineer to testify in a product liability suit brought against the carmaker by the family of a Missouri woman killed in a 1990 auto crash while driving a GM–made pickup truck. GM had previously obtained an injunction from a Michigan state court prohibiting the engineer, Ronald Elwell, from testifying against the company in any civil suits. When Elwell was subpoenaed in the Missouri case, the judge hearing the case rejected GM's effort to block his testimony. But the Eighth U.S. Circuit Court of Appeals ruled that the Constitution's Full Faith and Credit Clause—which says courts in one state should accept the validity of orders issued by courts in other states—required the court in Missouri to enforce the Michigan injunction.

In a unanimous decision, the Court disagreed. Writing for five justices, Ginsburg stressed that the plaintiffs in the Missouri case had not been parties to the Michigan case and could not be bound by it. "Michigan has no authority to shield a witness from another jurisdiction's subpoena power in a case involving persons and causes outside Michigan's governance," she wrote.

Four justices concurred separately. In a lengthy opinion concurring in the judgment, Kennedy, joined by O'Connor and Thomas, said Ginsburg's opinion gave state courts broad discretion to disregard the Full Faith and Credit Clause in order to protect their own proceedings. In a footnote, Ginsburg termed Kennedy's interpretation of the opinion "inexplicabl[e]." Scalia also wrote a separate, but brief, concurring opinion, saying the case could have been decided on "well-settled" legal principles.

Criminal Law and Procedure

Capital Punishment

Buchanan v. Angelone, Director, Virginia Department of Corrections, decided by a 6–3 vote, January 21, 1998; Rehnquist wrote the opinion; Breyer, Stevens, and Ginsburg dissented.

A defendant in a capital case has no constitutional right to have the jury instructed that it must consider mitigating evidence against imposing a death sentence.

The ruling rejected a federal habeas corpus petition by a Virginia death row inmate, Douglas Buchanan, who had been sentenced to death for the 1987 shotgun slayings of his father, stepmother, and two brothers. In the sentencing hearing, Buchanan's lawyer presented evidence that he was under extreme stress at the time of the killings because of the way his family had dealt with his mother's death. In his habeas corpus petition, Buchanan attacked the judge's refusal to instruct the jury that it was required to consider mitigating factors specified in state law. A lower federal court and the Fourth U.S. Circuit Court of Appeals rejected Buchanan's arguments.

In a divided decision, the Court agreed that the refusal to give the requested jury instructions did not violate the Eighth or Fourteenth Amendments. "We have never . . . held that the state must affirmatively structure in a particular way the manner in which juries consider mitigating evidence," Rehnquist wrote for the majority. He added that the judge's instruction "did not foreclose the jury's consideration of any mitigating evidence" and that the jury had been "informed" that it could consider mitigating evidence by the opposing lawyers in their final arguments.

Writing for the dissenters, Breyer argued that the judge's instruction misled the jury. The effect of the instructions, he said, was "to tell the jury that evidence of mitigating circumstances . . . is not relevant to their sentencing decision." He also noted that Virginia had recently changed its death penalty instructions to include a statement that jurors must consider evidence that "may extenuate or reduce the degree of moral culpability and punishment."

Hopkins, Warden v. Reeves, decided by an 8–1 vote, June 8, 1998; Thomas wrote the opinion; Stevens dissented.

States have no constitutional responsibility to allow judges or juries in capital murder cases to consider lesser degrees of homicide, such as manslaughter.

The ruling reinstated the felony murder convictions and death sentences of a Nebraska inmate, Randolph Reeves, for the 1980 rape-slayings of two women committed during a break-in at a religious meetinghouse. The Eighth U.S. Circuit Court of Appeals had granted Reeves's petition for habeas corpus on the ground that the trial judge should have instructed the jury on two lower degrees of homicide: second-degree murder and manslaughter. The appeals court based its ruling on the Supreme Court's 1980 decision in an Alabama case that overturned a state law barring instructions for so-called "lesser included offenses" in capital cases.

In a nearly unanimous decision, the Court said that the appeals court had misread the prior ruling. Thomas stressed that Nebraska law did not recognize manslaughter or second-degree murder as lesser offenses for felony murder. The appeals court ruling, Thomas said, would have imposed an "unprecedented" and "unworkable" requirement on states to give instructions on less serious crimes "when no lesser included offense exists."

In a lone dissent, Stevens said the procedure violated the rule established in other cases that the death penalty cannot be imposed without proving that a defendant intended to kill the victim.

Ohio Adult Parole Authority v. Woodard, decided by an 8–1 vote, March 25, 1998; Rehnquist wrote the main opinion; O'Connor wrote a concurring opinion; Stevens dissented in part.

The Court rejected a constitutional challenge to Ohio's executive clemency procedures for death penalty cases, but a majority of the justices said due process may set some limits on the practice.

The ruling rejected a claim by an Ohio inmate, Eugene Woodard, that the state's executive clemency procedure violated his rights under the Fifth Amendment's privilege against self-incrimination and the Fourteenth Amendment's Due Process Clause. A federal district court dismissed the claim, but the Sixth U.S. Circuit Court of Appeals said the procedure violated the Fifth Amendment by requiring an interview with the state parole authority in order to request clemency. The appeals court also held that due process applied to the procedure and remanded the case to the district court for further consideration of that issue.

The Court unanimously rejected Woodard's Fifth Amendment claim and voted 8–1 to reject his due process argument. On the Fifth Amendment issue, Rehnquist said the parole authority interview was not "compelled" simply because of the "pressure to speak in the hope of improving his chance of being granted clemency." All justices joined that part of the opinion. Rehnquist also said that due process sets no limits on the procedures states use for determining clemency pleas. He described clemency as "a matter of grace committed to the executive authority." Three justices—Scalia, Kennedy, and Thomas—joined that part of the opinion.

In a partial concurring opinion, O'Connor said "some *minimal* standards apply to clemency proceedings," but she agreed that Ohio's procedures satisfied any possible requirements. Souter, Ginsburg, and Breyer joined her opinion.

In a partial dissent, Stevens said that due process applied to clemency procedures and that the case should be returned to the district court for further proceedings on that issue.

Criminal Offenses

Bates v. United States, decided by a 9–0 vote, November 4, 1997; Ginsburg wrote the opinion.

The crime of willful misapplication of federally insured student loan funds does not require proof of an intent to defraud the federal government or the private lender that made the loans.

The ruling cleared the way for the prosecution of the former treasurer of a defunct Chicago trade school on charges of failing to make more than $139,000 in refunds to private banks for loans made to students who later withdrew from the school. The defendant, Garrit Bates, won a lower court ruling dismissing the indictment on the ground that it failed to allege that he intended to defraud the government. The federal appeals court in Chicago reinstated the indictment, but the Court agreed to review the case because the decision conflicted with a ruling by another federal appeals court in a separate case.

Unanimously, the Court held that it was unnecessary to prove a fraudulent intent in a prosecution for misapplying the federally guaranteed loan funds. "The text of [the statute] does not include an 'intent to defraud' state of mind requirement," Ginsburg wrote, "and we ordinarily resist reading words or elements into a statute that do not appear on its face."

Brogan v. United States, decided by a 7–2 vote, January 26, 1998; Scalia wrote the opinion; Stevens and Breyer dissented.

Someone can be prosecuted under the federal false-statements law for a false denial of guilt.

The ruling rejected the so-called "exculpatory no" doctrine recognized by several federal appeals courts that barred a separate prosecution of someone for falsely denying to investigators an accusation of a crime. The issue reached the Court when the Second U.S. Circuit Court of Appeals upheld the dual prosecutions of a former labor union official for violating a federal law against accepting money from an employer and for denying the charge when questioned by investigators.

In a 7–2 decision, the Court held the federal statute did not permit any exception for an initial denial of guilt. The federal statute "covers 'any' false statement," Scalia said. In an opinion concurring in the judgment, Ginsburg, joined by Souter, warned against what she called "the dubious propriety of bringing felony prosecutions for bare exculpatory denials informally made to Government agents."

Stevens, joined by Breyer, dissented. "The mere fact that a false denial fits within the unqualified language of [the false statement law] is not, in my opinion, a sufficient reason for rejecting a well-settled interpretation of that statute," Stevens wrote.

Bryan v. United States, decided by a 6–3 vote, June 15, 1998; Stevens wrote the opinion; Scalia, Rehnquist, and Ginsburg dissented.

The Court eased the prosecution's burden for convicting someone of violating the federal law against dealing in firearms without a federal license.

By a 6–3 vote, the Court held that a defendant can be convicted of "willfully" violating the law even if he does not know about the provision as long as he is aware that his conduct is unlawful in some other respect.

The decision settled a split between federal appeals courts on the interpretation of a 1986 provision that required proof of a willful violation of the law. In the case that reached the Court, the Second U.S. Circuit Court of Appeals upheld the conviction of a defendant, Sillasse Bryan, who had bought guns in another state through intermediaries, defaced their serial numbers, and sold them on New York street corners where drugs were sold. The government did not show that Bryan knew about the licensing requirement.

Writing for the majority, Stevens said the prosecution's evidence satisfied the willfulness requirement. "Knowledge that the conduct is unlawful is all that is required," Stevens said. In a dissent, Scalia, joined by Rehnquist and Ginsburg, said the statute was ambiguous and any ambiguity should be resolved in the defendant's favor.

Caron v. United States, decided by a 6–3 vote, June 22, 1998; Kennedy wrote the opinion; Thomas, Scalia, and Souter dissented.

Someone can be subject to a federal law prohibiting repeat offenders from possessing firearms even if state law permits them to own the weapons in question.

The ruling involved a federal law that prohibited someone convicted of a serious crime from possessing any firearm and imposed a longer term on someone with three prior violent felonies who violated the provision. The law stipulated that a state conviction would not count if the offender's civil rights had been restored "unless . . . such restoration of civil rights expressly provides that the person may not . . . possess . . . firearms." The federal government invoked the law against a Massachusetts man, Gerald Caron, for possessing a rifle. He contended that the law did not apply because his civil rights had been restored under state law and he was allowed to possess rifles and shotguns, though not handguns. A federal district court agreed with Caron's interpretation of the law, but the First U.S. Circuit Court of Appeals sided with the government.

By a 6–3 vote, the Court adopted the government's interpretation that the federal law applied as long as an ex-offender was subject to some state law firearms restrictions. "[T]he Federal government has an interest in a single, national, protective policy, broader than required under state law," Kennedy wrote.

In a dissent, Thomas, joined by Scalia and Souter, argued that the majority opinion contradicted the "plain language" of the federal law. "[I]t is bizarre to hold that the *legal* possession of firearms under state law subjects a person to a sentence enhancement under federal law," Thomas wrote.

Lewis v. United States, decided by an 8–1 vote, March 9, 1998; Breyer wrote the opinion; Kennedy dissented.

The federal murder statute, rather than state law, applies to homicides committed on military bases or other federal enclaves.

The ruling involved application of the Assimilative Crimes Act, a federal law dating to the 1820s aimed at filling in gaps in the federal criminal code. The act provides that under certain conditions state criminal laws can be "assimilated" into federal law and made applicable to federal enclaves located within the state.

Applying that law, a federal court in Louisiana convicted Debra Faye Lewis and her husband, James Lewis, of first-degree murder under the state's murder statute for the beating death of their four-year-old daughter while on the grounds of Fort Polk, a U.S. Army base. The state law established a minimum sentence of life imprisonment without parole for the deliberate murder of a child under the age of twelve; the federal murder statute would have defined the offense as second-degree murder, with a normal punishment of 168 to 210 months. Ruling in an appeal by Debra Lewis, the Fifth U.S. Circuit Court of Appeals held that the federal law should have applied.

But it upheld the conviction and sentence anyway on the ground that the defendant could have been given a life sentence under the federal law.

The Court used the case to set out a general approach to deciding when state laws are assimilated into federal law under the act. Breyer said federal law applies if a parallel state law "would interfere with the achievement of a federal policy" or "effectively rewrite an offense definition that Congress carefully considered" or if the federal statutes "reveal an intent to occupy so much of the field as to exclude use of the particular statute at issue." Under that test, Breyer said the federal murder statute applied in the case because of its "detailed" provisions and because of Congress's "considered legislative judgment" in drawing lines between first- and second-degree murder.

Five justices joined Breyer's opinion. In an opinion concurring in the judgment, Scalia, joined by Thomas, argued for a historical approach to applying the law. He said state law should be assimilated into federal law only if the offense would not have been treated as a crime under common law.

In a lone dissent, Kennedy argued that federalism required that state law should be assimilated "except where Congress has manifested a contrary intention in 'specific [federal] laws.' "

The ruling returned the case for resentencing. Breyer explained that the appeals court should have set aside the life term and allowed the district court to use federal sentencing guidelines in setting Lewis's sentence.

Muscarello v. United States, decided by a 5–4 vote, June 8, 1998; Breyer wrote the opinion; Ginsburg, Rehnquist, Scalia, and Souter dissented.

The Court broadly applied a federal firearms provision imposing a mandatory five-year sentence to someone who "carries" a weapon during a drug trafficking crime.

By a 5–4 vote, the Court held that the provision applies to a defendant who carries a weapon in the trunk or locked glove compartment of a car while driving to commit a drug trafficking offense. The decision upheld rulings in unrelated cases by federal appeals courts in the First and Fifth Circuits. Some other federal appeals courts had limited the statute by imposing the sentence only if the weapon was "immediately accessible" during the crime.

Writing for the majority, Breyer surveyed sources ranging from dictionaries to the Bible before concluding that "the 'generally accepted contemporary meaning' of 'carries' includes the carrying of a firearm in a vehicle." He also said that the broad meaning was consistent with the law's purpose and that any "misuse" of the statute would be prevented by the qualification that it applies only to carrying a weapon "during or in relation to" a drug trafficking crime.

The dissenters included two of the Court's liberals, Ginsburg and Souter, and two conservatives, Rehnquist and Scalia. Writing for the four, Ginsburg said the provision should apply only to "bearing [a firearm] in such a manner as to be ready for use as a weapon." She noted that if the mandatory five-year term was not imposed, a defendant could still receive some additional punishment under the "more finely tuned" sentencing guidelines.

Salinas v. United States, decided by a 9–0 vote, December 2, 1997; Kennedy wrote the opinion.

The federal bribery statute applies to bribes paid to officials of any state or local agency receiving federal funds even if the payments do not involve federal funds. In a second holding, the Court eased the requirements for a conspiracy conviction under the federal racketeering law.

The decision upheld the bribery and racketeering conspiracy convictions of a local deputy sheriff in Texas, Mario Salinas. He was found guilty of accepting a pair of designer watches and a pickup truck from a federal prisoner being housed at the county jail in exchange for allowing the inmate to have conjugal visits with his wife and his girlfriend. The federal bribery statute was invoked because the sheriff's department received reimbursement from the federal government for housing federal prisoners. In seeking to overturn the bribery convictions, Salinas argued the statute should apply only if federal moneys were diverted or misappropriated.

The Court cited the statute's "expansive and unqualified language" in rejecting the argument. The bribery statute, Kennedy wrote, "does not require the Government to prove the bribe in question had any particular influence on federal funds." On the second issue, the Court settled a conflict among the federal appeals courts by holding that a conspiracy conviction under the federal Racketeering Influenced and Corrupt Organizations Act (RICO) does not require proof—as the general federal conspiracy statute does—that the defendant committed one or more "overt acts" to further the conspiracy.

Double Jeopardy

Hudson v. United States, decided by 9–0 and 5–4 votes, December 10, 1997; Rehnquist wrote the opinion; Stevens, Souter, Ginsburg, and Breyer concurred in the result but not the legal holding.

The imposition of civil penalties ordinarily does not prevent the government from prosecuting someone for the same conduct unless the legislature intended the civil enforcement scheme to be punitive.

The unanimous decision, overruling a 1989 precedent, rejected arguments by three former Oklahoma bankers that the Double Jeopardy Clause blocked their criminal prosecutions for making unlawful insider loans from two banks they controlled during the 1980s. The three men had already been fined and barred from banking by the Office of the Comptroller of the Currency, one of the federal bank regulatory agencies. A trial judge dismissed the indictments on double jeopardy grounds, but the Tenth U.S.

Circuit Court of Appeals reinstated the charges. It applied the Court's 1989 decision, *Halper v. United States,* in holding that the civil penalties were not so "grossly disproportionate" to the proven damages to the government as to be punitive for double jeopardy purposes.

In upholding the ruling, the Court rejected the 1989 precedent as "ill considered" and adopted a more lenient standard for double jeopardy claims. Writing for a five-justice majority, Rehnquist said civil penalties ordinarily do not amount to punishment for double jeopardy purposes if Congress intended the sanctions to be civil unless there is the "clearest proof" that they are so punitive as to be criminal "despite Congress' intent to the contrary."

The four other justices concurred in the result, but not in Rehnquist's opinion. In separate opinions, Breyer, joined by Ginsburg, and Souter all agreed that *Halper* should be discarded, but they objected to the part of Rehnquist's opinion requiring "clearest proof" to find that a civil penalty scheme could amount to criminal punishment. Stevens said that there was no need to reconsider *Halper* and emphasized that the Court's opinion left open the possibility that civil penalties could prevent prosecutions in some cases.

Monge v. California, decided by a 5–4 vote, June 26, 1998; O'Connor wrote the opinion; Scalia, Stevens, Souter, and Ginsburg dissented.

The Double Jeopardy Clause does not prevent the prosecution from having a second chance to prove a defendant's prior criminal record for purposes of enhancing a sentence for a new offense.

The ruling eased the use of so-called "three-strikes" laws enacted in California and other states that provided for substantially increased sentences for defendants with two or more prior convictions. Under the California law, Angel Monge's sentence for using a minor to sell marijuana was increased to eleven years from five years because of two prior criminal convictions for assault. On appeal, the California Court of Criminal Appeal held that the evidence on one of the prior convictions was insufficient and that the Double Jeopardy Clause barred a retrial on the issue. The California Supreme Court disagreed. Monge brought the issue to the U.S. Supreme Court, citing a 1981 decision, *Bullington v. Missouri,* that barred a retrial on allegations introduced by the prosecution in the sentencing phase of death penalty cases.

In a narrowly divided ruling, the Court held that the Double Jeopardy Clause did not bar a retrial on a prior conviction allegation in noncapital sentencing proceedings. Writing for the majority, O'Connor said that historically the Double Jeopardy Clause had not been applied to sentencing proceedings and that the *Bullington* decision should not be extended to noncapital cases.

Of the four dissenters, only Stevens argued that the Double Jeopardy Clause should apply to sentencing proceedings in noncapital as well as capital cases. "[T]he Double Jeopardy Clause prohibits a 'second bite at the apple,' " Stevens said.

Writing for the other three dissenters, Scalia contended that the prior convictions used to trigger the three-strikes law amounted to separate offenses rather than sentencing factors and were therefore subject to the Double Jeopardy Clause. "Giving the State a second chance to prove [Monge] guilty of that same crime would violate the very core of the Double Jeopardy prohibition," Scalia wrote. O'Connor answered the argument in her opinion by pointing to the Court's 5–4 decision earlier in the term, *Almendarez-Torres v. United States,* allowing lawmakers broad discretion in determining what factors can be used to enhance sentences in repeat-offender statutes. Scalia led the four dissenters in that decision.

Evidence

Gray v. Maryland, decided by a 5–4 vote, March 9, 1998; Breyer wrote the opinion; Scalia, Rehnquist, Kennedy, and Thomas dissented.

The Court made it harder for the prosecution to use a confession by one defendant that also implicates a codefendant being tried at the same time.

The ruling tightened a restriction first established in a 1968 case, *Bruton v. United States.* The so-called *Bruton* rule prohibited the use of a confession by one defendant as evidence against the other. In joint trials, the rule essentially required prosecutors to edit out—or "redact"—any references in a defendant's confession to any codefendants. Prosecutors in a Maryland murder case redacted a confession by one defendant by leaving a blank space or inserting the word "deleted" wherever a codefendant's name had appeared. The codefendant challenged the procedure as a violation of *Bruton,* but the state's highest court upheld the conviction.

In a narrowly divided decision, the Court held that the use of "an obvious blank symbol or a word such as 'deleted' " did not comply with the rule requiring redactions of confessions implicating other defendants. "[T]he jury will often realize that the confession refers specifically to the defendant," Breyer wrote.

Writing for the four dissenters, Scalia said jurors should be trusted to follow instructions not to consider the statement by one defendant as evidence against another. "Though the jury may speculate," he wrote, "the statement expressly implicates no one but the speaker."

United States v. Scheffer, decided by an 8–1 vote, March 31, 1998; Thomas wrote the main opinion; Kennedy wrote a concurring opinion; Stevens dissented.

The Court held that an accused has no constitutional right to present evidence of a lie detector test, even though a majority of the justices said they opposed a complete ban on polygraph evidence.

The ruling reinstated a per se exclusion on the use of polygraph evidence in military courts, Military Rule of Evidence 707, adopted in 1991. The ban had been challenged by a former airman, Edward Scheffer, in his

1992 court-martial for several charges, including using methamphetamine. Scheffer took a lie detector test, and the polygraph examiner said the results "indicated no deception." The military judge barred the evidence, but the U.S. Court of Appeals for the Armed Forces held, by a 3–2 vote, that the rule barring polygraph evidence violated Scheffer's Sixth Amendment right to present a defense.

In a nearly unanimous but nonetheless divided decision, the Court rejected the argument that the Sixth Amendment entitles a defendant to present lie detector evidence at trial. Thomas said the military's ban on polygraph evidence served the government's interests of ensuring use of "reliable evidence" at trial, "preserving the jury's core function of making credibility determinations in criminal trials," and "avoiding litigation over issues other than the guilt or innocence of the accused."

Four justices—Kennedy, O'Connor, Ginsburg, and Breyer—said they agreed only that the rule excluding lie detector evidence was "not so arbitrary or disproportionate" as to be unconstitutional. But, writing for the four, Kennedy said, "I doubt, though, that the rule of *per se* exclusion is wise." And he specifically rejected two of Thomas's three rationales: protecting the jury's role and avoiding collateral litigation.

In a dissenting opinion, Stevens said the decision "rests on a serious undervaluation of the importance of the citizen's constitutional right to present a defense to a criminal charge and an unrealistic appraisal of the importance of the governmental interests that undergird the Rule." Stevens also argued it was inconsistent for the government to use polygraph evidence in investigations but to bar its use by an accused. Thomas responded in a footnote by saying "limited, out of court uses" of polygraph tests "carry less severe consequences" than their use in trials.

Extradition

New Mexico ex rel. Ortiz v. Reed, decided by a 9–0 vote, June 8, 1998; *per curiam* (unsigned) opinion.

The Court reinforced states' obligation in extradition proceedings to return a fugitive to another state without considering any legal issues besides the procedural formalities of the request.

The decision required New Mexico authorities to return a prominent Indian-rights activist, Timothy Reed, to Ohio to face a parole violation charge. Reed had told New Mexico courts that he fled Ohio because he feared that his parole would be revoked without a hearing and that he faced physical harm if returned to prison. The New Mexico Supreme Court, in a 4–1 decision, refused Ohio's extradition request, saying that Reed was not a "fugitive" but a "refugee from injustice."

In an unsigned decision issued without hearing oral argument, the Court said Reed's claims could be considered only in Ohio, the "demanding state," not in "the asylum state," New Mexico. "[C]laims relating to what actually happened in the demanding State, the law of the demanding State, and what may be expected to happen in the demanding State when the fugitive returns, are issues that must be tried in the courts of that State, and not in those of the asylum State," the Court wrote.

Forfeitures

United States v. Bajakajian, decided by a 5–4 vote, June 22, 1998; Thomas wrote the opinion; Kennedy, Rehnquist, O'Connor, and Scalia dissented.

The Court, citing the Eighth Amendment's Excessive Fines Clause, struck down as "grossly disproportional" the government's attempt to seize $357,144 from a California man for failing to report the currency as he was leaving the United States.

The ruling favored a Syrian immigrant, Hosep Bajakajian, who was arrested at Los Angeles International Airport in June 1994 for violating a federal money laundering statute by failing to report that he was leaving the country with more than $10,000 in cash. The reporting provision required forfeiture of any money that had not been reported. A federal district court judge, however, found the penalty "grossly disproportional" and instead ordered $15,000 forfeited; he also fined Bajakajian $5,000 and placed him on three-years' probation. On the government's appeal, the Ninth U.S. Circuit Court of Appeals ruled that any forfeiture would be disproportional but said it had no jurisdiction to overturn the $15,000 forfeiture because Bajakajian had not appealed.

In a narrowly divided ruling, the Court upheld the appeals court's decision. Thomas said the forfeiture was a criminal penalty, subject to the Excessive Fines Clause, because the forfeiture served no "remedial" purpose. He then said a punitive forfeiture violates the Excessive Fines Clause if it is "grossly disproportional to the gravity of a defendant's offense." Applying that test, Thomas concluded the forfeiture of all $357,144 was grossly disproportional because it bore "no articulable correlation to any injury suffered by the Government."

Writing for the four dissenters, Kennedy said the ruling understated the seriousness of the offense. "[T]he Government needs the information to investigate other serious crimes," Kennedy said, "and it needs the penalties to ensure compliance." *(See story, pp. 55–58; excerpts, pp. 154–164.)*

Guilty Pleas

Bousley v. United States, decided by a 7–2 vote, May 18, 1998; Rehnquist wrote the opinion; Scalia and Thomas dissented.

A defendant may bring a belated challenge to a guilty plea by showing that he or she is probably innocent of the charge.

The ruling allowed a convicted drug dealer, Kenneth Bousley, to seek to withdraw his 1990 guilty plea to a separate charge of using a firearm in connection with the drug offense. Bousley filed a habeas corpus petition, claiming his guilty plea was not "knowing and intelligent" because of a 1995 Court decision tightening the requirements for proving the firearms offense. The Eighth U.S. Circuit Court of Appeals, however, ruled that Bousley could not use a habeas corpus petition to claim a defect in his guilty plea on the basis of having been misinformed about the elements of the offense.

In a 7–2 decision, the Court disagreed and reinstated the habeas petition. Rehnquist said that rulings limiting the ability to use habeas corpus petitions to challenge procedural errors did not apply to cases involving the interpretation of substantive criminal statutes. Even though Bousley had failed to challenge the guilty plea earlier, Rehnquist concluded, his claim "may still be reviewed . . . if he can establish that the constitutional error in his plea colloquy has probably resulted in the conviction of one who is actually innocent."

In a dissenting opinion, Scalia, joined by Thomas, called the ruling "a grave mistake" that would invite "extremely frequent" challenges.

Habeas Corpus

Calderon, Warden v. Ashmus, decided by a 9–0 vote, May 26, 1998; Rehnquist wrote the opinion.

The Court blocked a class action suit by California death row inmates seeking an early determination whether the state met the requirements of a new law for expedited procedures in federal habeas corpus cases.

The ruling involved the habeas corpus revisions in the 1996 Antiterrorism and Effective Death Penalty Act. The law established a number of restrictions on the ability of inmates to file habeas corpus challenges in death penalty cases, including a short, 180-day deadline for filing a petition and a limit on amending a petition after the state has filed an answer. A state could invoke the restrictions only if it met certain standards for providing legal representation for death row inmates.

A California death row inmate, Troy Ashmus, filed a class action suit under the federal Declaratory Judgment Act asking a federal court to determine whether California met those requirements. He argued that uncertainty about the state's compliance created a dilemma for death row inmates because they did not know whether they had to meet the 180-day deadline at the risk of filing a "bare-bones" petition that they could not amend later. A lower federal court and the Ninth U.S. Circuit Court of Appeals both held the suit was properly filed and that the state had not met the law's requirements.

In a unanimous opinion, the Court held that the suit was not "justiciable"—or not appropriate for judicial decision—under the Constitution's "case or controversy" requirement for federal court jurisdiction. Rehnquist said the suit did not meet the requirement that a declaratory judgment action provide a "final or conclusive determination" of a controversy between the opposing parties. "Any judgment in this action," Rehnquist wrote, "would not resolve the entire case or controversy . . . , but would merely determine a collateral legal issue governing certain aspects of their pending or future suits."

In a brief concurring opinion, Breyer, joined by Stevens, noted that some inmates could obtain a "relatively expeditious judicial answer" to the question of the state's compliance with the law "and thereby provide legal guidance for others."

Calderon, Warden v. Thompson, decided by a 5–4 vote, April 29, 1998; Kennedy wrote the opinion; Souter, Stevens, Ginsburg, and Breyer dissented.

A federal appeals court was sharply rebuked for its last-minute change of mind to grant a new trial to a California death row inmate convicted of a rape-murder fifteen years earlier.

The bluntly worded ruling reversed a procedurally complex decision by the Ninth U.S. Circuit Court of Appeals to grant habeas corpus relief to an inmate, Thomas Thompson, who had been convicted and sentenced to death in 1983 for the rape-murder of a young woman in a Southern California beach community in 1981. A federal district court in March 1995 granted Thompson's plea for a new trial because of ineffective assistance of counsel, but the appeals court reversed that decision in June 1996. Over the next year, Thompson tried but failed to get a new hearing from the appeals court, review by the Supreme Court, or relief from the state courts. Then, just two days before his scheduled execution on August 5, 1997, the appeals court voted 7–4 to withdraw its previous order—in legal terms, "recall its mandate"—and order a new trial for Thompson. California authorities appealed the decision on procedural and substantive grounds.

By a 5–4 vote, the Court ruled that the appeals court had committed "a grave abuse of discretion" in granting the new trial. Kennedy acknowledged that appellate courts have "inherent power to recall their mandates" but said that the procedural lapses in the handling of Thompson's case cited by the Ninth Circuit provided only "the slightest bases" for doing so. He also said that even though the restrictive habeas corpus provisions contained in the Antiterrorism and Effective Death Penalty Act did not specifically govern the case, a court nonetheless "must exercise its discretion in a manner consistent with the object of that statute." With that background, Kennedy concluded that an appellate court commits an abuse of discretion by recalling its mandate in order to reexamine the merits of an inmate's habeas petition "unless it acts to avoid a miscarriage of justice"—a test that was not met, Kennedy said, in Thompson's case.

Kennedy included in his opinion several strongly worded passages about the importance of "finality" in criminal cases, both for the state and for crime victims. In his opinion for the four dissenters, Souter acknowledged that the timing of the appeals court's decision was "a matter of regret." But he said the majority had decided to "jettison" a flexible abuse of discretion standard "for the sake of solving a systemic problem that does not exist."

Hohn v. United States, decided by a 5–4 vote, June 15, 1998; Kennedy wrote the opinion; Scalia, Rehnquist, O'Connor, and Thomas dissented.

The Court reduced the impact of a recently enacted habeas corpus law aimed at making it harder for prison inmates to appeal a federal judge's refusal to overturn their convictions or sentences.

By a 5–4 vote, the Court held that it has the power to review an action by a federal appeals judge or court denying an inmate a "certificate of appealability" needed to appeal the lower court judge's ruling. The requirement was one of many provisions that Congress included in the 1996 Antiterrorism and Effective Death Penalty Act in an effort to reduce prisoners' ability to use habeas corpus to challenge convictions or sentences.

The issue reached the Court in the case of a Nebraska man, Arnold Hohn, convicted in 1992 of a number of drug-related offenses, including use of a firearm during a drug crime. Hohn later filed a federal habeas corpus petition, claiming that his conviction on the firearm count was inconsistent with the Court's interpretation of the provision in a 1995 decision. A federal district court judge ruled the plea did not present a "substantial constitutional question," and the Eighth U.S. Circuit Court of Appeals refused to issue a certificate of appealability. When Hohn asked the Court to review the case, the justices had to decide whether his application for the certificate amounted to a "case" that was "in" the Court of Appeals—the normal requirements for the Court to review an appeals court ruling.

Writing for the majority, Kennedy concluded that the Court did have jurisdiction. "The application moved through the Eighth Circuit in the same manner as cases in general do," Kennedy wrote. In reaching that conclusion, the majority overruled an old precedent, *House v. Mayo* (1945), that held the Court had no power to consider an appellate court's refusal to issue a "certificate of probable cause" needed under old procedural rules to appeal an adverse lower court decision.

In a sharply written dissent, Scalia accused the majority of "judicial willfulness" by ignoring "the obvious intent" of the law. Rehnquist, O'Connor, and Thomas joined his opinion.

Spencer v. Kemna, Superintendent, Western Missouri Correctional Center, decided by an 8–1 vote, March 3, 1998; Scalia wrote the opinion; Stevens dissented.

A former inmate cannot use federal habeas corpus to challenge a parole revocation after the expiration of his or her sentence.

The ruling upheld the dismissal of a habeas corpus petition by a former Missouri inmate whose parole was revoked because of a rape accusation that he denied. The inmate's sentence ended, however, before the federal district court could rule on the petition. On that basis, the district court and the Eighth U.S. Court of Appeals dismissed the petition, even though other appeals courts had allowed parole revocation challenges after an inmate's sentence was over.

In a nearly unanimous decision, the Court held the inmate's habeas corpus petition was moot, or legally over. "The reincarceration that he incurred as a result of [the parole revocation] is now over, and cannot be undone," Scalia wrote.

In a concurring opinion, Souter argued that the inmate could still bring a federal civil rights suit to contest the parole revocation; Scalia left that issue open.

In a lone dissent, Stevens said the dispute was not moot because of the inmate's interest in vindicating his reputation. "Such an interest is sufficient to defeat a claim of mootness," he wrote.

Stewart, Director, Arizona Department of Correction v. Martinez-Villareal, decided by a 7–2 vote, May 18, 1998; Rehnquist wrote the opinion; Scalia and Thomas dissented.

The Court somewhat eased the effect of a recently enacted law aimed at limiting the ability of state prison inmates to file repeated habeas corpus petitions in federal court.

The 7–2 ruling allowed an Arizona death row inmate, Ramon Martinez-Villareal, to proceed with a federal habeas corpus petition seeking to block his execution on grounds of mental incompetency. The state had sought to bar consideration of the claim by invoking a provision of the 1996 Antiterrorism and Effective Death Penalty Act that barred state inmates from filing a "second or successive habeas corpus application" except under limited circumstances. Martinez-Villareal had earlier filed a series of habeas corpus petitions, but the federal courts put off a ruling on the mental incompetency claim until state courts determined whether he was fit to be executed.

Writing for the majority, Rehnquist said Martinez-Villareal's return to federal court with the mental incompetency issue did not amount to a "second or successive" application under the 1996 law. To order the petition dismissed, Rehnquist said, "would mean that a dismissal of a first habeas petition for technical procedural reasons would bar the prisoner from ever obtaining federal habeas review."

In dissenting opinions, Thomas and Scalia both harshly criticized the ruling as inconsistent with what Scalia called "the unmistakable language of the statute." Wrote Thomas: "[H]abeas petitioners cannot be permitted to evade [the law's] prohibitions simply by moving to reopen claims already presented in a prior habeas application."

Trest v. Cain, Warden, decided by a 9–0 vote, December 9, 1997; Breyer wrote the opinion.

A federal appeals court is not required to raise on its own the question whether a state inmate's habeas corpus petition should be barred for failing to properly challenge his conviction in state court.

The limited ruling sent back for further proceedings a habeas corpus petition filed by a Louisiana inmate challenging a thirty-five-year prison sentence imposed under the state's habitual offender law after a robbery conviction. Even though the state did not raise the issue, the Fifth U.S. Circuit Court of Appeals ruled that the inmate's petition should be dismissed for "procedural default."

In a brief and unanimous opinion, the Court rejected the appeals court's conclusion that it was required to raise the issue. "We are not aware of any precedent stating that a habeas corpus *must* raise such a matter where the State itself does not do so," Breyer wrote. But the Court declined to decide whether the appeals court had discretion to raise the issue on its own.

Jury Selection

Campbell v. Louisiana, decided by a 7–2 vote, April 21, 1998; Kennedy wrote the opinion; Thomas and Scalia dissented in part.

A white criminal defendant may challenge his conviction on grounds that blacks were discriminated against in the selection of grand jurors.

The ruling overturned the second-degree murder conviction of a Louisiana man, Terry Campbell, for the killing of another white man. Campbell introduced evidence that no black had served as foreperson of the Evangeline Parish grand jury over a seventeen-year period, from January 1976 to August 1993, even though blacks comprised about 20 percent of the parish's population. The Louisiana Supreme Court rejected the challenge, saying that Campbell had no standing to raise an equal protection claim on behalf of potential black jurors. The state court also said Campbell could not raise a due process challenge because the grand jury foreperson's role was "ministerial" and had "little, if any, effect" on the fairness of the trial.

By a 7–2 vote, the Court held that Campbell had so-called "third-party" standing to assert what it called "the well-established equal protection rights of black persons not to be excluded from grand jury service on the basis of their race." "Regardless of his or her skin color," Kennedy wrote, "the accused suffers a significant injury in fact when the composition of the grand jury is tainted by racial discrimination." Citing factors from a 1991 ruling on discrimination in selection of trial juries, *Powers v. Ohio,* Kennedy added that a white defendant would have the same interest as the excluded grand jurors in seeking to eradicate discrimination but would not have the disincentives an individual juror would face in bringing the claim.

In a dissenting opinion, Thomas, joined by Scalia, rejected Campbell's equal protection claim and called for overruling the *Powers* decision. "I fail to understand how the rights of blacks excluded from jury service can be vindicated by letting a white murderer go free," Thomas wrote. The dissenting justices agreed with the majority that Campbell could raise a due process challenge but voiced doubts that he could prevail on that claim.

Parole

Pennsylvania Board of Probation and Parole v. Scott, decided by a 5–4 vote, June 22, 1998; Thomas wrote the opinion; Souter, Stevens, Ginsburg, and Breyer dissented.

Illegally obtained evidence may be introduced against a parolee at a parole revocation hearing.

The ruling cleared the way for reinstating a decision by the Pennsylvania parole board to revoke the parole of a former prison inmate, Keith Scott, for possession of firearms. Parole officers found the weapons during a search of Scott's home. The Pennsylvania Supreme Court held that officers had no basis for the search and that the exclusionary rule barring use of illegally obtained evidence should be extended to parole revocation hearings in some circumstances.

By a 5–4 vote, the Court rejected any extension of the exclusionary rule to parole revocation hearings. Thomas said application of the exclusionary rule "would provide only minimal deterrence benefits" while it would "hinder the functioning of state parole systems and alter the traditionally flexible, administrative nature of parole revocation proceedings."

In a dissenting opinion, Souter challenged Thomas's arguments that parole officers did not need to be deterred from conducting illegal searches. "If the police need the deterrence of an exclusionary rule to offset the temptations to forget the Fourth Amendment, parole officers need it quite as much," he wrote. Ginsburg and Breyer joined Souter's opinion. In a brief dissent, Stevens endorsed Souter's arguments, but added—in contrast to the majority opinion—that he believed the exclusionary rule was a constitutionally required protection.

Search and Seizure

United States v. Ramirez, decided by a 9–0 vote, March 4, 1998; Rehnquist wrote the opinion.

Police executing a no-knock search warrant do not need special justification if they damage or destroy property while entering the premises.

The ruling reinstated the firearms conviction of an Oregon man, Hernan Ramirez, who was arrested after police, searching for a prison escapee, forced their way into his garage by breaking a window. The escapee was not found. In overturning the conviction, the Ninth U.S. Circuit Court of Appeals held that police need "specific inferences of exigency" to justify a no-knock entry when property is destroyed.

In a unanimous decision, the Court disagreed. Rehnquist said that the

Court's recent decisions had confirmed the legality of no-knock entries if police have a "reasonable suspicion" that knocking and announcing would be futile or dangerous. "Whether such a 'reasonable suspicion' exists depends in no way on whether police must destroy property in order to enter," he wrote.

Self-Incrimination

United States v. Balsys, decided by a 7–2 vote, June 25, 1998; Souter wrote the opinion; Breyer and Ginsburg dissented.

The Fifth Amendment's privilege against self-incrimination does not protect someone from being compelled to give testimony in a civil proceeding that might subject him to criminal prosecution in another country.

The ruling rejected an effort by a suspected Nazi war criminal, Aloyzas Balsys, to avoid giving a deposition in an investigation that could have led to his deportation to his native Latvia or some other country. The Justice Department's Office of Special Investigation was seeking to determine whether Balsys lied about his activities during World War II when he entered the United States in 1961. Although the statute of limitations had expired on any possible criminal prosecution in the United States, Balsys refused to answer any questions on the ground that he feared prosecution in Latvia, Germany, or Israel. A federal district court rejected the plea, but the Second U.S. Circuit Court of Appeals held Balsys was entitled to invoke the Fifth Amendment.

By a 7–2 vote, the Court held that someone cannot invoke the Fifth Amendment based on fear of prosecution by a foreign nation. The amendment's language prohibiting compelled testimony in "any criminal case" applied only to proceedings in the United States, Souter said. He also rejected as "fatally flawed" a broader, policy-based rationale for the privilege included in two companion decisions in 1964 that first applied the Fifth Amendment to states as well as to the federal government.

Four justices joined all of Souter's opinion; Scalia and Thomas did not join two final sections in which Souter concluded that the costs to law enforcement of extending the privilege outweighed any potential benefits in individual rights. Stevens added a brief concurrence, suggesting that the ruling would have little impact on the fairness of trials in the United States or in other countries.

In a dissenting opinion, Breyer, joined by Ginsburg, criticized both the rationale and the effect of the ruling. "The basic values which this Court has said underlie the Fifth Amendment's protections are each diminished if the privilege may not be claimed here," he wrote.

Sentencing

Almendarez-Torres v. United States, decided by a 5–4 vote, March 24, 1998; Breyer wrote the opinion; Scalia, Stevens, Souter, and Ginsburg dissented.

The Court eased the burden on federal prosecutors to seek heightened prison sentences for aliens who return to the United States after having been deported because of criminal convictions.

The ruling involved a 1988 immigration law amendment providing for a prison term of up to twenty years for an alien who returns to the United States after having been deported because of prior convictions for an "aggravated" felony. The previous law—left on the books—set a prison term of up to two years for the offense for an alien deported without a criminal conviction. Hugo Almendalez-Torres, who had been given a prison term of seventy-seven to ninety-six months under the amended law, sought to reduce the sentence by arguing that the law created a new offense and that federal prosecutors had not included it in his indictment. The Fifth U.S. Circuit Court of Appeals rejected the argument, agreeing with seven out of eight other courts to rule on the issue that the provision was a sentence enhancement rather than a separate offense.

In a closely divided decision, the Court agreed. After examining the text and history of the provision, Breyer concluded the provision "simply authorizes a court to increase the sentence for a recidivist. It does not define a separate offense." On that basis, Breyer said that the statute did not require the government to cite the provision in an indictment. He went on to reject the defendant's argument that the Constitution generally requires Congress to treat recidivism as a separate offense rather than a sentencing factor.

Writing for the dissenters, Scalia argued for interpreting the provision to be a separate offense in order to avoid what he called "serious constitutional doubts." Prior to the ruling, Scalia said, it was uncertain "whether the Constitution permits a defendant's sentencing exposure to be increased tenfold on the basis of a fact that is not charged, tried to a jury, and found beyond a reasonable doubt."

Edwards v. United States, decided by a 9–0 vote, April 28, 1998; Breyer wrote the opinion.

The Court, interpreting the federal Sentencing Guidelines, strengthened the power of federal judges to determine sentences in cocaine trafficking cases.

The ruling rejected pleas by five gang members in an Illinois drug case to limit their sentences in a case charging them with conspiracy to traffic in powdered and "crack" cocaine. They argued on appeal that the jury's verdict had been ambiguous as to which type of drug was involved and that the judge was required to sentence them only on the shorter terms prescribed for powdered cocaine. The Seventh U.S. Circuit Court of Appeals rejected the argument.

In a brief and unanimous opinion, the Court agreed. "Regardless of the jury's actual, or assumed beliefs about the conspiracy," Breyer wrote, "the Guidelines nonetheless require the judge to determine whether the 'controlled substances' at issue—and how much of those substances—consisted of cocaine, crack, or both."

Venue

United States v. Cabrales, decided by a 9–0 vote, June 1, 1998; Ginsburg wrote the opinion.

A defendant cannot be prosecuted for money laundering in one state if the transactions took place entirely in another state.

The decision upheld a ruling by the Eighth U.S. Circuit Court of Appeals dismissing two money laundering counts of a three-count indictment brought in federal court in Missouri against Vickie Cabrales. She had been charged with depositing $40,000 in drug proceeds in a South Florida bank and withdrawing the funds within a week in four separate $9,500 transactions. The appeals court dismissed counts charging Cabrales with avoiding financial reporting requirements and engaging in a transaction with criminal proceeds greater than $10,000 on the ground the charges should have been brought in Florida. It sustained a third count that charged Cabrales with conspiracy to avoid a transaction-reporting requirement.

In a brief and unanimous opinion, the Court agreed. Ginsburg said the charges "portray her and the money she deposited and withdrew as moving inside Florida only." But she noted that the effect of the decision would be "negligible," since the government could still try Cabrales on the first count in Missouri and introduce evidence of the money laundering at sentencing.

Election Law

Congressional Elections

Foster, Governor of Louisiana v. Love, decided by a 9–0 vote, December 2, 1997; Souter wrote the opinion.

The Court struck down Louisiana's "open primary" system that allowed members of Congress to be elected in balloting among candidates of all parties conducted before the general election in November.

The Louisiana system, unique among the states, provided for the election of any congressional candidate who received a majority of the votes cast in a so-called "open primary" in October or a runoff in November between the top two candidates if no one received a majority. Four one-time congressional candidates challenged the procedure as a violation of federal law, which established the Tuesday after the first Monday in November in even-numbered years as the date for congressional elections. The state argued that the system, established in 1975, fell within the federal law provision giving states discretion to control the "manner" of electing members of Congress.

In a brief and unanimous opinion, the Court rejected Louisiana's argument. "[A] contested selection of candidates for a congressional office that is concluded as a matter of law before the federal election day . . . clearly violates" the federal law, Souter wrote. The ruling left the state free to continue the open primary system for state offices.

Federal Election Commission

Federal Election Commission v. Akins, decided by a 6–3 vote, June 1, 1998; Breyer wrote the opinion; Scalia, O'Connor, and Thomas dissented.

Voters have legal standing to sue the Federal Election Commission (FEC) for failing to bring an action to enforce political contribution and expenditure reporting requirements.

The ruling was a significant procedural victory for a group of voters, including a former member of Congress, seeking to compel the American Israel Public Affairs Committee (AIPAC) to disclose how much money it contributes to political candidates. The plaintiffs—critics of U.S. policy toward Israel—claimed that AIPAC was a "political committee" under the Federal Election Campaign Act and subject to the act's requirement to disclose spending aimed at influencing a federal election. When the FEC refused to bring an enforcement action against AIPAC, they filed suit under a provision of the law granting standing to "any person aggrieved by" an agency action. The federal appeals court in Washington agreed that AIPAC was required to disclose the political contributions; however, the FEC contended before the Supreme Court that the voters had not suffered sufficient legal injury to bring the suit.

By a 6–3 vote, the Court disagreed. Breyer said the plaintiffs' "failure to obtain relevant information" was an "injury of a kind that [the law] seeks to address." But the Court sent the case back to the FEC to reconsider the issue whether AIPAC's expenditures amounted to communications with members that did not have to be disclosed under the law.

Writing for the dissenters, Scalia called the decision to recognize standing "too much of a stretch." If similar standing provisions were "commonplace," Scalia said, "the role of the Executive Branch . . . would be greatly reduced, and that of the Judiciary greatly expanded."

Voting Rights

City of Monroe v. United States, decided by a 7–2 vote, November 17, 1997; *per curiam* (unsigned) opinion; Souter and Breyer dissented.

The city of Monroe, Georgia, was allowed to use a majority voting system for local elections even though it did not obtain specific approval under the Voting Rights Act to change from a plurality system.

The ruling rejected a suit by the Justice Department contesting the shift from plurality to majority elections, which had been adopted in 1966. The government claimed the city needed to obtain approval for the change under the Voting Rights Act's preclearance requirement. The city contended that the Justice Department had approved the new system by preclearing a 1968 Georgia state law that provided for majority voting in local elections unless a city charter required plurality voting. A three-judge federal court sustained the government's suit.

Without hearing argument, the Court agreed with the city's position. "[B]y preclearing the 1968 code, the Attorney General approved the state law default rule," the Court wrote in an unsigned opinion. The Court said the case was not controlled by a 1980 decision involving another Georgia city that, unlike Monroe, had a specific charter provision requiring plurality voting prior to shifting to majority voting.

In separate dissents, Souter and Breyer both said that the state's submission of the 1968 law for preclearance did not provide sufficient notice of the cities that would be affected. Both justices joined the other's dissent.

Texas v. United States, decided by a 9–0 vote, March 31, 1998; Scalia wrote the opinion.

The Court declined to decide whether the Voting Rights Act limits the ability of Texas officials to use a state law permitting the displacement of elected local school boards in certain circumstances.

The 1995 state law gave the state commissioner of education authority to appoint a master or management team if local school systems failed to meet student achievement standards. Texas officials sought a ruling from the Justice Department that the law did not affect voting and did not trigger the Voting Rights Act's requirement to obtain preclearance from the government or the federal court in Washington. When the Justice Department said some steps under the law could violate the act, Texas filed suit in federal court seeking a declaratory judgment that the federal law did not apply. The federal court dismissed the suit, saying it was not "ripe" for adjudication.

In a brief and unanimous opinion, the Court agreed, saying the suit was too "speculative." Since the state had not pointed to any impending application of the state law, Scalia wrote, "the issue is not fit for adjudication."

Environmental Law

National Forests

Ohio Forestry Association, Inc. v. Sierra Club, decided by a 9–0 vote, May 18, 1998; Breyer wrote the opinion.

The Court rejected as premature an environmental organization's legal challenge to a National Forest Service management plan for the Wayne National Forest in southern Ohio.

The Sierra Club claimed that the service's management plan for the 178,000-acre forest violated various federal environmental and administrative laws by authorizing clear-cutting and below-cost timber sales. The government and the Ohio Forestry Association, a timber industry group that intervened in the suit, both argued that the challenge was premature because the plan did not authorize logging on any specific sites. The Sixth U.S. Circuit Court of Appeals held that the suit was "justiciable" and that the plan violated the National Forest Management Act by impermissibly favoring clear-cutting.

In a unanimous opinion, the Court held that the suit was "not yet ripe for judicial review" and ordered the action dismissed. "The Sierra Club will have ample opportunity later to bring its legal challenge at a time when harm is more imminent and more certain," Breyer wrote. He also said that allowing the suit to proceed at this point "could hinder agency efforts to refine its policies" and "require time-consuming judicial consideration" of issues that ultimately might not need to be decided.

"Right to Know" Laws

Steel Co. v. Citizens for a Better Environment, decided by 9–0 and 6–3 votes, March 4, 1998; Scalia wrote the opinion; Stevens, Souter, and Ginsburg agreed with the outcome but disagreed with the legal holding.

The Court left unresolved the issue of whether businesses can be sued by private citizens for past violations of a federal law requiring public disclosure of the use of toxic chemicals. Instead, the Court used the case to narrow the doctrine of legal standing in cases where plaintiffs are not seeking damages or future injunctive relief.

The issue arose in a suit brought by an environmental group against a Chicago steel-finishing company under the Emergency Planning and Community Right-to-Know Act of 1986. The company failed to comply with the law's provisions requiring disclosure of the use of toxic chemicals but corrected the violation before the suit was filed. A federal district court judge dismissed the suit, but the Seventh U.S. Circuit Court of Appeals reinstated the action. Another federal appeals court had ruled no suits were allowed under the law for "historic violations."

Without settling that issue, the Court held that the environmental group did not meet the constitutional requirements for legal standing to bring the suit. Scalia said the law provided for a civil fine to the government but no damages to private plaintiffs; he also noted that the group was not seeking an injunction against future violations. Instead, he said, the group was asking only for a declaratory judgment that the company had violated the law and for authority to periodically inspect its records and facilities.

On that basis, Scalia concluded, the group did not satisfy the requirement of "redressability"—"the likelihood that the requested relief will redress [the plaintiff's] injury." "None of the specific items of relief sought . . . ," Scalia wrote, "would serve to reimburse [the group] for losses caused by the late reporting, or to eliminate any effects of that late reporting on respondent."

In an opinion concurring in the result, Stevens argued that the Court should have resolved the case by ruling that the law did not allow citizen suits for past violations. He called the Court's ruling "new constitutional law" that was unnecessary to decide the case. Souter joined his opinion; Ginsburg joined part of it.

Toxic Waste

United States v. Bestfoods, decided by a 9–0 vote, June 8, 1998; Souter wrote the opinion.

A corporation can be held liable for the costs of cleaning up toxic wastes at a subsidiary's plant if the parent company participated in and controlled the plant's operations.

The ruling was a partial setback for the government in enforcing the 1980 federal "Superfund" law—formally called the Comprehensive Environmental Response, Compensation, and Liability Act. The issue arose in connection with the planned cleanup of the site of a former chemical manufacturing plant near Muskegon, Michigan. The government sought to impose some of the cleanup costs on the corporation that bought the site— CPC International, later called Bestfoods—and then set up subsidiary companies to operate the facility. A federal district court judge ruled that CPC could be held liable under a doctrine known as "piercing the corporate veil," which allows a parent company to be held responsible for a subsidiary's action under certain circumstances. But in a 7–6 decision, the Sixth U.S. Circuit Court of Appeals held that the doctrine did not apply and that CPC was not responsible for any of the cleanup costs.

In a unanimous decision, the Court agreed that the "piercing the corporate veil" doctrine did not apply. But Souter also said that CPC might be directly responsible for the cleanup costs if its officers or directors were involved in operating the plant. "[A] corporate parent that actively participated in, and exercised control over, the operations of the facility itself may be held directly liable in its own right as an operator of the facility," Souter wrote. The decision returned the case to lower courts to apply that standard.

Federal Government

Federal Employees

LaChance, Acting Director, Office of Personnel Management v. Erickson, decided by a 9–0 vote, January 21, 1998; Rehnquist wrote the opinion.

Federal employees can be disciplined for lying to agency investigators about allegations of employment-related misconduct.

The ruling came in six consolidated cases involving federal employees who were punished for various instances of misconduct and for making false statements during the investigations. The Merit Systems Protection Board, the administrative appeals board for federal workers, overturned the false statement charges, and the Court of Appeals for the Federal Circuit upheld its action. In its ruling, the appeals court said due process prohibited punishing a government employee for denying accusations of job-related misconduct.

In a unanimous and very brief decision, the Court disagreed. "A citizen may decline to answer the question," Rehnquist wrote, quoting from a 1969 precedent, "but he cannot with impunity knowingly and willfully answer with a falsehood."

Federal Regulation

American Telephone & Telegraph Co. v. Central Office Telephone, Inc., decided by a 7–1 vote, June 15, 1998; Scalia wrote the opinion; Stevens dissented; O'Connor did not participate.

Customers cannot sue federally regulated telephone companies for breach of contract in state court for failing to provide services as specified in rate tariffs filed with the Federal Communications Commission (FCC).

The decision nullified a $1.15 million judgment won by a long-distance service reseller, Central Office Telephone, against American Telephone & Telegraph (AT&T), the country's largest long-distance telephone company. Central Office, which bought bulk long-distance service from AT&T for resale to business customers, won the damage award after claiming that AT&T failed to live up to terms of their agreement regarding service and billing of customers. Both the lower court and the Ninth U.S. Circuit Court of Appeals rejected AT&T's arguments that Central Office's claims for breach of contract and tortious interference with contract were barred by the so-called "filed rate" doctrine, which generally requires common carriers to charge rates and provide services according to the tariffs filed with the FCC.

In a nearly unanimous decision, the Court held that the filed rate doctrine barred both counts of Central Office's state court suits. Scalia explained that the doctrine was intended to prevent regulated companies from discriminating between customers and that the appeals court was wrong to hold that it applied only to rates, not to services. "Any claim for inadequate excessive rates can be couched as a claim for inadequate services and vice versa," he said.

In a lone dissent, Stevens contended that Central Office's claims that AT&T improperly interfered with its business by soliciting its customers and disclosing the amount of Central Office's mark-up were not preempted. Rehnquist, in a concurring opinion, also suggested that the filed rate doctrine would not block all state law claims.

Regions Hospital v. Shalala, Secretary of Health and Human Services, decided by a 6–3 vote, February 24, 1998; Ginsburg wrote the opinion; Scalia, O'Connor, and Thomas dissented.

The Court upheld a federal regulation aimed at limiting Medicare and Medicaid reimbursements to hospitals for the costs of training medical residents.

The disputed rule, issued on the authority of a 1986 law, allowed the Department of Health and Human Services (HHS) to reaudit a hospital's 1984 figures for the cost of "graduate medical education" to determine payments in subsequent years. A Minnesota hospital challenged the rule after a reaudit determined that its allowable reimbursements for 1984 should have been about $5.9 million instead of about $9.9 million. The hospital claimed the rule was impermissibly retroactive and an improper interpretation of the law, but the Eighth U.S. Circuit Court of Appeals rejected the argument.

In a divided decision, the Court upheld the rule as "a reasonable interpretation" of the 1986 law. Ginsburg said the reaudit rule "enables the Secretary . . . to carry out that official's responsibility to reimburse only reasonable costs." She also said the rule was not retroactive, since it did not reduce payments for closed years but applied only to reimbursements in the future or within the normal three-year period for audits.

Writing for the dissenters, Scalia said the majority misinterpreted the law. The statutory language, he said, "cannot reasonably be understood to authorize a new composite cost determination."

Native Americans

Alaska v. Native Village of Venetie Tribal Government, decided by a 9–0 vote, February 25, 1998; Thomas wrote the opinion.

Native Alaskans failed in an effort to establish sovereign "Indian country" status for a 1.8-million-acre swath of land surrounding two villages north of the Arctic Circle.

The decision stemmed from a dispute over an effort by the tribal government in the village of Venetie to collect $161,000 in taxes from a private contractor constructing a state-financed school. But it involved a potentially far-reaching issue under the Alaska Native Claims Settlement Act. The 1971 law extinguished historic Indian titles to land in exchange for cash payments to state-chartered private corporations to be formed by Alaskan Natives. In upholding the village's power to impose the tax, the Ninth U.S. Circuit Court of Appeals held that the area qualified as "Indian country" under a six-part test. Alaskan officials argued the ruling misinterpreted the law and warned it could result in declaring vast areas of the state to be Indian country.

In a unanimous decision, the Court held that the villages and surrounding areas were not Indian country. Thomas rejected the appeals court's six-part test. Instead, he said that the 1971 law established two requirements: first, that the land be set aside by the federal government for the use of Indians as Indian land; and second, that the lands be "under federal superintendence." He concluded that the villages did not meet those conditions because the 1971 act "revoked" the existing Venetie reservation and "ended federal superintendence over the Tribe's lands."

Cass County, Minnesota v. Leech Lake Band of Chippewa Indians, decided by a 9–0 vote, June 8, 1998; Thomas wrote the opinion.

The Court strictly enforced procedures for exempting lands owned by Indian tribes from state or local property taxation.

The ruling involved the common situation of property once part of an Indian reservation that was allotted to Indians for private ownership or sold to non-Indians and later repurchased by a tribe. Indian reservations are exempt from state and local property taxes. On that basis, the Eighth U.S. Circuit Court of Appeals exempted from local property taxes eight parcels of land that been repurchased by a band of Chippewa Indians in northern Minnesota in recent years to rebuild its land base.

In a unanimous decision, the Court said the property was subject to local taxation. Thomas said that the federal laws establishing the allotment policy provided for taxation of former reservation lands once they passed into private ownership. "The subsequent repurchase of reservation land by a tribe does not manifest any congressional intent . . . to oust taxing authority," Thomas wrote.

The ruling's impact was limited, however, because another law—the Indian Reorganization Act—allowed tribes to regain the tax exemption by having the Interior Department hold lands in trust for the tribe's benefit. The Chippewas followed that procedure for seven of the eight parcels at issue while the case was being litigated.

Kiowa Tribe of Oklahoma v. Manufacturing Technologies, Inc., decided by a 6–3 vote, May 26, 1998; Kennedy wrote the opinion; Stevens, Thomas, and Ginsburg dissented.

The Court reaffirmed the rule of tribal immunity barring suits against Indian tribes in state courts but appeared to invite Congress to consider limiting the doctrine.

The decision overturned a ruling by an Oklahoma appeals court that had allowed a suit against the Kiowa tribe for defaulting on a $285,000 note for the purchase of stock. The state appeals court held that the doctrine of tribal immunity did not apply to suits involving commercial activities conducted outside tribal reservations.

By a 6–3 vote, the Court rejected the limitation. "Tribes enjoy immunity from suits on contracts, whether those contracts involve governmental or commercial activities and whether they were made on or off a reservation," Kennedy wrote. But Kennedy also said that the growth of tribal business activities and other factors created "reasons to doubt the wisdom of perpetuating the doctrine" and stressed that Congress could revise the rule if it wanted.

Writing for the dissenters, Stevens said earlier cases had not recognized tribal immunity for off-reservation activities. He called the extension of the doctrine "strikingly anomalous" and "unjust."

Montana v. Crow Tribe of Indians, decided by 9–0 and 7–2 votes, May 18, 1998; Ginsburg wrote the opinion; Souter and O'Connor dissented in part.

The Court rejected the Crow tribe's effort to recover about $58 million that a mining company paid in coal severance taxes under a Montana levy that was later invalidated as an intrusion on the tribe's powers.

The ruling came in what the Court described as a "tangled, long-pending" dispute over the power to tax the right to mine subsurface coal on a 1.1-million-acre strip of land lying just north of the Crow reservation in Montana. The tribe had ceded the land to the state but retained the right to minerals under the surface. Montana enacted an unusually high—30 percent—state-wide mineral severance tax in 1975. The tribe sought to impose a 25 percent severance tax six months later, but it did not obtain necessary permission from the U.S. Department of the Interior until 1983.

In the meantime, the tribe filed what proved to be a successful suit in federal court claiming the state could not tax the coal mined from underneath the so-called "ceded strip." After winning that case in 1987, the tribe began a new action seeking to recover the $58.2 million that the mining company had paid under the state levy between 1975 and 1983. While that case was pending, the Supreme Court ruled in 1989 in a New Mexico case that states could impose a severance tax on minerals from Indian lands as long as the levy was not "excessive." Relying on that case, a federal district court rejected the Crow tribe's effort to recover the funds, but the Ninth U.S. Circuit Court of Appeals ruled in 1996 that the tribe was entitled to the "disgorgement" of the funds.

In a mostly unanimous decision, the Court rejected the tribe's effort to recover all the funds. Ginsburg explained that because the tribe itself had not established a legal tax prior to 1983, disgorgement was "not warranted." In a partial dissent, Souter, joined by O'Connor, said the tribe still might be entitled to a partial recovery for the state's "excess revenues" under the severance tax.

South Dakota v. Yankton Sioux Tribe, decided by a 9–0 vote, January 26, 1998; O'Connor wrote the opinion.

Resolving a dispute over state versus federal authority of a municipal landfill site, the Court ruled that an 1894 law had taken out of tribal control most of the Yankton Sioux Indian reservation.

The Court's interpretation of the century-old congressional action, upholding state authority over the land, eased the way for construction of a landfill by several South Dakota municipalities. The dispute involved an 1894 law ratifying an agreement with the tribe to cede back to the United States all but 30,000 acres of the 430,000-acre reservation created by an 1858 treaty.

The plan for the landfill forced the issue of authority over the land into the courts, resulting in a federal appeals court decision that the tribe had not ceded control over the land.

In a unanimous decision, the Court disagreed. O'Connor said the "explicit language" of the 1894 law "bears the hallmarks of congressional intent to diminish a reservation."

Separation of Powers

Clinton, President of the United States v. City of New York, decided by a 6–3 vote, June 25, 1998; Stevens wrote the opinion; Scalia, O'Connor, and Breyer dissented.

The Line Item Veto Act's provision giving the president the power to cancel individual items in spending or certain tax laws violates the procedures for enacting laws in the Constitution's Presentment Clause.

The ruling upheld separate challenges filed by groups affected by President Clinton's use of the 1996 law in August 1997. In one suit, the city of New York and others attacked Clinton's cancellation of a Medicaid reimbursement provision. In the other, an Idaho potato growers cooperative challenged the disapproval of a tax provision aimed at encouraging the sale of agricultural processing plants to farmer co-ops. A federal district judge in Washington ruled the measure unconstitutional as a violation of the Presentment Clause, which requires that a bill be passed in identical form by both the House and the Senate and signed by the president before it can become law. The judge also said the measure violated general separation of powers principles.

By a 6–3 vote, the Court agreed that the measure violated the Presentment Clause by giving the president "the unilateral power to change the text of duly enacted statutes." The act, Stevens wrote, "would authorize the President to create a different law—one whose text was not voted on by either House of Congress or presented to the President for signature."

Scalia and Breyer wrote separate dissents. Scalia, but not Breyer, contended the co-operatives had no legal standing to challenge the president's action. On the substantive issue, Scalia said the law was "no broader than the discretion traditionally granted the President in his execution of spending laws." Breyer similarly said the law did not improperly shift lawmaking power from Congress to the president. O'Connor joined Scalia's dissent in full; Breyer joined in part. O'Connor and Scalia both joined part of Breyer's. *(See story, pp. 47–51; excerpts, pp. 219–233.)*

Social Security

Forney v. Apfel, Commissioner of Social Security, decided by a 9–0 vote, June 15, 1998; Breyer wrote the opinion.

Someone contesting a denial of Social Security disability benefits may immediately appeal a federal judge's order returning the case to an administrative law judge (ALJ) for further proceedings.

The ruling came in a federal court suit by an Oregon woman, Sandra Forney, challenging an agency judge's determination that she was ineligible for disability benefits. The federal court judge remanded the case to the ALJ for more evidence. Forney appealed, but the Ninth U.S. Circuit Court of Appeals refused to consider the plea on the ground that she had won a ruling in her favor.

In a brief and unanimous opinion, the Court held that Forney could appeal the ruling because the she had won "some, but not all, of the relief she requested."

First Amendment

Freedom of Speech

National Endowment for the Arts v. Finley, decided by an 8–1 vote, June 25, 1998; O'Connor wrote the opinion; Souter dissented.

The National Endowment for the Arts (NEA) may consider "general standards of decency" in awarding grants to artists without violating the First Amendment's protections for freedom of speech.

The ruling upheld but significantly softened a restriction passed by Congress in 1990 after controversies had arisen over the use of some NEA grants for works criticized as sexually indecent or sacrilegious. The spending provision required the NEA in awarding grants to "tak[e] into consideration general standards of decency and respect for the diverse beliefs and values of the American public." Four individual artists and the National Association of Artists' Organizations challenged the provision as a violation of the First Amendment; a lower court and the Ninth U.S. Circuit Court of Appeals both agreed.

By a deceptively lopsided vote, the Court upheld the provision, but only after saying that its "advisory language" imposed no "categorical requirement" for issuing grants. "[T]he provision does not introduce considerations that, in practice, would effectively preclude or punish the expression of particular views," O'Connor wrote for six justices. She also said the provision was not unconstitutionally vague.

In an opinion concurring in the judgment, Scalia, joined by Thomas, argued that the provision did bar funding for "offensive" works but that such a restriction would be constitutional. "[T]he Government may earmark NEA funds for projects it deems to be in the public interest without thereby abridging speech," Scalia wrote.

In a lone dissent, Souter also said that the provision imposed "viewpoint-based" restrictions on NEA funding, but contended that such a restriction would be a free speech violation. The general rule, Souter said, is that "viewpoint discrimination in the exercise of public authority over expressive activity is unconstitutional." *(See story, pp. 63–67; excerpts, pp. 206–218.)*

Public Television

Arkansas Educational Television Commission v. Forbes, decided by a 6–3 vote, May 18, 1998; Kennedy wrote the opinion; Stevens, Ginsburg, and Breyer dissented.

Government-owned public television stations have discretion to exclude minor candidates from campaign debates if the decisions are reasonable and not based on the candidates' views.

The ruling rejected a claim by an independent candidate for a congressional seat in Arkansas, Ralph Forbes, that the state-owned public television station violated his First Amendment rights by not inviting him to participate in a candidate debate that it sponsored in 1992. The Eighth U.S. Circuit Court of Appeals had ruled that the candidate debate amounted to a "public forum" to which all legally qualified candidates had a presumptive right of access. It then went on to hold that Forbes's "political viability" was not the kind of "compelling" or "narrowly tailored" reason needed to justify excluding him.

In a 6–3 decision, the Court held the candidate debate to be a more limited "nonpublic forum" and then upheld the station's decision to exclude Forbes as a "reasonable, viewpoint-neutral exercise of journalistic discretion." The debate amounted to a nonpublic forum, Kennedy said, because the station had reserved the right to make "candidate-by-candidate determinations" as to whom to invite. The decision not to invite Forbes satisfied First Amendment standards, Kennedy concluded, because it was based on his "objective lack of support" rather than because his views were "unpopular or out of the mainstream."

The dissenting justices agreed that the station was not required to invite all qualified candidates but faulted what Stevens called the "standardless character" of the decision not to include Forbes. He said the Court should have required stations to adopt "pre-established, objective criteria" for what candidates to invite or not to invite.

Immigration Law

Citizenship

Miller v. Albright, Secretary of State, decided by a 6–3 vote, April 22, 1998; Stevens wrote the main opinion; O'Connor and Scalia wrote opinions concurring in the judgment, each on different grounds; Ginsburg, Souter, and Breyer dissented.

The Court left on the books a law setting different citizenship requirements for an illegitimate child born abroad depending on whether the mother or father is a U.S. citizen. But a majority of the justices cast doubt that the provision would be upheld if challenged in a different case.

The fractured ruling rejected a citizenship plea by Lorelyn Penero Miller, the adult child of a Filipina mother and a former U.S. serviceman, Charlie Miller, once stationed in the Philippines. Under a provision of immigration law dating to 1938, a child born out of wedlock in another country is automatically a U.S. citizen if the mother is a U.S. citizen and meets certain residency requirements. But if the father and not the mother is a U.S. citizen, the child can become a U.S. citizen only if the father acknowledges paternity or paternity is otherwise established before the child reaches the age of eighteen.

Lorelyn Miller filed for a U.S. passport in 1991, at the age of twenty-one. The State Department rejected the application on the ground that her father had not acknowledged paternity earlier. Both Lorelyn and Charlie challenged the law as sex discrimination in violation of equal protection requirements. A federal district court in Texas found that Charlie Miller had no legal standing to challenge the law and transferred the case to a federal court in Washington, where Lorelyn Miller continued the case. Both the federal district court and the federal appeals court in Washington rejected her claim.

The Court split four ways—and issued opinions totaling seventy-four pages—in rejecting Lorelyn's challenge to the law. In the main opinion, Stevens, joined only by Rehnquist, said the law's different treatment of citizen mothers and citizen fathers was justified by "strong governmental interests." Those interests, Stevens said, included "ensuring reliable proof of a biological relationship between the potential citizen and its citizen parent" and "encouraging . . . the development of a healthy relationship between the citizen parent and the child while the child is a minor" as well as "the related interest in fostering ties between the foreign-born child and the United States."

The four other justices in the majority concurred on different grounds. O'Connor, joined by Kennedy, said that Lorelyn Miller had no standing to raise the sex discrimination claim because what O'Connor called "the *discriminatory impact*" of the law fell on her father rather than on her. Scalia, joined by Thomas, said that the Court had "no power" to confer citizenship "on a basis other than that prescribed by Congress."

In a dissenting opinion—which he emphasized by reading from the bench—Breyer said the law was unconstitutional because it relied on outmoded "gender-based generalizations." "What sense does it make," Breyer wrote, to treat parents differently "in today's world—where paternity can readily be proved and where women and men both are likely to earn a living in the workplace?" He also rejected O'Connor's position on standing and Scalia's objection to the Court's power to recognize citizenship. Souter and Ginsburg joined in the dissent. Ginsburg wrote a separate dissent, joined by Souter and Breyer. She criticized the law for "shaping government policy to fit and reinforce [a gender-based] stereotype" and expressed the hope that Congress would revise the law "before the century is out."

In her opinion, O'Connor said that the challenged law had a sufficient basis to be upheld under a lenient, rational-basis test. But she continued by saying that it was "unlikely . . . that any gender classifications based on stereotypes can survive heightened scrutiny" applicable in equal protection cases. Breyer noted that passage in his dissent, saying that it was agreed to by "a majority of the Court"—meaning the three dissenters, O'Connor, and Kennedy.

Individual Rights

Age Discrimination

Oubre v. Entergy Operations, Inc., decided by a 6–3 vote, January 26, 1998; Kennedy wrote the opinion; Thomas, Rehnquist, and Scalia dissented.

The Court, strictly interpreting federal law, made it harder for employers to enforce provisions in severance agreements with older workers giving up their right to sue for age discrimination.

The ruling reinstated a complaint brought by a Louisiana woman, Dolores Oubre, under the federal Age Discrimination in Employment Act (ADEA). Oubre left her job at a power plant in 1995 after signing an agreement providing for $6,258 in severance pay and waiving "any and all claims" against the company. The waiver did not comply, however, with several requirements for such releases established by a 1990 law, the Older Workers Benefit Protection Act. When Oubre brought an age discrimination complaint, the company, Entergy Operations, Inc., conceded the waiver was invalid but argued Oubre "ratified" the agreement by failing to return the severance pay. A trial judge and the Fifth U.S. Circuit Court of Appeals both agreed and dismissed the suit.

In a divided decision, the Court disagreed, holding that an employee "may not waive an age discrimination claim unless the employer complies with the statute." Kennedy said the 1990 law was designed "to protect the rights and benefits of older workers . . . via a strict, unqualified stricture on waivers, and we are bound to take Congress at its word."

The three dissenting justices argued that the statute did not supersede a common-law doctrine known as "tender back," which requires anyone receiving money under a release of legal claims to return the money before bringing suit. In a concurring opinion, Breyer, joined by O'Connor, suggested that the company would be entitled to seek "restitution" by offsetting the severance pay against any award won by Oubre.

Damage Suits

Bogan v. Scott-Harris, decided by a 9–0 vote, March 3, 1998; Thomas wrote the opinion.

Local lawmakers are entitled to absolute immunity from liability in federal civil rights suits.

The ruling—extending the doctrine of immunity for members of Congress and state legislators—threw out a damage award won by a former Fall River, Massachusetts, official. She claimed that the mayor and city council abolished her position in retaliation for her filing a racial harassment claim against one of her employees. The federal district court and the First U.S. Circuit Court of Appeals both rejected the defendants' pleas for legislative immunity, saying the decision to abolish the plaintiff's position was administrative rather than legislative.

Unanimously, the Court decided that local lawmakers should enjoy absolute immunity and that the abolition of plaintiff's position was legislative in nature. "Regardless of the level of government," Thomas wrote, "the exercise of legislative discretion should not be inhibited by judicial interference or distorted by the fear of personal liability."

County of Sacramento v. Lewis, decided by a 9–0 vote, May 26, 1998; Souter wrote the opinion.

Police officers cannot be held liable for injuries or deaths resulting from automobile chases unless they intend to hurt the suspects being pursued.

The ruling ordered the dismissal of a federal civil rights suit filed by the parents of a California teenager, Philip Lewis, who was killed in 1990 after a high-speed chase by a Sacramento County sheriff's deputy, James Smith. Lewis was a passenger on a motorcycle being driven by a friend, who refused Smith's order to stop as the boys arrived on the scene of a fight that Smith was investigating. Lewis was thrown off the motorcycle during the chase and killed when Smith's patrol car hit him at high speed. A federal court judge barred the suit against Smith. But the Ninth U.S. Circuit Court of Appeals reinstated the suit, saying Smith could be held liable if he was shown to have demonstrated "reckless indifference" toward Lewis's life.

The Court held that the officer could not be liable unless his conduct met a higher, so-called "shocks the conscience" test and that only an intentional action would satisfy that standard. "[H]igh-speed chases with no intent to harm suspects physically or to worsen their legal plight do not give rise to liability" for a due process violation covered by the federal civil rights statute, Souter wrote. Evaluating Smith's conduct, Souter said the deputy "exaggerated" the need to pursue the boys, but concluded that his actions were not "tainted by an improper or malicious motive."

Five justices joined Souter's opinion; three others concurred on separate grounds. Stevens said he would have dismissed the suit on grounds of qualified immunity, reasoning that there was no established right to be free from unreasonable police chases at the time of the incident.

Scalia, joined by Thomas, wrote a broader opinion concurring in the judgment that rejected the Court's use of the "shocks-the-conscience" test. Scalia complained of the "subjectivity" of the test and called instead for evaluating claims of due process violations on a historical standard: "whether our Nation has traditionally protected the right."

In a response to Scalia, Kennedy, joined by O'Connor, said that history and tradition were "the starting point, but not in all cases the ending point of the substantive due process inquiry."

Crawford-El v. Britton, decided by a 5–4 vote, May 4, 1998; Stevens wrote the opinion; Rehnquist, O'Connor, Scalia, and Thomas dissented.

The Court rejected a heightened standard of proof for plaintiffs claiming that state or local officials violated their civil rights by retaliating against them for exercising their freedom of speech.

The ruling threw out a splintered decision by the U.S. Court of Appeals Court for the District of Columbia in a suit brought by a prison inmate, Leonard Crawford-El, under the federal civil rights statute, section 1983 of Title 42 of the U.S. Code. Crawford-El claimed a corrections officer delayed his receipt of personal belongings because of critical interviews he had given about prison conditions. The official moved to dismiss the suit on grounds of qualified immunity because the action violated no established legal right. To overcome qualified immunity, the appeals court said, Crawford-El had to prove an improper motive by "clear and convincing" evidence instead of the normal, lower standard: preponderance of the evidence.

By a 5–4 vote, the Court said the appeals court had no basis under federal statutes or federal procedural rules for what it called "the unprecedented change" in the evidentiary standard. Stevens said the ruling "undermines the very purpose of section 1983—to provide a remedy for the violation of federal rights."

Stevens noted that Congress had recently enacted a law aimed at reducing prisoners' suits in federal courts. In a concurring opinion, Kennedy also referred to Congress, saying that the authority to enact procedural changes to limit "frivolous" lawsuits "lies with the Legislative Branch, not with us."

In a dissenting opinion, Rehnquist, joined by O'Connor, said he would grant an official's qualified immunity defense if the official shows "a lawful reason" for the action and the plaintiff cannot show that the reason was "actually a pretext." In a separate dissent, Scalia, joined by Thomas, went further and said he would bar any evidence of improper motive if a government official could show some "objectively valid" reasons for an action.

Gebser v. Lago Vista Independent School District, decided by a 5–4 vote, June 22, 1998; O'Connor wrote the opinion; Stevens, Souter, Ginsburg, and Breyer dissented.

A school district cannot be ordered to pay damages under federal law for sexual harassment of a student by a teacher unless a ranking official knows of and is "deliberately indifferent" to the conduct.

The ruling rejected a damage suit by a former Texas high school student, Alida Star Gebser, and her mother against the Lago Vista school district for damages stemming from the girl's sexual affair with a former teacher, Frank Waldrop. Gebser brought the suit under Title IX of the Education Amendments of 1972, which prohibits sexual discrimination by school districts that receive federal funds. The Court in prior rulings had held that a student could recover damages from a school district for intentional conduct; however, a lower court judge and the Fifth U.S. Circuit Court of Appeals both held that the school district could not be held liable unless it knew of the sexual misconduct.

By a 5–4 vote, the Court agreed, saying that a stricter standard of liability would "frustrate" the purposes of Title IX. "[D]amages may not be recovered," O'Connor wrote for the majority, "unless an official of the school district who at a minimum has authority to institute corrective measures on the district's behalf has actual notice of, and is deliberately indifferent to, the teacher's misconduct." O'Connor said the ruling would not affect the possibility of recovering damages under federal law from the teacher or under state law from either the teacher or the school district.

Writing for the four dissenters, Stevens said the ruling "thwarts the purposes of Title IX" by encouraging school districts to "insulate themselves from knowledge about this sort of conduct." In a separate dissent, Ginsburg, joined by Souter and Breyer but not Stevens, said school districts should be allowed to point to a anti–sexual harassment policy as a defense in such suits. The majority had said that the lack of such a policy would not establish "deliberate indifference" on a school district's part. *(See story, pp. 39–42; excerpts, pp. 164–176.)*

Jefferson v. City of Tarrant, Alabama, decided by an 8–1 vote, December 9, 1997; Ginsburg wrote the opinion; Stevens dissented.

The Court declined to decide whether damages in a suit for federal civil rights violations are limited by a state law that bars compensatory damages in wrongful-death suits.

The ruling sent back to Alabama state courts a suit by the survivors of an African American woman who blamed her death in a house fire on racial discrimination by the city's fire department in failing to respond promptly to the fire. The plaintiffs brought the case to the Court after the Alabama Supreme Court issued a preliminary ruling that the state's wrongful-death law barred them from recovering compensatory damages for their federal civil rights claims.

In a nearly unanimous opinion, the Court dismissed the petition for certiorari on grounds that the state court litigation was not over. "This case . . . was brought to this Court too soon," Ginsburg wrote, pointing to a long-standing federal law limiting the Court's review to final state judgments.

In a limited dissent, Stevens said the case was governed by *Pennsylvania v. Ritchie,* a 1987 decision that allowed an exception to the finality rule. He said he would vote to overrule the decision but felt obligated to follow it until it was overruled. In her opinion, Ginsburg said the earlier decision was an "extraordinary" case that "does not augur expansion" of exceptions to the finality requirement.

Kalina v. Fletcher, decided by a 9–0 vote, December 10, 1997; Stevens wrote the opinion.

Prosecutors may be held liable in a federal civil rights suit for making false statements of fact in an affidavit supporting an application for an arrest warrant.

The ruling cleared the way for trial of a suit by a Washington State man, Rodney Fletcher, against a deputy prosecuting attorney in Kings County (Seattle) for false statements she included in a warrant for his arrest for a school burglary. Fletcher was cleared of the charge and then filed a federal civil rights suit against the prosecutor, Lynne Kalina. She sought to have the suit dismissed on the ground that she was entitled to absolute immunity as a prosecutor, but two lower federal courts rejected her argument.

In a unanimous opinion, the Court held that the prosecutor was not entitled to absolute immunity because she was acting as a complaining witness rather than an in-court prosecutor when making the statements in the arrest warrant. "Testifying about facts is the function of a the witness, not of the lawyer," Stevens wrote.

The ruling seemed likely to have limited impact since—as Stevens noted —federal prosecutors and most state prosecutors typically do not personally attest to facts used in obtaining an arrest warrant.

Disability Rights

Bragdon v. Abbott, decided by a 5–4 vote, June 25, 1998; Kennedy wrote the opinion; Rehnquist, O'Connor, Scalia, and Thomas dissented.

Persons with HIV, the virus that causes AIDS, are protected by the Americans with Disabilities Act (ADA) from discrimination in employment, housing, or public accommodations even if they have no outward symptoms of the disease.

The ruling—an important victory for AIDS organizations and disability rights groups—nonetheless gave a Maine dentist, Randon Bragdon, another opportunity to prove that he did not violate the ADA in refusing to treat an HIV-positive woman, Sidney Abbott, in his dental office. A federal district court and the First U.S. Circuit Court of Appeals both ruled in favor of Abbott's suit under the law. Bragdon asked the Court to consider two issues. First, he argued that HIV disability did not meet the definition of disability under the law: "a physical or mental impairment that substantially limits one or more of the major life activities." Second, he argued he was entitled to refuse to treat Abbott in his office because she posed—in the words of the law—"a direct threat to the health or safety or others."

In a narrowly divided opinion, the Court agreed with Abbott's argument that HIV disease amounted to an impairment and that it substantially limited her reproductive abilities, which met the law's definition of a major life activity. Writing for the majority, Kennedy said HIV disease amounted to "an impairment from the moment of infection" because of "the immediacy" of its effects and "the severity of the disease." He said that reproduction amounted to a major life activity for purposes of the law and that HIV disease limited her reproductive abilities because of the risk of spreading the disease during sex and the risk of transmitting the disease to her fetus if she became pregnant.

Four justices dissented from the legal holding. Rehnquist, joined by Scalia and Thomas, argued that reproduction was not "a major life activity" and that HIV disease did not limit Abbott's "voluntary choices" about whether to engage in sexual intercourse or give birth to a child. O'Connor wrote separately to say that reproduction was not covered under the law.

Kennedy said the case should be returned to the First Circuit because Bragdon had not had a full opportunity to argue whether treating Abbott in his office created a risk of transmitting the disease to himself or other dental workers. But he said Bragdon had to show "objective medical evidence" rather than his subjective beliefs to justify his conclusion. Stevens, joined by Breyer, argued that the medical evidence on the issue was sufficient to reject Bragdon's argument. The four dissenting justices agreed in returning the case for further proceedings. *(See story, pp. 43–47; excerpts, pp. 177–191.)*

Pennsylvania Department of Corrections v. Yeskey, decided by a 9–0 vote, June 15, 1998; Scalia wrote the opinion.

The federal Americans with Disabilities Act prohibits state prisons from discriminating against persons with disabilities in determining eligibility for programs or services.

The decision came in connection with a suit filed by a Pennsylvania inmate, Ronald Yeskey, who had been refused admission because of high blood pressure to the state's "motivational boot camp" for first offenders.

Yeskey, who stood to be released from prison early after completion of the program, claimed the denial violated the ADA. A federal district court judge dismissed the complaint, but the Third U.S. Circuit Court of Appeals reinstated the suit.

In a brief and unanimous ruling, the Court agreed that state prisons were covered by the law. The "plain text" of the act "unambiguously extends to state prison inmates," Scalia wrote.

The Court did not rule, however, on two arguments by Pennsylvania's attorneys that Congress had no constitutional power under either the Commerce Clause or the Fourteenth Amendment to apply the law to state prisons. Scalia said those issues had not been addressed by lower courts. In addition, Scalia said nothing about what accommodations prison authorities would have to make in programs or services for prisoners with disabilities to comply with the law.

Job Discrimination

Burlington Industries, Inc. v. Ellerth, decided by a 7–2 vote, June 26, 1998; Kennedy wrote the opinion; Thomas and Scalia dissented.

An employer may be liable for sexual harassment of an employee by a supervisor even if the employee suffers no tangible consequences. The employer can avoid liability, however, by proving that it took reasonable steps to prevent the conduct and that the employee failed to take reasonable steps to prevent or avoid harm.

The ruling—and the companion decision *Faragher v. City of Boca Raton* issued the same day *(see p. 124)*—sought to clarify the rules for holding employers responsible for sexual harassment by supervisors. Plaintiff Kimberly Ellerth, a former sales associate with Burlington Industries, sued the clothing manufacturer under Title VII's sex discrimination provisions because of a series of sexually suggestive comments allegedly made to her by a supervisor, Ted Slowik. A lower court granted summary judgment for Burlington on the ground that the company had no way of knowing about the conduct. The Seventh U.S. Circuit Court of Appeals reinstated the suit by an 8–3 vote, but with no majority opinion.

The Court agreed that the case should be returned to the lower court for trial. Writing for the majority, Kennedy said that basic principles of agency law called for imposing so-called "vicarious liability" on employers for "misuse of supervisory authority" even if an employee did not suffer tangible consequences. Allowing a defense for employers in such cases, he continued, would encourage employers to develop antiharassment policies and employees to report harassing conduct before it became severe. Five justices joined Kennedy's opinion; Ginsburg wrote a separate concurrence but did not specify her reason for not joining the majority opinion.

In a dissenting opinion, Thomas, joined by Scalia, said that an employer should be liable for a supervisor's sexual harassment only if it was negligent in permitting the conduct to occur. *(See story, pp. 29–36; excerpts, pp. 250–261.)*

Faragher v. City of Boca Raton, decided by a 7–2 vote, June 26, 1998; Souter wrote the opinion; Thomas and Scalia dissented.

An employer is liable for sexual harassment of an employee by a supervisor if the conduct results in any tangible employment action, including discharge, demotion, or undesirable reassignment.

The ruling—and a companion decision issued the same day, *Burlington Industries, Inc. v. Ellerth (see p. 123)*—was aimed at setting clear guidelines for employer responsibility for sexual harassment by supervisors. Plaintiff Beth Ann Faragher, a former lifeguard for the city of Boca Raton, Florida, sued the city under Title VII's sex discrimination provisions because of a series of lewd comments and gestures allegedly made by two of her supervisors, Bill Terry and David Silverman. A trial court awarded Faragher nominal damages, but the Eleventh U.S. Circuit Court of Appeals reversed, saying there was no basis for holding the city liable.

The Court reinstated the award for Faragher. Writing for the majority, Souter set out the same standard as in *Burlington:* vicarious liability for employers for a supervisor's sexual harassment, but subject to a defense if there were no tangible consequences from the conduct. Applying that standard to Faragher's case, Souter said the city was "negligent as a matter of law" because of its failure to disseminate its sexual harassment policies.

In a dissenting opinion, Thomas, joined by Scalia, repeated his view in *Burlington* that employers should be liable only if negligent in permitting sexual harassment by a supervisor to occur. He said the case should be returned to the trial court on that issue. *(See story, pp. 29–36; excerpts, pp. 240–250.)*

Oncale v. Sundowner Offshore Services, Inc., decided by a 9–0 vote, March 4, 1998; Scalia wrote the opinion.

Federal civil rights law prohibits sexual harassment in the workplace by someone of the same sex.

The ruling—a victory for gay rights groups—reinstated a suit filed by a Lousiana oil rig worker, Joseph Oncale, who claimed he was forced to quit his job after being subjected to sexual abuse, humiliation, and threats by two male supervisors. The Fifth U.S. Circuit Court of Appeals held that the job-discrimination provisions of the Civil Rights Act of 1964 did not apply to same-sex harassment.

In a unanimous and compact decision, the Court disagreed. "[S]ex discrimination consisting of same-sex harassment is actionable under Title VII," Scalia wrote. But he stressed that the law "does not prohibit all verbal or physical harassment" in the workplace. A plaintiff must prove the conduct complained of "was not merely tinged with offensive sexual connotations, but actually constituted 'discrimina[tion] . . . because of . . . sex,'" he said, quoting the statute's language.

In a one-sentence concurring opinion, Thomas also stressed that the ruling required plaintiffs to "plead and ultimately prove" discrimination. *(See story, pp. 36–39; excerpts, pp. 151–154.)*

Labor Law

Agency Shop Fees

Air Line Pilots Association v. Miller, decided by a 7–2 vote, May 26, 1998; Ginsburg wrote the opinion; Breyer and Stevens dissented.

Nonunion members who object to the amount they are required to pay the union for collective bargaining purposes can go directly to federal court without being forced to take their dispute to arbitration.

The decision upheld a ruling by the federal appeals court in Washington, D.C., in a dispute that began in 1992 between some 150 Delta Air Lines pilots and the Air Line Pilots Association (ALPA). Federal law requires a union to represent all employees within a bargaining unit but permits the union to charge nonunion members a so-called "agency shop" fee to cover the costs. The Court has ruled that the agency shop fee cannot be used to cover political expenses to which the nonunion members object. In addition, it ruled in a 1986 case, *Teachers v. Hudson,* that a union must set up an impartial procedure for resolving complaints about the amount of the fees. When a number of Delta pilots objected to the amount of the fee charged by ALPA in 1992, they bypassed the union's arbitration procedure and filed suit in federal court. A federal district court ruled they must first go through arbitration; the appeals court disagreed.

By a 7–2 vote, the Court ruled that its prior decision did not require nonunion members to submit their dispute to arbitration before they could file suit in court. "We . . . decline to read *Hudson* as a decision that protects nonunion members at a cost—delayed access to federal court—they do not wish to pay," Ginsburg wrote.

Writing for the dissenters, Breyer said that the earlier ruling did envision mandatory arbitration and that the procedure would reduce the cost of resolving agency fee disputes without adversely affecting the interests of nonunion members.

Labor-Management Relations

Allentown Mack Sales and Service, Inc. v. National Labor Relations Board, decided by separate 5–4 votes, January 26, 1998; Scalia wrote the opinion;

Rehnquist, O'Connor, Kennedy, and Thomas dissented in part; Breyer, Stevens, Souter, and Ginsburg dissented in part.

The Court upheld but weakened a National Labor Relations Board (NLRB) policy limiting the ability of employers to poll workers to determine whether a union has lost majority support.

The mixed decision overturned the NLRB's finding that a Pennsylvania truck dealer had committed an unfair labor practice by polling its thirty-two workers to test the union's majority status. The agency's long-standing policy required an employer to have a "good-faith reasonable doubt" about a union's support before conducting such a poll, and it said the company did not have enough evidence to justify taking the survey. On appeal, the company argued the NLRB's policy was too restrictive, but the federal appeals court in Washington upheld both the policy and the board's finding against the company.

By separate 5–4 votes, the Court declined to overturn the NLRB's policy but ruled the agency had applied it too strictly. After noting the board's reasoning that employer-conducted polls are "disruptive to established bargaining relationships," Scalia said the policy was "not so irrational as to be arbitrary and capricious." But after reviewing the evidence in the case and the NLRB's decisions in prior cases, Scalia said the board had established "an arbitrary rule" limiting the kind of information that an employer could use to demonstrate doubts about the union's status.

The Court's four other conservative justices dissented from the decision to uphold the NLRB policy. Rehnquist said that there was "no support" for the rule in the main federal labor statute, the National Labor Relations Act, and that the board's treatment of polling was also "irrational." But they voted with Scalia to set aside the finding against the company.

The four liberal justices disagreed with that part of the decision. Breyer said the majority had "rewritten a Board rule without adequate justification" and "failed to give . . . leeway to the Board's factfinding authority."

Pensions and Benefits

Bay Area Laundry and Dry Cleaning Pension Trust Fund v. Ferbar Corporation of California, Inc., decided by a 9–0 vote, December 15, 1997; Ginsburg wrote the opinion.

The Court adopted an expansive time limit for industrywide pension plans to sue an employer for failing to make mandatory payments after withdrawing from the plan.

In a unanimous ruling, the Court held that a suit by the trustees of a pension plan may be brought within six years after an employer fails to make any monthly installment required under the federal law governing industrywide pension plans. The decision settled a conflict between federal courts of appeals on what statute of limitations should be applied under the Multiemployer Pension Plan Amendments Act of 1980.

The case before the Court stemmed from a suit by a pension fund for San Francisco–area laundry workers against the Ferbar Corporation, which failed to make any of the legally required installment payments after withdrawing from the pension plan in 1985. The plan filed suit in February 1987, six years and eight days after having notified the company that it was in default. Both the trial court and the Ninth U.S. Circuit Court of Appeals ruled the suit was too late, though on different grounds.

In her opinion for the Court, Ginsburg said that the applicable time period of six years begins to run when an employer "misses a scheduled withdrawal liability payment" and that a separate suit could be brought for each unpaid monthly installment. On that basis, the Court ruled that the pension fund was too late for the first monthly installment but could maintain its suit to recover all other payments that were due and unpaid.

Eastern Enterprises v. Apfel, Commissioner of Social Security, decided by a 5–4 vote, June 25, 1998; O'Connor wrote the plurality opinion; Breyer, Stevens, Souter, and Ginsburg dissented.

The Court ruled unconstitutional a federal law requiring companies that had once been in the coal business to pay for lifetime health benefits for retired miners and families of miners who had worked for them decades earlier.

The decision struck down part of a 1992 law, the Coal Industry Retiree Health Benefit Act, aimed at guaranteeing the solvency of an industrywide health benefits fund. One provision of the complex law assigned liability for lifetime benefits for some retirees to whatever company had employed the miners the longest period of time prior to a 1978 industry agreement even if the company was no longer in the coal business. The law was challenged by a Massachusetts-based energy company, Eastern Enterprises, which had transferred its coal operations to a subsidiary in 1965 and sold off the subsidiary in 1987. Eastern argued that it had never agreed to provide lifetime health benefits while it was in the coal business and that imposing retroactive liability amounted to a taking of its property without compensation and a violation of its due process rights. A lower federal court and the First U.S. Court of Appeals both upheld the law.

Four justices voted to strike down the law as a violation of the Takings Clause, while a fifth—Kennedy—said the act violated the company's due process rights.

In the plurality opinion, O'Connor said that the "disproportionate and severely retroactively burden" upon the company "implicates fundamental principles of fairness underlying the Takings Clause." "Eastern cannot be forced to bear the expenses of lifetime health benefits for miners based on its activities decades before those benefits were promised," she wrote.

Kennedy agreed that the law was unconstitutional because of what he termed the law's "retroactive effect of unprecedented scope." But he said the law did not violate the Takings Clause. The law, Kennedy said, "does not operate on or alter an identified property interest."

Writing for the dissenters, Breyer said that the Takings Clause did not apply and that Congress "did not act unreasonably or otherwise unjustly" in imposing retroactive liability for the retired miners' health benefits. Eastern, he wrote, "benefited from the labor of those miners," "helped to create conditions that led the miners to expect continued health care benefits," and until 1987 "continued to draw sizable profits from the coal industry." *(See story, pp. 59–63; excerpts, pp. 191–206.)*

Geissal v. Moore Medical Corp., decided by a 9–0 vote, June 8, 1998; Souter wrote the opinion.

Employers must offer former workers continuation of their health insurance coverage even if they are also covered by their spouses' health plans.

The ruling settled a conflict among federal appeals courts on the interpretation of a provision of the Consolidated Omnibus Budget Reconciliation Act of 1985—called COBRA. The law required employers to offer former workers the chance to pay for continuation of their health insurance coverage after leaving employment. The Eighth U.S. Circuit Court of Appeals was one of three appeals courts that ruled the provision did not apply if a former employee was covered under a spouse's health insurance; two other appeals courts disagreed.

In a unanimous decision, the Court held that the law's "plain language" required employers to offer continuation coverage even if the former worker had other health insurance. Souter discounted the possibility that the ruling would create a "windfall" by allowing for overlapping coverage, noting that the law required a former employee "to pay for whatever COBRA coverage he obtains."

Remedies

Textron Lycoming Reciprocating Engine Division, Avco Corp. v. United Automobile, Aerospace and Agricultural Implement Workers of America, decided by a 9–0 vote, May 18, 1998; Scalia wrote the opinion.

A labor union was blocked from using a federal law allowing suits for violation of collective bargaining agreements to win damages for a contract that it claimed resulted from fraud by the employer.

The decision stemmed from a dispute between the United Auto Workers (UAW) and the Textron division of the Avco Corp. at the company's Williamsport, Pennsylvania, plant. In April 1994 the union and the company entered into a collective bargaining agreement that included a prohibition on strikes for any reason. Three months later, the company subcontracted a major part of the plant's work, resulting in the layoff of about half of the plant's 500 union members. The union claimed that the company had fraudulently concealed its plans to subcontract the work and filed a suit seeking damages under section 301(a) of the Labor Management Relations Act. That law gives federal courts jurisdiction over "suits for violations of contracts between an employer and a labor organization." A federal district court dismissed the suit, but the Third U.S. Circuit Court of Appeals said the suit could proceed.

In a unanimous decision, the Court reversed and barred the union's suit. Quoting the statutory language, Scalia wrote, " 'Suits for violation under contracts' under 301(a) are not suits that claim a contract is invalid, but suits that claim a contract has been violated." Scalia also rejected the union's effort to use the federal Declaratory Judgment Act as a basis for jurisdiction.

In a concurring opinion, Stevens noted that the union might be able to bring a complaint for unfair labor practices before the National Labor Relations Board. In a separate partial concurrence, Breyer said the union might have been able to sue under the Declaratory Judgment Act if it had shown that a strike in violation of the contract's terms was imminent.

Property Law

Interest on Lawyers' Trust Accounts

Phillips v. Washington Legal Foundation, decided by a 5–4 vote, June 15, 1998; Rehnquist wrote the opinion; Breyer, Stevens, Souter, and Ginsburg dissented.

Interest earned on client funds held in trust accounts set up by state bars to generate funds for legal aid for the poor is the client's property for purposes of the Takings Clause.

The ruling cast doubt on the constitutionality of legal aid funding programs operating in all fifty states and the District of Columbia. The so-called "IOLTA" programs—an acronym for "Interest on Lawyers' Trust Accounts"—pooled nominal funds held by lawyers for clients and funneled the interest from the accounts to legal aid organizations. The Fifth U.S. Circuit Court of Appeals, ruling on an unconstitutional takings claim brought by the conservative Washington Legal Foundation on behalf of a Texas client, held that the interest belonged to the client but did not determine whether there had been a taking. The Texas Supreme Court, which established the program, asked the Court to review the ruling.

In a closely divided decision, the Court also held that the interest was the client's property and sent the case back to the appeals court for further proceedings. Rehnquist cited a rule that he said dated to the 1700s that "interest follows principal." Since the funds belonged to the client, Rehnquist said, "any interest that does accrue attaches as a property right incident to the ownership of the underlying principal." Rehnquist said the Court expressed "no view" as to whether the funds had been "taken" or what compensation, "if any," would be due.

In separate dissents, Souter criticized the majority on procedural grounds, while Breyer disagreed with its holding. Souter argued the Court should have sent the case back to the appeals court for a complete decision on the takings claim; the limited holding, he said, amounted to an "abstract proposition" that might have no significance in resolving the real issue. In his dissent, Breyer said that the client funds could not have generated interest except for the state-operated program. "I consequently believe," he concluded, "that the interest earned is *not* the client's 'private property.' "

States

Border Disputes

New Jersey v. New York, decided by a 6–3 vote, May 26, 1998; Souter wrote the opinion; Scalia, Stevens, and Thomas dissented.

The Court awarded sovereignty over most of Ellis Island, the historic gateway to the United States for 12 million immigrants between 1890 and 1954, to New Jersey, not New York.

The ruling, settling a border dispute that dated to the 1600s, gave New Jersey authority over about twenty-four and one-half acres of filled land added to the island by the federal government beginning in the 1880s. New York retained authority under an 1834 compact between the two states over the island's original three acres. The island—entirely owned by the federal government since 1800—lies in New York Harbor, about 1,300 feet from Jersey City, New Jersey, and one mile from the southern tip of Manhattan.

The decision largely followed the recommendation of a special master appointed by the Court to resolve the dispute, which New Jersey filed as an original case before the Court in 1993. But the Court rejected the special master's recommendation to adjust the border to avoid dividing three buildings on the island, including the main immigration building, between the two states.

In his opinion for the Court, Souter rejected New York's arguments that the 1834 compact should be interpreted to apply to the filled part of the island, not just its original three acres. He also rejected New York's effort to invoke a doctrine called "prescription" to establish sovereignty based on New York's claimed exercise of authority over the island and New Jersey's purported acquiescence in New York's actions. Souter said the evidence—including voting lists, marriages, and birth and death certificates registered in New York—was inadequate to meet New York's "substantial burden to establish that it gave good notice to New Jersey of its designs on the made land."

In a dissenting opinion, Scalia, joined by Thomas, said he would interpret the 1834 compact confirming New York's authority to apply to the entire island. Separately, Stevens said he would recognize New York's authority based on prescription, saying there was "clear, convincing, and uncontradicted evidence" that both New Jersey and New York had "treated Ellis Island as part of a single State"—New York.

Immunity

California v. Deep Sea Research, Inc., decided by a 9–0 vote, April 22, 1998; O'Connor wrote the opinion.

Federal courts have jurisdiction to rule on a state's claim to own a sunken ship despite the general rule barring suits against states in federal courts.

The ruling allowed a treasure-hunting concern, Deep Sea Research, Inc., to proceed with a federal court suit seeking to establish its right to the *S.S. Brother Jonathan.* The vessel sank off the coast of California in 1865 while carrying an estimated $2 million in gold bars and an army payroll of $250,000. After the treasure hunters located the shipwreck, the state of California claimed title under federal and state statutes. The state argued the suit belonged in state courts because of the Eleventh Amendment, which bars most suits against states in federal court. But two lower federal courts rejected the argument and allowed the suit to proceed.

In a unanimous opinion, the Court agreed that federal courts could rule on the so-called *in rem* action—a suit to determine ownership of property—because the state did not have possession of the ship. "We conclude that the Eleventh Amendment does not bar the jurisdiction of a federal court over an *in rem* admiralty action where the res [property] is not within the State's possession," O'Connor wrote. The decision returned the case to lower federal courts to rule on other issues.

Taxation

Lunding v. New York Tax Appeals Tribunal, decided by a 6–3 vote, January 21, 1998; O'Connor wrote the opinion; Ginsburg, Rehnquist, and Kennedy dissented.

States cannot deny to nonresidents a tax deduction for alimony payments that is allowed to resident taxpayers.

The ruling upheld a constitutional attack on a New York state law brought by Christopher Lunding, who lived in Connecticut but worked for a New York City–based law firm. The law, enacted in 1987 to reverse a ruling three years earlier by the state's highest court, barred nonresidents from taking a deduction on their state income tax for alimony payments even though residents could. Lunding, representing himself, claimed the law discriminated against nonresidents in violation of the Constitution's Privileges and Immunities Clause. A trial judge agreed, but the New York Tax Appeals Tribunal upheld the provision, saying that the state had "substantial reasons for the disparity."

In a 6–3 decision, the Court agreed with Lunding that the measure was unconstitutional. O'Connor said that the tax provision violated what she described as "a rule of substantial equality of treatment" for residents and nonresidents and that the state had failed to provide "a substantial justification" needed to uphold the difference in treatment. "The state's failure to provide more than a cursory justification for [the law] smacks of an effort to 'penalize the citizens of other states,'" she wrote, quoting an earlier case.

Writing for the dissenters, Ginsburg said the alimony payments were a personal expense that New York need not recognize as deductible. "Lunding's alimony payments cannot be said to take place in New York, nor do they inure to New York's benefit," she wrote. "New York is not constitutionally compelled to subsidize them."

The ruling directly affected six other states that denied nonresidents tax deductions for alimony payments: Alabama, California, Illinois, Ohio, West Virginia, and Wisconsin. In addition, a group of states argued in a brief supporting New York's position that a ruling to strike down the law could jeopardize rules in many states that deny nonresidents tax deductions for other personal expenses, such as medical bills or moving expenses.

Newsweek, Inc. v. Florida Department of Revenue, decided by a 9–0 vote, February 23, 1998; *per curiam* (unsigned) opinion.

The Court broadened the right of taxpayers to receive a refund for payments made under a tax later ruled invalid.

The ruling backed an effort by *Newsweek* magazine to recover a refund for sales taxes paid under a Florida law that was held unconstitutional in 1990 because it exempted newspapers but not magazines. Florida tax authorities refused the refund, saying *Newsweek* should have contested the tax before paying it.

In a unanimous opinion issued without hearing argument, the Court held Florida had violated the magazine's due process rights because the state had previously interpreted its law to allow postpayment refunds. The magazine had "reasonably relied on the apparent availability of a postpayment refund when paying the tax," the Court stated.

Torts

Airline Crashes

Dooley v. Korean Air Lines Co., Ltd., decided by a 9–0 vote, June 8, 1998; Thomas wrote the opinion.

The federal law governing deaths on the high seas does not allow an air crash victim's survivors to recover damages for their pain and suffering before death.

The ruling rejected claims by relatives of some of the victims of Korean Air Lines Flight 007, which was shot down over the Sea of Japan in 1983. A federal trial judge and the U.S. Court of Appeals for the District of Columbia had both ruled that the federal Death on the High Seas Act did not permit recovery for so-called "pre-death pain and suffering."

Unanimously, the Court agreed. The federal law provided "the exclusive recovery" for deaths on the high seas, Thomas said, and limited recovery to "the pecuniary losses suffered by surviving relatives." The Court had ruled two years earlier, in another case arising from the same crash, that the law also did not allow survivors to recover for loss of companionship.

Preview of the 1998–1999 Term

Jesus Morales was walking home, on crutches, from a hospital on Chicago's west side on April 4, 1993, when he stopped to speak with some other Hispanic youths. Morales, like his friends, was dressed in blue and black, the colors of the Gangster Disciples, one of Chicago's major street gangs. Morales, however, was not a gang member.

Chicago police officer Ray Frano noticed the group and, thinking them out of place in the predominantly white neighborhood, asked whether they lived in the area. They told him no. At that point, according to Frano's account later in court, he told them he would arrest them if they did not disperse. Morales denied being given any warning. In any event, Frano did arrest the group, acting under the authority of a novel Chicago ordinance aimed at controlling gang-related street crime.

The ordinance, enacted in 1992, gave police broad powers to order anyone they "reasonably believed" to be a gang member who was found "loitering" on the public streets to "disperse." Anyone who disobeyed was subject to arrest and up to six months in jail after conviction. Loitering was defined as being on the public streets "with no apparent purpose."

Over the next three years, Chicago's anti–gang loitering ordinance resulted in a total of 42,967 arrests. Most defendants were African American or Hispanic youths. Sentences imposed under the ordinance were typically short—rarely even as long as one month. Morales himself was given a one-day sentence when he went to court. Still, Chicago police insisted the law was helping to reduce gang-related street crime.

Defense attorneys and civil rights and civil liberties organizations disputed those claims. In addition, they said the ordinance was unconstitutional. It gave police too much discretion, they said, and interfered with the right of innocent persons to walk the public streets.

Lawyers for defendants charged under the ordinance pressed those arguments in appealing their convictions. Morales's appeal was one of seventy that were eventually consolidated in arguments before the Illinois Supreme Court. In November 1996 the seven-member court unanimously ruled the ordinance unconstitutional. The state justices said the law was unconstitutionally vague and also infringed on a "constitutional right to loiter."

The city appealed to the U.S. Supreme Court, claiming the law was necessary to combat "chronic disorder" in the streets. The Court had previously struck down some local anti–loitering laws, but it had not dealt with the issue in depth for a quarter century. So, on April 19, the Court issued a one-sentence statement saying it had agreed to review *City of Chicago v. Morales.*

The gang loitering case was one of thirty-three disputes that the Court put on its calendar for the 1998–1999 term before the justices adjourned for their summer recess at the end of June. The total number was low: the Court had accepted fifty-eight cases at the same point in 1997 and forty-six in 1996. The number of cases of major legal or policy significance was even lower. Hot-button issues such as abortion, privacy, free speech, religion, and states' rights were not to be found.

Among the few cases that had attracted much attention, the one with the broadest effect perhaps was a regulatory dispute over the effort by the Federal Communications Commission (FCC) to implement a federal law aimed at introducing competition into local telephone service. The case pitted long-distance carriers such as AT&T against the so-called "Baby Bells," the local telephone companies created when the federal government split up AT&T in the early 1980s. The FCC lined up with the long-distance companies that wanted to enter the local telephone market; the "local exchange carriers" joined with state regulators in opposing the timing and details of the FCC's order.

In criminal law cases, the justices agreed to decide whether the Fifth Amendment privilege against self-incrimination applies at sentencing proceedings. They also took up two new cases testing police authority in search-and-seizure cases. One important labor-related case pitted business interests against civil rights groups on the question whether union workers with discrimination complaints could be forced under a collective bargaining agreement to arbitrate their disputes rather than file suit in federal court. In another significant case, disability rights advocates and school boards squared off over the interpretation of the federal law requiring public schools to provide children with disabilities health-related services needed to attend classes. And the Court agreed to test a 1996 immigration law passed by Congress to cut off judicial review of proceedings to deport aliens.

Two issues fell off the Court's agenda after the justices accepted cases for review. In March, the Court agreed to consider a criminal case from California that included a states' rights challenge to the recent federal carjacking law. One week later, however, the justices decided to limit their review to other issues in the case. In a second case, the Court agreed in June to hear an effort by the state of Pennsylvania to bar a citizens group from the city of Chester—which has a predominantly African American population—from using federal civil rights laws to try to block a permit for the construction of a waste processing facility. The "environmental justice" case raised an important, unsettled legal issue both for civil rights and environmental organizations and for state and local governments. But the state revoked the construction permit after the company developed financial problems, and the Court in August dismissed the state's petition on the ground that the case was moot, or legally over.

Over the summer, the justices did add one major, politically charged case to their calendar: a legal challenge to the Clinton administration's plan to use statistical sampling in conducting the national census in the year 2000. The Census Bureau, part of the Commerce Department, said that sampling would produce a more accurate and less expensive population count for use in the constitutionally required apportionment of seats in the House of Representatives among the states. But Republicans objected that sampling could be politically manipulated and violated the constitutional requirement for an "actual enumeration." A three-judge federal court, ruling in August in a suit brought by the GOP-controlled House, held that sampling violated the statutes governing the census without reaching the constitutional issue. In appealing the case, the administration argued that the House lacked standing to bring the suit and that sampling would not violate either the statute or the Constitution. The Court promptly agreed to hear the case and scheduled it for an early argument, on November 30, to permit a decision in early 1999. *(United States Department of Commerce v. United States House of Representatives)*

Continuing a recent practice, the Court also added more cases to the calendar in the week before the official beginning of the new term. The orders list released on September 29 included twelve cases, bringing the justices' workload at the start of the new term to a more respectable number: forty-five disputes in all. The new cases also spiced up the justices' agenda, with issues ranging from sexual harassment and racial redistricting to welfare benefits and automobile searches.

The new sexual harassment case raised a question left undecided in the Court's ruling in the Lago Vista School District case in June: whether school districts could be held liable under federal civil rights law for sexual misconduct between students. The case stemmed from a suit brought by the family of LaShonda Davis, a Macon, Georgia, youngster who claimed that a fellow fifth-grade student in 1992 and 1993 made obscene comments and tried to touch her in a sexual manner over a five-month period. The girl's family claimed that the classroom teacher and principal failed to take any action to prevent the misbehavior. But the federal appeals court in Atlanta held that the prohibition on sex discrimination contained in Title IX of the Education Amendments of 1972 did not permit a student to recover damages for sexual harassment by another student. *(Davis v. Monroe County Board of Education)*

The justices also decided to look for a third time at a congressional redistricting plan in North Carolina. Twice before, the Court had blocked a remapping plan with an oddly shaped, majority-black district that white voters attacked as racially motivated. The state redrew the district, reducing the African American population to 43 percent; but the federal appeals court in Richmond, Virginia, said the plan was still "race driven." *(Hunt v. Cromartie)*

Among other cases, the Court agreed to rule on an equal protection challenge to a California law that set special limits on welfare benefits for new residents. *(Anderson v. Roe)* The justices accepted an appeal by the state of Wyoming from a ruling that barred police from searching the personal belongings of a passenger during a traffic investigation. *(Wyoming v. Houghton)* And, in an important business-related dispute, the justices agreed to take up a legal challenge by insurers and employers to a federal appeals court decision that they said limited their ability to control health care costs under state workers' compensation programs. *(American Manufacturers Mutual Insurance Co. v. Sullivan)*

Anti–Gang Loitering Law

Chicago's anti–gang loitering law reached the Court at a time of widespread concern about gang crime. A Justice Department agency estimated that as of 1993 there were more than 16,000 youth gangs across the country with more than 550,000 members. State and local government groups and pro–law enforcement organizations, stressing the importance of the issue, joined Chicago in urging the Court to hear its plea to reinstate the law. Ohio's attorney general submitted a brief noting that nearly twenty states had recently passed laws that imposed special criminal penalties for gang membership or gang-related offenses.

The lawyers representing the Chicago defendants, Eileen Pahl, an assistant public defender with the Cook County public defender's office, and Harvey Grossman, legal director of the American Civil Liberties Union of Illinois, argued in response that the Illinois court's decision was correct and in line with the Court's own precedents. The Illinois court "properly concluded that the law arbitrarily impedes the personal liberties of free movement and association," Grossman wrote in urging the justices to leave the decision alone.

The Court had last dealt with laws prohibiting loitering in 1972. In that case, *Papachristou v. City of Jacksonville,* the Court unanimously struck down a Jacksonville, Florida, ordinance that allowed broad categories of people—including "rogues and vagabonds," "dissolute persons who go about begging," and "common night walkers"—to be prosecuted as "vagrants." Justice William O. Douglas said the ordinance was "plainly unconstitutional." The measure, he said, "makes criminal activities which by modern standards are normally innocent."

In the course of the opinion, Douglas quoted the writings of the poet Walt Whitman and the essayist Henry David Thoreau. Lawrence Rosenthal, Chicago's lawyer in the new Supreme Court appeal, scoffed at the opinion as "an homage to the vagrant." A lot had changed since that time, said Rosenthal, the city's deputy corporation counsel for appeals. "We think that there has been not only an enormous change in the Court but an enormous change in society's understanding of the functions of the criminal law," he

Luis Guiterrez was one of thousands of Chicago youths arrested under an anti–gang loitering law challenged as unconstitutional. Guiterrez, arrested while walking to his parents' home, was not a gang member; the case against him was thrown out.

explained. "In the succeeding twenty-five years, it has become clear that public order laws play a much larger role in maintaining community stability than anybody thought."

Grossman countered that the law was a throwback to a discredited police practice. "It is really an effort to put a legal gloss on street-sweeping, which is an archaic and universally condemned police tactic," he said. In addition, Grossman and other critics of the law insisted that the law had no appreciable effect on gang-related crime. "Locking someone up for a few hours on an ordinance violation," Grossman said, "is quite frankly no more than putting a thumb in the dike."

The city and its supporters, however, claimed that statistics proved the effectiveness of the law. The major types of gang-related crimes—aggravated battery with a firearm, drive-by shootings, and homicides—all decreased "dramatically" in 1995, the Justice Department said in a supporting brief. But gang-related homicides and aggravated batteries "climbed back to their prior levels" in 1996, the year after a lower court injunction against enforcement of the law went into effect.

Grossman, however, noted that gang-related homicides in the city fell in 1997 both in absolute numbers and as a percentage of all homicides in the city. "As time passes," Grossman concluded, "those statistics prove to be erratic."

Supporters and opponents of the law had a corresponding disagreement about the deterrent effects of the law. Dan Kahan, a law professor at the University of Chicago who coauthored a brief in support of the law on behalf of Chicago Neighborhood Organizations, said the ordinance fortified young people to turn away from gangs. "The kids who join gangs don't particularly like them," Kahan said. Enforcement of the law over time, he said, would convince young people that "being out on the street at night is no longer the way to show that you're a tough guy."

But Steven Drizin, supervising attorney for Northwestern University Law School's legal clinic for juvenile and family court, said that the law did nothing to deter crime among young people. "It causes them to disrespect police officers and the system," Drizin said, "and it doesn't provide any helpful kind of intervention for them."

The critics also objected to the discretion that the law gave police. Loitering was broadly defined to mean being in a public place "with no apparent purpose." "It leads to arbitrary and discriminatory enforcement against who[m]ever the police officer doesn't like," Pahl said. She noted that Morales was arrested just on the basis of his blue and black clothes. "Obviously, anyone wearing a pair of blue jeans and a black T-shirt would fall within that [category]," she said.

But Rosenthal said that police had no problem identifying gang members. "They tell you, they brag about it," Rosenthal said. "The last thing they would do is deny that they are gang members or refuse to answer that question." In addition, Rosenthal, who was the ordinance's principal draftsman, said that police had to have some leeway in enforcing the law. "No system of law works if the police are not allowed to exercise some discretion," he said.

Grossman and Rosenthal had both previously appeared before the Court. Grossman was the winning lawyer in a 1996 First Amendment decision and Rosenthal had argued in two cases decided in 1994 and 1995. The city lost both. "I got two votes and one recusal," Rosenthal recalled wryly.

In the current case Rosenthal conceded that the city had to persuade the Court to take a different approach than it did in the last loitering case. "As long as *Papachristou* stands on the books unaltered, we're in a very tough position to win this case," he said. But, he added, "I think it's clear that no member of the current Supreme Court would write the *Papachristou* opinion this day."

For his part, Grossman expressed confidence in the outcome. "There is a majority of justices on this Court who have displayed in previous cases a strong regard for fairness in the law enforcement process as well as a high degree of respect for striking a reasonable balance between the rights of persons and public safety issues," he said. "When the Court examines this law with the kind of scrutiny that can be expected, it will find this law wanting in many regards."

Following are some of the other major cases on the Court's calendar as it began its 1998–1999 term.

Business Law

Antitrust. A twelve-year-old dispute between a local telephone carrier and one of its former suppliers raised the question whether antitrust law applies to a company's decision to terminate a contract with a supplier.

The case involved Nynex Corp., the New York–based "Baby Bell" later acquired by Bell Atlantic, and Discon, Inc., a New York company that provided a little-known auxiliary service: removing and salvaging obsolete telephone equipment from businesses. Discon had a contract to provide services for Nynex customers for two years in the mid-1980s. Nynex canceled the contract in 1986, claiming that Discon had made an improper loan to a Nynex contracting officer and then hired him once he left the company. Discon denied that allegation and responded with an antitrust suit. It charged Nynex with canceling the contract and shifting the work to another company, AT&T Corp., to stifle price competition in the equipment-removal market and pass on the added costs to telephone customers.

A federal judge dismissed the complaint, but the federal appeals court in New York cleared the way for a trial of some parts of the suit. In seeking to overturn the decision, Nynex's lawyers said that antitrust suits involving decisions to terminate suppliers would "chill efficient supplier changes and thereby harm the very competitive process. . . ." But Discon's lawyers insisted the case was about a "group boycott" formed by Nynex and AT&T "to eliminate competition in the unregulated removal services supplier market." (*Nynex Corp. v. Discon, Inc.*)

Courts and Procedure

Expert testimony. Business interests won an important victory in 1993 when the Court strengthened the power of lower court judges to exclude scientific testimony in personal injury, product liability, and other civil suits. The ruling in *Daubert v. Merrill Dow Pharmaceuticals, Inc.* outlined a four-factor test for evaluating scientific testimony that business groups said would help keep what they called "junk science" out of trials.

Federal appeals courts disagreed over the next few years about whether the *Daubert* test also applied to evidence offered by engineering experts. The Court agreed to resolve the issue in a case stemming from a fatal automobile accident that an Alabama family blamed on a defective tire made by a South Korean manufacturer, Kumho Tire Co. Patrick Carmichael, whose daughter died in the July 1993 accident, sought to introduce evidence from a mechanical engineer who claimed to be an expert in diagnosing tire defects. The trial judge barred the evidence and threw out the suit, but the federal appeals court in Atlanta said the judge was wrong to use *Daubert* to exclude the testimony.

In urging the Court to reverse the decision, Kumho's lawyers said that extending *Daubert* to testimony from engineering experts would help "[ensure] the reliability of their methods and analyses." But Carmichael's attorneys said the rule should apply only to scientific testimony. An engineering expert, they said, should not be blocked from testifying simply because he "has not written a book, performed a statistical analysis, or joined a scientific club." *(Kumho Tire Co. v. Carmichael)*

Criminal Law and Procedure

Self-incrimination. A confessed accomplice in a big cocaine-selling ring in Allentown, Pennsylvania, brought the Court an unsettled issue under the Fifth Amendment: whether a defendant who pleads guilty can invoke the privilege against self-incrimination at a later sentencing hearing.

Amanda Mitchell pleaded guilty in October 1995 to a charge of conspiracy to distribute cocaine, but she reserved the right to contest the quantities she sold. At sentencing, the government used the testimony of another defendant to show that Mitchell regularly sold cocaine over a period of several years—well above the amount, five kilograms, needed to trigger a mandatory ten-year prison sentence. Mitchell's attorneys attacked the testimony, but Mitchell did not testify. In imposing the ten-year term, the judge told Mitchell, "I held it against you that you didn't come forward today and tell me that you really only did this a couple of times."

In asking the Court to overturn the decision, Mitchell's lawyers argued that refusing to recognize the Fifth Amendment privilege at sentencing "improperly permits the defendant to be the instrument of her own sentencing increase as well as subjects her to the potentiality of new prosecutions." But the government disagreed. "It would make no sense to conclude that the defendant's waiver of the Fifth Amendment privilege, while applicable to [the plea proceeding] if the defendant is questioned about the offense . . . ceases to be applicable at sentencing if asked to supply additional details about the offense," the government argued. *(Mitchell v. United States)*

Criminal offenses. Nathaniel Jones was charged under the new federal carjacking law for allegedly taking part in stealing a car parked outside a Bakersfield, California, liquor store on December 7, 1992. At arraignment, the judge told Jones he faced a maximum prison sentence of fifteen years. After his conviction, though, the judge gave Jones a twenty-five year term, raising the sentence under a section of the law that allowed a longer term if the crime resulted in "serious bodily injury."

Jones's appeal to the Court included an argument that the carjacking law went beyond Congress's power to regulate interstate commerce. The Court agreed to hear the case on March 30 but issued an order on April 6 eliminating the Commerce Clause issue. Instead, the Court said it wanted to use the case to consider a different question: where to draw a line between criminal law provisions that define the "elements" of an offense to be proved at trial and those that merely list "sentencing factors" for a judge to consider after conviction.

Jones, represented by a federal public defender, argued that the "serious bodily injury" allegation was part of the definition of the crime and needed to be included in the indictment and proved by evidence at trial. But the government said the law simply specified a range of punishments for an offense depending on the "traditional sentencing factors." The law, the government said in its brief, "fairly defines a serious violent crime and defines a reasonable structure for punishing those who commit it." (*Jones v. United States*)

Search and seizure. The Court took up two cases involving people convicted on drug charges after police searches that the defendants challenged as illegal under the Fourth Amendment.

In the first case, a police officer in Eagan, Minnesota, alerted by a passerby, approached within a foot of an apartment window, peered through an opening in the venetian blinds, and observed Wayne Thomas Carter and Melvin Johns bagging a white-powdered substance that appeared to be cocaine. The Minnesota Supreme Court reversed the convictions, however, on the ground that the officer's initial look into the apartment was an unjustified search. In seeking to reinstate the convictions, the Dakota County Attorney's office argued that Carter and Johns had no standing to challenge the officer's actions because they were guests in the apartment and that the officer's actions did not amount to a search anyway. Lawyers for the two men disagreed. "[S]ociety has determined that the officer's decision to engage in a little window-peeping was unreasonable," they said. (*Minnesota v. Carter*)

In the second case, Patrick Knowles challenged an Iowa law that authorized police officers to search an automobile whenever they issued a traffic citation even if the driver was not placed under arrest. Knowles was convicted of marijuana charges after police stopped him for speeding and found a quantity of marijuana and a "pot pipe" under the driver's seat of his car. The Iowa Supreme Court upheld the conviction on a 5–4 vote. "[T]he authority to search incident to citation would be a frightening expansion of police power," Knowles's lawyer said in urging the Court to reverse the decision. But the Iowa attorney general's office called Knowles's warning "unfounded." (*Knowles v. Iowa*)

Election Law

Initiatives. The initiative process was created in the early twentieth century as a way for the public to circumvent the influence of special interest groups and adopt consumer protection or political reform laws directly through the ballot. By the 1970s, however, many critics thought special interests had distorted the process through well-financed, often misleading campaigns. One of the causes of the transformation, they said, was the widespread use of paid petition circulators to gather the signatures needed to put an initiative on the ballot.

Colorado enacted a law in 1984 to ban paid petition circulators, but the Court ruled it unconstitutional in 1988. Colorado tried again in 1993 by passing a law that required petition circulators to be registered electors, wear identification badges, and file reports disclosing their identities and the amounts paid them. That law too was challenged: plaintiffs included the libertarian American Constitutional Law Foundation and four individual activists representing a variety of viewpoints. A federal appeals court agreed with their arguments that the law discriminated against unregistered citizens and infringed on a First Amendment right of anonymous political speech.

In asking the Court to reinstate the law, the Colorado attorney general's office insisted that the act was "non-discriminatory" and served the purpose of "preserving the integrity of Colorado's initiative process." Lawyers for the challengers countered that the law infringed on what they called "pure political speech effectuated to peacefully redress grievances." *(Buckley v. American Constitutional Law Foundation)*

Federal Government

Telecommunications. The stakes in the battle between local telephone companies and long-distance carriers were high both for the companies and for consumers. Local telephone service was a $100 billion market that remained a regulated monopoly business after the breakup of AT&T and the creation of competition for long-distance service. In adopting the Telecommunications Act of 1996, Congress decided that consumers could benefit from competition for local service too. The complex law ordered the FCC to adopt rules to allow the long-distance carriers into the local market.

The rules the FCC adopted in August 1996 were themselves complex, but two provisions emerged as the major points of contention between the long-distance companies and the local Bells. In one section, the FCC set out a national pricing formula—viewed as favorable to the long-distance companies—to be used in determining how much the local companies could charge the long-distance companies to connect to their existing networks. The other provision—what the FCC called "dialing parity rules"—prohibited the local companies from separating or "unbundling" existing elements of the network before connecting the long-distance carriers. Local companies thought both provisions were unfair. State utility commissions joined in opposing the provisions on the ground that they intruded on state regulation.

Legal challenges to the rules were filed across the country, consolidated, and assigned by lottery to the federal appeals court in St. Louis. It ruled in July 1997 that the FCC had gone beyond its authority in regulating rates and misread the law on the "bundling" issue. The Court agreed in January 1998 to hear the appeals filed by the FCC and the long-distance companies. In urging the Court to reinstate the FCC's rules, the government argued that the court decision threatened "to impede the competition that Congress sought to bring to local markets." But the state regulators countered that what they called the FCC's "one size fits all" rules "could lead to pricing results that would impede rather than promote competition." *(AT&T Corp. v. Iowa Utilities Board; Federal Communications Commission v. Iowa Utilities Board)*

Immigration

Deportation. A long-running fight over the government's effort to deport eight non-American supporters of the Popular Front for the Liberation of Palestine (PFLP) gave the Court an opportunity to determine the reach of a new law aimed at limiting judicial review of deportation proceedings.

The government first sought to deport the aliens—seven Palestinians and one Kenyan—in 1987. Eventually, it charged six of them with violating the terms of their student visas and the other two—who had permanent resident status—with membership in a terrorist organization. The aliens insisted that they had not engaged in violent activities but had only raised funds for the group's humanitarian efforts. They claimed that the government improperly singled them out for deportation on the basis of their political views. The government denied the accusations but also argued that an immigration judge should complete the deportation proceeding before any hearing on the selective prosecution claim. In July 1997, however, a federal appeals court ruled that a preliminary injunction against the deportation should remain in effect while the group gathered additional evidence to support their claims.

In agreeing to hear the government's appeal, the Court asked both sides to address the effect of a 1996 law that generally barred judicial review of deportation proceedings. The Justice Department said the law "was enacted to strengthen and make explicit the preexisting limitation on judicial review" of deportation cases. But attorneys for the aliens said that the law did not apply to cases pending when it was enacted and, in any event, that it could not be used to prevent a hearing on a claim of "irreparable First Amendment injury." *(Reno v. Arab-American Anti-Discrimination Committee)*

Individual Rights

Disability rights. A Cedar Rapids, Iowa, boy identified in court papers as Garret F. was rendered a quadriplegic after suffering a spinal cord injury in a motorcycle accident at the age of four. Garret's mental faculties were unaffected, however, so he and his family naturally wanted him to go to a regular school. Unlike his classmates, though, Garret needed full-time nursing assistance to take care of his ventilator, help feed him, and empty a urinary catheter.

Garret's family and the Cedar Rapids school board disagreed about who would pay for his nurse. The issue involved conflicting interpretations of the federal Individuals with Disabilities Education Act. The 1975 law required local school districts to provide children with disabilities an "appropriate" education and with "related services" needed to enable them to stay in school. The law did not apply to most "medical services." In 1984 the Court ruled that "medical services" meant services performed by a physician. Applying that decision, the federal appeals court for Iowa ordered the school system to pay for Garret's nurse.

The National School Boards Association, in a brief supporting the Cedar Rapids district, argued that upholding those decisions would add to what it called the "already tremendous costs" of special education. "Schools lack adequate human and financial resources to fulfill a mandate for health services that transcends their educational mission," the group argued. But the National Association of Protection and Advocacy Systems, a national advocacy group for persons with disabilities, said the federal law required local school districts to provide the services. "The sole criterion" under the law, the organization contended in its brief, "is whether or not the student's unique needs make those services necessary for the child to receive meaningful educational benefit." *(Cedar Rapids Community School District v. Garret F.)*

Labor Law

Arbitration and discrimination. A dispute from the Charleston, South Carolina, docks brought the Court an important legal question concerning the interaction between federal labor law and federal civil rights statutes.

Ceasar Wright suffered what was diagnosed as a permanently and totally disabling injury to his foot while working as a longshoreman in Charleston in 1992. By 1995, though, the injury had healed. When Wright tried to go back to work, however, the local stevedore companies all told him that they would not hire anyone who had previously been certified as permanently and totally disabled.

Wright wanted to sue the employers in federal court under the Americans with Disabilities Act, but the International Longshoremen's Union had a contract with the companies that called for workplace disputes to be resolved through a grievance and arbitration procedure. A federal appeals court ruled that the arbitration clause barred Wright's suit.

The Court's decision to hear the case seemed likely to apply not only to the disability rights law but also other federal antidiscrimination statutes. Civil rights groups, plaintiffs' lawyers, and the Clinton administration all joined in backing Wright's right to sue. "[T]he collective bargaining agreement cannot alter or modify the right of each individual worker to pursue a federal employment discrimination claim in federal court," the American Civil Liberties Union argued in a supporting brief. But employers' groups insisted that antidiscrimination policies would not be sacrificed in arbitration. "[I]ndividuals' substantive rights under the [equal employment opportunity] laws can be protected as effectively through arbitration as through judicial processes," the Equal Employment Advisory Council argued. *(Wright v. Universal Maritime Service Corp.)*

Pension funds. Hughes Aircraft amassed a whopping $1 billion surplus in its pension plan for salaried employees during the 1980s, but the good fortune generated a bitter lawsuit over what to do with the funds. A group of employees who were covered under—and had contributed to—the plan filed a class action suit under the federal pension protection law known as ERISA: the Employee Retirement Income Security Act. They contended that the surplus should be used to raise their benefits. Hughes insisted that it had discretion to keep the money in the fund and that the employees were entitled to nothing more than the benefits defined in the plan.

The dispute was factually and legally complex and marked by sharp charges and countercharges. The employees claimed that Hughes—which had been acquired by General Motors Corp.—was using the surplus to pay its own obligations to the plan. The company responded that the employees were simply seeking "a pot of gold to which they are not entitled." *(Hughes Aircraft Co. v. Jacobson)*

Property Law

Regulatory takings. A developer's protracted and unsuccessful effort to build a residential complex on 38 acres of beachfront in the city of Monterey, California, posed an array of property rights issues for the Court.

Del Monte Dunes failed to win the city's approval to develop the property in the mid-1980s, despite revising its plans several times to meet demands to mitigate the environmental impact of the construction. The company then filed a federal civil rights suit that claimed the city had "taken" its property without compensation by denying any productive use of the land. Although the state eventually bought the property, the jury awarded the company $1.45 million for the period when it was blocked from developing the parcel. The federal appeals court for California upheld the award.

The city, backed by the Clinton administration and an array of planning and local government groups, asked the Court to throw out the jury award on three grounds. The city contended that the developer was not entitled to a jury trial and that the jury should not have been allowed to "reweigh" the evidence on the reasonableness of the city's decision denying the construction permit. In addition, the city said that the lower courts had misapplied the Court's 1994 ruling requiring a "rough proportionality" between local government demands on property owners and the public benefits.

Lawyers for the developer countered each of the legal arguments and then concluded by defending the company's right to compensation. "An owner who goes through five different administrative proceedings. . . , and is then turned down for reasons that preclude any private development, deserves compensation," they argued. *(City of Monterey v. Del Monte Dunes at Monterey, Ltd.)*

Torts

Racketeering. Some Nevada customers of the big health insurer Humana, Inc., thought they spotted something fishy. They discovered that the company had negotiated deep discounts with health care providers but was basing their 20 percent copayments on the full, undiscounted amount. They sued in federal court under several laws, including the federal antiracketeering law known as RICO: the Racketeer Influenced and Corrupt Organizations Act.

RICO allowed plaintiffs to recover triple damages not only from conventional crime syndicates but also from otherwise legitimate businesses that engaged in a "pattern" of illegal activity. Plaintiffs in several other cases had tried to use RICO to go after allegedly fraudulent insurance practices. But most federal courts had dismissed the suits because of another federal law, the McCarran-Ferguson Act. That law barred applying any federal statute to insurance companies unless the statute specifically mentioned insurance.

Humana denied any wrongdoing, but it also invoked the McCarran-Ferguson law to try to throw out the plaintiffs' RICO count. A federal appeals court, however, said the plaintiffs could proceed with their RICO claim. In urging the Court to overturn the decision, Humana's lawyers argued that allowing RICO suits against insurance companies would render state laws "superfluous" and create the risk of raising premiums or forcing some insurers into insolvency. But the Justice Department, siding with the plaintiffs, saw no conflict with state laws. "[I]f federal law and state law both prohibit the same conduct," the government argued, "RICO's additional remedies at most enhance the vindication of state norms." *(Humana, Inc. v. Forsyth)*

Appendix

Opinion Excerpts

Following are excerpts from some of the most important rulings of the Supreme Court's 1997–1998 term. They appear in the order in which they were announced. Footnotes and legal citations are omitted.

No. 96-568

Joseph Oncale, Petitioner v. Sundowner Offshore Services, Incorporated, et al.

On writ of certiorari to the United States Court of Appeals for the Fifth Circuit

[March 4, 1998]

JUSTICE SCALIA delivered the opinion of the Court.

This case presents the question whether workplace harassment can violate Title VII's prohibition against "discriminat[ion] . . . because of . . . sex," 42 U. S. C. §2000e-2(a)(1), when the harasser and the harassed employee are of the same sex.

I

The District Court having granted summary judgment for respondent, we must assume the facts to be as alleged by petitioner Joseph Oncale. The precise details are irrelevant to the legal point we must decide, and in the interest of both brevity and dignity we shall describe them only generally. In late October 1991, Oncale was working for respondent Sundowner Offshore Services on a Chevron U.S.A., Inc., oil platform in the Gulf of Mexico. He was employed as a roustabout on an eight-man crew which included respondents John Lyons, Danny Pippen, and Brandon Johnson. Lyons, the crane operator, and Pippen, the driller, had supervisory authority. On several occasions, Oncale was forcibly subjected to sex-related, humiliating actions against him by Lyons, Pippen and Johnson in the presence of the rest of the crew. Pippen and Lyons also physically assaulted Oncale in a sexual manner, and Lyons threatened him with rape.

Oncale's complaints to supervisory personnel produced no remedial action; in fact, the company's Safety Compliance Clerk, Valent Hohen, told Oncale that Lyons and Pippen "picked [on] him all the time too," and called him a name suggesting homosexuality. Oncale eventually quit—asking that his pink slip reflect that he "voluntarily left due to sexual harassment and verbal abuse." When asked at his deposition why he left Sundowner, Oncale stated "I felt that if I didn't leave my job, that I would be raped or forced to have sex."

Oncale filed a complaint against Sundowner in the United States District Court for the Eastern District of Louisiana, alleging that he was discriminated against in his employment because of his sex. Relying on the Fifth Circuit's decision in *Garcia v. Elf Atochem North America* (CA5 1994), the district court held that "Mr. Oncale, a male, has no cause of action under Title VII for harassment by male co-workers." On appeal, a panel of the Fifth Circuit concluded that *Garcia* was binding Circuit precedent, and affirmed (1996). We granted certiorari (1997).

II

Title VII of the Civil Rights Act of 1964 provides, in relevant part, that "[i]t shall be an unlawful employment practice for an employer . . . to discriminate against any individual with respect to his compensation, terms, conditions, or privileges of employment, because of such individual's race, color, religion, sex, or national origin." We have held that this not only covers "terms" and "conditions" in the narrow contractual sense, but "evinces a congressional intent to strike at the entire spectrum of disparate treatment of men and women in employment." *Meritor Savings Bank, FSB v. Vinson* (1986). "When the workplace is permeated with discriminatory intimidation, ridicule, and insult that is sufficiently severe or pervasive to alter the conditions of the victim's employment and create an abusive working environment, Title VII is violated." *Harris v. Forklift Systems, Inc.* (1993).

Title VII's prohibition of discrimination "because of . . . sex" protects men as well as women, *Newport News Shipbuilding & Dry Dock Co. v. EEOC* (1983), and in the related context of racial discrimination in the workplace we have rejected any conclusive presumption that an employer will not discriminate against members of his own race. . . . In *Johnson v. Transportation Agency, Santa Clara Cty.* (1987), a male employee claimed that his employer discriminated against him because of his sex when it preferred a female employee for promotion. Although we ultimately rejected the claim on other grounds, we did not consider it significant that the supervisor who made that decision was also a man. If our precedents leave any doubt on the question, we hold today that nothing in Title VII necessarily bars a claim of discrimination "because of . . . sex" merely because the plaintiff and the defendant (or the person charged with acting on behalf of the defendant) are of the same sex.

Courts have had little trouble with that principle in cases like *Johnson,* where an employee claims to have been passed over for a job or promotion. But when the issue arises in the context of a "hostile environment" sexual harassment claim, the state and federal courts have taken a bewildering variety of stances. Some, like the Fifth Circuit in this case, have held that same-sex sexual harassment claims are never cognizable under Title VII. Other decisions say that such claims are actionable only if the plaintiff can prove that the harasser is homosexual (and thus presumably motivated by sexual desire). Still others suggest that workplace harassment that is sexual in content is always actionable, regardless of the harasser's sex, sexual orientation, or motivations.

We see no justification in the statutory language or our precedents for a categorical rule excluding same-sex harassment claims from the coverage of Title VII. As some courts have observed, male-on-male sexual harassment in the workplace was assuredly not the principal evil Congress was concerned with when it enacted Title VII. But statutory prohibitions often go beyond the principal evil to cover reasonably comparable evils, and it is ultimately the provisions of our laws rather than the principal concerns of our legislators by which we are governed. Title VII prohibits "discriminat[ion] . . . because of . . . sex" in the "terms" or "conditions" of employment. Our holding that this includes sexual harassment must extend to sexual harassment of any kind that meets the statutory requirements.

Respondents and their *amici* contend that recognizing liability for same-sex harassment will transform Title VII into a general civility code for the American workplace. But that risk is no greater for same-sex than for opposite-sex harassment, and is adequately met by careful attention to the requirements of the statute. Title VII does not prohibit all verbal or physical harassment in the workplace; it is directed only at "*discriminat[ion]* . . . because of . . . sex." We have never held that workplace harassment, even harassment between men and women, is automatically discrimination because of sex merely because the words used have sexual content or connotations. "The critical issue, Title VII's text indicates, is whether members of one sex are exposed to disadvantageous terms or conditions of employment to which members of the other sex are not exposed." *Harris* (GINSBURG, J., concurring).

Courts and juries have found the inference of discrimination easy to draw in most male-female sexual harassment situations, because the challenged conduct typically involves explicit or implicit proposals of sexual activity; it is reasonable to assume those proposals would not have been made to someone of the same sex. The same chain of inference would be available to a plaintiff alleging same-sex harassment, if there were credible evidence that the harasser was homosexual. But harassing conduct need not be motivated by sexual desire to support an inference of discrimination on the basis of sex. A trier of fact might reasonably find such discrimination, for example, if a female victim is harassed in such sex-specific and derogatory terms by another woman as to make it clear that the harasser is motivated by general hostility to the presence of women in the workplace. A same-sex harassment plaintiff may also, of course, offer direct comparative evidence about how the alleged harasser treated members of both sexes in a mixed-sex workplace. Whatever evidentiary route the plaintiff chooses to follow, he or she must always prove that the conduct at issue was not merely tinged with offensive sexual connotations, but actually constituted "*discrimina[tion]* . . . because of . . . sex."

And there is another requirement that prevents Title VII from expanding into a general civility code: As we emphasized in *Meritor* and *Harris,* the statute does not reach genuine but innocuous differences in the ways men and women routinely interact with members of the same sex and of the opposite sex. The prohibition of harassment on the basis of sex requires neither asexuality nor androgyny in the workplace; it forbids only behavior so objectively offensive as to alter the "conditions" of the victim's employment. "Conduct that is not severe or pervasive enough to create an objectively hostile or abusive work environment—an environment that a reasonable person would find hostile or abusive—is beyond Title VII's purview." *Harris,* citing *Meritor.* We have always regarded that requirement as crucial, and as sufficient to ensure that courts and juries do not mistake ordinary socializing in the workplace—such as male-on-male horseplay or intersexual flirtation—for discriminatory "conditions of employment."

We have emphasized, moreover, that the objective severity of harassment should be judged from the perspective of a reasonable person in the plaintiff's position, considering "all the circumstances." *Harris.* In same-sex (as in all) harassment cases, that inquiry requires careful consideration of the social context in which particular behavior occurs and is experienced by its target. A professional football player's working environment is not severely or pervasively abusive, for example, if the coach smacks him on the buttocks as he heads onto the field—even if the same behavior would reasonably be experienced as abusive by the coach's secretary (male or female) back at the office. The real social impact of workplace behavior often depends on a constellation of surrounding circumstances, expectations, and relationships which are not fully captured by a simple recitation of the words used or the physical acts performed. Common sense, and an appropriate sensitivity to social context, will enable courts and juries to distinguish between simple teasing or roughhousing among members of the same sex, and conduct which a reasonable person in the plaintiff's position would find severely hostile or abusive.

III

Because we conclude that sex discrimination consisting of same-sex sexual harassment is actionable under Title VII, the judgment of the Court of Appeals for the Fifth Circuit is reversed, and the case is remanded for further proceedings consistent with this opinion.

It is so ordered.

JUSTICE THOMAS, concurring.

I concur because the Court stresses that in every sexual harassment case, the plaintiff must plead and ultimately prove Title VII's statutory requirement that there be discrimination "because of . . . sex."

☐☐☐

No. 96-1487

United States, Petitioner v. Hosep Krikor Bajakajian

On writ of certiorari to the United States Court
of Appeals for the Ninth Circuit

[June 22, 1998]

JUSTICE THOMAS delivered the opinion of the Court.

Respondent Hosep Bajakajian attempted to leave the United States without reporting, as required by federal law, that he was transporting more than $10,000 in currency. Federal law also provides that a person convicted of willfully violating this reporting requirement shall forfeit to the government "any property . . . involved in such offense." 18 U. S. C. § 982(a)(1). The question in this case is whether forfeiture of the entire $357,144 that respondent failed to declare would violate the Excessive Fines Clause of the Eighth Amendment. We hold that it would, because full forfeiture of respondent's currency would be grossly disproportional to the gravity of his offense.

I

On June 9, 1994, respondent, his wife, and his two daughters were waiting at Los Angeles International Airport to board a flight to Italy; their final destination was Cyprus. Using dogs trained to detect currency by its smell, customs inspectors discovered some $230,000 in cash in the Bajakajians' checked baggage. A customs inspector approached respondent and his wife and told them that they were required to report all money in excess of $10,000 in their possession or in their baggage. Respondent said that he had $8,000 and that his wife had another $7,000, but that the family had no additional currency to declare. A search of their carry-on bags, purse, and wallet revealed more cash; in all, customs inspectors found $357,144. The currency was seized and respondent was taken into custody.

A federal grand jury indicted respondent on three counts. Count One charged him with failing to report, as required by 31 U. S. C. § 5316(a)(1)(A), 1 that he was transporting more than $10,000 outside the United States, and with doing so "willfully," in violation of § 5322(a). Count Two charged him with making a false material statement to the United States Customs Service, in violation of 18 U. S. C. § 1001. Count Three sought forfeiture of the $357,144 pursuant to 18 U. S. C. § 982(a)(1), which provides:

> "The court, in imposing sentence on a person convicted of an offense in violation of section . . . 5316, . . . shall order that the person forfeit to the United States any property, real or personal, involved in such offense, or any property traceable to such property." 18 U. S. C. § 982(a)(1).

Respondent pleaded guilty to the failure to report in Count One; the Government agreed to dismiss the false statement charge in Count Two; and respondent elected to have a bench trial on the forfeiture in Count Three. After the bench trial, the District Court found that the entire $357,144 was subject to forfeiture because it was "involved in" the offense. The court also found that the funds were not connected to any other crime and that respondent was transporting the money to repay a lawful debt. The District Court further found that respondent had failed to report that he was taking the currency out of the United States because of fear stemming from "cultural differences": Respondent, who had grown up as a member of the Armenian minority in Syria, had a "distrust for the Government."

Although § 982(a)(1) directs sentencing courts to impose full forfeiture, the District Court concluded that such forfeiture would be "extraordinarily harsh" and "grossly disproportionate to the offense in question," and that it would therefore violate the Excessive Fines Clause. The court instead ordered forfeiture of $15,000, in addition to a sentence of three years of probation and a fine of $5,000—the maximum fine under the Sentencing Guidelines—because the court believed that the maximum Guidelines fine was "too little" and that a $15,000 forfeiture would "make up for what I think a reasonable fine should be."

The United States appealed, seeking full forfeiture of respondent's currency as provided in § 982(a)(1). The Court of Appeals for the Ninth Circuit affirmed. (1996). Applying Circuit precedent, the Court held that, to satisfy the Excessive Fines Clause, a forfeiture must fulfill two conditions: The property forfeited must be an "instrumentality" of the crime committed, and the value of the property must be proportional to the culpability of the owner. A majority of the panel determined that the currency was not an "instrumentality" of the crime of failure to report because " '[t]he crime [in a currency reporting offense] is the withholding of information, . . . not the possession or the transportation of the money.' " The majority therefore held that § 982(a)(1) could never satisfy the Excessive Fines Clause in cases involving forfeitures of currency and that it was unnecessary to apply the "proportionality" prong of the test. Although the panel majority concluded that the Excessive Fines Clause did not permit forfeiture of any of the unreported currency, it held that it lacked jurisdiction to set the $15,000 forfeiture aside because respondent had not cross-appealed to challenge that forfeiture.

Judge Wallace concurred in the result. He viewed respondent's currency as an instrumentality of the crime because "without the currency, there can be no offense," and he criticized the majority for "strik[ing] down a portion of" the statute. He nonetheless agreed that full forfeiture would violate the Excessive Fines Clause in respondent's case, based upon the "proportionality" prong of the Ninth Circuit test. Finding no clear error in the District Court's factual findings, he concluded that the reduced forfeiture of $15,000 was proportional to respondent's culpability.

Because the Court of Appeals' holding—that the forfeiture ordered by § 982(a)(1) was *per se* unconstitutional in cases of currency forfeiture—invalidated a portion of an act of Congress, we granted certiorari (1997).

II

The Eighth Amendment provides: "Excessive bail shall not be required, nor excessive fines imposed, nor cruel and unusual punishments inflicted." This Court has had little occasion to interpret, and has never actually applied, the Excessive Fines Clause. We have, however, explained that at the time the Constitution was adopted, "the word 'fine' was understood to mean a payment to a sovereign as punishment for some offense." *Browning-Ferris Industries of Vt., Inc. v. Kelco Disposal, Inc.* (1989). The Excessive Fines Clause thus "limits the government's power to extract payments, whether in cash or in kind, 'as punishment for some offense.' " *Austin v. United States* (1993). Forfeitures—payments in kind—are thus "fines" if they constitute punishment for an offense.

We have little trouble concluding that the forfeiture of currency ordered by § 982(a)(1) constitutes punishment. The statute directs a court to order forfeiture as an additional sanction when "imposing sentence on a person convicted of" a willful violation of § 5316's reporting requirement. The forfeiture is thus imposed at the culmination of a criminal proceeding and requires conviction of an underlying felony, and it cannot be imposed upon an innocent owner of unreported currency, but only upon a person who has himself been convicted of a § 5316 reporting violation. Cf. *Austin v. United States* (holding forfeiture to be a "fine" in part because the forfeiture statute "expressly provide[d] an 'innocent owner' defense" and thus "look[ed] . . . like punishment").

The United States argues, however, that the forfeiture of currency under § 982(a)(1) "also serves important remedial purposes." The Government asserts that it has "an overriding sovereign interest in controlling what property leaves and enters the country." It claims that full forfeiture of unreported currency supports that interest by serving to "dete[r] illicit movements of cash" and aiding in providing the Government with "valuable information to investigate and detect criminal activities associated with that cash." Deterrence, however, has traditionally been viewed as a goal of punishment, and forfeiture of the currency here does not serve the remedial purpose of compensating the Government for a loss. . . . Although the Government has asserted a loss of information regarding the amount of currency leaving the country, that loss would not be remedied by the Government's confiscation of respondent's $357,144.

The United States also argues that the forfeiture mandated by § 982(a)(1) is constitutional because it falls within a class of historic forfeitures of property tainted by crime. In so doing, the Government relies upon a series of cases involving traditional civil *in rem* forfeitures that are inapposite because such forfeitures were historically considered nonpunitive.

The theory behind such forfeitures was the fiction that the action was directed against "guilty property," rather than against the offender himself. . . . Historically, the conduct of the property owner was irrelevant; indeed, the owner of forfeited property could be entirely innocent of any crime. . . .

Traditional *in rem* forfeitures were thus not considered punishment against the individual for an offense. . . . Because they were viewed as nonpunitive, such forfeitures traditionally were considered to occupy a place outside the domain of the Excessive Fines Clause. Recognizing the nonpunitive character of such proceedings, we have held that the Double Jeopardy Clause does not bar the institution of a civil, *in rem* forfeiture action after the criminal conviction of the defendant. [*United States v. Ursery* (1996).]

The forfeiture in this case does not bear any of the hallmarks of traditional civil *in rem* forfeitures. The Government has not proceeded against the currency itself, but has instead sought and obtained a criminal conviction of respondent personally. The forfeiture serves no remedial purpose, is designed to punish the offender, and cannot be imposed upon innocent owners.

Section 982(a)(1) thus descends not from historic *in rem* forfeitures of guilty property, but from a different historical tradition: that of *in personam*, criminal forfeitures. Such forfeitures have historically been treated as punitive, being part of the punishment imposed for felonies and treason in the Middle Ages and at common law. Although *in personam* criminal forfeitures were well established in England at the time of the Founding, they were rejected altogether in the laws of this country until very recently.

The Government specifically contends that the forfeiture of respondent's currency is constitutional because it involves an "instrumentality" of respondent's crime. According to the Government, the unreported cash is an instrumentality because it "does not merely facilitate a violation of law," but is " 'the very *sine qua non* of the crime.' " . . . The Government reasons that "there would be no violation at all without the exportation (or attempted exportation) of the cash."

Acceptance of the Government's argument would require us to expand the traditional understanding of instrumentality forfeitures. This we decline to do. Instrumentalities historically have been treated as a form of "guilty property" that can be forfeited in civil *in rem* proceedings. In this case, however, the Government has sought to punish respondent by proceeding against him criminally, *in personam*, rather than proceeding *in rem* against the currency. It is therefore irrelevant whether respondent's currency is an instrumentality; the forfeiture is punitive, and the test for the excessiveness of a punitive forfeiture involves solely a proportionality determination.

III

Because the forfeiture of respondent's currency constitutes punishment and is thus a "fine" within the meaning of the Excessive Fines Clause, we now turn to the question of whether it is "excessive."

A

The touchstone of the constitutional inquiry under the Excessive Fines Clause is the principle of proportionality: The amount of the forfeiture must bear some relationship to the gravity of the offense that it is designed to punish.... Until today, however, we have not articulated a standard for determining whether a punitive forfeiture is constitutionally excessive. We now hold that a punitive forfeiture violates the Excessive Fines Clause if it is grossly disproportional to the gravity of a defendant's offense.

The text and history of the Excessive Fines Clause demonstrate the centrality of proportionality to the excessiveness inquiry; nonetheless, they provide little guidance as to how disproportional a punitive forfeiture must be to the gravity of an offense in order to be "excessive." Excessive means surpassing the usual, the proper, or a normal measure of proportion.... The constitutional question that we address, however, is just how proportional to a criminal offense a fine must be, and the text of the Excessive Fines Clause does not answer it.

Nor does its history. The Clause was little discussed in the First Congress and the debates over the ratification of the Bill of Rights.... [T]he Clause was taken verbatim from the English Bill of Rights of 1689. That document's prohibition against excessive fines was a reaction to the abuses of the King's judges during the reigns of the Stuarts, but the fines that those judges imposed were described contemporaneously only in the most general terms. Similarly, Magna Charta—which the Stuart judges were accused of subverting—required only that amercements (the medieval predecessors of fines) should be proportioned to the offense and that they should not deprive a wrongdoer of his livelihood.... None of these sources suggests how disproportional to the gravity of an offense a fine must be in order to be deemed constitutionally excessive.

We must therefore rely on other considerations in deriving a constitutional excessiveness standard, and there are two that we find particularly relevant. The first, which we have emphasized in our cases interpreting the Cruel and Unusual Punishments Clause, is that judgments about the appropriate punishment for an offense belong in the first instance to the legislature.... The second is that any judicial determination regarding the gravity of a particular criminal offense will be inherently imprecise. Both of these principles counsel against requiring strict proportionality between the amount of a punitive forfeiture and the gravity of a criminal offense, and we therefore adopt the standard of gross disproportionality articulated in our Cruel and Unusual Punishments Clause precedents.

In applying this standard, the district courts in the first instance, and the courts of appeals, reviewing the proportionality determination *de novo,* must compare the amount of the forfeiture to the gravity of the defendant's offense. If the amount of the forfeiture is grossly disproportional to the gravity of the defendant's offense, it is unconstitutional.

B

Under this standard, the forfeiture of respondent's entire $357,144 would violate the Excessive Fines Clause. Respondent's crime was solely a reporting offense. It was permissible to transport the currency out of the country so long as he reported it. Section 982(a)(1) orders currency to be forfeited for a "willful" violation of the reporting requirement. Thus, the essence of respondent's crime is a willful failure to report the removal of currency from the United States. Furthermore, as the District Court found, respondent's violation was unrelated to any other illegal activities. The money was the proceeds of legal activity and was to be used to repay a lawful debt. Whatever his other vices, respondent does not fit into the class of persons for whom the statute was principally designed: He is not a money launderer, a drug trafficker, or a tax evader. And under the Sentencing Guidelines, the maximum sentence that could have been imposed on respondent was six months, while the maximum fine was $5,000. Such penalties confirm a minimal level of culpability.

The harm that respondent caused was also minimal. Failure to report his currency affected only one party, the Government, and in a relatively minor way. There was no fraud on the United States, and respondent caused no loss to the public fisc. Had his crime gone undetected, the Government would have been deprived only of the information that $357,144 had left the country. The Government and the dissent contend that there is a correlation between the amount forfeited and the harm that the Government would have suffered had the crime gone undetected. We disagree. There is no inherent proportionality in such a forfeiture. It is impossible to conclude, for example, that the harm respondent caused is anywhere near 30 times greater than that caused by a hypothetical drug dealer who willfully fails to report taking $12,000 out of the country in order to purchase drugs.

Comparing the gravity of respondent's crime with the $357,144 forfeiture the Government seeks, we conclude that such a forfeiture would be grossly disproportional to the gravity of his offense. It is larger than the $5,000 fine imposed by the District Court by many orders of magnitude, and it bears no articulable correlation to any injury suffered by the Government.

C

Finally, we must reject the contention that the proportionality of full forfeiture is demonstrated by the fact that the First Congress enacted statutes requiring full forfeiture of goods involved in customs offenses or the payment of monetary penalties proportioned to the goods' value. It is argued that the enactment of these statutes at roughly the same time that the Eighth Amendment was ratified suggests that full forfeiture, in the customs context at least, is a proportional punishment. The early customs statutes, however, do not support such a conclusion because, unlike § 982(a)(1), the type of forfeiture that they imposed was not considered punishment for a criminal offense. [Remainder of section omitted.]

* * *

For the foregoing reasons, the full forfeiture of respondent's currency would violate the Excessive Fines Clause. The judgment of the Court of Appeals is

Affirmed.

JUSTICE KENNEDY, with whom THE CHIEF JUSTICE, JUSTICE O'CONNOR, and JUSTICE SCALIA join, dissenting.

For the first time in its history, the Court strikes down a fine as excessive under the Eighth Amendment. The decision is disturbing both for its specific holding and for the broader upheaval it foreshadows. At issue is a fine Congress fixed in the amount of the currency respondent sought to smuggle or to transport without reporting. If a fine calibrated with this accuracy fails the Court's test, its decision portends serious disruption of a vast range of statutory fines. The Court all but says the offense is not serious anyway. This disdain for the statute is wrong as an empirical matter and disrespectful of the separation of powers. The irony of the case is that, in the end, it may stand for narrowing constitutional protection rather than enhancing it. To make its rationale work, the Court appears to remove important classes of fines from any excessiveness inquiry at all. This, too, is unsound; and with all respect, I dissent.

I

A

In striking down this forfeiture, the majority treats many fines as "remedial" penalties even though they far exceed the harm suffered. Remedial penalties, the Court holds, are not subject to the Excessive Fines Clause at all. Proceeding from this premise, the majority holds customs fines are remedial and not at all punitive, even if they amount to many times the duties due on the goods. In the majority's universe, a fine is not a punishment even if it is much larger than the money owed. This confuses whether a fine is excessive with whether it is a punishment.

This novel, mistaken approach requires reordering a tradition existing long before the Republic and confirmed in its early years. The Court creates its category to reconcile its unprecedented holding with a six-century-long tradition of *in personam* customs fines equal to one, two, three, or even four times the value of the goods at issue. [Citations omitted.]

In order to sweep all these precedents aside, the majority's remedial analysis assumes the settled tradition was limited to "reimbursing the Government for" unpaid duties. The assumption is wrong. Many offenses did not require a failure to pay a duty at all. . . . None of these *in personam* penalties depended on a compensable monetary loss to the government. True, these offenses risked causing harm, but so does smuggling or not reporting cash. A sanction proportioned to potential rather than actual harm is punitive, though the potential harm may make the punishment a reasonable one. The majority nonetheless treats the historic penalties as nonpunitive and thus not subject to the Excessive Fines Clause, though they are indistinguishable from the fine in this case. . . .

B

The majority's novel holding creates another anomaly as well. The majority suggests *in rem* forfeitures of the instrumentalities of crimes are not fines at all. The point of the instrumentality theory is to distinguish goods having a "close enough relationship to the offense" from those incidentally related to it. *Austin v. United States* [1993] (SCALIA, J., concurring in part and concurring in judgment). From this, the Court concludes the money in a cash smuggling or non-reporting offense cannot be an instrumentality, unlike, say, a car used to transport goods concealed from taxes. There is little logic in this rationale. The car plays an important role in the offense but is not essential; one could also transport goods by jet or by foot. The link between the cash and the cash-smuggling offense is closer, as the offender must fail to report while smuggling more than $10,000. The cash is not just incidentally related to the offense of cash smuggling. It is essential, whereas the car is not. Yet the car plays an important enough role to justify forfeiture, as the majority concedes. *A fortiori*, the cash does as well. Even if there were a clear distinction between instrumentalities and incidental objects, when the Court invokes the distinction it gets the results backwards.

II

Turning to the question of excessiveness, the majority states the test: A defendant must prove a gross disproportion before a court will strike down a fine as excessive. This test would be a proper way to apply the Clause, if only the majority were faithful in applying it. The Court does not, however, explain why in this case forfeiture of all of the cash would have suffered from a gross disproportion. The offense is a serious one, and respondent's smuggling and failing to report were willful. The cash was lawful to own, but this fact shows only that the forfeiture was a fine; it cannot also prove that the fine was excessive.

The majority illuminates its test with a principle of deference. Courts " 'should grant substantial deference to the broad authority that legislatures necessarily possess' " in setting punishments. Again, the principle is sound but the implementation is not. The majority's assessment of the crime accords no deference, let alone substantial deference, to the judgment of Congress. Congress deems the crime serious, but the Court does not. Under the congressional statute, the crime is punishable by a prison sentence, a heavy fine, and the forfeiture here at issue. As the statute makes clear, the Government needs the information to investigate other serious crimes, and it needs the penalties to ensure compliance.

A

By affirming, the majority in effect approves a meager $15,000 forfeiture. The majority's holding purports to be narrower, saying only that forfeiture of the entire $357,144 would be excessive. This narrow holding is artificial in constricting the question presented for this Court's review. The statute mandates forfeiture of the entire $357,144. The only ground for reducing the forfeiture, then, is that any higher amount would be unconstitutional. The majority affirms the reduced $15,000 forfeiture on *de novo* review, which it can do only if a forfeiture of even $15,001 would have suffered from a gross disproportion. Indeed, the majority leaves open whether the $15,000 forfeiture itself was too great. Money launderers, among the principal targets of this statute, may get an even greater return from their crime.

The majority does not explain why respondent's knowing, willful, serious crime deserves no higher penalty than $15,000. It gives only a cursory explanation of why forfeiture of all of the money would have suffered from a gross disproportion. The majority justifies its evisceration of the fine because the money was legal to have and came from a legal source. This fact, however, shows only that the forfeiture was a fine, not that it was excessive. As the majority puts it, respondent's money was lawful to possess, was acquired in a lawful manner, and was lawful to export. It was not, however, lawful to possess the money while concealing and smuggling it. . . .

B

1

In assessing whether there is a gross disproportion, the majority concedes, we must grant " 'substantial deference' " to Congress' choice of penalties. Yet, ignoring its own command, the Court sweeps aside Congress' reasoned judgment and substitutes arguments that are little more than speculation.

Congress considered currency smuggling and non-reporting a serious crime and imposed commensurate penalties. It authorized punishments of five years' imprisonment, a $250,000 fine, plus forfeiture of all the undeclared cash. Congress found the offense standing alone is a serious crime, for the same statute doubles the fines and imprisonment for failures to report cash "while violating another law of the United States." Congress experimented with lower penalties on the order of one year in prison plus a $1,000 fine, but it found the punishments inadequate to deter lucrative money laundering. The Court today rejects this judgment.

The Court rejects the congressional judgment because, it says, the Sentencing Guidelines cap the appropriate fine at $5,000. The purpose of the Guidelines, however, is to select punishments with precise proportion, not to opine on what is a gross disproportion. In addition, there is no authority for elevating the Commission's judgment of what is prudent over the congressional judgment of what is constitutional. The majority, then, departs from its promise of deference in the very case announcing the standard.

The Court's argument is flawed, moreover, by a serious misinterpretation of the Guidelines on their face. The Guidelines do not stop at the $5,000 fine the majority cites. They augment it with this vital point: "Forfeiture is to be imposed upon a convicted defendant as provided by statute." United States Sentencing Commission, Guidelines Manual § 5E1.4. The fine thus supplements the forfeiture; it does not replace it. Far from contradicting congressional judgment on the offense, the Guidelines implement and mandate it.

2

The crime of smuggling or failing to report cash is more serious than the Court is willing to acknowledge. The drug trade, money laundering, and tax evasion all depend in part on smuggled and unreported cash. Congress enacted the reporting requirement because secret exports of money were being used in organized crime, drug trafficking, money laundering, and other crimes. Likewise, tax evaders were using cash exports to dodge hundreds of millions of dollars in taxes owed to the Government.

The Court does not deny the importance of these interests but claims they are not implicated here because respondent managed to disprove any link to other crimes. Here, to be sure, the Government had no affirmative proof that the money was from an illegal source or for an illegal purpose. This will often be the case, however. By its very nature, money laundering is difficult to prove; for if the money launderers have done their job, the money appears to be clean. The point of the statute, which provides for even heavier penalties if a second crime can be proved, is to mandate forfeiture regardless. . . .

In my view, forfeiture of all the unreported currency is sustainable whenever a willful violation is proven. The facts of this case exemplify how hard it can be to prove ownership and other crimes, and they also show respondent is far from an innocent victim. For one thing, he was guilty of repeated lies to Government agents and suborning lies by others. Customs inspectors told respondent of his duty to report cash. He and his wife claimed they had only $15,000 with them, not the $357,144 they in fact had concealed. He then told customs inspectors a friend named Abe Ajemian had lent him about $200,000. Ajemian denied this. A month later, respondent said Saeed Faroutan had lent him $170,000. Faroutan, however, said he had not made the loan and respondent had asked him to lie. Six months later, respondent resurrected the fable of the alleged loan from Ajemian, though Ajemian had already contradicted the story. As the District Court found, respondent "has lied, and has had his friends lie." He had proffered a "suspicious and confused story, documented in the poorest way, and replete with past misrepresentation."

Respondent told these lies, moreover, in most suspicious circumstances. His luggage was stuffed with more than a third of a million dollars. All of it was in cash, and much of it was hidden in a case with a false bottom.

The majority ratifies the District Court's see-no-evil approach. The District Court ignored respondent's lies in assessing a sentence. It gave him a two-level downward adjustment for acceptance of responsibility, instead of an increase for obstruction of justice. It dismissed the lies as stemming from "distrust for the Government" arising out of "cultural differences." . . . This patronizing excuse demeans millions of law-abiding American immigrants by suggesting they cannot be expected to be as truthful as every other citizen. Each American, regardless of culture or ethnicity, is equal before the law. Each has the same obligation to refrain from perjury and false statements to the Government.

In short, respondent was unable to give a single truthful explanation of the source of the cash. The multitude of lies and suspicious circumstances points to some form of crime. Yet, though the Government rebutted each and every fable respondent proffered, it was unable to adduce affirmative proof of another crime in this particular case.

Because of the problems of individual proof, Congress found it necessary to enact a blanket punishment. . . . One of the few reliable warning signs of some serious crimes is the use of large sums of cash. So Congress punished all cash smuggling or non-reporting, authorizing single penalties for the offense alone and double penalties for the offense coupled with proof of other crimes. The requirement of willfulness, it judged, would be enough to protect the innocent. The majority second-guesses this judgment without explaining why Congress' blanket approach was unreasonable.

Money launderers will rejoice to know they face forfeitures of less than 5% of the money transported, provided they hire accomplished liars to carry their money for them. Five percent, of course, is not much of a deterrent or punishment; it is comparable to the fee one might pay for a mortgage lender or broker. . . . It is far less than the 20–26% commissions some drug dealers pay money launderers. . . . Since many couriers evade detection, moreover, the average forfeiture per dollar smuggled could amount, courtesy of today's decision, to far less than 5%. In any event, the fine permitted by the majority would be a modest cost of doing business in the world of drugs and crime. . . .

Given the severity of respondent's crime, the Constitution does not forbid forfeiture of all of the smuggled or unreported cash. Congress made a considered judgment in setting the penalty, and the Court is in serious error to set it aside.

III

The Court's holding may in the long run undermine the purpose of the Excessive Fines Clause. One of the main purposes of the ban on excessive fines was to prevent the King from assessing unpayable fines to keep his enemies in debtor's prison. . . . Concern with imprisonment may explain why the Excessive Fines Clause is coupled with, and follows right after, the Excessive Bail Clause. While the concern is not implicated here—for of necessity the money is there to satisfy the forfeiture—the Court's restrictive approach could subvert this purpose. Under the Court's holding, legislators may rely on mandatory prison sentences in lieu of fines. Drug lords will be heartened by this, knowing the prison terms will fall upon their couriers while leaving their own wallets untouched.

At the very least, today's decision will encourage legislatures to take advantage of another avenue the majority leaves open. The majority subjects this forfeiture to scrutiny because it is *in personam,* but it then suggests most *in rem* forfeitures (and perhaps most civil forfeitures) may not be fines at all. The suggestion, one might note, is inconsistent or at least in tension with *Austin v. United States.* In any event, these remarks may encourage a legislative shift from *in personam* to *in rem* forfeitures, avoiding *mens rea* as a predicate and giving owners fewer procedural protections. By invoking the Excessive Fines Clause with excessive zeal, the majority may in the long run encourage Congress to circumvent it.

IV

The majority's holding may not only jeopardize a vast range of fines but also leave countless others unchecked by the Constitution. Non-remedial fines may be subject to deference in theory but overbearing scrutiny in fact. So-called remedial penalties, most *in rem* forfeitures, and perhaps civil fines may not be subject to scrutiny at all. I would not create these exemptions from the Excessive Fines Clause. I would also accord genuine deference to Congress' judgments about the gravity of the offenses it creates. I would further follow the long tradition of fines calibrated to the value of the goods smuggled. In these circumstances, the Constitution does not forbid forfeiture of all of the $357,144 transported by respondent. I dissent.

No. 96-1866

Alida Star Gebser and Alida Jean McCullough, Petitioners v. Lago Vista Independent School District

On writ of certiorari to the United States Court of Appeals for the Fifth Circuit

[June 22, 1998]

JUSTICE O'CONNOR delivered the opinion of the Court.

The question in this case is when a school district may be held liable in damages in an implied right of action under Title IX of the Education Amendments of

1972, as amended, 20 U. S. C. § 1681 *et seq.*, for the sexual harassment of a student by one of the district's teachers. We conclude that damages may not be recovered in those circumstances unless an official of the school district who at a minimum has authority to institute corrective measures on the district's behalf has actual notice of, and is deliberately indifferent to, the teacher's misconduct.

I

In the spring of 1991, when petitioner Alida Star Gebser was an eighth-grade student at a middle school in respondent Lago Vista Independent School District, she joined a high school book discussion group led by Frank Waldrop, a teacher at Lago Vista's high school. Lago Vista received federal funds at all pertinent times. During the book discussion sessions, Waldrop often made sexually suggestive comments to the students. Gebser entered high school in the fall and was assigned to classes taught by Waldrop in both semesters. Waldrop continued to make inappropriate remarks to the students, and he began to direct more of his suggestive comments toward Gebser, including during the substantial amount of time that the two were alone in his classroom. He initiated sexual contact with Gebser in the spring, when, while visiting her home ostensibly to give her a book, he kissed and fondled her. The two had sexual intercourse on a number of occasions during the remainder of the school year. Their relationship continued through the summer and into the following school year, and they often had intercourse during class time, although never on school property.

Gebser did not report the relationship to school officials, testifying that while she realized Waldrop's conduct was improper, she was uncertain how to react and she wanted to continue having him as a teacher. In October 1992, the parents of two other students complained to the high school principal about Waldrop's comments in class. The principal arranged a meeting, at which, according to the principal, Waldrop indicated that he did not believe he had made offensive remarks but apologized to the parents and said it would not happen again. The principal also advised Waldrop to be careful about his classroom comments and told the school guidance counselor about the meeting, but he did not report the parents' complaint to Lago Vista's superintendent, who was the district's Title IX coordinator. A couple of months later, in January 1993, a police officer discovered Waldrop and Gebser engaging in sexual intercourse and arrested Waldrop. Lago Vista terminated his employment, and subsequently, the Texas Education Agency revoked his teaching license. During this time, the district had not promulgated or distributed an official grievance procedure for lodging sexual harassment complaints; nor had it issued a formal anti-harassment policy.

Gebser and her mother filed suit against Lago Vista and Waldrop in state court in November 1993, raising claims against the school district under Title IX, 42 U. S. C. § 1983, and state negligence law, and claims against Waldrop primarily under state law. They sought compensatory and punitive damages from both defendants. After the case was removed, the United States District Court for the Western District of Texas granted summary judgment in favor of Lago Vista on all claims, and remanded the allegations against Waldrop to state court. In rejecting the Title IX claim against the school district, the court reasoned that the statute "was enacted to counter *policies* of discrimination . . . in federally funded education programs," and that "[o]nly if school administrators have some type of notice of the gender discrimination and fail to respond in good faith can the discrimination be interpreted as a *policy* of the school district." Here, the court determined, the parents' complaint to the principal concerning Waldrop's comments in class was the only one Lago Vista had received about Waldrop, and that evidence was inadequate to raise a genuine issue on whether the school district had actual or constructive notice that Waldrop was involved in a sexual relationship with a student.

Petitioners appealed only on the Title IX claim. The Court of Appeals for the Fifth Circuit affirmed, *Doe v. Lago Vista Independent School Dist.* (1997), relying in large part on two of its recent decisions, *Rosa H. v. San Elizario Independent School Dist.* (CA5 1997) and *Canutillo Independent School Dist. v. Leija* (CA5 1996), cert. denied (1997). The court first declined to impose strict liability on school districts for a teacher's sexual harassment of a student, reiterating its conclusion in *Leija* that strict liability is inconsistent with "the Title IX contract." The court then determined that Lago Vista could not be liable on the basis of constructive notice, finding that there was insufficient evidence to suggest that a school official should have known about Waldrop's relationship with Gebser. Finally, the court refused to invoke the common law principle that holds an employer vicariously liable when an employee is "aided in accomplishing [a] tort by the existence of the agency relation," Restatement (Second) of Agency § 219(2)(d), explaining that application of that principle would result in school district liability in essentially every case of teacher-student harassment.

The court concluded its analysis by reaffirming its holding in *Rosa H.* that, "school districts are not liable in tort for teacher-student sexual harassment under Title IX unless an employee who has been invested by the school board with supervisory power over the offending employee actually knew of the abuse, had the power to end the abuse, and failed to do so," and ruling that petitioners could not satisfy that standard. The Fifth Circuit's analysis represents one of the varying approaches adopted by the Courts of Appeals in assessing a school district's liability under Title IX for a teacher's sexual harassment of a student. [Listing of cases from other federal appeals courts omitted.] We granted certiorari to address the issue (1997), and we now affirm.

II

Title IX provides in pertinent part that, "[n]o person . . . shall, on the basis of sex, be excluded from participation in, be denied the benefits of, or be subjected to discrimination under any education program or activity receiving Federal financial assistance." 20 U. S. C. § 1681(a). The express statutory means of enforcement is administrative: The statute directs federal agencies who distribute education funding to establish requirements to effectuate the nondiscrimination mandate, and permits the agencies to enforce those requirements through "any . . . means authorized by law," including ultimately the termination of federal funding. § 1682. The Court held in *Cannon v. University of Chicago* (1979) that Title IX is also enforceable through an implied private right of action, a conclusion we do not revisit here. We subsequently established in *Franklin v. Gwinnett County Public Schools* (1992) that monetary damages are available in the implied private action.

In *Franklin,* a high school student alleged that a teacher had sexually abused her on repeated occasions and that teachers and school administrators knew about the harassment but took no action, even to the point of dissuading her from initiating charges. The lower courts dismissed Franklin's complaint against the school district on the ground that the implied right of action under Title IX, as a categorical matter, does not encompass recovery in damages. We reversed the lower courts' blanket rule, concluding that Title IX supports a private action for damages, at least "in a case such as this, in which intentional discrimination is alleged." *Franklin* thereby establishes that a school district can be held liable in damages in cases involving a teacher's sexual harassment of a student; the decision, however, does not purport to define the contours of that liability.

We face that issue squarely in this case. Petitioners, joined by the United States as *amicus curiae*, would invoke standards used by the Courts of Appeals in Title VII cases involving a supervisor's sexual harassment of an employee in the workplace. In support of that approach, they point to a passage in *Franklin* in which we stated: "Unquestionably, Title IX placed on the Gwinnett County Public Schools the duty not to discriminate on the basis of sex, and 'when a supervisor sexually harasses a subordinate because of the subordinate's sex, that supervisor "discriminate[s]" on the basis of sex.' *Meritor Sav. Bank, FSB v. Vinson* (1986). We believe the same rule should apply when a teacher sexually harasses and abuses a student." *Meritor Savings Bank, FSB v. Vinson* directs courts to look to common-law agency principles when assessing an employer's liability under Title VII for sexual harassment of an employee by a supervisor. Petitioners and the United States submit that, in light of *Franklin's* comparison of teacher-student harassment with supervisor-employee harassment, agency principles should likewise apply in Title IX actions.

Specifically, they advance two possible standards under which Lago Vista would be liable for Waldrop's conduct. First, relying on a 1997 "Policy Guidance" issued by the Department of Education, they would hold a school district liable in damages under Title IX where a teacher is " 'aided in carrying out the sexual harassment of students by his or her position of authority with the institution,' " irrespective of whether school district officials had any knowledge of the harassment and irrespective of their response upon becoming aware. [Quoting Dept. of Education, Office of Civil Rights, Sexual Harassment Policy Guidance (1997).] That rule is an expression of *respondeat superior* liability, i.e., vicarious or imputed liability, under which recovery in damages against a school district would generally follow whenever a teacher's authority over a student facilitates the harassment. Second, petitioners and the United States submit that a school district should at a minimum be liable for damages based on a theory of constructive notice, i.e., where the district knew or "should have known" about harassment but failed to uncover and eliminate it. Both standards would allow a damages recovery in a broader range of situations than the rule adopted by the Court of Appeals, which hinges on actual knowledge by a school official with authority to end the harassment.

Whether educational institutions can be said to violate Title IX based solely on principles of *respondeat superior* or constructive notice was not resolved by *Franklin's* citation of *Meritor*. That reference to *Meritor* was made with regard to the general proposition that sexual harassment can constitute discrimination on the basis of sex under Title IX, an issue not in dispute here. In fact, the school district's liability in *Franklin* did not necessarily turn on principles of imputed liability or constructive notice, as there was evidence that school officials knew about the harassment but took no action to stop it. Moreover, *Meritor's* rationale for concluding that agency principles guide the liability inquiry under Title VII rests on an aspect of that statute not found in Title IX: Title VII, in which the prohibition against employment discrimination runs against "an employer," 42 U.S.C. § 2000e-2(a), explicitly defines "employer" to include "any agent," § 2000e(b). Title IX contains no comparable reference to an educational institution's "agents," and so does not expressly call for application of agency principles.

In this case, moreover, petitioners seek not just to establish a Title IX violation but to recover *damages* based on theories of *respondeat superior* and constructive notice. . . . Unlike Title IX, Title VII contains an express cause of action, § 2000e-5(f), and specifically provides for relief in the form of monetary damages, § 1981a. Congress therefore has directly addressed the subject of damages relief under Title VII and has set out the particular situations in which damages are available as well as the maximum amounts recoverable. § 1981a(b). With respect to Title IX, however, the private right of action is judicially implied, and there is thus no legislative expression of the scope of available remedies, including when it is appropriate to award monetary damages. In addition, although the general presumption that courts can award any appropriate relief in an established cause of action, coupled with Congress' abrogation of the States' Eleventh Amendment immunity under Title IX, led us to conclude in *Franklin* that Title IX recognizes a damages remedy, we did so in response to lower court decisions holding that Title IX does not support damages relief at all. We made no effort in *Franklin* to delimit the circumstances in which a damages remedy should lie.

III

Because the private right of action under Title IX is judicially implied, we have a measure of latitude to shape a sensible remedial scheme that best comports with the statute. That endeavor inherently entails a degree of speculation, since it addresses an issue on which Congress has not specifically spoken. To guide the analysis, we generally examine the relevant statute to ensure that we do not fashion the parameters of an implied right in a manner at odds with the statutory structure and purpose.

Those considerations, we think, are pertinent not only to the scope of the implied right, but also to the scope of the available remedies. . . .

Applying those principles here, we conclude that it would "frustrate the purposes" of Title IX to permit a damages recovery against a school district for a teacher's sexual harassment of a student based on principles of *respondeat superior* or constructive notice, i.e., without actual notice to a school district official. [Quoting from *Cannon.*] Because Congress did not expressly create a private right of action under Title IX, the statutory text does not shed light on Congress' intent with respect to the scope of available remedies. Instead, "we attempt to infer how the [1972] Congress would have addressed the issue had the . . . action been included as an express provision in the" statute. *Central Bank of Denver, N. A. v. First Interstate Bank of Denver, N. A.* (1994).

As a general matter, it does not appear that Congress contemplated unlimited recovery in damages against a funding recipient where the recipient is unaware of discrimination in its programs. When Title IX was enacted in 1972, the principal civil rights statutes containing an express right of action did not provide for recovery of monetary damages at all, instead allowing only injunctive and equitable relief. It was not until 1991 that Congress made damages available under Title VII, and even then, Congress carefully limited the amount recoverable in any individual case, calibrating the maximum recovery to the size of the employer. See 42 U. S. C. § 1981a(b)(3). Adopting petitioners' position would amount, then, to allowing unlimited recovery of damages under Title IX where Congress has not spoken on the subject of either the right or the remedy, and in the face of evidence that when Congress expressly considered both in Title VII it restricted the amount of damages available.

Congress enacted Title IX in 1972 with two principal objectives in mind: "to avoid the use of federal resources to support discriminatory practices" and "to provide individual citizens effective protection against those practices." *Cannon*. The statute was modeled after Title VI of the Civil Rights Act of 1964, which is parallel to Title IX except that it prohibits race discrimination, not sex discrimination, and applies in all programs receiving federal funds, not only in education programs. The two statutes operate in the same manner, conditioning an offer of federal funding on a promise by the recipient not to discriminate, in what amounts essentially to a contract between the Government and the recipient of funds.

That contractual framework distinguishes Title IX from Title VII, which is framed in terms not of a condition but of an outright prohibition. Title VII applies to all employers without regard to federal funding and aims broadly to "eradicat[e] discrimination throughout the economy." *Landgraf v. USI Film Products* (1994). Title VII, moreover, seeks to "make persons whole for injuries suffered through past discrimination." Thus, whereas Title VII aims centrally to compensate victims of discrimination, Title IX focuses more on "protecting" individuals from discriminatory practices carried out by recipients of federal funds. That might explain why, when the Court first recognized the implied right under Title IX in *Cannon*, the opinion referred to injunctive or equitable relief in a private action, but not to a damages remedy.

Title IX's contractual nature has implications for our construction of the scope of available remedies. When Congress attaches conditions to the award of federal funds under its spending power, as it has in Title IX and Title VI, we examine closely the propriety of private actions holding the recipient liable in monetary damages for noncompliance with the condition. Our central concern in that regard is with ensuring "that the receiving entity of federal funds [has] notice that it will be liable for a monetary award." *Franklin*. Justice White's opinion announcing the Court's judgment in *Guardians Assn. v. Civil Serv. Comm'n of New York City* [1983], for instance, concluded that the relief in an action under Title VI alleging unintentional discrimination should be prospective only. . . . We confront similar concerns here. If a school district's liability for a teacher's sexual harassment rests on principles of constructive notice or *respondeat superior,* it will likewise be the case that the recipient of funds was unaware of the discrimination. It is sensible to assume that Congress did not envision a recipient's liability in damages in that situation. . . .

Most significantly, Title IX contains important clues that Congress did not intend to allow recovery in damages where liability rests solely on principles of vicarious liability or constructive notice. Title IX's express means of enforcement—by administrative agencies—operates on an assumption of actual notice to officials of the funding recipient. The statute entitles agencies who disburse education funding to enforce their rules implementing the non-discrimination mandate through proceedings to suspend or terminate funding or through "other means authorized by law." 20 U. S. C. § 1682. Significantly, however, an agency may not initiate enforcement proceedings until it "has advised the appropriate person or persons of the failure to comply with the requirement and has determined that compliance cannot be secured by voluntary means." The administrative regulations implement that obligation, requiring resolution of compliance issues "by informal means whenever possible," and prohibiting commencement of enforcement proceedings until the agency has determined that voluntary compliance is unobtainable and "the recipient . . . has been notified of its failure to comply and of the action to be taken to effect compliance."

In the event of a violation, a funding recipient may be required to take "such remedial action as [is] deem[ed] necessary to overcome the effects of [the] discrimination." While agencies have conditioned continued funding on providing equitable relief to the victim, the regulations do not appear to contemplate a condition ordering payment of monetary damages, and there is no indication that payment of damages has been demanded as a condition of finding a recipient to be in compliance with the statute. In *Franklin*, for instance, the Department of Education found a violation of Title IX but determined that the school district came into compliance by virtue of the offending teacher's resignation and the district's institution of a grievance procedure for sexual harassment complaints.

Presumably, a central purpose of requiring notice of the violation "to the appropriate person" and an opportunity for voluntary compliance before administrative enforcement proceedings can commence is to avoid diverting education funding from beneficial uses where a recipient was unaware of discrimination in its programs and is willing to institute prompt corrective measures. The scope of private damages relief proposed by petitioners is at odds with that basic objective. When a teacher's sexual harassment is imputed to a school district or when a school district is deemed to have "constructively" known of the teacher's harassment, by assumption the district had no actual knowledge of the teacher's conduct. Nor, of course, did the district have an opportunity to take action to end the harassment or to limit further harassment.

It would be unsound, we think, for a statute's express system of enforcement to require notice to the recipient and an opportunity to come into voluntary compliance while a judicially *implied* system of enforcement permits substantial liability without regard to the recipient's knowledge or its corrective actions upon receiving notice. . . . Moreover, an award of damages in a particular case might well exceed a recipient's level of federal funding. See Tr. of Oral Arg. (Lago Vista's federal funding for 1992–1993 was roughly $120,000). Where a statute's express enforcement scheme hinges its most severe sanction on notice and unsuccessful efforts to obtain compliance, we cannot attribute to Congress the intention to have implied an enforcement scheme that allows imposition of greater liability without comparable conditions.

IV

Because the express remedial scheme under Title IX is predicated upon notice to an "appropriate person" and an opportunity to rectify any violation, we conclude, in the absence of further direction from Congress, that the implied damages remedy should be fashioned along the same lines. An "appropriate person" . . . is, at a minimum, an official of the recipient entity with authority to take corrective action to end the discrimination. Consequently, in cases like this one that do not involve official policy of the recipient entity, we hold that a damages remedy will not lie under Title IX unless an official who at a minimum has authority to address the alleged discrimination and to institute corrective measures on the recipient's behalf has actual knowledge of discrimination in the recipient's programs and fails adequately to respond.

We think, moreover, that the response must amount to deliberate indifference to discrimination. The administrative enforcement scheme presupposes that an official who is advised of a Title IX violation refuses to take action to bring the recipient into compliance. The premise, in other words, is an official decision by the recipient not to remedy the violation. That framework finds a rough parallel in the standard of deliberate indifference. Under a lower standard, there would be a risk that the recipient would be liable in damages not for its own official decision but instead for its employees' independent actions. Comparable considerations led to our adoption of a deliberate indifference standard for claims under § 1983 alleging that a municipality's actions in failing to prevent a deprivation of federal rights was the cause of the violation.

Applying the framework to this case is fairly straightforward, as petitioners do not contend they can prevail under an actual notice standard. The only official alleged to have had information about Waldrop's misconduct is the high school principal. That information, however, consisted of a complaint from parents of other students charging only that Waldrop had made inappropriate comments during class, which was plainly insufficient to alert the principal to the possibility that Waldrop was involved in a sexual relationship with a student. Lago Vista, moreover, terminated Waldrop's employment upon learning of his relationship with Gebser. JUSTICE STEVENS points out in his dissenting opinion that Waldrop of course had knowledge of his own actions. Where a school district's liability rests on actual notice principles, however, the knowledge of the wrongdoer himself is not pertinent to the analysis.

Petitioners focus primarily on Lago Vista's asserted failure to promulgate and publicize an effective policy and grievance procedure for sexual harassment claims. They point to Department of Education regulations requiring each funding recipient to "adopt and publish grievance procedures providing for prompt and equitable resolution" of discrimination complaints, and to notify students and others "that it does not discriminate on the basis of sex in the educational programs or activities which it operates." Lago Vista's alleged failure to comply with the regulations, however, does not establish the requisite actual notice and deliberate indifference. And in any event, the failure to promulgate a grievance procedure does not itself constitute "discrimination" under Title IX. Of course, the Department of Education could enforce the requirement administratively: Agencies generally have authority to promulgate and enforce requirements that effectuate the statute's non-discrimination mandate, even if those requirements do not purport to represent a definition of discrimination under the statute. . . . We have never held, however, that the implied private right of action under Title IX allows recovery in damages for violation of those sorts of administrative requirements.

V

The number of reported cases involving sexual harassment of students in schools confirms that harassment unfortunately is an all too common aspect of the educational experience. No one questions that a student suffers extraordinary harm when subjected to sexual harassment and abuse by a teacher, and that the teacher's conduct is reprehensible and undermines the basic purposes of the educational system. The issue in this case, however, is whether the independent misconduct of a teacher is attributable to the school district that employs him under a specific federal statute designed primarily to prevent recipients of federal financial assistance from using the funds in a discriminatory manner. Our decision does not affect any right of recovery that an individual may have against a school district as a matter of state law or against the teacher in his individual capacity under state law or under 42 U. S. C. § 1983. Until Congress speaks directly on the subject, however, we will not hold a school district liable in damages under Title IX for a teacher's sexual harassment of a student absent actual notice and deliberate indifference. We therefore affirm the judgment of the Court of Appeals.

It is so ordered.

JUSTICE STEVENS, with whom JUSTICE SOUTER, JUSTICE GINSBURG, and JUSTICE BREYER join, dissenting.

The question that the petition for certiorari asks us to address is whether the Lago Vista Independent School District (respondent) is liable in damages for a violation of Title IX of the Education Amendments of 1972, 20 U. S. C. § 1681 *et seq.* (Title IX). The Court provides us with a negative answer to that question because respondent did not have actual notice of, and was not deliberately indifferent to, the odious misconduct of one of its teachers. As a basis for its decision, the majority relies heavily on the notion that because the private cause of action under Title IX is "judicially implied," the Court has "a measure of latitude" to use its own judgment in shaping a remedial scheme. This assertion of lawmaking authority is not faithful either to our precedents or to our duty to interpret, rather than to revise, congressional commands. Moreover, the majority's policy judgment about the appropriate remedy in this case thwarts the purposes of Title IX.

I

It is important to emphasize that in *Cannon v. University of Chicago* (1979), the Court confronted a question of statutory construction. The decision represented our considered judgment about the intent of the Congress that enacted Title IX in 1972. After noting that Title IX had been patterned after Title VI of the Civil Rights Act of 1964, which had been interpreted to include a private right of action, we concluded that Congress intended to authorize the same private enforcement of Title IX. As long as the intent of Congress is clear, an implicit command has the same legal force as one that is explicit. . . .

In *Franklin v. Gwinnett County Public Schools* (1992), we unanimously concluded that Title IX authorized a high school student who had been sexually harassed by a sports coach/teacher to recover damages from the school district. . . .

Because these constructions of the statute have been accepted by Congress and are unchallenged here, they have the same legal effect as if the private cause of action seeking damages had been explicitly, rather than implicitly, authorized by Congress. We should therefore seek guidance from the text of the statute and settled legal principles rather than from our views about sound policy.

II

We have already noted that the text of Title IX should be accorded " 'a sweep as broad as its language.' " *North Haven Bd. of Ed. v. Bell* (1982). That sweep is broad indeed. "No person . . . shall, on the basis of sex, . . . be subjected to discrimination under any education program or activity receiving Federal financial assistance. . . ." 20 U. S. C. § 1681(a). . . . [T]he use of passive verbs in Title IX, focusing on the victim of the discrimination rather than the particular wrongdoer, gives this statute broader coverage than Title VII. Moreover, because respondent assumed the statutory duty set out in Title IX as part of its consideration for the receipt of federal funds, that duty constitutes an affirmative undertaking that is more significant than a mere promise to obey the law.

Both of these considerations are reflected in our decision in *Franklin*. Explaining why Title IX is violated when a teacher sexually abuses a student, we wrote:

> "Unquestionably, Title IX placed on the Gwinnett County Public Schools the duty not to discriminate on the basis of sex, and 'when a supervisor sexually harasses a subordinate because of the subordinate's sex, that supervisor "discriminate[s]" on the basis of sex.' *Meritor Sav. Bank, FSB v. Vinson* (1986). We believe the same rule should apply when a teacher sexually harasses and abuses a student. *Congress surely did not intend for federal moneys to be expended to support the intentional actions it sought by statute to proscribe.*" (emphasis added).

Franklin therefore stands for the proposition that sexual harassment of a student by her teacher violates the duty—assumed by the school district in exchange for federal funds—not to discriminate on the basis of sex, and that a student may recover damages from a school district for such a violation.

Although the opinion the Court announces today is not entirely clear, it does not purport to overrule *Franklin*. Moreover, I do not understand the Court to question the conclusion that an intentional violation of Title IX, of the type we recognized in *Franklin*, has been alleged in this case. During her freshman and sophomore years of high school, petitioner Alida Star Gebser was repeatedly subjected to sexual abuse by her teacher, Frank Waldrop, whom she had met in the eighth grade when she joined his high school book discussion group. Waldrop's conduct was surely intentional and it occurred during, and as a part of, a curriculum activity in which he wielded authority over Gebser that had been delegated to him by respondent. Moreover, it is undisputed that the activity was subsidized, in part, with federal moneys.

The Court nevertheless holds that the law does not provide a damages remedy for the Title IX violation alleged in this case because no official of the school district with "authority to institute corrective measures on the district's behalf" had actual notice of Waldrop's misconduct. That holding is at odds with settled principles of agency law, under which the district is responsible for Waldrop's misconduct because "he was aided in accomplishing the tort by the existence of the agency relation." Restatement (Second) of Agency, § 219(2)(d). This case presents a paradigmatic example of a tort that was made possible, that was effected, and that was repeated over a prolonged period because of the powerful influence that Waldrop had over Gebser by reason of the authority that his employer, the school district, had delegated to him. As a secondary school teacher, Waldrop exercised even greater authority and control over his students than employers and supervisors exercise over their employees. His gross misuse of that authority allowed him to abuse his young student's trust.

Reliance on the principle set out in § 219(2)(b) of the Restatement comports with the relevant agency's interpretation of Title IX. The United States Department of Education, through its Office for Civil Rights, recently issued a policy "Guidance" stating that a school district is liable under Title IX if one of its teachers "was aided in carrying out the sexual harassment of students by his or her position of authority with the institution." Dept. of Ed., Office for Civil Rights, Sexual Harassment Guidance: Harassment of Students by School Employees, Other Students, or Third Parties (1997). As the agency charged with administering and enforcing Title IX, the Department of Education has a special interest in ensuring that federal funds are not used in contravention of Title IX's mandate. It is therefore significant that the Department's interpretation of the statute wholly supports the conclusion that respondent is liable in damages for Waldrop's sexual abuse of his student, which was made possible only by Waldrop's affirmative misuse of his authority as her teacher.

The reason why the common law imposes liability on the principal in such circumstances is the same as the reason why Congress included the prohibition against discrimination on the basis of sex in Title IX: to induce school boards to adopt and enforce practices that will minimize the danger that vulnerable students will be exposed to such odious behavior. The rule that the Court has crafted creates the opposite incentive. As long as school boards can insulate themselves from knowledge about this sort of conduct, they can claim immunity from damages liability. Indeed, the rule that the Court adopts would preclude a damages remedy even if every teacher at the school knew about the harassment but did not have "authority to institute corrective measures on the district's behalf." It is not my function to determine whether this newly fashioned rule is wiser than the established common-law rule. It is proper, however, to suggest that the Court bears the burden of justifying its rather dramatic departure from settled law, and to explain why its opinion fails to shoulder that burden.

III

The Court advances several reasons why it would "frustrate the purposes" of Title IX to allow recovery against a school district that does not have actual notice of a teacher's sexual harassment of a student. As the Court acknowledges, however, the two principal purposes that motivated the enactment of Title IX were: (1) " 'to avoid the use of federal resources to support discriminatory practices' "; and (2) " 'to provide individual citizens effective protection against those practices.' " (quoting *Cannon*). It seems quite obvious that both of those purposes would be served—not frustrated—by providing a damages remedy in a case of this kind. To the extent that the Court's reasons for its policy choice have any merit, they suggest that no damages should ever be awarded in a Title IX case—in other words, that our unanimous holding in *Franklin* should be repudiated.

First, the Court observes that at the time Title IX was enacted, "the principal civil rights statutes containing an express right of action did not provide for recovery of monetary damages at all." *Franklin,* however, forecloses this reevaluation of legislative intent; in that case, we "evaluate[d] the state of the law when the Legislature passed Title IX" and concluded that "the same contextual approach used to justify an implied right of action more than amply demonstrates the lack of any legislative intent to abandon the traditional presumption in favor of all available remedies." The Court also suggests that the fact that Congress has imposed a ceiling on the amount of damages that may be recovered in Title VII cases, see 42 U. S. C. § 1981a, is somehow relevant to the question whether any damages at all may be awarded in a Title IX case. The short answer to this creative argument is that the Title VII ceiling does not have any bearing on when damages may be recovered from a defendant in a Title IX case. Moreover, this case does not present any issue concerning the amount of any possible damages award.

Second, the Court suggests that the school district did not have fair notice when it accepted federal funding that it might be held liable " 'for a monetary award' " under Title IX. The Court cannot mean, however, that respondent was not on notice that sexual harassment of a student by a teacher constitutes an "intentional" violation of Title IX for which damages are available, because we so held shortly before Waldrop began abusing Gebser. Given the fact that our holding in *Franklin* was unanimous, it is not unreasonable to assume that it could have been foreseen by counsel for the recipients of Title IX funds. Moreover, the nondiscrimination requirement set out in Title IX is clear, and this Court held that sexual harassment constitutes intentional sex discrimination long before the sexual abuse in this case began. Normally, of course, we presume that the citizen has knowledge of the law.

The majority nevertheless takes the position that a school district that accepts federal funds under Title IX should not be held liable in damages for an intentional violation of that statute if the district itself "was unaware of the discrimination." The Court reasons that because administrative proceedings to terminate funding cannot be commenced until after the grant recipient has received notice of its noncompliance and the agency determines that voluntary compliance is not possible, there should be no damages liability unless the grant recipient has actual notice of the violation (and thus an opportunity to end the harassment).

The fact that Congress has specified a particular administrative procedure to be followed when a subsidy is to be terminated, however, does not illuminate the question of what the victim of discrimination on the basis of sex must prove in order to recover damages in an implied private right of action. Indeed, in *Franklin*, we noted that the Department of Education's Office of Civil Rights had declined to terminate federal funding of the school district at issue—despite its finding that a Title IX violation had occurred—because "the district had come into compliance with Title IX" after the harassment at issue. That fact did not affect the Court's analysis, much less persuade the Court that a damages remedy was unavailable. . . .

The majority's inappropriate reliance on Title IX's administrative enforcement scheme to limit the availability of a damages remedy leads the Court to require not only actual knowledge on the part of "an official who at a minimum has authority to address the alleged discrimination and to institute corrective measures on the recipient's behalf," but also that official's "refus[al] to take action," or "deliberate indifference" toward the harassment. Presumably, few Title IX plaintiffs who have been victims of intentional discrimination will be able to recover damages under this exceedingly high standard. The Court fails to recognize that its holding will virtually "render inutile causes of action authorized by Congress through a decision that no remedy is available." *Franklin*.

IV

We are not presented with any question concerning the affirmative defenses that might eliminate or mitigate the recovery of damages for a Title IX violation. It has been argued, for example, that a school district that has adopted and vigorously enforced a policy that is designed to prevent sexual harassment and redress the harms that such conduct may produce should be exonerated from damages liability. The Secretary of Education has promulgated regulations directing grant recipients to adopt such policies and disseminate them to students. A rule providing an affirmative defense for districts that adopt and publish such policies pursuant to the regulations would not likely be helpful to respondent, however, because it is not at all clear whether respondent adopted any such policy, and there is no evidence that such a policy was made available to students, as required by regulation.

A theme that seems to underlie the Court's opinion is a concern that holding a school district liable in damages might deprive it of the benefit of the federal subsidy—that the damages remedy is somehow more onerous than a possible termination of the federal grant. . . . It is possible, of course, that in some cases the recoverable damages, in either a Title IX action or a state-law tort action, would exceed the amount of a federal grant. That is surely not relevant to the question whether the school district or the injured student should bear the risk of harm—a risk against which the district, but not the student, can insure. It is not clear to me why the well-settled rules of law that impose responsibility on the principal for the misconduct of its agents should not apply in this case. As a matter of policy, the Court ranks protection of the school district's purse above the protection of immature high school students that those rules would provide. Because those students are members of the class for whose special benefit Congress enacted Title IX, that policy choice is not faithful to the intent of the policymaking branch of our Government.

I respectfully dissent.

JUSTICE GINSBURG, with whom JUSTICE SOUTER and JUSTICE BREYER join, dissenting.

JUSTICE STEVENS' opinion focuses on the standard of school district liability for teacher-on-student harassment in secondary schools. I join that opinion, which reserves the question whether a district should be relieved from damages liability if it has in place, and effectively publicizes and enforces, a policy to curtail and redress injuries caused by sexual harassment. I think it appropriate to answer that question. . . .

In line with the tort law doctrine of avoidable consequences, I would recognize as an affirmative defense to a Title IX charge of sexual harassment, an effective policy for reporting and redressing such misconduct. . . .

The burden would be the school district's to show that its internal remedies were adequately publicized and likely would have provided redress without exposing the complainant to undue risk, effort, or expense. Under such a regime, to the extent that a plaintiff unreasonably failed to avail herself of the school district's preventive and remedial measures, and consequently suffered avoidable harm, she would not qualify for Title IX relief.

No. 97-156

Randon Bragdon, Petitioner v. Sidney Abbott et al.

On writ of certiorari to the United States Court of Appeals for the First Circuit

[June 25, 1998]

JUSTICE KENNEDY delivered the opinion of the Court.

We address in this case the application of the Americans with Disabilities Act of 1990 (ADA), 42 U. S. C. § 12101 *et seq.,* to persons infected with the human immunodeficiency virus (HIV). We granted certiorari to review, first, whether HIV infection is a disability under the ADA when the infection has not yet progressed to the so-called symptomatic phase; and, second, whether the Court of Appeals, in affirming a grant of summary judgment, cited sufficient material in the record to determine, as a matter of law, that respondent's infection with HIV posed no direct threat to the health and safety of her treating dentist.

I

Respondent Sidney Abbott has been infected with HIV since 1986. When the incidents we recite occurred, her infection had not manifested its most serious symptoms. On September 16, 1994, she went to the office of petitioner Randon Bragdon in Bangor, Maine, for a dental appointment. She disclosed her HIV infection on the patient registration form. Petitioner completed a dental examination, discovered a cavity, and informed respondent of his policy against filling cavities of HIV-infected patients. He offered to perform the work at a hospital with no added fee for his services, though respondent would be responsible for the cost of using the hospital's facilities. Respondent declined.

Respondent sued petitioner under state law and § 302 of the ADA, 42 U. S. C. § 12182, alleging discrimination on the basis of her disability. The state law claims are not before us. Section 302 of the ADA provides:

"No individual shall be discriminated against on the basis of disability in the full and equal enjoyment of the goods, services, facilities, privileges, advantages, or accommodations of any place of public accommodation by any person who . . . operates a place of public accommodation." § 12182(a).

The term "public accommodation" is defined to include the "professional office of a health care provider." § 12181(7)(F).

A later subsection qualifies the mandate not to discriminate. It provides:

"Nothing in this subchapter shall require an entity to permit an individual to participate in or benefit from the goods, services, facilities, privileges, advantages and accommodations of such entity where such individual poses a direct threat to the health or safety of others." § 12182(b)(3).

The United States and the Maine Human Rights Commission intervened as plaintiffs. After discovery, the parties filed cross-motions for summary judgment. The District Court ruled in favor of the plaintiffs, holding that respondent's HIV infection satisfied the ADA's definition of disability. (Me. 1995). The court held further that petitioner raised no genuine issue of material fact as to whether respondent's HIV infection would have posed a direct threat to the health or safety of others during the course of a dental treatment. The court relied on affidavits submitted by Dr. Donald Wayne Marianos, Director of the Division of Oral Health of the Centers for Disease Control and Prevention (CDC). The Marianos affidavits asserted it is safe for dentists to treat patients infected with HIV in dental offices if the dentist follows the so-called universal precautions described in the Recommended Infection-Control Practices for Dentistry issued by CDC in 1993.

The Court of Appeals affirmed. It held respondent's HIV infection was a disability under the ADA, even though her infection had not yet progressed to the symptomatic stage. (CA1 1997). The Court of Appeals also agreed that treating the respondent in petitioner's office would not have posed a direct threat to the health and safety of others. Unlike the District Court, however, the Court of Appeals declined to rely on the Marianos affidavits. Instead the court relied on the 1993 CDC Dentistry Guidelines, as well as the Policy on AIDS, HIV Infection and the Practice of Dentistry, promulgated by the American Dental Association in 1991.

II

We first review the ruling that respondent's HIV infection constituted a disability under the ADA. The statute defines disability as:

"(A) a physical or mental impairment that substantially limits one or more of the major life activities of such individual;

"(B) a record of such an impairment; or

"(C) being regarded as having such impairment." § 12102(2).

We hold respondent's HIV infection was a disability under subsection (A) of the definitional section of the statute. In light of this conclusion, we need not consider the applicability of subsections (B) or (C).

Our consideration of subsection (A) of the definition proceeds in three steps. First, we consider whether respondent's HIV infection was a physical impairment. Second, we identify the life activity upon which respondent relies (reproduction and child bearing) and determine whether it constitutes a major life activity under the ADA. Third, tying the two statutory phrases together, we ask whether the impairment substantially limited the major life activity. In construing the statute, we are informed by interpretations of parallel definitions in previous statutes and the views of various administrative agencies which have faced this interpretive question.

A

The ADA's definition of disability is drawn almost verbatim from the definition of "handicapped individual" included in the Rehabilitation Act of 1973, 29 U. S. C. § 706(8)(B), and the definition of "handicap" contained in the Fair Housing Amendments Act of 1988, 42 U. S. C. § 3602(h)(1). Congress' repetition of a well-established term carries the implication that Congress intended the term to be construed in accordance with pre-existing regulatory interpretations. In this case, Congress did more than suggest this construction; it adopted a specific statutory provision in the ADA directing as follows:

"Except as otherwise provided in this chapter, nothing in this chapter shall be construed to apply a lesser standard than the standards applied under title V of the Rehabilitation Act of 1973 (29 U. S. C. 790 *et seq.*) or the regulations issued by Federal agencies pursuant to such title." 42 U. S. C. § 12201(a).

The directive requires us to construe the ADA to grant at least as much protection as provided by the regulations implementing the Rehabilitation Act.

1

The first step in the inquiry under subsection (A) requires us to determine whether respondent's condition constituted a physical impairment. The Department of Health, Education and Welfare (HEW) issued the first regulations interpreting the Rehabilitation Act in 1977. The regulations are of particular significance because, at the time, HEW was the agency responsible for coordinating the implementation and enforcement of § 504. The HEW regulations, which appear without change in the current regulations issued by the Department of Health and Human Services, define "physical or mental impairment" to mean:

"(A) any physiological disorder or condition, cosmetic disfigurement, or anatomical loss affecting one or more of the following body systems: neurological; musculoskeletal; special sense organs; respiratory, including speech organs; cardiovascular; reproductive, digestive, genito-urinary; hemic and lymphatic; skin; and endocrine; or

"(B) any mental or psychological disorder, such as mental retardation, organic brain syndrome, emotional or mental illness, and specific learning disabilities." 45 CFR § 84.3(j)(2)(i) (1997).

In issuing these regulations, HEW decided against including a list of disorders constituting physical or mental impairments, out of concern that any specific enumeration might not be comprehensive. The commentary accompanying the regulations, however, contains a representative list of disorders and conditions constituting physical impairments, including "such diseases and conditions as orthopedic, visual, speech, and hearing impairments, cerebral palsy, epilepsy, muscular dystrophy, multiple sclerosis, cancer, heart disease, diabetes, mental retardation, emotional illness, and . . . drug addiction and alcoholism."

In 1980, the President transferred responsibility for the implementation and enforcement of § 504 to the Attorney General. The regulations issued by the Justice Department, which remain in force to this day, adopted verbatim the HEW definition of physical impairment quoted above. In addition, the representative list of diseases and conditions originally relegated to the commentary accompanying the HEW regulations were incorporated into the text of the regulations.

HIV infection is not included in the list of specific disorders constituting physical impairments, in part because HIV was not identified as the cause of AIDS until 1983. [Medical citations omitted.] HIV infection does fall well within the general definition set forth by the regulations, however.

The disease follows a predictable and, as of today, an unalterable course. Once a person is infected with HIV, the virus invades different cells in the blood and in body tissues. Certain white blood cells, known as helper T-lymphocytes or CD4+

cells, are particularly vulnerable to HIV. The virus attaches to the CD4 receptor site of the target cell and fuses its membrane to the cell's membrane. HIV is a retrovirus, which means it uses an enzyme to convert its own genetic material into a form indistinguishable from the genetic material of the target cell. The virus' genetic material migrates to the cell's nucleus and becomes integrated with the cell's chromosomes. Once integrated, the virus can use the cell's own genetic machinery to replicate itself. Additional copies of the virus are released into the body and infect other cells in turn. Although the body does produce antibodies to combat HIV infection, the antibodies are not effective in eliminating the virus.

The virus eventually kills the infected host cell. CD4+ cells play a critical role in coordinating the body's immune response system, and the decline in their number causes corresponding deterioration of the body's ability to fight infections from many sources. Tracking the infected individual's CD4+ cell count is one of the most accurate measures of the course of the disease.

The initial stage of HIV infection is known as acute or primary HIV infection. In a typical case, this stage lasts three months. The virus concentrates in the blood. The assault on the immune system is immediate. The victim suffers from a sudden and serious decline in the number of white blood cells. There is no latency period. Mononucleosis-like symptoms often emerge between six days and six weeks after infection, at times accompanied by fever, headache, enlargement of the lymph nodes (lymphadenopathy), muscle pain (myalgia), rash, lethargy, gastrointestinal disorders, and neurological disorders. Usually these symptoms abate within 14 to 21 days. HIV antibodies appear in the bloodstream within 3 weeks; circulating HIV can be detected within 10 weeks.

After the symptoms associated with the initial stage subside, the disease enters what is referred to sometimes as its asymptomatic phase. The term is a misnomer, in some respects, for clinical features persist throughout, including lymphadenopathy, dermatological disorders, oral lesions, and bacterial infections. Although it varies with each individual, in most instances this stage lasts from 7 to 11 years. The virus now tends to concentrate in the lymph nodes, though low levels of the virus continue to appear in the blood. It was once thought the virus became inactive during this period, but it is now known that the relative lack of symptoms is attributable to the virus' migration from the circulatory system into the lymph nodes. The migration reduces the viral presence in other parts of the body, with a corresponding diminution in physical manifestations of the disease. The virus, however, thrives in the lymph nodes, which, as a vital point of the body's immune response system, represents an ideal environment for the infection of other CD4+ cells. Studies have shown that viral production continues at a high rate. CD4+ cells continue to decline an average of 5% to 10% (40 to 80 cells/mm3) per year throughout this phase.

A person is regarded as having AIDS when his or her CD4+ count drops below 200 cells/mm3 of blood or when CD4+ cells comprise less than 14% of his or her total lymphocytes. During this stage, the clinical conditions most often associated with HIV, such as *pneumocystis carninii* pneumonia, Kaposi's sarcoma, and non-Hodgkins lymphoma, tend to appear. In addition, the general systemic disorders present during all stages of the disease, such as fever, weight loss, fatigue, lesions, nausea, and diarrhea, tend to worsen. In most cases, once the patient's CD4+ count drops below 10 cells/mm3, death soon follows.

In light of the immediacy with which the virus begins to damage the infected person's white blood cells and the severity of the disease, we hold it is an impairment from the moment of infection. As noted earlier, infection with HIV causes immediate abnormalities in a person's blood, and the infected person's white cell count continues to drop throughout the course of the disease, even when the attack is concentrated in the lymph nodes. In light of these facts, HIV infection must be regarded as a physiological disorder with a constant and detrimental effect on the infected person's hemic and lymphatic systems from the moment of infection. HIV infection satisfies the statutory and regulatory definition of a physical impairment during every stage of the disease.

2

The statute is not operative, and the definition not satisfied, unless the impairment affects a major life activity. Respondent's claim throughout this case has been that the HIV infection placed a substantial limitation on her ability to reproduce and to bear children. Given the pervasive, and invariably fatal, course of the disease, its effect on major life activities of many sorts might have been relevant to our inquiry. Respondent and a number of *amici* make arguments about HIV's profound impact on almost every phase of the infected person's life. In light of these submissions, it may seem legalistic to circumscribe our discussion to the activity of reproduction. We have little doubt that had different parties brought the suit they would have maintained that an HIV infection imposes substantial limitations on other major life activities.

From the outset, however, the case has been treated as one in which reproduction was the major life activity limited by the impairment. It is our practice to decide cases on the grounds raised and considered in the Court of Appeals and included in the question on which we granted certiorari. We ask, then, whether reproduction is a major life activity.

We have little difficulty concluding that it is. As the Court of Appeals held, "[t]he plain meaning of the word 'major' denotes comparative importance" and "suggest[s] that the touchstone for determining an activity's inclusion under the statutory rubric is its significance." Reproduction falls well within the phrase "major life activity." Reproduction and the sexual dynamics surrounding it are central to the life process itself.

While petitioner concedes the importance of reproduction, he claims that Congress intended the ADA only to cover those aspects of a person's life which have a public, economic, or daily character. The argument founders on the statutory language. Nothing in the definition suggests that activities without a public, economic, or daily dimension may somehow be regarded as so unimportant or insignificant as to fall outside the meaning of the word "major." The breadth of the term confounds the attempt to limit its construction in this manner.

As we have noted, the ADA must be construed to be consistent with regulations issued to implement the Rehabilitation Act. Rather than enunciating a general principle for determining what is and is not a major life activity, the Rehabilitation Act regulations instead provide a representative list, defining term to include "functions such as caring for one's self, performing manual tasks, walking, seeing, hearing, speaking, breathing, learning, and working." As the use of the term "such as" confirms, the list is illustrative, not exhaustive.

These regulations are contrary to petitioner's attempt to limit the meaning of the term "major" to public activities. The inclusion of activities such as caring for one's self and performing manual tasks belies the suggestion that a task must have a public or economic character in order to be a major life activity for purposes of the ADA. On the contrary, the Rehabilitation Act regulations support the inclusion of reproduction as a major life activity, since reproduction could not be regarded as any less important than working and learning. Petitioner advances no credible basis for confining major life activities to those with a public, economic, or daily aspect. In the absence of any reason to reach a contrary conclusion, we agree with the Court of Appeals' determination that reproduction is a major life activity for the purposes of the ADA.

3

The final element of the disability definition in subsection (A) is whether respondent's physical impairment was a substantial limit on the major life activity she asserts. The Rehabilitation Act regulations provide no additional guidance.

Our evaluation of the medical evidence leads us to conclude that respondent's infection substantially limited her ability to reproduce in two independent ways. First, a woman infected with HIV who tries to conceive a child imposes on the man a significant risk of becoming infected. The cumulative results of 13 studies collected in a 1994 textbook on AIDS indicates that 20% of male partners of women with HIV became HIV-positive themselves, with a majority of the studies finding a statistically significant risk of infection.

Second, an infected woman risks infecting her child during gestation and childbirth, i.e., perinatal transmission. Petitioner concedes that women infected with HIV face about a 25% risk of transmitting the virus to their children. Published reports available in 1994 confirm the accuracy of this statistic. . . .

Petitioner points to evidence in the record suggesting that antiretroviral therapy can lower the risk of perinatal transmission to about 8%. The Solicitor General questions the relevance of the 8% figure, pointing to regulatory language requiring the substantiality of a limitation to be assessed without regard to available mitigating measures. We need not resolve this dispute in order to decide this case, however. It cannot be said as a matter of law that an 8% risk of transmitting a dread and fatal disease to one's child does not represent a substantial limitation on reproduction.

The Act addresses substantial limitations on major life activities, not utter inabilities. Conception and childbirth are not impossible for an HIV victim but, without doubt, are dangerous to the public health. This meets the definition of a substantial limitation. The decision to reproduce carries economic and legal consequences as well. There are added costs for antiretroviral therapy, supplemental insurance, and long-term health care for the child who must be examined and, tragic to think, treated for the infection. The laws of some States, moreover, forbid persons infected with HIV from having sex with others, regardless of consent. [Citations omitted.]

In the end, the disability definition does not turn on personal choice. When significant limitations result from the impairment, the definition is met even if the difficulties are not insurmountable. For the statistical and other reasons we have cited, of course, the limitations on reproduction may be insurmountable here. Testimony from the respondent that her HIV infection controlled her decision not to have a child is unchallenged. In the context of reviewing summary judgment, we must take it to be true. We agree with the District Court and the Court of Appeals that no triable issue of fact impedes a ruling on the question of statutory coverage. Respondent's HIV infection is a physical impairment which substantially limits a major life activity, as the ADA defines it. In view of our holding, we need not address the second question presented, i.e., whether HIV infection is a *per se* disability under the ADA.

B

Our holding is confirmed by a consistent course of agency interpretation before and after enactment of the ADA. Every agency to consider the issue under the Rehabilitation Act found statutory coverage for persons with asymptomatic HIV. [Summary and excerpt of 1988 legal opinion by Justice Department's Office of Legal Counsel omitted.]

Every court which addressed the issue before the ADA was enacted in July 1990, moreover, concluded that asymptomatic HIV infection satisfied the Rehabilitation Act's definition of a handicap. [Citations omitted.]

Had Congress done nothing more than copy the Rehabilitation Act definition into the ADA, its action would indicate the new statute should be construed in light of this unwavering line of administrative and judicial interpretation. All indications are that Congress was well aware of the position taken by [the Justice Department's Office of Legal Counsel] when enacting the ADA and intended to give that position its active endorsement. . . .

We find the uniformity of the administrative and judicial precedent construing the definition significant. When administrative and judicial interpretations have settled the meaning of an existing statutory provision, repetition of the same language in a new statute indicates, as a general matter, the intent to incorporate its administrative and judicial interpretations as well. The uniform body of administrative and judicial precedent confirms the conclusion we reach today as the most faithful way to effect the congressional design.

C

Our conclusion is further reinforced by the administrative guidance issued by the Justice Department to implement the public accommodation provisions of Title III of the ADA. . . .

The Justice Department's interpretation of the definition of disability is consistent with our analysis. The regulations acknowledge that Congress intended the ADA's definition of disability to be given the same construction as the definition of handicap in the Rehabilitation Act. The regulatory definition developed by HEW to implement the Rehabilitation Act is incorporated verbatim in the ADA regulations. The Justice Department went further, however. It added "HIV infection (symptomatic and asymptomatic)" to the list of disorders constituting a physical impairment. The technical assistance the Department has issued pursuant to 42 U. S. C. § 12206 similarly concludes that persons with asymptomatic HIV infection fall within the ADA's definition of disability. Any other conclusion, the Department reasoned, would contradict Congress' affirmative ratification of the administrative interpretations given previous versions of the same definition. . . .

The regulatory authorities we cite are consistent with our holding that HIV infection, even in the so-called asymptomatic phase, is an impairment which substantially limits the major life activity of reproduction.

III

The petition for certiorari presented three other questions for review. The questions stated:

"3. When deciding under title III of the ADA whether a private health care provider must perform invasive procedures on an infectious patient in his office, should courts defer to the health care provider's professional judgment, as long as it is reasonable in light of then-current medical knowledge?

"4. What is the proper standard of judicial review under title III of the ADA of a private health care provider's judgment that the performance of certain invasive procedures in his office would pose a direct threat to the health or safety of others?

"5. Did petitioner, Randon Bragdon, D. M. D., raise a genuine issue of fact for trial as to whether he was warranted in his judgment that the performance of certain invasive procedures on a patient in his office would have posed a direct threat to the health or safety of others?" Pet. for Cert. i.

Of these, we granted certiorari only on question three. The question is phrased in an awkward way, for it conflates two separate inquiries. In asking whether it is appropriate to defer to petitioner's judgment, it assumes that petitioner's assessment of the objective facts was reasonable. The central premise of the question and the assumption on which it is based merit separate consideration.

Again, we begin with the statute. Notwithstanding the protection given respondent by the ADA's definition of disability, petitioner could have refused to treat her if her infectious condition "pose[d] a direct threat to the health or safety of others." 42 U. S. C. § 12182(b)(3). The ADA defines a direct threat to be "a significant risk to the health or safety of others that cannot be eliminated by a modification of policies, practices, or procedures or by the provision of auxiliary aids or services." Parallel provisions appear in the employment provisions of Title I. § § 12111(3), 12113(b).

The ADA's direct threat provision stems from the recognition in *School Bd. of Nassau Cty. v. Arline* (1987) of the importance of prohibiting discrimination against individuals with disabilities while protecting others from significant health and safety risks, resulting, for instance, from a contagious disease. In *Arline,* the Court reconciled these objectives by construing the Rehabilitation Act not to require the hiring of a person who posed "a significant risk of communicating an infectious disease to others." Congress amended the Rehabilitation Act and the Fair Housing Act to incorporate the language. It later relied on the same language in enacting the ADA. Because few, if any, activities in life are risk free, *Arline* and the ADA do not ask whether a risk exists, but whether it is significant.

The existence, or nonexistence, of a significant risk must be determined from the standpoint of the person who refuses the treatment or accommodation, and the risk assessment must be based on medical or other objective evidence. As a health care professional, petitioner had the duty to assess the risk of infection based on the objective, scientific information available to him and others in his profession. His belief that a significant risk existed, even if maintained in good faith, would not relieve him from liability. To use the words of the question presented, petitioner receives no special deference simply because he is a health care professional. . . .

Our conclusion that courts should assess the objective reasonableness of the views of health care professionals without deferring to their individual judgments does not answer the implicit assumption in the question presented, whether petitioner's actions were reasonable in light of the available medical evidence. In assessing the reasonableness of petitioner's actions, the views of public health authorities, such as the U. S. Public Health Service, CDC, and the National Institutes of Health, are of special weight and authority. The views of these organizations are not conclusive, however. A health care professional who disagrees with the prevailing medical consensus may refute it by citing a credible scientific basis for deviating from the accepted norm.

We have reviewed so much of the record as necessary to illustrate the application of the rule to the facts of this case. For the most part, the Court of Appeals followed the proper standard in evaluating the petitioner's position and conducted a thorough review of the evidence. Its rejection of the District Court's reliance on the Marianos affidavits was a correct application of the principle that petitioner's actions must be evaluated in light of the available, objective evidence. The record did not show that CDC had published the conclusion set out in the affidavits at the time petitioner refused to treat respondent.

A further illustration of a correct application of the objective standard is the Court of Appeals' refusal to give weight to the petitioner's offer to treat respondent in a hospital. Petitioner testified that he believed hospitals had safety measures, such as air filtration, ultraviolet lights, and respirators, which would reduce the risk of HIV transmission. Petitioner made no showing, however, that any area hospital had these safeguards or even that he had hospital privileges. His expert also admitted the lack of any scientific basis for the conclusion that these measures would lower the risk of transmission. Petitioner failed to present any objective, medical evidence showing that treating respondent in a hospital would be safer or more efficient in preventing HIV transmission than treatment in a well-equipped dental office.

We are concerned, however, that the Court of Appeals might have placed mistaken reliance upon two other sources. In ruling no triable issue of fact existed on this point, the Court of Appeals relied on the 1993 CDC Dentistry Guidelines and the 1991 American Dental Association Policy on HIV. This evidence is not definitive. . . . The Guidelines set out CDC's recommendation that the universal precautions are the best way to combat the risk of HIV transmission. They do not assess the level of risk.

Nor can we be certain, on this record, whether the 1991 American Dental Association Policy on HIV carries the weight the Court of Appeals attributed to it. The Policy does provide some evidence of the medical community's objective assessment of the risks posed by treating people infected with HIV in dental offices. It indicates:

> "Current scientific and epidemiologic evidence indicates that there is little risk of transmission of infectious diseases through dental treatment if recommended infection control procedures are routinely followed. Patients with HIV infection may be safely treated in private dental offices when appropriate infection control procedures are employed. Such infection control procedures provide protection both for patients and dental personnel."

We note, however, that the Association is a professional organization, which, although a respected source of information on the dental profession, is not a public health authority. It is not clear the extent to which the Policy was based on the Association's assessment of dentists' ethical and professional duties in addition to its scientific assessment of the risk to which the ADA refers. Efforts to clarify dentists' ethical obligations and to encourage dentists to treat patients with HIV infection with compassion may be commendable, but the question under the statute is one of statistical likelihood, not professional responsibility. Without more information on the manner in which the American Dental Association formulated this Policy, we are unable to determine the Policy's value in evaluating whether petitioner's assessment of the risks was reasonable as a matter of law.

The court considered materials submitted by both parties on the cross motions for summary judgment. The petitioner was required to establish that there existed a genuine issue of material fact. Evidence which was merely colorable or not significantly probative would not have been sufficient.

We acknowledge the presence of other evidence in the record before the Court of Appeals which, subject to further arguments and examination, might support affirmance of the trial court's ruling. For instance, the record contains substantial testimony from numerous health experts indicating that it is safe to treat patients infected with HIV in dental offices. We are unable to determine the import of this evidence, however. The record does not disclose whether the expert testimony submitted by respondent turned on evidence available in September 1994.

There are reasons to doubt whether petitioner advanced evidence sufficient to raise a triable issue of fact on the significance of the risk. Petitioner relied on two principal points: First, he asserted that the use of high-speed drills and surface cooling with water created a risk of airborne HIV transmission. The study on which petitioner relied was inconclusive, however, determining only that "[f]urther work is required to determine whether such a risk exists." Petitioner's expert witness conceded, moreover, that no evidence suggested the spray could transmit HIV. His opinion on airborne risk was based on the absence of contrary evidence, not on positive data. Scientific evidence and expert testimony must have a traceable, analytical basis in objective fact before it may be considered on summary judgment.

Second, petitioner argues that, as of September 1994, CDC had identified seven dental workers with possible occupational transmission of HIV. These dental workers were exposed to HIV in the course of their employment, but CDC could not determine whether HIV infection had resulted. It is now known that CDC could not ascertain whether the seven dental workers contracted the disease because they did not present themselves for HIV testing at an appropriate time after their initial exposure. It is not clear on this record, however, whether this information was available to petitioner in September 1994. If not, the seven cases might have provided some, albeit not necessarily sufficient, support for petitioner's position. Standing alone, we doubt it would meet the objective, scientific basis for finding a significant risk to the petitioner.

Our evaluation of the evidence is constrained by the fact that on these and other points we have not had briefs and arguments directed to the entire record. In accepting the case for review, we declined to grant certiorari on question five, which asked whether petitioner raised a genuine issue of fact for trial. As a result, the briefs and arguments presented to us did not concentrate on the question of sufficiency in light all of the submissions in the summary judgment proceeding. "When attention has been focused on other issues, or when the court from which a case comes has expressed no views on a controlling question, it may be appropriate to remand the case rather than deal with the merits of that question in this Court." *Dandridge v. Williams* (1970). This consideration carries particular force where, as here, full briefing directed at the issue would help place a complex factual record in proper perspective. Resolution of the issue will be of importance to health care workers not just for the result but also for the precision and comprehensiveness of the reasons given for the decision.

We conclude the proper course is to give the Court of Appeals the opportunity to determine whether our analysis of some of the studies cited by the parties would change its conclusion that petitioner presented neither objective evidence nor a triable issue of fact on the question of risk. In remanding the case, we do not foreclose the possibility that the Court of Appeals may reach the same conclusion it did earlier. A remand will permit a full exploration of the issue through the adversary process.

The determination of the Court of Appeals that respondent's HIV infection was a disability under the ADA is affirmed. The judgment is vacated, and the case is remanded for further proceedings consistent with this opinion.

It is so ordered.

JUSTICE STEVENS, with whom JUSTICE BREYER joins, concurring.

The Court's opinion demonstrates that respondent's HIV infection easily falls within the statute's definition of "disability." Moreover, the Court's discussion in Part III of the relevant evidence has persuaded me that the judgment of the Court of Appeals should be affirmed. . . .

There are not, however, five Justices who agree that the judgment should be affirmed. . . . Because I am in agreement with the legal analysis in JUSTICE KENNEDY's opinion, in order to provide a judgment supported by a majority, I join that opinion even though I would prefer an outright affirmance.

JUSTICE GINSBURG, concurring.

HIV infection, as the description set out in the Court's opinion documents, has been regarded as a disease limiting life itself. The disease inevitably pervades life's choices: education, employment, family and financial undertakings. It affects the need for and, as this case shows, the ability to obtain health care because of the reaction of others to the impairment. No rational legislator . . . would require non-discrimination once symptoms become visible but permit discrimination when the disease, though present, is not yet visible. I am therefore satisfied that the statutory and regulatory definitions are well met. . . .

I further agree . . . that it is wise to remand, erring, if at all, on the side of caution. By taking this course, the Court ensures a fully informed determination whether respondent Abbott's disease posed "a significant risk to the health or safety of [petitioner Bragdon] that [could not] be eliminated by a modification of policies, practices, or procedures. . . ."

CHIEF JUSTICE REHNQUIST, with whom JUSTICE SCALIA and JUSTICE

THOMAS join, and with whom JUSTICE O'CONNOR joins as to Part II, concurring in the judgment in part and dissenting in part.

I

Is respondent—who has tested positive for the human immunodeficiency virus (HIV) but was asymptomatic at the time she suffered discriminatory treatment—a person with a "disability" as that term is defined in the Americans with Disabilities Act of 1990 (ADA)? [Definition of "disability" omitted; see majority opinion.] It is important to note that whether respondent has a disability covered by the ADA is an individualized inquiry. . . .

The individualized nature of the inquiry is particularly important in this case because the District Court disposed of it on summary judgment. Thus all disputed issues of material fact must be resolved against respondent. She contends that her asymptomatic HIV status brings her within the first definition of a "disability." She must therefore demonstrate, *inter alia,* that she was (1) physically or mentally impaired and that such impairment (2) substantially limited (3) one or more of her major life activities.

Petitioner does not dispute that asymptomatic HIV-positive status is a physical impairment. I therefore assume this to be the case, and proceed to the second and third statutory requirements for "disability."

According to the Court, the next question is "whether reproduction is a major life activity." That, however, is only half of the relevant question. As mentioned above, the ADA's definition of a "disability" requires that the major life activity at issue be one "of such individual." The Court truncates the question, perhaps because there is not a shred of record evidence indicating that, prior to becoming infected with HIV, respondent's major life activities included reproduction (assuming for the moment that reproduction is a major life activity at all). At most, the record indicates that after learning of her HIV status, respondent, whatever her previous inclination, conclusively decided that she would not have children. There is absolutely no evidence that, absent the HIV, respondent would have had or was even considering having children. Indeed, when asked during her deposition whether her HIV infection had in any way impaired her ability to carry out any of her life functions, respondent answered "No." . . .

But even aside from the facts of this particular case, the Court is simply wrong in concluding as a general matter that reproduction is a "major life activity." Unfortunately, the ADA does not define the phrase "major life activities." But the Act does incorporate by reference a list of such activities contained in regulations issued under the Rehabilitation Act. The Court correctly recognizes that this list of major life activities "is illustrative, not exhaustive," but then makes no attempt to demonstrate that reproduction is a major life activity in the same sense that "caring for one's self, performing manual tasks, walking, seeing, hearing, speaking, breathing, learning, and working" are.

Instead, the Court argues that reproduction is a "major" life activity in that it is "central to the life process itself." In support of this reading, the Court focuses on the fact that " 'major' " indicates " 'comparative importance,' " . . . ignoring the alternative definition of "major" as "greater in quantity, number, or extent." It is the latter definition that is most consistent with the ADA's illustrative list of major life activities.

No one can deny that reproductive decisions are important in a person's life.

But so are decisions as to who to marry, where to live, and how to earn one's living. Fundamental importance of this sort is not the common thread linking the statute's listed activities. The common thread is rather that the activities are repetitively performed and essential in the day-to-day existence of a normally functioning individual. They are thus quite different from the series of activities leading to the birth of a child. Both respondent and the United States as *amicus curiae* argue that reproduction must be a major life activity because regulations issued under the ADA define the term "physical impairment" to include physiological disorders affecting the reproductive system. If reproduction were not a major life activity, they argue, then it would have made little sense to include the reproductive disorders in the roster of physical impairments. This argument is simply wrong. There are numerous disorders of the reproductive system, such as dysmenorrhea and endometriosis, which are so painful that they limit a woman's ability to engage in major life activities such as walking and working. And, obviously, cancer of the various reproductive organs limits one's ability to engage in numerous activities other than reproduction.

But even if I were to assume that reproduction is a major life activity of respondent, I do not agree that an asymptomatic HIV infection "substantially limits" that activity. The record before us leaves no doubt that those so infected are still entirely able to engage in sexual intercourse, give birth to a child if they become pregnant, and perform the manual tasks necessary to rear a child to maturity. While individuals infected with HIV may choose not to engage in these activities, there is no support in language, logic, or our case law for the proposition that such voluntary choices constitute a "limit" on one's own life activities.

The Court responds that the ADA "addresses substantial limitations on major life activities, not utter inabilities." I agree, but fail to see how this assists the Court's cause. Apart from being unable to demonstrate that she is utterly unable to engage in the various activities that comprise the reproductive process, respondent has not even explained how she is less able to engage in those activities.

Respondent contends that her ability to reproduce is limited because "the fatal nature of HIV infection means that a parent is unlikely to live long enough to raise and nurture the child to adulthood." But the ADA's definition of a disability is met only if the alleged impairment substantially "limits" (present tense) a major life activity. Asymptomatic HIV does not presently limit respondent's ability to perform any of the tasks necessary to bear or raise a child. Respondent's argument, taken to its logical extreme, would render every individual with a genetic marker for some debilitating disease "disabled" here and now because of some possible future effects.

In my view, therefore, respondent has failed to demonstrate that any of her major life activities were substantially limited by her HIV infection.

II

While the Court concludes to the contrary as to the "disability" issue, it then quite correctly recognizes that petitioner could nonetheless have refused to treat respondent if her condition posed a "direct threat." The Court of Appeals affirmed the judgment of the District Court granting summary judgment to respondent on this issue. The Court vacates this portion of the Court of Appeals' decision, and remands the case to the lower court, presumably so that it may "determine whether our analysis of some of the studies cited by the parties would change its conclusion that petitioner presented neither objective evidence nor a triable issue of fact on the question of risk." I agree that the judgment should be vacated, although I am not sure I understand the Court's cryptic direction to the lower court.

"[D]irect threat" is defined as a "significant risk to the health or safety of others that cannot be eliminated by a modification of policies, practices, or procedures or by the provision of auxiliary aides or services." § 12182(b)(3). This statutory definition of a direct threat consists of two parts. First, a court must ask whether treating the infected patient *without precautionary techniques* would pose a "significant risk to the heath or safety of others." Whether a particular risk is significant depends on:

> " '(a) the nature of the risk (how the disease is transmitted), (b) the duration of the risk (how long is the carrier infectious), (c) the severity of the risk (what is the potential harm to third parties) and (d) the probabilities the disease will be transmitted and will cause varying degrees of harm.' " *School Bd. of Nassau Cty. v. Arline* (1987).

Even if a significant risk exists, a health practitioner will still be required to treat the infected patient if "a modification of policies, practices, or procedures" (in this case, universal precautions) will "eliminat[e]" the risk. § 12182(b)(3).

I agree with the Court that "the existence, or nonexistence, of a significant risk must be determined from the standpoint of the person who refuses the treatment or accommodation," as of the time that the decision refusing treatment is made. I disagree with the Court, however, that "[i]n assessing the reasonableness of petitioner's actions, the views of public health authorities . . . are of special weight and authority." Those views are, of course, entitled to a presumption of validity when the actions of those authorities themselves are challenged in court, and even in disputes between private parties where Congress has committed that dispute to adjudication by a public health authority. But in litigation between private parties originating in the federal courts, I am aware of no provision of law or judicial practice that would require or permit courts to give some scientific views more credence than others simply because they have been endorsed by a politically appointed public health authority (such as the Surgeon General). In litigation of this latter sort, . . . the credentials of the scientists employed by the public health authority, and the soundness of their studies, must stand on their own. . . .

Applying these principles here, it is clear to me that petitioner has presented more than enough evidence to avoid summary judgment on the "direct threat" question. In June 1994, the Centers for Disease Control and Prevention published a study identifying seven instances of possible transmission of HIV from patients to dental workers. While it is not entirely certain whether these dental workers contracted HIV during the course of providing dental treatment, the potential that the disease was transmitted during the course of dental treatment is relevant evidence. One need only demonstrate "risk," not certainty of infection. . . . Given the "severity of the risk" involved here, i.e., near certain death, and the fact that no public health authority had outlined a protocol for *eliminating* this risk in the context of routine dental treatment, it seems likely that petitioner can establish that it was objectively reasonable for him to conclude that treating respondent in his office posed a "direct threat" to his safety.

In addition, petitioner offered evidence of 42 documented incidents of occupational transmission of HIV to healthcare workers other than dental professionals. The Court of Appeals dismissed this evidence as irrelevant because these health professionals were not dentists. But the fact that the health care workers were not dentists is no more valid a basis for distinguishing these transmissions of HIV than the fact that the health care workers did not practice in Maine. At a minimum, petitioner's evidence was sufficient to create a triable issue on this question, and summary judgment was accordingly not appropriate.

JUSTICE O'CONNOR, concurring in the judgment in part and dissenting in part.

I agree with THE CHIEF JUSTICE that respondent's claim of disability should be evaluated on an individualized basis and that she has not proven that her asymptomatic HIV status substantially limited one or more of her major life activities. In my view, the act of giving birth to a child, while a very important part of the lives of many women, is not generally the same as the representative major life activities of all persons—"caring for one's self, performing manual tasks, walking, seeing, hearing, speaking, breathing, learning, and working"—listed in regulations relevant to the Americans with Disabilities Act of 1990. Based on that conclusion, there is no need to address whether other aspects of intimate or family relationships not raised in this case could constitute major life activities; nor is there reason to consider whether HIV status would impose a substantial limitation on one's ability to reproduce if reproduction were a major life activity.

I join in Part II of THE CHIEF JUSTICE's opinion concurring in the judgment in part and dissenting in part, which concludes that the Court of Appeals failed to properly determine whether respondent's condition posed a direct threat. Accordingly, I agree that a remand is necessary on that issue.

No. 97-42

Eastern Enterprises, Petitioner v. Kenneth S. Apfel, Commissioner of Social Security, et al.

On writ of certiorari to the United States
Court of Appeals for the First Circuit

[June 25, 1998]

JUSTICE O'CONNOR announced the judgment of the Court and delivered an opinion, in which THE CHIEF JUSTICE, JUSTICE SCALIA, and JUSTICE THOMAS join.

In this case, the Court considers a challenge under the Due Process and Takings Clauses of the Constitution to the Coal Industry Retiree Health Benefit Act of 1992 (Coal Act), 26 U. S. C. § § 9701-9722, which establishes a mechanism for funding health care benefits for retirees from the coal industry and their dependents. We conclude that the Coal Act, as applied to petitioner Eastern Enterprises, effects an unconstitutional taking.

I

A

For a good part of this century, employers in the coal industry have been involved in negotiations with the United Mine Workers of America (UMWA or Union) regarding the provision of employee benefits to coal miners. When petitioner Eastern Enterprises was formed in 1929, coal operators provided health care to their employees through a prepayment system funded by payroll deductions. Because of the rural location of most mines, medical facilities were frequently substandard, and many of the medical professionals willing to work in mining areas were "company doctors," often selected by the coal operators for reasons other than their skills or training. The health care available to coal miners and their families was deficient in many respects. In addition, the cost of company-provided services, such as housing and medical care, often consumed the bulk of miners' compensation. . . .

In the late 1930's, the UMWA began to demand changes in the manner in which essential services were provided to miners, and by 1946, the subject of miners' health care had become a critical issue in collective bargaining negotiations between the Union and bituminous coal companies. When a breakdown in those negotiations resulted in a nationwide strike, President Truman issued an Executive order directing Secretary of the Interior Julius Krug to take possession of all bituminous coal mines and to negotiate "appropriate changes in the terms and conditions of employment" of miners with the UMWA. A week of negotiations between Secretary Krug and UMWA President John L. Lewis produced the historic Krug-Lewis Agreement that ended the strike.

That agreement . . . led to the creation of benefit funds, financed by royalties on coal produced and payroll deductions. The funds compensated miners and their dependents and survivors for wages lost due to disability, death, or retirement. The funds also provided for the medical expenses of miners and their dependents, with the precise benefits determined by UMWA-appointed trustees. . . .

Shortly after the study was issued, the mines returned to private control and the UMWA and several coal operators entered into the National Bituminous Coal Wage Agreement of 1947, which established the "United Mine Workers of America Welfare and Retirement Fund" (1947 W&R Fund), modeled after the Krug-Lewis benefit trusts. The Fund was to use the proceeds of a royalty on coal production to provide pension and medical benefits to miners and their families. The 1947 NBCWA did not specify the benefits to which miners and their dependents were entitled. Instead, three trustees appointed by the parties were given authority to determine "coverage and eligibility, priorities among classes of benefits, amounts of benefits, methods of providing or arranging for provisions for benefits, investment of trust funds, and all other related matters."

Disagreement over benefits continued, however, leading to the execution of another NBCWA in 1950, which created a new multiemployer trust, the "United Mine Workers of America Welfare and Retirement Fund of 1950" (1950 W&R Fund). The 1950 W&R Fund established a 30-cents-per-ton royalty on coal produced, payable by signatory operators on a "several and not joint" basis for the duration of the 1950 Agreement. As with the 1947 W&R Fund, the 1950 W&R Fund was governed by three trustees chosen by the parties and vested with responsibility to determine the level of benefits. Between 1950 and 1974, the 1950 NBCWA was amended on occasion, and new NBCWA's were adopted in 1968 and 1971. Except for increases in the amount of royalty payments, however, the terms and structure of the 1950 W&R Fund remained essentially unchanged. A 1951 amendment recognized the creation of the Bituminous Coal Operators' Association (BCOA), a multiemployer bargaining association, which became the primary representative of coal operators in negotiations with the Union.

Under the 1950 W&R Fund, miners and their dependents were not promised specific benefits. . . . [T]he Fund operated using a fixed amount of royalties, with the trustees having the authority to establish and adjust the level of benefits provided so as to remain within the budgetary constraints.

Subsequent annual reports of the 1950 W&R Fund reiterated that benefits were subject to change. . . . Thus, although persons involved in the coal industry may have made occasional statements intimating that the 1950 W&R Fund promised lifetime health benefits, it is clear that the 1950 W&R Fund did not, by its terms, guarantee lifetime health benefits for retirees and their dependents. In fact, as to widows of miners, the 1950 W&R Fund expressly limited health benefits to the time period during which widows would also receive death benefits.

Between 1950 and 1974, the trustees often exercised their prerogative to alter the level of benefits according to the Fund's budget. . . .

Reductions in benefits were not always acceptable to the miners, and some wildcat strikes erupted in the 1960's. . . . Nonetheless, the 1950 W&R Fund continued to provide benefits on a "pay-as-you-go" basis, with the level of benefits fully subject to revision, until the Employee Retirement Income Security Act of 1974 (ERISA), introduced specific funding and vesting requirements for pension plans. To comply with ERISA, the UMWA and the BCOA entered into a new agreement, the 1974 NBCWA, which created four trusts, funded by royalties on coal production and premiums based on hours worked by miners, to replace the 1950 W&R Fund. Two of the new trusts, the UMWA 1950 Benefit Plan and Trust (1950 Benefit Plan) and the UMWA 1974 Benefit Plan and Trust (1974 Benefit Plan), provided nonpension benefits, including medical benefits. Miners who retired before January 1, 1976, and their dependents were covered by the 1950 Benefit Plan, while active miners and those who retired after 1975 were covered by the 1974 Benefit Plan.

The 1974 NBCWA thus was the first agreement between the UMWA and the BCOA to expressly reference health benefits for retirees. . . . The 1974 NBCWA explained that it was amending previous medical benefits to provide a Health Services card for retired miners until their death, and to their widows until their death or remarriage. Despite the expanded benefits, the 1974 NBCWA did not alter the employers' obligation to contribute only a fixed amount of royalties, nor did it extend employers' liability beyond the life of the agreement.

As a result of the broadened coverage under the 1974 NBCWA, the number of eligible benefit recipients jumped dramatically. . . .

The increase in benefits, combined with various other circumstances—such as a decline in the amount of coal produced, the retirement of a generation of miners, and rapid escalation of health care costs—quickly resulted in financial problems for the 1950 and 1974 Benefit Plans. In response, the next NBCWA, executed in 1978, assigned responsibility to signatory employers for the health care of their own active and retired employees. The 1974 Benefit Plan remained in effect, but only to cover retirees whose former employers were no longer in business.

To ensure the Plans' solvency, the 1978 NBCWA included a "guarantee" clause obligating signatories to make sufficient contributions to maintain benefits during that agreement, and "evergreen" clauses were incorporated into the Plans so that signatories would be required to contribute as long as they remained in the coal business, regardless whether they signed a subsequent agreement. As a result, the coal operators' liability to the Benefit Plans shifted from a defined contribution obligation, under which employers were responsible only for a predetermined amount of royalties, to a form of defined benefit obligation, under which employers were to fund specific benefits.

Despite the 1978 changes, the Benefit Plans continued to suffer financially as costs increased and employers who had signed the 1978 NBCWA withdrew from the agreement, either to continue in business with nonunion employees or to exit the coal business altogether. As more and more coal operators abandoned the Benefit Plans, the remaining signatories were forced to absorb the increasing cost of covering retirees left behind by exiting employers. A spiral soon developed, with the rising cost of participation leading more employers to withdraw from the plans, resulting in more onerous obligations for those that remained. In 1988, the UMWA and BCOA attempted to relieve the situation by imposing withdrawal liability on NBCWA signatories who seceded from the Benefit Plans. Even so, by 1990, the 1950 and 1974 Benefit Plans had incurred a deficit of about $110 million, and obligations to beneficiaries were continuing to surpass revenues.

B

In response to unrest among miners, such as the lengthy strike that followed Pittston Coal Company's refusal to sign the 1988 NBCWA, Secretary of Labor Elizabeth Dole announced the creation of the Advisory Commission on United Mine Workers of America Retiree Health Benefits (Coal Commission). The Coal Commission was charged with "recommend[ing] a solution for ensuring that orphan retirees in the 1950 and 1974 Benefit Trusts will continue to receive promised medical care." ... The Commission agreed that "a statutory obligation to contribute to the plans should be imposed on current and former signatories to the [NBCWA]," but disagreed about "whether the entire [coal] industry should contribute to the resolution of the problem of orphan retirees." Therefore, the Commission proposed two alternative funding plans for Congress' consideration.

First, the Commission recommended that Congress establish a fund financed by an industrywide fee to provide health care to orphan retirees at the level of benefits they were entitled to receive at that fund's inception. To cover the cost of medical benefits for retirees from signatories to the 1978 or subsequent NBCWA's who remained in the coal business, the Commission proposed the creation of another fund financed by the retirees' most recent employers. The Commission also recommended that Congress codify the "evergreen" obligation of the 1978 and subsequent NBCWA's.

As an alternative to imposing industrywide liability, the Commission suggested that Congress spread the cost of retirees' health benefits across "a broadened base of current and past signatories to the contracts," apparently referring to the 1978 and subsequent NBCWA's. Not all Commission members agreed, however, that it would be fair to assign such a burden to signatories of the 1978 agreement. Four Commissioners explained that "[i]ssues of elemental fairness are involved" in imposing obligations on "respectable operators who made decisions in the past to move to different locales, invest in different technology, or pursue their business with or without respect to union presence."

After the Coal Commission issued its report, Congress considered several proposals to fund health benefits for UMWA retirees.

In 1992, as part of a larger bill, both Houses passed legislation based on the Coal Commission's first proposal, which required signatories to the 1978 or any subsequent NBCWA to fund their own retirees' health care costs and provided for orphan retirees' benefits through a tax on future coal production. President Bush, however, vetoed the entire bill.

Congress responded by passing the Coal Act, a modified version of the Coal Commission's alternative funding plan. In the Act, Congress purported "to identify persons most responsible for [1950 and 1974 Benefit Plan] liabilities in order to stabilize plan funding and allow for the provision of health care benefits to . . . retirees." § 19142(a)(2). . . .

The Coal Act merged the 1950 and 1974 Benefit Plans into a new multiemployer plan called the United Mine Workers of America Combined Benefit Fund (Combined Fund). The Combined Fund provides "substantially the same" health benefits to retirees and their dependents that they were receiving under the 1950 and 1974 Benefit Plans. It is financed by annual premiums assessed against "signatory coal operators," i.e., coal operators that signed any NBCWA or any other agreement requiring contributions to the 1950 or 1974 Benefit Plans. See § § 9701(b)(1), (3); § 9701(c)(1). Any signatory operator who "conducts or derives revenue from any business activity, whether or not in the coal industry," may be liable for those premiums. § 9706(a); § 9701(c)(7). Where a signatory is no longer involved in any business activity, premiums may be levied against "related person[s]," including successors in interest and businesses or corporations under common control. § § 9706(a); § 9701(c)(2)(A).

The Commissioner of Social Security (Commissioner) calculates the premiums due from any signatory operator based on the following formula, by which retirees are assigned to particular operators:

"For purposes of this chapter, the Commissioner of Social Security shall . . . assign each coal industry retiree who is an eligible beneficiary to a signatory operator which (or any related person with respect to which) remains in business in the following order:

"(1) First, to the signatory operator which—

"(A) was a signatory to the 1978 coal wage agreement or any subsequent coal wage agreement, and

"(B) was the most recent signatory operator to employ the coal industry retiree in the coal industry for at least 2 years.

"(2) Second, if the retiree is not assigned under paragraph (1), to the signatory operator which—

"(A) was a signatory to the 1978 coal wage agreement or any subsequent coal wage agreement, and

"(B) was the most recent signatory operator to employ the coal industry retiree in the coal industry.

"(3) Third, if the retiree is not assigned under paragraph (1) or (2), to the signatory operator which employed the coal industry retiree in the coal industry for a longer period of time than any other signatory operator prior to the effective date of the 1978 coal wage agreement." § 9706(a).

It is the application of the third prong of the allocation formula, § 9706(a)(3), to Eastern that we review in this case.

II

A

Eastern was organized as a Massachusetts business trust in 1929, under the name Eastern Gas and Fuel Associates. . . . Until 1965, Eastern conducted extensive coal mining operations centered in West Virginia and Pennsylvania. As a signatory to each NBCWA executed between 1947 and 1964, Eastern made contributions of over $60 million to the 1947 and 1950 W&R Funds.

In 1963, Eastern decided to transfer its coal-related operations to a subsidiary, Eastern Associated Coal Corp. (EACC). The transfer was completed by the end of 1965. . . .

Eastern retained its stock interest in EACC through a subsidiary corporation, Coal Properties Corp. (CPC), until 1987, and it received dividends of more than $100 million from EACC during that period. In 1987, Eastern sold its interest in CPC to respondent Peabody Holding Company, Inc. Under the terms of the agreement effecting the transfer, Peabody, CPC, and EACC assumed responsibility for payments to certain benefit plans, including the "Benefit Plan for UMWA Represented Employees of EACC and Subs." As of June 30, 1987, the 1950 and 1974 Benefit Plans reported surplus assets, totaling over $33 million.

B

Following enactment of the Coal Act, the Commissioner assigned to Eastern the obligation for Combined Fund premiums respecting over 1,000 retired miners who had worked for the company before 1966, based on Eastern's status as the pre-1978 signatory operator for whom the miners had worked for the longest period of time. Eastern's premium for a 12-month period exceeded $5 million.

Eastern responded by suing the Commissioner, as well as the Combined Fund and its trustees, in the United States District Court for the District of Massachusetts. Eastern asserted that the Coal Act, either on its face or as applied, violates substantive due process and constitutes a taking of its property in violation of the Fifth Amendment. Eastern also challenged the Commissioner's interpretation of the Coal Act. The District Court granted summary judgment for respondents on all claims . . . (1996).

The Court of Appeals for the First Circuit affirmed. *Eastern Enterprises v. Chater* (1997). [Summary of decision omitted.]

Other Courts of Appeals have also upheld the Coal Act against constitutional challenges. In view of the importance of the issues raised in this case, we granted certiorari (1997).

III [omitted]

IV

A

The Takings Clause of the Fifth Amendment provides: "[N]or shall private property be taken for public use, without just compensation." The aim of the Clause is to prevent the government "from forcing some people alone to bear public burdens which, in all fairness and justice, should be borne by the public as a whole." *Armstrong v. United States* (1960).

This case does not present the "classi[c] taking" in which the government directly appropriates private property for its own use. . . . [E]conomic regulation such as the Coal Act may nonetheless effect a taking. . . . By operation of the Act, Eastern is "permanently deprived of those assets necessary to satisfy its statutory obligation, not to the Government, but to [the Combined Benefit Fund]" [quoting *Connolly v. Pension Benefit Guaranty Corporation* (1986)]. . . .

B

Our analysis in this case is informed by previous decisions considering the constitutionality of somewhat similar legislative schemes. In *Usery v. Turner Elkhorn Mining Co.* (1976), we had occasion to review provisions of the Black Lung Benefits Act of 1972, which required coal operators to compensate certain miners and their survivors for death or disability due to black lung disease caused by employment in coal mines. Coal operators challenged the provisions of the Act relating to miners who were no longer employed in the industry. . . .

[W]e . . . concluded that the assignment of liability for black lung benefits was "justified as a rational measure to spread the costs of the employees' disabilities to those who have profited from the fruits of their labor."

[O'Connor summarized three other decisions that rejected challenges to the Multiemployer Pension Plan Amendments Act of 1980 (MPPAA). That law required any company that withdrew from industrywide pension plans to make a contribution to cover its share of unfunded vested benefits; the act applied retroactively to withdrawals in the five months preceding its enactment. The Court rejected substantive due process and taking clause challenges to the act in three cases: *Pension Benefit Guaranty Corporation v. R. A. Gray & Co.* (1984); *Connolly v. Pension Benefit Guaranty Corporation* (1986); and *Concrete Pipe & Products of Cal., Inc. v. Construction Laborers Pension Trust for Southern Cal.* (1993).]

Our opinions in *Turner Elkhorn, Connolly*, and *Concrete Pipe* make clear that Congress has considerable leeway to fashion economic legislation, including the power to affect contractual commitments between private parties. Congress also may impose retroactive liability to some degree, particularly where it is "confined to short and limited periods required by the practicalities of producing national legislation." *Gray*. Our decisions, however, have left open the possibility that legislation might be unconstitutional if it imposes severe retroactive liability on a limited class of parties that could not have anticipated the liability, and the extent of that liability is substantially disproportionate to the parties' experience.

C

We believe that the Coal Act's allocation scheme, as applied to Eastern, presents such a case. We reach that conclusion by applying the three factors that traditionally have informed our regulatory takings analysis. Although JUSTICE KENNEDY and JUSTICE BREYER would pursue a different course in evaluating the constitutionality of the Coal Act, they acknowledge that this Court's opinions in *Connolly* and *Concrete Pipe* indicate that the regulatory takings framework is germane to legislation of this sort.

As to the first factor relevant in assessing whether a regulatory taking has occurred, economic impact, there is no doubt that the Coal Act has forced a considerable financial burden upon Eastern. The parties estimate that Eastern's cumulative payments under the Act will be on the order of $50 to $100 million. Eastern's liability is thus substantial, and the company is clearly deprived of the amounts it must pay the Combined Fund. . . .

That liability is not, of course, a permanent physical occupation of Eastern's property. . . . But our decisions upholding the MPPAA suggest that an employer's statutory liability for multiemployer plan benefits should reflect some "proportion[ality] to its experience with the plan." *Concrete Pipe* . . . In *Concrete Pipe* and *Connolly,* the employers had "voluntarily negotiated and maintained a pension plan. . . , and consequently, the statutory liability was linked to the employers' conduct.

Here, however, while Eastern contributed to the 1947 and 1950 W&R Funds, it ceased its coal mining operations in 1965 and neither participated in negotiations nor agreed to make contributions in connection with the Benefit Plans under the 1974, 1978, or subsequent NBCWA's. It is the latter agreements that first suggest an industry commitment to the funding of lifetime health benefits for both retirees and their family members. Although EACC continued mining coal until 1987 as a subsidiary of Eastern, Eastern's liability under the Act bears no relationship to its ownership of EACC; the Act assigns Eastern responsibility for benefits relating to miners that Eastern itself, not EACC, employed, while EACC would be assigned the responsibility for any miners that it had employed. . . . The company's obligations under the Act depend solely on its roster of employees some 30 to 50 years before the statute's enactment, without any regard to responsibilities that Eastern accepted under any benefit plan the company itself adopted.

It is true that Eastern may be able to seek indemnification from EACC or Peabody. But although the Act preserves Eastern's right to pursue indemnification, it does not confer any right of reimbursement. . . . Moreover, the possibility of indemnification does not alter the fact that Eastern has been assessed over $5 million in Combined Fund premiums and that its liability under the Coal Act will continue for many years. To the extent that Eastern may have entered into contractual arrangements to insure itself against liabilities arising out of its former coal operations, that indemnity is neither enhanced nor supplanted by the Coal Act and does not affect the availability of the declaratory relief Eastern seeks.

We are also not persuaded by respondents' argument that the Coal Act "moderate[s] and mitigate[s] the economic impact" upon Eastern. Although Eastern is not assigned the premiums for former employees who later worked for companies that signed the 1978 NBCWA, Eastern had no control over the activities of its former employees subsequent to its departure from the coal industry in 1965. . . . The mere fact that Eastern is not forced to bear the burden of lifetime benefits respecting all of its former employees does not mean that the company's liability for some of those employees is not a significant economic burden.

For similar reasons, the Coal Act substantially interferes with Eastern's reasonable investment-backed expectations. The Act's beneficiary allocation scheme reaches back 30 to 50 years to impose liability against Eastern based on the company's activities between 1946 and 1965. Thus, even though the Act mandates only the payment of future health benefits, it nonetheless "attaches new legal consequences to [an employment relationship] completed before its enactment." *Landgraf v. USI Film Products* (1994).

Retroactivity is generally disfavored in the law. . . . "Retroactive legislation," we have explained, "presents problems of unfairness that are more serious than those posed by prospective legislation, because it can deprive citizens of legitimate expectations and upset settled transactions." *General Motors Corp. v. Romein* (1992).

Our Constitution expresses concern with retroactive laws through several of its provisions, including the *Ex Post Facto* and Takings Clauses. In *Calder v. Bull* (1798), this Court held that the *Ex Post Facto* Clause is directed at the retroactivity of penal legislation, while suggesting that the Takings Clause provides a similar safeguard against retrospective legislation concerning property rights. . . .

[T]he Coal Act operates retroactively, divesting Eastern of property long after the company believed its liabilities under the 1950 W&R Fund to have been settled. And the extent of Eastern's retroactive liability is substantial and particularly far reaching. Even in areas in which retroactivity is generally tolerated, such as tax legislation, some limits have been suggested. . . . The distance into the past that the Act reaches back to impose a liability on Eastern and the magnitude of that liability raise substantial questions of fairness. . . .

Respondents and their *amici curiae* assert that the extent of retroactive liability is justified because there was an implicit, industrywide agreement during the time that Eastern was involved in the coal industry to fund lifetime health benefits for qualifying miners and their dependents. That contention, however, is not supported by the pre-1974 NBCWA's. No contrary conclusion can be drawn from the few isolated statements of individuals involved in the coal industry or from statements of Members of Congress while considering legislative responses to the issue of funding retiree benefits. Moreover, even though retirees received medical benefits before 1974, and perhaps developed a corresponding expectation that those benefits would continue, the Coal Act imposes liability respecting a much broader range of beneficiaries. In any event, the question is not whether miners had an expectation of lifetime benefits, but whether Eastern should bear the cost of those benefits as to miners it employed before 1966.

Eastern only participated in the 1947 and 1950 W&R Funds, which operated on a pay-as-you-go basis, and under which the degree of benefits and the classes of beneficiaries were subject to the trustees' discretion. Not until 1974, when ERISA forced revisions to the 1950 W&R Fund, could lifetime medical benefits under the multiemployer agreement have been viewed as promised. Eastern was no longer in the industry when the Evergreen and Guarantee clauses of the 1978 and subsequent NBCWA's shifted the 1950 and 1974 Benefit Plans from a defined contribution framework to a guarantee of defined benefits, at least for the life of the agreements. . . . Thus, . . . the Coal Act's scheme for allocation of Combined Fund premiums is not calibrated either to Eastern's past actions or to any agreement—implicit or otherwise—by the company. Nor would the pattern of the Federal Government's involvement in the coal industry have given Eastern "sufficient notice" that lifetime health benefits might be guaranteed to retirees several decades later.

Eastern's liability also differs from coal operators' responsibility for benefits under the Black Lung Benefits Act of 1972. . . . Eastern might be responsible for employment-related health problems of all former employees whether or not the cost was foreseen at the time of employment, but there is no such connection here. There is no doubt that many coal miners sacrificed their health on behalf of this country's industrial development, and we do not dispute that some members of the industry promised lifetime medical benefits to miners and their dependents during the 1970's. Nor do we, as JUSTICE STEVENS suggests, question Congress' policy decision that the miners are entitled to relief. But the Constitution does not permit a solution to the problem of funding miners' benefits that imposes such a disproportionate and severely retroactive burden upon Eastern.

Finally, the nature of the governmental action in this case is quite unusual. That Congress sought a legislative remedy for what it perceived to be a grave problem in the funding of retired coal miners' health benefits is understandable; complex problems of that sort typically call for a legislative solution. When, however, that solution singles out certain employers to bear a burden that is substantial in amount, based on the employers' conduct far in the past, and unrelated to any commitment that the employers made or to any injury they caused, the governmental action implicates fundamental principles of fairness underlying the Takings Clause. Eastern cannot be forced to bear the expense of lifetime health benefits for miners based on its activities decades before those benefits were promised. Accordingly, in the specific circumstances of this case, we conclude that the Coal Act's application to Eastern effects an unconstitutional taking.

D

Eastern also claims that the manner in which the Coal Act imposes liability upon it violates substantive due process. . . . Our analysis of legislation under the Takings and Due Process Clauses is correlated to some extent, and there is a question whether the Coal Act violates due process in light of the Act's severely retroactive impact. At the same time, this Court has expressed concerns about using the Due Process Clause to invalidate economic legislation. [Citations omitted.] Because we have determined that the third tier of the Coal Act's allocation scheme violates the Takings Clause as applied to Eastern, we need not address Eastern's due process claim. Nor do we consider the first two tiers of the Act's allocation scheme, 26 U. S. C. § § 9706(a)(1) and (2), as the liability that has been imposed on Eastern arises only under the third tier.

V

In enacting the Coal Act, Congress was responding to a serious problem with the funding of health benefits for retired coal miners. While we do not question Congress' power to address that problem, the solution it crafted improperly places a severe, disproportionate, and extremely retroactive burden on Eastern. Accordingly, we conclude that the Coal Act's allocation of liability to Eastern violates the

Takings Clause, and that 26 U. S. C. § 9706(a)(3) should be enjoined as applied to Eastern. The judgment of the Court of Appeals is reversed, and the case is remanded for further proceedings.

It is so ordered.

JUSTICE THOMAS, concurring.

JUSTICE O'CONNOR's opinion correctly concludes that the Coal Act's imposition of retroactive liability on petitioner violates the Takings Clause. I write separately to emphasize that the *Ex Post Facto* Clause of the Constitution, Art. I., § 9, cl. 3, even more clearly reflects the principle that "[r]etrospective laws are, indeed, generally unjust." 2 J. Story, Commentaries on the Constitution § 1398. Since *Calder v. Bull* (1798), however, this Court has considered the *Ex Post Facto* Clause to apply only in the criminal context. I have never been convinced of the soundness of this limitation, which in *Calder* was principally justified because a contrary interpretation would render the Takings Clause unnecessary. In an appropriate case, therefore, I would be willing to reconsider *Calder* and its progeny to determine whether a retroactive civil law that passes muster under our current Takings Clause jurisprudence is nonetheless unconstitutional under the *Ex Post Facto* Clause. Today's case, however, does present an unconstitutional taking, and I join JUSTICE O'CONNOR's well-reasoned opinion in full.

JUSTICE KENNEDY, concurring in the judgment and dissenting in part.

The plurality's careful assessment of the history and purpose of the statute in question demonstrates the necessity to hold it arbitrary and beyond the legitimate authority of the Government to enact. In my view, which is in full accord with many of the plurality's conclusions, the relevant portions of the Coal Industry Retiree Health Benefit Act of 1992 (Coal Act), 26 U. S. C. § 9701 *et seq.*, must be invalidated as contrary to essential due process principles, without regard to the Takings Clause of the Fifth Amendment. I concur in the judgment holding the Coal Act unconstitutional but disagree with the plurality's Takings Clause analysis, which, it is submitted, is incorrect and quite unnecessary for decision of the case. I must record my respectful dissent on this issue.

I

... Our cases do not support the plurality's conclusion that the Coal Act takes property. The Coal Act imposes a staggering financial burden on the petitioner, Eastern Enterprises, but it regulates the former mine owner without regard to property. It does not operate upon or alter an identified property interest, and it is not applicable to or measured by a property interest. ... The law simply imposes an obligation to perform an act, the payment of benefits. The statute is indifferent as to how the regulated entity elects to comply or the property it uses to do so. To the extent it affects property interests, it does so in a manner similar to many laws; but until today, none were thought to constitute takings. To call this sort of governmental action a taking ... is both imprecise and, with all due respect, unwise. ...

II

When the constitutionality of the Coal Act is tested under the Due Process Clause, it must be invalidated. Accepted principles forbidding retroactive legislation of this type are sufficient to dispose of the case.

Although we have been hesitant to subject economic legislation to due process scrutiny as a general matter, the Court has given careful consideration to due process challenges to legislation with retroactive effects. . . .

. . . [R]etroactive lawmaking is a particular concern for the courts because of the legislative "tempt[ation] to use retroactive legislation as a means of retribution against unpopular groups or individuals." *Landgraf v. USI Film Products* (1994). . . . If retroactive laws change the legal consequences of transactions long closed, the change can destroy the reasonable certainty and security which are the very objects of property ownership. As a consequence, due process protection for property must be understood to incorporate our settled tradition against retroactive laws of great severity. Groups targeted by retroactive laws, were they to be denied all protection, would have a justified fear that a government once formed to protect expectations now can destroy them. Both stability of investment and confidence in the constitutional system, then, are secured by due process restrictions against severe retroactive legislation.

The case before us represents one of the rare instances where the Legislature has exceeded the limits imposed by due process. The plurality opinion demonstrates in convincing fashion that the remedy created by the Coal Act bears no legitimate relation to the interest which the Government asserts in support of the statute. In our tradition, the degree of retroactive effect is a significant determinant in the constitutionality of a statute. [Citations omitted.] As the plurality explains today, in creating liability for events which occurred 35 years ago the Coal Act has a retroactive effect of unprecedented scope.

While we have upheld the imposition of liability on former employers based on past employment relationships, the statutes at issue were remedial, designed to impose an "actual, measurable cost of [the employer's] business" which the employer had been able to avoid in the past. [Citations omitted.] The Coal Act, however, does not serve this purpose. Eastern was once in the coal business and employed many of the beneficiaries, but it was not responsible for their expectation of lifetime health benefits or for the perilous financial condition of the 1950 and 1974 Plans which put the benefits in jeopardy. As the plurality opinion discusses in detail, the expectation was created by promises and agreements made long after Eastern left the coal business. Eastern was not responsible for the resulting chaos in the funding mechanism caused by other coal companies leaving the framework of the National Bituminous Coal Wage Agreement. This case is far outside the bounds of retroactivity permissible under our law.

. . . Statutes may be invalidated on due process grounds only under the most egregious of circumstances. This case represents one of the rare instances in which even such a permissive standard has been violated.

Application of the Coal Act to Eastern would violate the proper bounds of settled due process principles, and I concur in the plurality's conclusion that the judgment of the Court of Appeals must be reversed.

JUSTICE STEVENS, with whom JUSTICE SOUTER, JUSTICE GINSBURG, and JUSTICE BREYER join, dissenting.

. . . During . . . [the 1950's and 1960's] there was an implicit understanding on both sides of the bargaining table that the [coal] operators would provide the miners with lifetime health benefits. It was this understanding that kept the mines in operation and enabled Eastern to earn handsome profits before it transferred its coal business to a wholly owned subsidiary in 1965.

. . . Given the critical importance of the reasonable expectations of both the miners and the operators during the period before their implicit agreement was made explicit in 1974, I am unable to agree with the plurality's conclusion that the retroactive application of the 1992 Act is an unconstitutional "taking" of Eastern's property. Rather, it seems to me that the plurality and JUSTICE KENNEDY have substituted their judgment about what is fair for the better informed judgment of the Members of the Coal Commission and Congress. . . .

JUSTICE BREYER, with whom JUSTICE STEVENS, JUSTICE SOUTER, and JUSTICE GINSBURG join, dissenting.

We must decide whether it is fundamentally unfair for Congress to require Eastern Enterprises to pay the health care costs of retired miners who worked for Eastern before 1965, when Eastern stopped mining coal. For many years Eastern benefited from the labor of those miners. Eastern helped to create conditions that led the miners to expect continued health care benefits for themselves and their families after they retired. And Eastern, until 1987, continued to draw sizable profits from the coal industry though a wholly owned subsidiary. For these reasons, I believe that Congress did not act unreasonably or otherwise unjustly in imposing these health care costs upon Eastern. Consequently, in my view, the statute before us is constitutional.

I

As a preliminary matter, I agree with JUSTICE KENNEDY, that the plurality views this case through the wrong legal lens. The Constitution's Takings Clause does not apply. That Clause refers to the taking of "private property . . . for public use without just compensation." . . .

The "private property" upon which the Clause traditionally has focused is a specific interest in physical or intellectual property. It requires compensation when the government takes that property for a public purpose. . . . This case involves, not an interest in physical or intellectual property, but an ordinary liability to pay money, and not to the Government, but to third parties. . . .

II

The substantive question before us is whether or not it is fundamentally unfair to require Eastern to make future payments for health care costs of retired miners and their families, on the basis of Eastern's past association with these miners. Congress might have assessed all those who now use coal, or the taxpayer, in order to pay for those retired coal miners' health benefits. But Congress, instead, imposed this liability on Eastern. Coal Industry Retiree Health Benefit Act of 1992 (Coal Act), 26 U. S. C. § § 9701-9722. The "fairness" question is, why Eastern?

The answer cannot lie in a contractual promise to pay, for Eastern made no such contractual promise. Nor did Eastern participate in any benefit plan that made such a contractual promise, prior to its departure from the coal industry in 1965. But . . . this case is not a civil law suit for breach of contract. It is a constitutional challenge to Congress' decision to assess a new future liability on the basis of an old employment relationship. Unless it is fundamentally unfair and unjust, in terms of

Eastern's reasonable reliance and settled expectations, to impose that liability, the Coal Act's "reachback" provision meets that challenge.

I believe several features of this case demonstrate that the relationship between Eastern and the payments demanded by the Act is special enough to pass the Constitution's fundamental fairness test. That is, even though Eastern left the coal industry in 1965, the historical circumstances, taken together, prevent Eastern from showing that the Act's "reachback" liability provision so frustrates Eastern's reasonable settled expectations as to impose an unconstitutional liability.

For one thing, the liability that the statute imposes upon Eastern extends only to miners whom Eastern itself employed. . . . They are miners whose labor benefited Eastern when they were younger and healthier. Insofar as working conditions created a risk of future health problems for those miners, Eastern created those conditions. And these factors help to distinguish Eastern from others with respect to a later obligation to pay the health care costs that inevitably arise in old age. . . .

Congress has sometimes imposed liability, even "retroactive" liability, designed to prevent degradation of a natural resource, upon those who have used and benefited from it. See, e.g., Comprehensive Environmental Response, Compensation, and Liability Act of 1980 (CERCLA). That analogy, while imperfect, calls attention to the special tie between a firm and its former employee, a human resource, that helps to explain the special retroactive liability. That connection, while not by itself justifying retroactive liability here, helps to distinguish a firm like Eastern, which employed a miner but no longer makes coal, from other funding sources, say current coal producers or coal consumers, who now make or use coal but who have never employed that miner or benefited from his work.

More importantly, the record demonstrates that Eastern, before 1965, contributed to the making of an important "promise" to the miners. That "promise," even if not contractually enforceable, led the miners to "develo[p]" a reasonable "expectation" that they would continue to receive "[retiree] medical benefits." The relevant history . . . shows that industry action (including action by Eastern), combined with Federal Government action and the miners' own forbearance, produced circumstances that made it natural for the miners to believe that either industry or government (or both) would make every effort to see that they received health benefits after they retired—regardless of what terms were explicitly included in previously signed bargaining agreements.

(1) Before the 1940's, health care for miners, insofar as it existed, was provided by "company doctors" in company towns. . . . By the late 1940's, health care and pension rights had become the issue for miners, a central demand in collective bargaining, and a rallying cry for those who urged a nationwide coal strike. . . . In 1946, the workers struck. The Government seized the mines. And the Government, together with the Union, effectively imposed a managed health care agreement on the coal operators.

(2) The resulting 1946 "Krug-Lewis Agreement" created a Medical and Hospital Fund designed to "provide, or to arrange for the availability of, medical, hospital, and related services for the miners and their dependents." One year later, this fund was consolidated with a "Welfare and Retirement Fund" also established in 1946 (W&R Fund). Under the 1947 and successive agreements, the Fund's three trustees (union, management, and "neutral") determined the specific benefits provided under the plan.

(3) Between 1947 and 1965, the benefits that the W&R Fund provided included retiree benefits quite similar to those at issue here. The bargaining agreements between the coal operators and miners and the Fund's Annual Reports make clear that the W&R Fund provided benefits to all "employees. . . , their families and dependents for medical or hospital care." The Fund's Annual Reports specified that eligible family members included miners' spouses, children, dependent parents, (and, at least after 1955) *retired miners and their dependents,* and widows and orphans (for a 12-month period). . . . The only significant difference between the coverage provided before 1974 and after 1974 consists of greater generosity after 1974 with respect to widows, for the earlier 12-month limitation was repealed and health benefits extended to widows' remarriage or death.

(4) In return for what the miners thought was an assurance (though not a contractual obligation) from management of continued pension and health care benefits, the Union agreed to accept mechanization of mining, a concession that meant significant layoffs and a smaller future workforce. . . . The President of the Southern Coal Operators' Association said in 1953 that the miners "have been promised and grown accustomed to" health benefits. Those benefits, the management's W&R Fund trustee said in 1951, covered "mine worker[s], including pensioners, and dependents . . . without limit as to duration." This Court, too, has said that the UMWA "agreed not to oppose the rapid mechanization of the mines" in exchange for "increased wages" and "payments into the welfare fund." *Mine Workers v. Pennington* (1965). . . . And numerous supporters of the present law read the history as showing, for example, that the "miners went to work each day under the assumption that their health benefits would be there when they retired." [Quoting Sen. Harrison Wofford, D-Pa., from 1992 debate.]

Further, the Federal Government played a significant role in developing the expectations that these "promises" created. In 1946, as mentioned above, during a strike related to health and pension benefits, the Government seized the mines and imposed the "Krug-Lewis Agreement," which established the basic health benefits framework. . . . In 1948, during a strike related to pension benefits, the Government again intervened to ensure continued availability of these benefits. . . . In later years, but before 1965, Congress provided the W&R Fund with special tax benefits, helped the Fund to build hospitals, and established health and safety standards. . . .

[I]n labor relations, as in human relations, one can create promises and understandings which, even in the absence of a legally enforceable contract, others reasonably expect will be honored. Indeed, in labor relations such industrywide understandings may spell the difference between labor war and labor peace, for the parties may look to a strike, not to a court, for enforcement. It is that kind of important, mutual understanding that is at issue here. For the record shows that pre-1965 statements and other conduct led management to understand, and labor legitimately to expect, that health care benefits for retirees and their dependents would continue to be provided.

Finally, Eastern continued to obtain profits from the coal mining industry long after 1965, for it operated a wholly owned coal-mining subsidiary, Eastern Associated Coal Corp. (EACC), until the late 1980's. Between 1966 and 1987, Eastern effectively ran EACC, sharing officers, supervising management, and receiving 100% of EACC's approximately $100 million in dividends. . . . Eastern officials, in their role as EACC directors, ratified the post-1965 bargaining agreements and must have remained aware of the W&R Fund's deepening financial crisis.

Taken together, these circumstances explain why it is not fundamentally unfair for Congress to impose upon Eastern liability for the future health care costs of miners whom it long ago employed—rather than imposing that liability, for example, upon the present industry, coal consumers, or taxpayers. Each diminishes the reasonableness of Eastern's expectation that, by leaving the industry, it could fall within the Constitution's protection against unfairly retroactive liability. . . .

These circumstances . . . mean that Eastern knew of the potential funding problems that arise in any multiemployer benefit plan before it left the industry. Eastern knew or should have known that, in light of the structure of the benefit plan and the frequency with which coal operators went out of business, a "last man out" problem could exacerbate the health plan's funding difficulties. . . . Eastern also knew or should have known that because of prior federal involvement, future federal intervention to solve any such problem was a serious possibility. Eastern knew . . . that any legislative effort to solve such a problem could well occur many years into the future. And, most importantly, Eastern played a significant role in creating the miners' expectations that led to this legislation. Add to these circumstances the two others I have mentioned—that Eastern had benefited from the labor of the miners for whose future health care it must provide, and that Eastern remained in the industry, drawing from it substantial profits. . . .

The upshot . . . is that I cannot say the Government's regulation has unfairly interfered with Eastern's "distinct investment-backed expectations." . . .

The law imposes upon Eastern the burden of showing that the statute, because of its retroactive effect, is fundamentally unfair or unjust. The circumstances I have mentioned convince me that Eastern cannot show a sufficiently reasonable expectation that it would remain free of future health care cost liability for the workers whom it employed. Eastern has therefore failed to show that the law unfairly upset its legitimately settled expectations. Because, in my view, Eastern has not met its burden, I would uphold the "reachback" provision of the Coal Act as constitutional.

No. 97-371

National Endowment for the Arts, et al., Petitioners v. Karen Finley et al.

On writ of certiorari to the United States
Court of Appeals for the Ninth Circuit

[June 25, 1998]

JUSTICE O'CONNOR delivered the opinion of the Court.[*]
The National Foundation on the Arts and Humanities Act, as amended in 1990, requires the Chairperson of the National Endowment for the Arts (NEA) to ensure

---

[*]JUSTICE GINSBURG joins all but Part II-B of this opinion.

that "artistic excellence and artistic merit are the criteria by which [grant] applications are judged, taking into consideration general standards of decency and respect for the diverse beliefs and values of the American public." 20 U. S. C. § 954(d)(1). In this case, we review the Court of Appeals' determination that § 954(d)(1), on its face, impermissibly discriminates on the basis of viewpoint and is void for vagueness under the First and Fifth Amendments. We conclude that § 954(d)(1) is facially valid, as it neither inherently interferes with First Amendment rights nor violates constitutional vagueness principles.

I

A

With the establishment of the NEA in 1965, Congress embarked on a "broadly conceived national policy of support for the . . . arts in the United States," see § 953(b), pledging federal funds to "help create and sustain not only a climate encouraging freedom of thought, imagination, and inquiry but also the material conditions facilitating the release of . . . creative talent." § 951(7). The enabling statute vests the NEA with substantial discretion to award grants; it identifies only the broadest funding priorities, including "artistic and cultural significance, giving emphasis to American creativity and cultural diversity," "professional excellence," and the encouragement of "public knowledge, education, understanding, and appreciation of the arts." See § § 954(c)(1)-(10).

Applications for NEA funding are initially reviewed by advisory panels composed of experts in the relevant field of the arts. Under the 1990 Amendments to the enabling statute, those panels must reflect "diverse artistic and cultural points of view" and include "wide geographic, ethnic, and minority representation," as well as "lay individuals who are knowledgeable about the arts." § § 959(c)(1)-(2). The panels report to the 26-member National Council on the Arts (Council), which, in turn, advises the NEA Chairperson. The Chairperson has the ultimate authority to award grants but may not approve an application as to which the Council has made a negative recommendation. § 955(f).

Since 1965, the NEA has distributed over three billion dollars in grants to individuals and organizations, funding that has served as a catalyst for increased state, corporate, and foundation support for the arts. Congress has recently restricted the availability of federal funding for individual artists, confining grants primarily to qualifying organizations and state arts agencies, and constraining sub-granting. By far the largest portion of the grants distributed in fiscal year 1998 were awarded directly to state arts agencies. In the remaining categories, the most substantial grants were allocated to symphony orchestras, fine arts museums, dance theater foundations, and opera associations.

Throughout the NEA's history, only a handful of the agency's roughly 100,000 awards have generated formal complaints about misapplied funds or abuse of the public's trust. Two provocative works, however, prompted public controversy in 1989 and led to congressional revaluation of the NEA's funding priorities and efforts to increase oversight of its grant-making procedures. The Institute of Contemporary Art at the University of Pennsylvania had used $30,000 of a visual arts grant it received from the NEA to fund a 1989 retrospective of photographer Robert Mapplethorpe's work. The exhibit, entitled *The Perfect Moment,* included homoerotic photographs that several Members of Congress condemned as pornographic. Members also denounced artist Andres Serrano's work *Piss Christ,* a photograph of a crucifix immersed in urine. Serrano had been awarded a $15,000 grant from the Southeast Center for Contemporary Art, an organization that received NEA support.

When considering the NEA's appropriations for fiscal year 1990, Congress reacted to the controversy surrounding the Mapplethorpe and Serrano photographs by eliminating $45,000 from the agency's budget, the precise amount contributed to the two exhibits by NEA grant recipients. Congress also enacted an amendment providing that no NEA funds "may be used to promote, disseminate, or produce materials which in the judgment of [the NEA] may be considered obscene, including but not limited to, depictions of sadomasochism, homoeroticism, the sexual exploitation of children, or individuals engaged in sex acts and which, when taken as a whole, do not have serious literary, artistic, political, or scientific value." Department of the Interior and Related Agencies Appropriations Act, 1990. The NEA implemented Congress' mandate by instituting a requirement that all grantees certify in writing that they would not utilize federal funding to engage in projects inconsistent with the criteria in the 1990 appropriations bill. That certification requirement was subsequently invalidated as unconstitutionally vague by a Federal District Court, *Bella Lewitzky Dance Foundation v. Frohnmayer* (CD Cal. 1991), and the NEA did not appeal the decision.

In the 1990 appropriations bill, Congress also agreed to create an Independent Commission of constitutional law scholars to review the NEA's grant-making procedures and assess the possibility of more focused standards for public arts funding. The Commission's report, issued in September 1990, concluded that there is no constitutional obligation to provide arts funding, but also recommended that the NEA rescind the certification requirement and cautioned against legislation setting forth any content restrictions. Instead, the Commission suggested procedural changes to enhance the role of advisory panels and a statutory reaffirmation of "the high place the nation accords to the fostering of mutual respect for the disparate beliefs and values among us."

Informed by the Commission's recommendations, and cognizant of pending judicial challenges to the funding limitations in the 1990 appropriations bill, Congress debated several proposals to reform the NEA's grant-making process when it considered the agency's reauthorization in the fall of 1990. The House rejected the Crane Amendment, which would have virtually eliminated the NEA, and the Rohrabacher Amendment, which would have introduced a prohibition on awarding any grants that could be used to "promote, distribute, disseminate, or produce matter that has the purpose or effect of denigrating the beliefs, tenets, or objects of a particular religion" or "of denigrating an individual, or group of individuals, on the basis of race, sex, handicap, or national origin." Ultimately, Congress adopted the Williams/Coleman Amendment, a bipartisan compromise between Members opposing any funding restrictions and those favoring some guidance to the agency. In relevant part, the Amendment became § 954(d)(1), which directs the Chairperson, in establishing procedures to judge the artistic merit of grant applications, to "tak[e] into consideration general standards of decency and respect for the diverse beliefs and values of the American public."

The NEA has not promulgated any official interpretation of the provision, but in December 1990, the Council unanimously adopted a resolution to implement § 954(d)(1) merely by ensuring that the members of the advisory panels that conduct the initial review of grant applications represent geographic, ethnic, and aesthetic diversity. John Frohnmayer, then Chairperson of the NEA, also declared that he would "count on [the] procedures" ensuring diverse membership on the peer review panels to fulfill Congress' mandate.

B

The four individual respondents in this case, Karen Finley, John Fleck, Holly Hughes, and Tim Miller, are performance artists who applied for NEA grants before § 954(d)(1) was enacted. An advisory panel recommended approval of respondents' projects, both initially and after receiving Frohnmayer's request to reconsider three of the applications. A majority of the Council subsequently recommended disapproval, and in June 1990, the NEA informed respondents that they had been denied funding. Respondents filed suit, alleging that the NEA had violated their First Amendment rights by rejecting the applications on political grounds, had failed to follow statutory procedures by basing the denial on criteria other than those set forth in the NEA's enabling statute, and had breached the confidentiality of their grant applications through the release of quotations to the press, in violation of the Privacy Act of 1974. Respondents sought restoration of the recommended grants or reconsideration of their applications, as well as damages for the alleged Privacy Act violations. When Congress enacted § 954(d)(1), respondents, now joined by the National Association of Artists' Organizations (NAAO), amended their complaint to challenge the provision as void for vagueness and impermissibly viewpoint based.

The District Court denied the NEA's motion for judgment on the pleadings [1992], and, after discovery, the NEA agreed [in 1993] to settle the individual respondents' statutory and as-applied constitutional claims by paying the artists the amount of the vetoed grants, damages, and attorney's fees.

The District Court then granted summary judgment in favor of respondents on their facial constitutional challenge to § 954(d)(1) and enjoined enforcement of the provision. The court rejected the argument that the NEA could comply with § 954(d)(1) by structuring the grant selection process to provide for diverse advisory panels. The provision, the court stated, "fails adequately to notify applicants of what is required of them or to circumscribe NEA discretion." Reasoning that "the very nature of our pluralistic society is that there are an infinite number of values and beliefs, and correlatively, there may be no national 'general standards of decency,'" the court concluded that § 954(d)(1) "cannot be given effect consistent with the Fifth Amendment's due process requirement." Drawing an analogy between arts funding and public universities, the court further ruled that the First Amendment constrains the NEA's grant-making process, and that because § 954(d)(1) "clearly reaches a substantial amount of protected speech," it is impermissibly overbroad on its face. The Government did not seek a stay of the District Court's injunction, and consequently the NEA has not applied § 954(d)(1) since June 1992.

A divided panel of the Court of Appeals affirmed the District Court's ruling. (CA9 1996). The majority agreed with the District Court that the NEA was compelled by the adoption of § 954(d)(1) to alter its grant-making procedures to ensure that applications are judged according to the "decency and respect" criteria. The Chairperson, the court reasoned, "has no discretion to ignore this obligation, enforce only part of it, or give it a cramped construction." Concluding that the "decency and respect" criteria are not "susceptible to objective definition," the court held that § 954(d)(1) "gives rise to the danger of arbitrary and discriminatory application" and is void for vagueness under the First and Fifth Amendments. In the alternative, the court ruled that § 954(d)(1) violates the First Amendment's prohibition on viewpoint-based restrictions on protected speech. Government funding of the arts, the court explained, is both a "traditional sphere of free expression" and an area in which the Government has stated its intention to "encourage a diversity of views from private speakers." Accordingly, finding that § 954(d)(1) "has a speech-based restriction as its sole rationale and operative principle" and noting the NEA's failure to articulate a compelling interest for the provision, the court declared it facially invalid.

The dissent asserted that the First Amendment protects artists' rights to express themselves as indecently and disrespectfully as they like, but does not compel the Government to fund that speech. (Kleinfeld, J., dissenting). The challenged provision, the dissent contended, did not prohibit the NEA from funding indecent or offensive art, but merely required the agency to consider the "decency and respect" criteria in the grant selection process. Moreover, according to the dissent's reasoning, the vagueness principles applicable to the direct regulation of speech have no bearing on the selective award of prizes, and the Government may draw distinctions based on content and viewpoint in making its funding decisions. Three judges dissented from the denial of rehearing en banc, maintaining that the panel's decision gave the statute an "implausible construction," applied the " 'void for vagueness' doctrine where it does not belong," and extended "First Amendment principles to a situation that the First Amendment doesn't cover." (CA9 1997).

We granted certiorari (1997) and now reverse the judgment of the Court of Appeals.

II

A

Respondents raise a facial constitutional challenge to § 954(d)(1), and consequently they confront "a heavy burden" in advancing their claim. . . . To prevail, respondents must demonstrate a substantial risk that application of the provision will lead to the suppression of speech.

Respondents argue that the provision is a paradigmatic example of viewpoint discrimination because it rejects any artistic speech that either fails to respect mainstream values or offends standards of decency. The premise of respondents' claim is that § 954(d)(1) constrains the agency's ability to fund certain categories of artistic expression. The NEA, however, reads the provision as merely hortatory, and contends that it stops well short of an absolute restriction. Section 954(d)(1) adds "considerations" to the grant-making process; it does not preclude awards to projects that might be deemed "indecent" or "disrespectful," nor place conditions on grants, or even specify that those factors must be given any particular weight in reviewing an application. Indeed, the agency asserts that it has adequately implemented § 954(d)(1) merely by ensuring the representation of various backgrounds and points of view on the advisory panels that analyze grant applications. See Declaration of Randolph McAusland, Deputy Chairman for Programs at the NEA, reprinted in App. 79 (stating that the NEA implements the provision "by ensuring that the peer review panels represent a variety of geographical areas, aesthetic views, professions, areas of expertise, races and ethnic groups, and gender, and include a lay person"). We do not decide whether the NEA's view—that the formulation of diverse advisory panels is sufficient to comply with Congress' command—is in fact a reasonable reading of the statute. It is clear, however, that the text of § 954(d)(1) imposes no categorical requirement. The advisory language stands in sharp contrast to congressional efforts to prohibit the funding of certain classes of speech. When Congress has in fact intended to affirmatively constrain the NEA's grant-making authority, it has done so in no uncertain terms. See § 954(d)(2) ("[O]bscenity is without artistic merit, is not protected speech, and shall not be funded").

Furthermore, like the plain language of § 954(d), the political context surrounding the adoption of the "decency and respect" clause is inconsistent with respondents' assertion that the provision compels the NEA to deny funding on the basis of viewpoint discriminatory criteria. The legislation was a bipartisan proposal introduced as a counterweight to amendments aimed at eliminating the NEA's funding or substantially constraining its grant-making authority. The Independent Commission had cautioned Congress against the adoption of distinct viewpoint-based standards for funding, and the Commission's report suggests that "additional criteria for selection, if any, should be incorporated as part of the selection process (perhaps as part of a definition of 'artistic excellence'), rather than isolated and treated as exogenous considerations." In keeping with that recommendation, the criteria in § 954(d)(1) inform the assessment of artistic merit, but Congress declined to disallow any particular viewpoints. . . .

That § 954(d)(1) admonishes the NEA merely to take "decency and respect" into consideration, and that the legislation was aimed at reforming procedures rather than precluding speech, undercut respondents' argument that the provision inevitably will be utilized as a tool for invidious viewpoint discrimination. In cases where we have struck down legislation as facially unconstitutional, the dangers were both more evident and more substantial. . . .

In contrast, the "decency and respect" criteria do not silence speakers by expressly "threaten[ing] censorship of ideas." Thus, we do not perceive a realistic danger that § 954(d)(1) will compromise First Amendment values. As respondents' own arguments demonstrate, the considerations that the provision introduces, by their nature, do not engender the kind of directed viewpoint discrimination that would prompt this Court to invalidate a statute on its face. Respondents assert, for example, that "[o]ne would be hard-pressed to find two people in the United States who could agree on what the 'diverse beliefs and values of the American public' are, much less on whether a particular work of art 'respects' them"; and they claim that " '[d]ecency' is likely to mean something very different to a septegenarian in Tuscaloosa and a teenager in Las Vegas." The NEA likewise views the considerations enumerated in § 954(d)(1) as susceptible to multiple interpretations. . . . Accordingly, the provision does not introduce considerations that, in practice, would effectively preclude or punish the expression of particular views. Indeed, one could hardly anticipate how "decency" or "respect" would bear on grant applications in categories such as funding for symphony orchestras.

Respondents' claim that the provision is facially unconstitutional may be reduced to the argument that the criteria in § 954(d)(1) are sufficiently subjective that the agency could utilize them to engage in viewpoint discrimination. Given the varied interpretations of the criteria and the vague exhortation to "take them into consideration," it seems unlikely that this provision will introduce any greater element of selectivity than the determination of "artistic excellence" itself. And we are reluctant, in any event, to invalidate legislation "on the basis of its hypothetical application to situations not before the Court." *FCC v. Pacifica Foundation* (1978).

The NEA's enabling statute contemplates a number of indisputably constitutional applications for both the "decency" prong of § 954(d)(1) and its reference to "respect for the diverse beliefs and values of the American public." Educational programs are central to the NEA's mission. . . . And it is well established that "decency" is a permissible factor where "educational suitability" motivates its consideration. . . .

Permissible applications of the mandate to consider "respect for the diverse beliefs and values of the American public" are also apparent. In setting forth the purposes of the NEA, Congress explained that "[i]t is vital to democracy to honor and preserve its multicultural artistic heritage." § 951(10). The agency expressly takes diversity into account, giving special consideration to "projects and productions . . . that reach, or reflect the culture of, a minority, inner city, rural, or tribal community," § 954(c)(4), as well as projects that generally emphasize "cultural diversity," § 954(c)(1). Respondents do not contend that the criteria in § 954(d)(1) are impermissibly applied when they may be justified, as the statute contemplates, with respect to a project's intended audience.

We recognize, of course, that reference to these permissible applications would not alone be sufficient to sustain the statute against respondents' First Amendment challenge. But neither are we persuaded that, in other applications, the language of § 954(d)(1) itself will give rise to the suppression of protected expression. Any content-based considerations that may be taken into account in the grant-making process are a consequence of the nature of arts funding. The NEA has limited resources and it must deny the majority of the grant applications that it receives, including many that propose "artistically excellent" projects. The agency may decide to fund particular projects for a wide variety of reasons, "such as the technical proficiency of the artist, the creativity of the work, the anticipated public interest in or appreciation of the work, the work's contemporary relevance, its educational value, its suitability for or appeal to special audiences (such as children or the disabled), its service to a rural or isolated community, or even simply that the work could increase public knowledge of an art form." As the dissent below noted, it would be "impossible to have a highly selective grant program without denying money to a large amount of constitutionally protected expression." The "very assumption" of the NEA is that grants will be awarded according to the "artistic worth of competing applications," and absolute neutrality is simply "inconceivable." . . .

Respondents do not allege discrimination in any particular funding decision. (In fact, after filing suit to challenge § 954(d)(1), two of the individual respondents received NEA grants.) Thus, we have no occasion here to address an as-applied challenge in a situation where the denial of a grant may be shown to be the product of invidious viewpoint discrimination. If the NEA were to leverage its power to award subsidies on the basis of subjective criteria into a penalty on disfavored viewpoints, then we would confront a different case. . . . In addition, as the NEA itself concedes, a more pressing constitutional question would arise if government funding resulted in the imposition of a disproportionate burden calculated to drive "certain ideas or viewpoints from the marketplace." Unless and until § 954(d)(1) is applied in a manner that raises concern about the suppression of disfavored viewpoints, however, we uphold the constitutionality of the provision. . . .

B

Finally, although the First Amendment certainly has application in the subsidy context, we note that the Government may allocate competitive funding according to criteria that would be impermissible were direct regulation of speech or a criminal penalty at stake. So long as legislation does not infringe on other constitutionally protected rights, Congress has wide latitude to set spending priorities. In the 1990 Amendments that incorporated § 954(d)(1), Congress modified the declaration of purpose in the NEA's enabling act to provide that arts funding should "contribute to public support and confidence in the use of taxpayer funds," and that "[p]ublic funds . . . must ultimately serve public purposes the Congress defines." § 951(5). And as we held in *Rust* [*v. Sullivan* (1991)], Congress may "selectively fund a program to encourage certain activities it believes to be in the public interest, without at the same time funding an alternative program which seeks to deal with the problem in another way." In doing so, "the Government has not discriminated on the basis of viewpoint; it has merely chosen to fund one activity to the exclusion of the other."

III

The lower courts also erred in invalidating § 954(d)(1) as unconstitutionally vague. Under the First and Fifth Amendments, speakers are protected from arbitrary and discriminatory enforcement of vague standards. The terms of the provision are undeniably opaque, and if they appeared in a criminal statute or regulatory scheme, they could raise substantial vagueness concerns. It is unlikely, however, that speakers will be compelled to steer too far clear of any "forbidden area" in the context of grants of this nature. [Citations omitted.] We recognize, as a practical matter, that artists may conform their speech to what they believe to be the decision-making criteria in order to acquire funding. But when the Government is acting as patron rather than as sovereign, the consequences of imprecision are not constitutionally severe.

In the context of selective subsidies, it is not always feasible for Congress to legislate with clarity. Indeed, if this statute is unconstitutionally vague, then so too are all government programs awarding scholarships and grants on the basis of subjective criteria such as "excellence." [Citing statutes establishing the Congressional Award Program, National Endowment for the Humanities, Fulbright grants, and grant programs by the Departments of Education and Energy.] To accept respondents' vagueness argument would be to call into question the constitutionality of these valuable government programs and countless others like them.

Section 954(d)(1) merely adds some imprecise considerations to an already subjective selection process. It does not, on its face, impermissibly infringe on First or Fifth Amendment rights. Accordingly, the judgment of the Court of Appeals is reversed and the case is remanded for further proceedings consistent with this opinion.

It is so ordered.

JUSTICE SCALIA, with whom JUSTICE THOMAS joins, concurring in the judgment.

"The operation was a success, but the patient died." What such a procedure is to medicine, the Court's opinion in this case is to law. It sustains the constitutionality of 20 U. S. C. § 954(d)(1) by gutting it. The most avid congressional opponents of the provision could not have asked for more. I write separately because, unlike the Court, I think that § 954(d)(1) must be evaluated as written, rather than as distorted by the agency it was meant to control. By its terms, it establishes content- and viewpoint-based criteria upon which grant applications are to be evaluated. And that is perfectly constitutional.

I

THE STATUTE MEANS WHAT IT SAYS

Section 954(d)(1) provides:

"No payment shall be made under this section except upon application therefor which is submitted to the National Endowment for the Arts in accordance with regulations issued and procedures established by the Chairperson. In establishing such regulations and procedures, the Chairperson shall ensure that—

"(1) artistic excellence and artistic merit are the criteria by which applications are judged, taking into consideration general standards of decency and respect for the diverse beliefs and values of the American public."

The phrase "taking into consideration general standards of decency and respect for the diverse beliefs and values of the American public" is what my grammar-school teacher would have condemned as a dangling modifier. . . . Even so, it is clear enough that the phrase is meant to apply to those who do the judging. The application reviewers must take into account "general standards of decency" and "respect for the diverse beliefs and values of the American public" when evaluating artistic excellence and merit. . . .

This is so apparent that I am at a loss to understand what the Court has in mind (other than the gutting of the statute) when it speculates that the statute is merely "advisory." General standards of decency and respect for Americans' beliefs and values *must* (for the statute says that the Chairperson "shall ensure" this result) be taken into account . . . in evaluating all applications. This does not mean that those factors must always be dispositive, but it *does* mean that they must always be considered. The method of compliance proposed by the National Endowment for the Arts (NEA)—selecting diverse review panels of artists and nonartists that reflect a wide range of geographic and cultural perspectives—is so obviously inadequate that it insults the intelligence. A diverse panel membership increases the odds that, *if and when* the panel takes the factors into account, it will reach an accurate assessment of what they demand. But it in no way increases the odds that the panel *will* take the factors into consideration—much less *ensures* that the panel will do so, which is the Chairperson's duty under the statute. . . .

The statute requires the decency and respect factors to be considered in evaluating all applications. . . . A reviewer may, of course, give varying weight to the factors depending on the context, and in some categories of cases (such as the Court's example of funding for symphony orchestras) the factors may rarely if ever affect the outcome; but § 954(d)(1) requires the factors to be considered in every case.

I agree with the Court that § 954(d)(1) "imposes no categorical requirement." . . . But the factors need not be conclusive to be discriminatory. To the extent a particular applicant exhibits disrespect for the diverse beliefs and values of the American public or fails to comport with general standards of decency, the likelihood that he will receive a grant diminishes. . . . [T]he decisionmaker, all else being equal, will favor applications that display decency and respect, and disfavor applications that do not.

This unquestionably constitutes viewpoint discrimination. . . . The applicant who displays "decency" . . . and the applicant who displays "respect" . . . will *always* have an edge over an applicant who displays the opposite. . . .

The "political context surrounding the adoption of the 'decency and respect' clause" . . . does not change its meaning or affect its constitutionality. . . . It is evident in the legislative history that § 954(d)(1) was prompted by, and directed at, the public funding of such offensive productions as Serrano's "Piss Christ," the portrayal of a crucifix immersed in urine, and Mapplethorpe's show of lurid homoerotic photographs. Thus, . . . it is perfectly clear that the statute was meant to disfavor—that is, to discriminate against—such productions. Not to ban their funding absolutely, to be sure (though as I shall discuss, that also would not have been unconstitutional); but to make their funding more difficult. . . .

II

WHAT THE STATUTE SAYS IS CONSTITUTIONAL

The Court devotes so much of its opinion to explaining why this statute means something other than what it says that it neglects to cite the constitutional text governing our analysis. The First Amendment reads: "Congress shall make no law . . . *abridging* the freedom of speech" (emphasis added). . . . With the enactment of § 954(d)(1), Congress did not abridge the speech of those who disdain the beliefs and values of the American public, nor did it abridge indecent speech. Those who wish to create indecent and disrespectful art are as unconstrained now as they were before the enactment of this statute. *Avant-garde artists* such as respondents remain entirely free to *épater* [spite] *les bourgeois;* they are merely deprived of the additional satisfaction of having the bourgeoisie taxed to pay for it. . . .

Section 954(d)(1) is no more discriminatory, and no less constitutional, than virtually every other piece of funding legislation enacted by Congress. "The Government can, without violating the Constitution, selectively fund a program to encourage certain activities it believes to be in the public interest, without at the same time funding an alternative program. . . ." *Rust v. Sullivan* (1991). . . . It takes a particularly high degree of chutzpah for the NEA to contradict this proposition, since the agency itself discriminates—and is required by law to discriminate—in favor of artistic (as opposed to scientific, or political, or theological) expression. . . .

The nub of the difference between me and the Court is that I regard the distinction between "abridging" speech and funding it as a fundamental divide, on this side of which the First Amendment is inapplicable. The Court, by contrast, seems to believe that the First Amendment, despite its words, has some ineffable effect upon funding, imposing constraints of an indeterminate nature which it announces . . . are not violated by the statute here—or, more accurately, are not violated by the quite different, emasculated statute that it imagines. . . .

Finally, what is true of the First Amendment is also true of the constitutional rule against vague legislation: it has no application to funding. . . .

* * *

In its laudatory description of the accomplishments of the NEA, the Court notes with satisfaction that "only a handful of the agency's roughly 100,000 awards have generated formal complaints." The Congress that felt it necessary to enact § 954(d)(1) evidently thought it much *more* noteworthy that *any* money exacted from American taxpayers had been used to produce a crucifix immersed in urine, or a display of homoerotic photographs. It is no secret that the provision was prompted by, and directed at, the funding of such offensive productions. Instead of banning the funding of such productions absolutely, which I think would have been entirely constitutional, Congress took the lesser step of requiring them to be disfavored in the evaluation of grant applications. The Court's opinion today renders even that lesser step a nullity. For that reason, I concur only in the judgment.

JUSTICE SOUTER, dissenting.

The question here is whether the italicized segment of this statute is unconstitutional on its face: "artistic excellence and artistic merit are the criteria by which applications [for grants from the National Endowment for the Arts] are judged, *taking into consideration general standards of decency and respect for the diverse beliefs and values of the American public.* " 20 U. S. C. § 954(d) (emphasis added). It is.

The decency and respect proviso mandates viewpoint-based decisions in the disbursement of government subsidies, and the Government has wholly failed to explain why the statute should be afforded an exemption from the fundamental rule of the First Amendment that viewpoint discrimination in the exercise of public authority over expressive activity is unconstitutional. The Court's conclusions that the proviso is not viewpoint based, that it is not a regulation, and that the NEA may permissibly engage in viewpoint-based discrimination, are all patently mistaken. Nor may the question raised be answered in the Government's favor on the assumption that some constitutional applications of the statute are enough to satisfy the demand of facial constitutionality, leaving claims of the proviso's obvious invalidity to be dealt with later in response to challenges of specific applications of the discriminatory standards. This assumption is irreconcilable with our long standing and sensible doctrine of facial overbreadth, applicable to claims brought under the First Amendment's speech clause. I respectfully dissent.

I [omitted]

II

. . . [T]he Court has its work cut out for it in seeking a constitutional reading of the statute. . . .

A

The Court says, first, that because the phrase "general standards of decency and respect for the diverse beliefs and values of the American public" is imprecise and capable of multiple interpretations, "the considerations that the provision introduces, by their nature, do not engender the kind of directed viewpoint discrimination that would prompt this Court to invalidate a statute on its face." Unquestioned case law, however, is clearly to the contrary.

"Sexual expression which is indecent but not obscene is protected by the First Amendment," *Sable Communications of Cal., Inc. v. FCC* (1989), and except when protecting children from exposure to indecent material, the First Amendment has never been read to allow the government to rove around imposing general standards of decency. . . . Because "the normal definition of 'indecent' . . . refers to nonconformance with accepted standards of morality," *FCC v. Pacifica Foundation* [1978], restrictions turning on decency, especially those couched in terms of "general standards of decency," are quintessentially viewpoint based: they require discrimination on the basis of conformity with mainstream mores. . . .

Just as self-evidently, a statute disfavoring speech that fails to respect America's "diverse beliefs and values" is the very model of viewpoint discrimination; it penalizes any view disrespectful to any belief or value espoused by someone in the American populace. Boiled down to its practical essence, the limitation obviously means that art that disrespects the ideology, opinions, or convictions of a significant segment of the American public is to be disfavored, whereas art that reinforces those values is not. After all, the whole point of the proviso was to make sure that works like Serrano's ostensibly blasphemous portrayal of Jesus would not be funded, while a reverent treatment, conventionally respectful of Christian sensibilities, would not run afoul of the law. Nothing could be more viewpoint based than that. . . .

B

Another alternative for avoiding unconstitutionality that the Court appears to regard with some favor is the Government's argument that the NEA may comply with § 954(d) merely by populating the advisory panels that analyze grant applications with members of diverse backgrounds. Would that it were so easy; this asserted implementation of the law fails even to "reflec[t] a plausible construction of the plain language of the statute." . . .

C

A third try at avoiding constitutional problems is the Court's disclaimer of any constitutional issue here because "[s]ection 954(d)(1) adds 'considerations' to the grant-making process; it does not preclude awards to projects that might be deemed 'indecent' or 'disrespectful,' nor place conditions on grants, or even specify that those factors must be given any particular weight in reviewing an application." Since "§ 954(d)(1) admonishes the NEA merely to take 'decency and respect' into consideration," not to make funding decisions specifically on those grounds, the Court sees no constitutional difficulty.

That is not a fair reading. Just as the statute cannot be read as anything but viewpoint based, or as requiring nothing more than diverse review panels, it cannot be read as tolerating awards to spread indecency or disrespect, so long as the review panel, the National Council on the Arts, and the Chairperson have given some thought to the offending qualities and decided to underwrite them anyway. That, after all, is presumably just what prompted the congressional outrage in the first place, and there was nothing naive about the Representative who said he voted for the bill because it does "not tolerate wasting Federal funds for sexually explicit photographs [or] sacrilegious works."

III

A second basic strand in the Court's treatment of today's question, and the heart of JUSTICE SCALIA's, in effect assumes that whether or not the statute mandates viewpoint discrimination, there is no constitutional issue here because government art subsidies fall within a zone of activity free from First Amendment restraints. The Government calls attention to the roles of government-as-speaker and government-as-buyer, in which the government is of course entitled to engage in viewpoint discrimination: if the Food and Drug Administration launches an advertising campaign on the subject of smoking, it may condemn the habit without also having to show a cowboy taking a puff on the opposite page; and if the Secretary of Defense wishes to buy a portrait to decorate the Pentagon, he is free to prefer George Washington over George the Third.

The Government freely admits, however, that it neither speaks through the expression subsidized by the NEA, nor buys anything for itself with its NEA grants. On the contrary, believing that "[t]he arts . . . reflect the high place accorded by the American people to the nation's rich cultural heritage," § 951(6), and that "[i]t is vital to a democracy . . . to provide financial assistance to its artists and the organizations that support their work," § 951(10), the Government acts as a patron, financially underwriting the production of art by private artists and impresarios for independent consumption. Accordingly, the Government would have us liberate government-as-patron from First Amendment strictures not by placing it squarely within the categories of government-as-buyer or government-as-speaker, but by recognizing a new category by analogy to those accepted ones. The analogy is, however, a very poor fit, and this patronage falls embarrassingly on the wrong side of the line between government-as-buyer or -speaker and government-as-regulator-of-private-speech.

The division is reflected quite clearly in our precedents. Drawing on the notion of government-as-speaker, we held in *Rust v. Sullivan* [1991] that the Government was entitled to appropriate public funds for the promotion of particular choices among alternatives offered by health and social service providers (e.g., family planning with, and without, resort to abortion). When the government promotes a particular governmental program, "it is entitled to define the limits of that program," and to dictate the viewpoint expressed by speakers who are paid to participate in it. But we added the important qualifying language that "[t]his is not to suggest that funding by the Government, even when coupled with the freedom of the fund recipients to speak outside the scope of the Government-funded project, is invariably sufficient to justify Government control over the content of expression." Indeed, outside of the contexts of government-as-buyer and government-as-speaker, we have held time and time again that Congress may not "discriminate invidiously in its subsidies in such a way as to aim at the suppression of . . . ideas." *Regan v. Taxation with Representation of Wash.* (1983). . . .

IV, V [omitted]

No. 97-1374

William J. Clinton, President of the United States, et al., Appellants v. City of New York et al.

On appeal from the United States District Court for the District of Columbia

[June 25, 1998]

JUSTICE STEVENS delivered the opinion of the Court.

The Line Item Veto Act (Act) 2 U. S. C. § 691 *et seq.*, was enacted in April 1996 and became effective on January 1, 1997. The following day, six Members of Congress who had voted against the Act brought suit in the District Court for the District of Columbia challenging its constitutionality. On April 10, 1997, the District Court entered an order holding that the Act is unconstitutional. *Byrd v. Raines.* In obedience to the statutory direction to allow a direct, expedited appeal to this Court, see § § 692(b)-(c), we promptly noted probable jurisdiction and expedited review (1997). We determined, however, that the Members of Congress did not have standing to sue because they had not "alleged a sufficiently concrete injury to have established Article III standing," *Raines v. Byrd* (1997); thus, "in . . . light of [the] overriding and time-honored concern about keeping the Judiciary's power within its proper constitutional sphere," we remanded the case to the District Court with instructions to dismiss the complaint for lack of jurisdiction.

Less than two months after our decision in that case, the President exercised his authority to cancel one provision in the Balanced Budget Act of 1997 and two provisions in the Taxpayer Relief Act of 1997. Appellees, claiming that they had been injured by two of those cancellations, filed these cases in the District Court. That Court again held the statute invalid (1998), and we again expedited our review (1998). We now hold that these appellees have standing to challenge the constitutionality of the Act and, reaching the merits, we agree that the cancellation procedures set forth in the Act violate the Presentment Clause, Art. I, § 7, cl. 2, of the Constitution.

I

We begin by reviewing the canceled items that are at issue in these cases.

Section 4722(c) of the Balanced Budget Act

Title XIX of the Social Security Act, as amended, authorizes the Federal Government to transfer huge sums of money to the States to help finance medical care for the indigent. In 1991, Congress directed that those federal subsidies be reduced by the amount of certain taxes levied by the States on health care providers. In 1994, the Department of Health and Human Services (HHS) notified the State of New York that 15 of its taxes were covered by the 1991 Act, and that as of June 30, 1994, the statute therefore required New York to return $955 million to the United States. The notice advised the State that it could apply for a waiver on certain statutory grounds. New York did request a waiver for those tax programs, as well as for a number of others, but HHS has not formally acted on any of those waiver requests. New York has estimated that the amount at issue for the period from October 1992 through March 1997 is as high as $2.6 billion.

Because HHS had not taken any action on the waiver requests, New York turned to Congress for relief. On August 5, 1997, Congress enacted a law that resolved the issue in New York's favor. Section 4722(c) of the Balanced Budget Act of 1997 identifies the disputed taxes and provides that they "are deemed to be permissible health care related taxes and in compliance with the requirements" of the relevant provisions of the 1991 statute.

On August 11, 1997, the President sent identical notices to the Senate and to the House of Representatives canceling "one item of new direct spending," specifying § 4722(c) as that item, and stating that he had determined that "this cancellation will reduce the Federal budget deficit." He explained that § 4722(c) would have permitted New York "to continue relying upon impermissible provider taxes to finance its Medicaid program" and that "[t]his preferential treatment would have increased Medicaid costs, would have treated New York differently from all other States, and would have established a costly precedent for other States to request comparable treatment."

Section 968 of the Taxpayer Relief Act
A person who realizes a profit from the sale of securities is generally subject to a capital gains tax. Under existing law, however, an ordinary business corporation can acquire a corporation, including a food processing or refining company, in a merger or stock-for-stock transaction in which no gain is recognized to the seller; the seller's tax payment, therefore, is deferred. If, however, the purchaser is a farmers' cooperative, the parties cannot structure such a transaction because the stock of the cooperative may be held only by its members; thus, a seller dealing with a farmers' cooperative cannot obtain the benefits of tax deferral.

In § 968 of the Taxpayer Relief Act of 1997, Congress amended § 1042 of the Internal Revenue Code to permit owners of certain food refiners and processors to defer the recognition of gain if they sell their stock to eligible farmers' cooperatives. The purpose of the amendment, as repeatedly explained by its sponsors, was "to facilitate the transfer of refiners and processors to farmers' cooperatives." The amendment to § 1042 was one of the 79 "limited tax benefits" authorized by the Taxpayer Relief Act of 1997 and specifically identified in Title XVII of that Act as "subject to [the] line item veto."

On the same date that he canceled the "item of new direct spending" involving New York's health care programs, the President also canceled this limited tax benefit. In his explanation of that action, the President endorsed the objective of encouraging "value-added farming through the purchase by farmers' cooperatives of refiners or processors of agricultural goods," but concluded that the provision lacked safeguards and also "failed to target its benefits to small-and-medium-size cooperatives."

II

Appellees filed two separate actions against the President and other federal officials challenging these two cancellations. The plaintiffs in the first case are the City of New York, two hospital associations, one hospital, and two unions representing health care employees. The plaintiffs in the second are a farmers' cooperative consisting of about 30 potato growers in Idaho and an individual farmer who is a member and officer of the cooperative. The District Court consolidated the two cases and determined that at least one of the plaintiffs in each had standing under Article III of the Constitution.

Appellee New York City Health and Hospitals Corporation (NYCHHC) is responsible for the operation of public health care facilities throughout the City of New York. If HHS ultimately denies the State's waiver requests, New York law will automatically require 10 NYCHHC to make retroactive tax payments to the State of about $4 million for each of the years at issue. This contingent liability for NYCHHC, and comparable potential liabilities for the other appellee health care providers, were eliminated by § 4722(c) of the Balanced Budget Act of 1997 and revived by the President's cancellation of that provision. The District Court held that the cancellation of the statutory protection against these liabilities constituted sufficient injury to give these providers Article III standing.

Appellee Snake River Potato Growers, Inc. (Snake River) was formed in May 1997 to assist Idaho potato farmers in marketing their crops and stabilizing prices, in part through a strategy of acquiring potato processing facilities that will allow the members of the cooperative to retain revenues otherwise payable to third-party processors. At that time, Congress was considering the amendment to the capital gains tax that was expressly intended to aid farmers' cooperatives in the purchase of processing facilities, and Snake River had concrete plans to take advantage of the amendment if passed. Indeed, appellee Mike Cranney, acting on behalf of Snake River, was engaged in negotiations with the owner of an Idaho potato processor that would have qualified for the tax benefit under the pending legislation, but these negotiations terminated when the President canceled § 968. Snake River is currently considering the possible purchase of other processing facilities in Idaho if the President's cancellation is reversed. Based on these facts, the District Court concluded that the Snake River plaintiffs were injured by the President's cancellation of § 968, as they "lost the benefit of being on equal footing with their competitors and will likely have to pay more to purchase processing facilities now that the sellers will not [be] able to take advantage of section 968's tax breaks."

On the merits, the District Court held that the cancellations did not conform to the constitutionally mandated procedures for the enactment or repeal of laws in two respects. First, the laws that resulted after the cancellations "were different from those consented to by both Houses of Congress." Moreover, the President violated Article I "when he unilaterally canceled provisions of duly enacted statutes." As a separate basis for its decision, the District Court also held that the Act "impermissibly disrupts the balance of powers among the three branches of government."

III

As in the prior challenge to the Line Item Veto Act, we initially confront jurisdictional questions. [Stevens rejected several arguments by the government contending that the plaintiffs lacked standing to bring the suits. First, he rejected an argument that the act authorized only "individuals," not corporations, to invoke its provision for expedited review. "There is no plausible reason," Stevens wrote, "why Congress would have intended to provide for such special treatment of actions filed by natural persons and to have precluded entirely jurisdiction over comparable cases brought by corporate persons."]

We are also unpersuaded by the Government's argument that appellees' challenge to the constitutionality of the Act is nonjusticiable. . . .

In both the New York and the Snake River cases, the Government argues that the appellees are not actually injured because the claims are too speculative and, in any event, the claims are advanced by the wrong parties. We find no merit in the suggestion that New York's injury is merely speculative because HHS has not yet acted on the State's waiver requests. The State now has a multibillion dollar contingent liability that had been eliminated by § 4722(c) of the Balanced Budget Act of 1997. The District Court correctly concluded that the State, and the appellees, "suffered an immediate, concrete injury the moment that the President used the Line Item Veto to cancel section 4722(c) and deprived them of the benefits of that law." . . .

We also reject the Government's argument that New York's claim is advanced by the wrong parties because the claim belongs to the State of New York, and not appellees. Under New York statutes that are already in place, it is clear that both the City of New York and the appellee health care providers will be assessed by the State for substantial portions of any recoupment payments that the State may have to make to the Federal Government. . . .

The Snake River farmers' cooperative also suffered an immediate injury when the President canceled the limited tax benefit that Congress had enacted to facilitate the acquisition of processing plants. Three critical facts identify the specificity and the importance of that injury. First, Congress enacted § 968 for the specific purpose of providing a benefit to a defined category of potential purchasers of a defined category of assets. The members of that statutorily defined class received the equivalent of a statutory "bargaining chip" to use in carrying out the congressional plan to facilitate their purchase of such assets. Second, the President selected § 968 as one of only two tax benefits in the Taxpayer Relief Act of 1997 that should be canceled. The cancellation rested on his determination that the use of those bargaining chips would have a significant impact on the Federal budget deficit. Third, the Snake River cooperative was organized for the very purpose of acquiring processing facilities, it had concrete plans to utilize the benefits of § 968, and it was engaged in ongoing negotiations with the owner of a processing plant who had expressed an interest in structuring a tax-deferred sale when the President canceled § 968. Moreover, it is actively searching for other processing facilities for possible future purchase if the President's cancellation is reversed; and there are ample processing facilities in the State that Snake River may be able to purchase. By depriving them of their statutory bargaining chip, the cancellation inflicted a sufficient likelihood of economic injury to establish standing under our precedents. . . .

As with the New York case, the Government argues that the wrong parties are before the Court—that because the sellers of the processing facilities would have received the tax benefits, only they have standing to challenge the cancellation of § 968. This argument not only ignores the fact that the cooperatives were the intended beneficiaries of § 968, but also overlooks the self-evident proposition that more than one party may have standing to challenge a particular action or inaction. Once it is determined that a particular plaintiff is harmed by the defendant, and that the harm will likely be redressed by a favorable decision, that plaintiff has standing—regardless of whether there are others who would also have standing to sue. Thus, we are satisfied that both of these actions are Article III "Cases" that we have a duty to decide.

IV

The Line Item Veto Act gives the President the power to "cancel in whole" three types of provisions that have been signed into law: "(1) any dollar amount of discretionary budget authority; (2) any item of new direct spending; or (3) any limited tax benefit." 2 U. S. C. § 691(a). It is undisputed that the New York case involves an "item of new direct spending" and that the Snake River case involves a "limited tax benefit" as those terms are defined in the Act. It is also undisputed that each of those provisions had been signed into law pursuant to Article I, § 7, of the Constitution before it was canceled.

The Act requires the President to adhere to precise procedures whenever he exercises his cancellation authority. In identifying items for cancellation he must consider the legislative history, the purposes, and other relevant information about the items. See 2 U. S. C. § 691(b). He must determine, with respect to each cancellation, that it will "(i) reduce the Federal budget deficit; (ii) not impair any essential Government functions; and (iii) not harm the national interest." § 691(a)(A). Moreover, he must transmit a special message to Congress notifying it of each cancellation within five calendar days (excluding Sundays) after the enactment of the canceled provision. See § 691(a)(B). It is undisputed that the President meticulously followed these procedures in these cases.

A cancellation takes effect upon receipt by Congress of the special message from the President. See § 691b(a). If, however, a "disapproval bill" pertaining to a special message is enacted into law, the cancellations set forth in that message become "null and void." The Act sets forth a detailed expedited procedure for the consideration of a "disapproval bill," see § 691d, but no such bill was passed for either of the cancellations involved in these cases. A majority vote of both Houses is sufficient to enact a disapproval bill. The Act does not grant the President the authority to cancel a disapproval bill, see § 691(c), but he does, of course, retain his constitutional authority to veto such a bill.

The effect of a cancellation is plainly stated in § 691e. . . . With respect to both an item of new direct spending and a limited tax benefit, the cancellation prevents the item "from having legal force or effect." 2 U. S. C. § § 691e(4)(B)-(C). . . .

In both legal and practical effect, the President has amended two Acts of Congress by repealing a portion of each. "[R]epeal of statutes, no less than enactment, must conform with Art. I." *INS v. Chadha* (1983). There is no provision in the Constitution that authorizes the President to enact, to amend, or to repeal statutes. Both Article I and Article II assign responsibilities to the President that directly relate to the lawmaking process, but neither addresses the issue presented by these cases. The President "shall from time to time give to the Congress Information on the State of the Union, and recommend to their Consideration such Measures as he shall judge necessary and expedient. . . ." Art. II, § 3. Thus, he may initiate and influence legislative proposals. Moreover, after a bill has passed both Houses of Congress, but "before it become[s] a Law," it must be presented to the President. If he approves it, "he shall sign it, but if not he shall return it, with his Objections to that House in which it shall have originated, who shall enter the Objections at large on their Journal, and proceed to reconsider it." Art. I, § 7, cl. 2. His "return" of a bill, which is usually described as a "veto," is subject to being overridden by a two-thirds vote in each House.

There are important differences between the President's "return" of a bill pursuant to Article I, § 7, and the exercise of the President's cancellation authority pursuant to the Line Item Veto Act. The constitutional return takes place *before* the bill becomes law; the statutory cancellation occurs *after* the bill becomes law. The constitutional return is of the entire bill; the statutory cancellation is of only a part. Although the Constitution expressly authorizes the President to play a role in the process of enacting statutes, it is silent on the subject of unilateral Presidential action that either repeals or amends parts of duly enacted statutes.

There are powerful reasons for construing constitutional silence on this profoundly important issue as equivalent to an express prohibition. The procedures governing the enactment of statutes set forth in the text of Article I were the product of the great debates and compromises that produced the Constitution itself. Familiar historical materials provide abundant support for the conclusion that the power to enact statutes may only "be exercised in accord with a single, finely wrought and exhaustively considered, procedure." *Chadha.* Our first President understood the text of the Presentment Clause as requiring that he either "approve all the parts of a Bill, or reject it in toto." What has emerged in these cases from the President's exercise of his statutory cancellation powers, however, are truncated versions of two bills that passed both Houses of Congress. They are not the product of the "finely wrought" procedure that the Framers designed.

At oral argument, the Government suggested that the cancellations at issue in these cases do not effect a "repeal" of the canceled items because under the special "lockbox" provisions of the Act, a canceled item "retain[s] real, legal budgetary effect" insofar as it prevents Congress and the President from spending the savings that result from the cancellation. The text of the Act expressly provides, however, that a cancellation prevents a direct spending or tax benefit provision "from having legal force or effect." That a canceled item may have "real, legal budgetary effect" as a result of the lockbox procedure does not change the fact that by canceling the items at issue in these cases, the President made them entirely inoperative as to appellees. Section 968 of the Taxpayer Relief Act no longer provides a tax benefit, and § 4722(c) of the Balanced Budget Act of 1997 no longer relieves New York of its contingent liability. Such significant changes do not lose their character simply because the canceled provisions may have some continuing financial effect on the Government. The cancellation of one section of a statute may be the functional equivalent of a partial repeal even if a portion of the section is not canceled.

V

The Government advances two related arguments to support its position that despite the unambiguous provisions of the Act, cancellations do not amend or repeal properly enacted statutes in violation of the Presentment Clause. First, relying primarily on *Field v. Clark* (1892), the Government contends that the cancellations were merely exercises of discretionary authority granted to the President by the Balanced Budget Act and the Taxpayer Relief Act read in light of the previously enacted Line Item Veto Act. Second, the Government submits that the substance of the authority to cancel tax and spending items "is, in practical effect, no more and no less than the power to 'decline to spend' specified sums of money, or to 'decline to implement' specified tax measures." Neither argument is persuasive.

In *Field v. Clark,* the Court upheld the constitutionality of the Tariff Act of 1890. That statute contained a "free list" of almost 300 specific articles that were exempted from import duties "unless otherwise specially provided for in this act." Section 3 was a special provision that directed the President to suspend that exemption for sugar, molasses, coffee, tea, and hides "whenever, and so often" as he should be satisfied that any country producing and exporting those products imposed duties on the agricultural products of the United States that he deemed to be "reciprocally unequal and unreasonable. . . ." The section then specified the duties to be imposed on those products during any such suspension. The Court provided this explanation for its conclusion that § 3 had not delegated legislative power to the President [excerpt from opinion omitted]. . . .

This passage identifies three critical differences between the power to suspend the exemption from import duties and the power to cancel portions of a duly enacted statute. First, the exercise of the suspension power was contingent upon a condition that did not exist when the Tariff Act was passed: the imposition of "reciprocally unequal and unreasonable" import duties by other countries. In contrast, the exercise of the cancellation power within five days after the enactment of the Balanced Budget and Tax Reform Acts necessarily was based on the same conditions that Congress evaluated when it passed those statutes. Second, under the Tariff Act, when the President determined that the contingency had arisen, he had a duty to suspend; in contrast, while it is true that the President was required by the Act to make three determinations before he canceled a provision, those determinations did not qualify his discretion to cancel or not to cancel. Finally, whenever the President suspended an exemption under the Tariff Act, he was executing the policy that Congress had embodied in the statute. In contrast, whenever the President cancels an item of new direct spending or a limited tax benefit he is rejecting the policy judgment made by Congress and relying on his own policy judgment. . . .

The Government's reliance upon other tariff and import statutes, discussed in *Field,* that contain provisions similar to the one challenged in *Field* is unavailing for the same reasons. Some of those statutes authorized the President to "suspen[d] and discontinu[e]" statutory duties upon his determination that discriminatory duties imposed by other nations had been abolished. . . .

The cited statutes all relate to foreign trade, and this Court has recognized that in the foreign affairs arena, the President has "a degree of discretion and freedom from statutory restriction which would not be admissible were domestic affairs alone involved." *United States v. Curtiss-Wright Export Corp.* (1936). . . . More important, when enacting the statutes discussed in *Field,* Congress itself made the decision to suspend or repeal the particular provisions at issue upon the occurrence of particular events subsequent to enactment, and it left only the determination of whether such events occurred up to the President. The Line Item Veto Act authorizes the President himself to effect the repeal of laws, for his own policy reasons, without observing the procedures set out in Article I, § 7. The fact that Congress intended such a result is of no moment. Although Congress presumably anticipated that the President might cancel some of the items in the Balanced Budget Act and in the Taxpayer Relief Act, Congress cannot alter the procedures set out in Article I, § 7, without amending the Constitution.

Neither are we persuaded by the Government's contention that the President's authority to cancel new direct spending and tax benefit items is no greater than his traditional authority to decline to spend appropriated funds. The Government has reviewed in some detail the series of statutes in which Congress has given the Executive broad discretion over the expenditure of appropriated funds. . . . The critical difference between this statute and all of its predecessors, however, is that unlike any of them, this Act gives the President the unilateral power to change the text of duly enacted statutes. None of the Act's predecessors could even arguably have been construed to authorize such a change.

VI

... [T]he profound importance of these cases makes it appropriate to emphasize three points.

First, we express no opinion about the wisdom of the procedures authorized by the Line Item Veto Act. Many members of both major political parties who have served in the Legislative and the Executive Branches have long advocated the enactment of such procedures for the purpose of "ensur[ing] greater fiscal accountability in Washington." [Citing 1996 conference report.] The text of the Act was itself the product of much debate and deliberation in both Houses of Congress and that precise text was signed into law by the President. We do not lightly conclude that their action was unauthorized by the Constitution. We have, however, twice had full argument and briefing on the question and have concluded that our duty is clear.

Second, although appellees challenge the validity of the Act on alternative grounds, the only issue we address concerns the "finely wrought" procedure commanded by the Constitution. We have been favored with extensive debate about the scope of Congress' power to delegate law-making authority, or its functional equivalent, to the President. The excellent briefs filed by the parties and their *amici curiae* have provided us with valuable historical information that illuminates the delegation issue but does not really bear on the narrow issue that is dispositive of these cases. Thus, because we conclude that the Act's cancellation provisions violate Article I, § 7, of the Constitution, we find it unnecessary to consider the District Court's alternative holding that the Act "impermissibly disrupts the balance of powers among the three branches of government."

Third, our decision rests on the narrow ground that the procedures authorized by the Line Item Veto Act are not authorized by the Constitution. The Balanced Budget Act of 1997 is a 500-page document that became "Public Law 105-33" after three procedural steps were taken: (1) a bill containing its exact text was approved by a majority of the Members of the House of Representatives; (2) the Senate approved precisely the same text; and (3) that text was signed into law by the President. The Constitution explicitly requires that each of those three steps be taken before a bill may "become a law." Art. I, § 7. If one paragraph of that text had been omitted at any one of those three stages, Public Law 105-33 would not have been validly enacted. If the Line Item Veto Act were valid, it would authorize the President to create a different law—one whose text was not voted on by either House of Congress or presented to the President for signature. Something that might be known as "Public Law 105-33 as modified by the President" may or may not be desirable, but it is surely not a document that may "become a law" pursuant to the procedures designed by the Framers of Article I, § 7, of the Constitution.

If there is to be a new procedure in which the President will play a different role in determining the final text of what may "become a law," such change must come not by legislation but through the amendment procedures set forth in Article V of the Constitution.

The judgment of the District Court is affirmed.

It is so ordered.

JUSTICE KENNEDY, concurring.

A nation cannot plunder its own treasury without putting its Constitution and its survival in peril. The statute before us, then, is of first importance, for it seems undeniable the Act will tend to restrain persistent excessive spending. Nevertheless, for the reasons given by JUSTICE STEVENS in the opinion for the Court, the statute must be found invalid. Failure of political will does not justify unconstitutional remedies.

I write to respond to my colleague JUSTICE BREYER, who observes that the statute does not threaten the liberties of individual citizens, a point on which I disagree. . . . Liberty is always at stake when one or more of the branches seek to transgress the separation of powers.

. . . [The Framers] used the principles of separation of powers and federalism to secure liberty in the fundamental political sense of the term, quite in addition to the idea of freedom from intrusive governmental acts. The idea and the promise were that when the people delegate some degree of control to a remote central authority, one branch of government ought not possess the power to shape their destiny without a sufficient check from the other two. In this vision, liberty demands limits on the ability of any one branch to influence basic political decisions. . . .

It follows that if a citizen who is taxed has the measure of the tax or the decision to spend determined by the Executive alone, without adequate control by the citizen's Representatives in Congress, liberty is threatened. Money is the instrument of policy and policy affects the lives of citizens. The individual loses liberty in a real sense if that instrument is not subject to traditional constitutional constraints.

The principal object of the statute, it is true, was not to enhance the President's power to reward one group and punish another, to help one set of taxpayers and hurt another, to favor one State and ignore another. Yet these are its undeniable effects. The law establishes a new mechanism which gives the President the sole ability to hurt a group that is a visible target, in order to disfavor the group or to extract further concessions from Congress. The law is the functional equivalent of a line item veto and enhances the President's powers beyond what the Framers would have endorsed.

It is no answer, of course, to say that Congress surrendered its authority by its own hand; nor does it suffice to point out that a new statute, signed by the President or enacted over his veto, could restore to Congress the power it now seeks to relinquish. That a congressional cession of power is voluntary does not make it innocuous. The Constitution is a compact enduring for more than our time, and one Congress cannot yield up its own powers, much less those of other Congresses to follow. Abdication of responsibility is not part of the constitutional design. . . .

JUSTICE SCALIA, with whom JUSTICE O'CONNOR joins, and with whom JUSTICE BREYER joins as to Part III, concurring in part and dissenting in part.

Today the Court acknowledges the " 'overriding and time-honored concern about keeping the Judiciary's power within its proper constitutional sphere.' " It proceeds, however, to ignore the prescribed statutory limits of our jurisdiction by permitting the expedited-review provisions of the Line Item Veto Act to be invoked by persons who are not "individual[s]," 2 U. S. C. § 692; and to ignore the constitutional limits of our jurisdiction by permitting one party to challenge the Government's denial *to another party* of favorable tax treatment from which the first party might, but just as likely might not, gain a concrete benefit. In my view, the Snake River appellees lack standing to challenge the President's cancellation of the "limited tax benefit," and the constitutionality of that action should not be addressed. I think the New York appellees have standing to challenge the President's cancellation of an "item of new direct spending"; I believe we have statutory authority (other than the expedited-review provision) to address that challenge; but unlike the Court I find the President's cancellation of spending items to be entirely in accord with the Constitution.

I

[Scalia concluded that none of the plaintiffs except Mike Cranney qualified as "individuals" under the expedited review provision of the act. However, he said that "in light of the public importance of the issues involved," the Court should exercise its certiorari power to review both cases.]

II

[Scalia argued at length that the Snake River appellees lacked standing to bring the case. He disputed the Court's conclusion that "harm to one's bargaining position" could amount to "a legally cognizable injury." In any event, he said, "Snake River has presented no evidence to show that it was engaged in bargaining, and that that bargaining was impaired by the President's cancellation of § 968."]

III

I agree with the Court that the New York appellees have standing to challenge the President's cancellation of § 4722(c) of the Balanced Budget Act of 1997 as an "item of new direct spending." The tax liability they will incur under New York law is a concrete and particularized injury, fairly traceable to the President's action, and avoided if that action is undone. Unlike the Court, however, I do not believe that Executive cancellation of this item of direct spending violates the Presentment Clause. . . .

Article I, § 7 of the Constitution obviously prevents the President from cancelling a law that Congress has not authorized him to cancel. . . . But that is not this case. . . .

I turn, then, to the crux of the matter: whether Congress's authorizing the President to cancel an item of spending gives him a power that our history and traditions show must reside exclusively in the Legislative Branch. . . .

Insofar as the degree of political, "law-making" power conferred upon the Executive is concerned, there is not a dime's worth of difference between Congress's authorizing the President to cancel a spending item, and Congress's authorizing money to be spent on a particular item at the President's discretion. And the latter has been done since the Founding of the Nation. From 1789–1791, the First Congress made lump-sum appropriations for the entire Government—"sum[s] not exceeding" specified amounts for broad purposes. [Citations omitted.] From a very early date Congress also made permissive individual appropriations, leaving the decision whether to spend the money to the President's unfettered discretion. In 1803, it appropriated $50,000 for the President to build "not exceeding fifteen gun boats, to be armed, manned and fitted out, and employed for such purposes as in his opinion the public service may require." President Jefferson reported that "[t]he sum of fifty thousand dollars appropriated by Congress for providing gun boats remains unexpended. The favorable and peaceable turn of affairs on the Mississippi rendered an immediate execution of that law unnecessary." Examples of appropriations committed to the discretion of the President abound in our history. During the Civil War, an Act appropriated over $76 million to be divided among various items "as the exigencies of the service may require." During the Great Depression, Congress appropriated $950 million "for such projects and/or purposes and under such rules and regulations as the President in his discretion may prescribe," and $4 billion for general classes of projects, the money to be spent "in the discretion and under the direction of the President." The constitutionality of such appropriations has never seriously been questioned. . . .

Certain Presidents have claimed Executive authority to withhold appropriated funds even *absent* an express conferral of discretion to do so. In 1876, for example, President Grant reported to Congress that he would not spend money appropriated for certain harbor and river improvements, because "[u]nder no circumstances [would he] allow expenditures upon works not clearly national," and in his view, the appropriations were for "works of purely private or local interest, in no sense national." President Franklin D. Roosevelt impounded funds appropriated for a flood control reservoir and levee in Oklahoma. President Truman ordered the impoundment of hundreds of millions of dollars that had been appropriated for military aircraft. President Nixon, the Mahatma Ghandi of all impounders, asserted at a press conference in 1973 that his "constitutional right" to impound appropriated funds was "absolutely clear." Our decision two years later in *Train v. City of New York* (1975) proved him wrong, but it implicitly confirmed that Congress may confer discretion upon the executive to withhold appropriated funds, even funds appropriated for a specific purpose. . . .

The short of the matter is this: Had the Line Item Veto Act authorized the President to "decline to spend" any item of spending contained in the Balanced Budget Act of 1997, there is not the slightest doubt that authorization would have been constitutional. What the Line Item Veto Act does instead—authorizing the President to "cancel" an item of spending—is technically different. But the technical difference does *not* relate to the technicalities of the Presentment Clause, which have been fully complied with; and the doctrine of unconstitutional delegation, which is at issue here, is preeminently *not* a doctrine of technicalities. The title of the Line Item Veto Act, which was perhaps designed to simplify for public comprehension, or perhaps merely to comply with the terms of a campaign pledge, has succeeded in faking out the Supreme Court. The President's action it authorizes in fact is not a line-item veto and thus does not offend Art. I, § 7; and insofar as the substance of that action is concerned, it is no different from what Congress has permitted the President to do since the formation of the Union.

IV

I would hold that the President's cancellation of § 4722(c) of the Balanced Budget Act as an item of direct spending does not violate the Constitution. Because I find no party before us who has standing to challenge the President's cancellation of § 968 of the Taxpayer Relief Act, I do not reach the question whether that violates the Constitution.

For the foregoing reasons, I respectfully dissent.

JUSTICE BREYER, with whom JUSTICE O'CONNOR and JUSTICE SCALIA join as to Part III, dissenting.

I

I agree with the Court that the parties have standing, but I do not agree with its ultimate conclusion. In my view the Line Item Veto Act does not violate any specific textual constitutional command, nor does it violate any implicit Separation of Powers principle. Consequently, I believe that the Act is constitutional.

II

I approach the constitutional question before us with three general considerations in mind. *First,* the Act represents a legislative effort to provide the President with the power to give effect to some, but not to all, of the expenditure and revenue-diminishing provisions contained in a single massive appropriations bill. And this objective is constitutionally proper. . . .

Second, the case in part requires us to focus upon the Constitution's generally phrased structural provisions, provisions that delegate all "legislative" power to Congress and vest all "executive" power in the President. The Court, when applying these provisions, has interpreted them generously in terms of the institutional arrangements that they permit. . . .

Third, we need not here referee a dispute among the other two branches. . . .

These three background circumstances mean that, when one measures the *literal* words of the Act against the Constitution's *literal* commands, the fact that the Act may closely resemble a different, literally unconstitutional, arrangement is beside the point. To drive exactly 65 miles per hour on an interstate highway closely resembles an act that violates the speed limit. But it does not violate that limit, for small differences matter when the question is one of literal violation of law. No more does this Act literally violate the Constitution's words. . . .

III

The Court believes that the Act violates the literal text of the Constitution. A simple syllogism captures its basic reasoning:

> Major Premise: The Constitution sets forth an exclusive method for enacting, repealing, or amending laws.

> Minor Premise: The Act authorizes the President to "repea[l] or amen[d]" laws in a different way, namely by announcing a cancellation of a portion of a previously enacted law.

> Conclusion: The Act is inconsistent with the Constitution.

I find this syllogism unconvincing, however, because its Minor Premise is faulty. When the President "canceled" the two appropriation measures now before us, he did not *repeal* any law nor did he *amend* any law. He simply *followed* the law, leaving the statutes, as they are literally written, intact. . . .

IV

Because I disagree with the Court's holding of literal violation, I must consider whether the Act nonetheless violates Separation of Powers principles—principles that arise out of the Constitution's vesting of the "executive Power" in "a President," U. S. Const., Art. II, § 1, and "[a]ll legislative Powers" in "a Congress," Art. I, § 1. There are three relevant Separation of Powers questions here: (1) Has Congress given the President the wrong kind of power, i.e., "non-Executive" power? (2) Has Congress given the President the power to "encroach" upon Congress' own constitutionally reserved territory? (3) Has Congress given the President too much power, violating the doctrine of "nondelegation?" These three limitations help assure "adequate control by the citizen's representatives in Congress," upon which JUSTICE KENNEDY properly insists. And with respect to this Act, the answer to all these questions is "no."

A

Viewed conceptually, the power the Act conveys is the right kind of power. It is "executive". . . . [A]n exercise of that power "executes" the Act. Conceptually speaking, it closely resembles the kind of delegated authority—to spend or not to spend appropriations, to change or not to change tariff rates—that Congress has frequently granted the President, any differences being differences in degree, not kind.

The fact that one could also characterize this kind of power as "legislative," say, if Congress itself (by amending the appropriations bill) prevented a provision from taking effect, is beside the point. . . .

If there is a Separation of Powers violation, then, it must rest, not upon purely conceptual grounds, but upon some important conflict between the Act and a significant Separation of Powers objective.

B

The Act does not undermine what this Court has often described as the principal function of the Separation of Powers, which is to maintain the tripartite structure of the Federal Government—and thereby protect individual liberty—by providing a "safeguard against the encroachment or aggrandizement of one branch at the expense of the other." *Buckley v. Valeo* (1976). . . .

[O]ne cannot say that the Act "encroaches" upon Congress' power, when Congress retained the power to insert, by simple majority, into any future appropriations bill, into any section of any such bill, or into any phrase of any section, a provision that says the Act will not apply. . . . Congress also retained the power to "disapprov[e]," and thereby reinstate, any of the President's cancellations. And it is Congress that drafts and enacts the appropriations statutes that are subject to the Act in the first place—and thereby defines the outer limits of the President's cancellation authority. . . .

Nor can one say that the Act's basic substantive objective is constitutionally improper, for the earliest Congresses could have, and often did, confer on the President this sort of discretionary authority over spending. . . .

Nor can one say the Act's grant of power "aggrandizes" the Presidential office. The grant is limited to the context of the budget. It is limited to the power to spend, or not to spend, particular appropriated items, and the power to permit, or not to permit, specific limited exemptions from generally applicable tax law from taking effect. These powers . . . resemble those the President has exercised in the past on other occasions. The delegation of those powers to the President may strengthen the Presidency, but any such change in Executive Branch authority seems minute when compared with the changes worked by delegations of other kinds of authority that the Court in the past has upheld. [Citations omitted.]

C

The "nondelegation" doctrine represents an added constitutional check upon Congress' authority to delegate power to the Executive Branch. And it raises a more serious constitutional obstacle here. . . . [I]n Chief Justice Taft's . . . familiar words, the Constitution permits only those delegations where Congress "shall lay down by legislative act an *intelligible principle* to which the person or body authorized to [act] is directed to conform." *J. W. Hampton* [*Jr., & Co. v. United States* (1938)] (emphasis added).

The Act before us seeks to create such a principle in three ways. The first is procedural. The Act tells the President that, in "identifying dollar amounts [or] . . . items . . . for cancellation" . . . he is to "consider," among other things, "the legislative history, construction, and purposes of the law which contains [those amounts or items, and] . . . any specific sources of information referenced in such law or . . . the best available information. . . ."

The second is purposive. The clear purpose behind the Act, confirmed by its legislative history, is to promote "greater fiscal accountability" and to "eliminate wasteful federal spending and . . . special tax breaks." [Quoting conference report.]

The third is substantive. The President must determine that, to "prevent" the item or amount "from having legal force or effect" will "reduce the Federal budget deficit; . . . not impair any essential Government functions; and . . . not harm the national interest."

The resulting standards are broad. But this Court has upheld standards that are equally broad, or broader. [Citations omitted.]

Indeed, the Court has only twice in its history found that a congressional delegation of power violated the "nondelegation" doctrine. [Summary of *Panama Refining Co. v. Ryan* (1935) and *Schechter Poultry Corp. v. United States* (1935) omitted.]

The case before us . . . is limited to one area of government, the budget, and it seeks to give the President the power, in one portion of that budget, to tailor spending and special tax relief to what he concludes are the demands of fiscal responsibility. Nor is the standard that governs his judgment, though broad, any broader than the standard that currently governs the award of television licenses, namely "public convenience, interest, *or* necessity." (emphasis added). To the contrary, (a) the broadly phrased limitations in the Act, together with (b) its evident deficit reduction purpose, and (c) a procedure that guarantees Presidential awareness of the reasons for including a particular provision in a budget bill, taken together, guide the President's exercise of his discretionary powers. . . .

V

In sum, I recognize that the Act before us is novel. In a sense, it skirts a constitutional edge. But that edge has to do with means, not ends. The means chosen do not amount literally to the enactment, repeal, or amendment of a law. Nor, for that matter, do they amount literally to the "line item veto" that the Act's title announces. Those means do not violate any basic Separation of Powers principle. They do not improperly shift the constitutionally foreseen balance of power from Congress to the President. Nor, since they comply with Separation of Powers principles, do they threaten the liberties of individual citizens. They represent an experiment that may, or may not, help representative government work better. The Constitution, in my view, authorizes Congress and the President to try novel methods in this way. Consequently, with respect, I dissent.

□□□

No. 97-1192

Swidler & Berlin and James Hamilton, Petitioners v. United States

On writ of certiorari to the United States
Court of Appeals for the District of Columbia Circuit

[June 25, 1998]

CHIEF JUSTICE REHNQUIST delivered the opinion of the Court.

Petitioner, an attorney, made notes of an initial interview with a client shortly before the client's death. The Government, represented by the Office of Independent Counsel, now seeks his notes for use in a criminal investigation. We hold that the notes are protected by the attorney-client privilege.

This dispute arises out of an investigation conducted by the Office of the Independent Counsel into whether various individuals made false statements, obstructed justice, or committed other crimes during investigations of the 1993 dismissal of employees from the White House Travel Office. Vincent W. Foster, Jr., was Deputy White House Counsel when the firings occurred. In July, 1993, Foster met with petitioner James Hamilton, an attorney at petitioner Swidler & Berlin, to seek legal representation concerning possible congressional or other investigations of the firings. During a 2-hour meeting, Hamilton took three pages of handwritten notes. One of the first entries in the notes is the word "Privileged." Nine days later, Foster committed suicide.

In December 1995, a federal grand jury, at the request of the Independent Counsel, issued subpoenas to petitioners Hamilton and Swidler & Berlin for, *inter alia,* Hamilton's handwritten notes of his meeting with Foster. Petitioners filed a motion to quash, arguing that the notes were protected by the attorney-client privilege and by the work product privilege. The District Court, after examining the notes *in camera,* concluded they were protected from disclosure by both doctrines and denied enforcement of the subpoenas.

The Court of Appeals for the District of Columbia Circuit reversed. *In re Sealed Case* (1997). While recognizing that most courts assume the privilege survives death, the Court of Appeals noted that holdings actually manifesting the posthumous force of the privilege are rare. Instead, most judicial references to the privilege's posthumous application occur in the context of a well recognized exception allowing disclosure for disputes among the client's heirs. It further noted that most commentators support some measure of posthumous curtailment of the privilege. The Court of

Appeals thought that the risk of posthumous revelation, when confined to the criminal context, would have little to no chilling effect on client communication, but that the costs of protecting communications after death were high. It therefore concluded that the privilege was not absolute in such circumstances, and that instead, a balancing test should apply. It thus held that there is a posthumous exception to the privilege for communications whose relative importance to particular criminal litigation is substantial. While acknowledging that uncertain privileges are disfavored, the Court of Appeals determined that the uncertainty introduced by its balancing test was insignificant in light of existing exceptions to the privilege. The Court of Appeals also held that the notes were not protected by the work product privilege.

The dissenting judge would have affirmed the District Court's judgment that the attorney-client privilege protected the notes. He concluded that the common-law rule was that the privilege survived death. He found no persuasive reason to depart from this accepted rule, particularly given the importance of the privilege to full and frank client communication.

Petitioners sought review in this Court on both the attorney-client privilege and the work product privilege. We granted certiorari (1998), and we now reverse.

The attorney-client privilege is one of the oldest recognized privileges for confidential communications. *Upjohn Co. v. United States* (1981); *Hunt v. Blackburn* (1888). The privilege is intended to encourage "full and frank communication between attorneys and their clients and thereby promote broader public interests in the observance of law and the administration of justice." *Upjohn.* The issue presented here is the scope of that privilege; more particularly, the extent to which the privilege survives the death of the client. Our interpretation of the privilege's scope is guided by "the principles of the common law . . . as interpreted by the courts . . . in the light of reason and experience." Fed. Rule Evid. 501; *Funk v. United States* (1933).

The Independent Counsel argues that the attorney-client privilege should not prevent disclosure of confidential communications where the client has died and the information is relevant to a criminal proceeding. There is some authority for this position. One state appellate court, *Cohen v. Jenkintown Cab Co.* (Pa. Super. 1976), and the Court of Appeals below have held the privilege may be subject to posthumous exceptions in certain circumstances. In *Cohen,* a civil case, the court recognized that the privilege generally survives death, but concluded that it could make an exception where the interest of justice was compelling and the interest of the client in preserving the confidence was insignificant.

But other than these two decisions, cases addressing the existence of the privilege after death—most involving the testamentary exception—uniformly presume the privilege survives, even if they do not so hold. [Citations omitted.] In *John Doe Grand Jury Investigation* [1990], for example, the Massachusetts Supreme Court concluded that survival of the privilege was "the clear implication" of its early pronouncements that communications subject to the privilege could not be disclosed at any time. The court further noted that survival of the privilege was "necessarily implied" by cases allowing waiver of the privilege in testamentary disputes.

Such testamentary exception cases consistently presume the privilege survives. [Citations omitted.] They view testamentary disclosure of communications as an exception to the privilege: "[T]he general rule with respect to confidential communications . . . is that such communications are privileged during the testator's lifetime and, also, after the testator's death unless sought to be disclosed in litigation between the testator's heirs." [*United States v.*] *Osborn* [CA9 1977]. The rationale for such disclosure is that it furthers the client's intent.

Indeed, in *Glover v. Patten* (1897), this Court, in recognizing the testamentary exception, expressly assumed that the privilege continues after the individual's death. The Court explained that testamentary disclosure was permissible because the privilege, which normally protects the client's interests, could be impliedly waived in order to fulfill the client's testamentary intent.

The great body of this caselaw supports, either by holding or considered dicta, the position that the privilege does survive in a case such as the present one. Given the language of Rule 501, at the very least the burden is on the Independent Counsel to show that "reason and experience" require a departure from this rule.

The Independent Counsel contends that the testamentary exception supports the posthumous termination of the privilege because in practice most cases have refused to apply the privilege posthumously. He further argues that the exception reflects a policy judgment that the interest in settling estates outweighs any posthumous interest in confidentiality. He then reasons by analogy that in criminal proceedings, the interest in determining whether a crime has been committed should trump client confidentiality, particularly since the financial interests of the estate are not at stake.

But the Independent Counsel's interpretation simply does not square with the caselaw's implicit acceptance of the privilege's survival and with the treatment of testamentary disclosure as an "exception" or an implied "waiver." And the premise of his analogy is incorrect, since cases consistently recognize that the rationale for the testamentary exception is that it furthers the client's intent. There is no reason to suppose as a general matter that grand jury testimony about confidential communications furthers the client's intent.

Commentators on the law also recognize that the general rule is that the attorney-client privilege continues after death. [Citations omitted.] Undoubtedly, as the Independent Counsel emphasizes, various commentators have criticized this rule, urging that the privilege should be abrogated after the client's death where extreme injustice would result, as long as disclosure would not seriously undermine the privilege by deterring client communication. See, *e.g.,* C. Mueller & L. Kirkpatrick, 2 Federal Evidence § 199, at 380–381 (2d ed. 1994); Restatement (Third) of the Law Governing Lawyers § 127, Comment d (Proposed Final Draft No. 1, Mar. 29, 1996). But even these critics clearly recognize that established law supports the continuation of the privilege and that a contrary rule would be a modification of the common law. [Citing Mueller & Kirkpatrick; Restatement of the Law Governing Lawyers; 24 C. Wright & K. Graham, Federal Practice and Procedure § 5498 (1986).]

Despite the scholarly criticism, we think there are weighty reasons that counsel in favor of posthumous application. Knowing that communications will remain confidential even after death encourages the client to communicate fully and frankly with counsel. While the fear of disclosure, and the consequent withholding of information from counsel, may be reduced if disclosure is limited to posthumous disclosure in a criminal context, it seems unreasonable to assume that it vanishes altogether. Clients may be concerned about reputation, civil liability, or possible harm to friends or family. Posthumous disclosure of such communications may be as feared as disclosure during the client's lifetime.

The Independent Counsel suggests, however, that his proposed exception would have little to no effect on the client's willingness to confide in his attorney. He reasons that only clients intending to perjure themselves will be chilled by a rule of disclosure after death, as opposed to truthful clients or those asserting their Fifth Amendment privilege. This is because for the latter group, communications disclosed by the attorney after the client's death purportedly will reveal only information that the client himself would have revealed if alive.

The Independent Counsel assumes, incorrectly we believe, that the privilege is analogous to the Fifth Amendment's protection against self-incrimination. But as suggested above, the privilege serves much broader purposes. Clients consult attorneys for a wide variety of reasons, only one of which involves possible criminal liability. Many attorneys act as counselors on personal and family matters, where, in the course of obtaining the desired advice, confidences about family members or financial problems must be revealed in order to assure sound legal advice. The same is true of owners of small businesses who may regularly consult their attorneys about a variety of problems arising in the course of the business. These confidences may not come close to any sort of admission of criminal wrongdoing, but nonetheless be matters which the client would not wish divulged.

The contention that the attorney is being required to disclose only what the client could have been required to disclose is at odds with the basis for the privilege even during the client's lifetime. In related cases, we have said that the loss of evidence admittedly caused by the privilege is justified in part by the fact that without the privilege, the client may not have made such communications in the first place. This is true of disclosure before and after the client's death. Without assurance of the privilege's posthumous application, the client may very well not have made disclosures to his attorney at all, so the loss of evidence is more apparent than real. In the case at hand, it seems quite plausible that Foster, perhaps already contemplating suicide, may not have sought legal advice from Hamilton if he had not been assured the conversation was privileged.

The Independent Counsel additionally suggests that his proposed exception would have minimal impact if confined to criminal cases, or, as the Court of Appeals suggests, if it is limited to information of substantial importance to a particular criminal case. However, there is no case authority for the proposition that the privilege applies differently in criminal and civil cases, and only one commentator ventures such a suggestion, see Mueller & Kirkpatrick. In any event, a client may not know at the time he discloses information to his attorney whether it will later be relevant to a civil or a criminal matter, let alone whether it will be of substantial importance. Balancing *ex post* the importance of the information against client interests, even limited to criminal cases, introduces substantial uncertainty into the privilege's application. For just that reason, we have rejected use of a balancing test in defining the contours of the privilege.

In a similar vein, the Independent Counsel argues that existing exceptions to the privilege, such as the crime-fraud exception and the testamentary exception, make the impact of one more exception marginal. However, these exceptions do not demonstrate that the impact of a posthumous exception would be insignificant, and there is little empirical evidence on this point. The established exceptions are consistent with the purposes of the privilege, while a posthumous exception in criminal cases appears at odds with the goals of encouraging full and frank communication and of protecting the client's interests. A "no harm in one more exception" rationale could contribute to the general erosion of the privilege, without reference to common law principles or "reason and experience."

Finally, the Independent Counsel, relying on cases such as *United States v. Nixon* (1974) and *Branzburg v. Hayes* (1972), urges that privileges be strictly construed because they are inconsistent with the paramount judicial goal of truth seeking. But both *Nixon* and *Branzburg* dealt with the creation of privileges not recognized by the common law, whereas here we deal with one of the oldest recognized privileges in the law. And we are asked, not simply to "construe" the privilege, but to narrow it, contrary to the weight of the existing body of caselaw.

It has been generally, if not universally, accepted, for well over a century, that the attorney-client privilege survives the death of the client in a case such as this. While the arguments against the survival of the privilege are by no means frivolous, they are based in large part on speculation—thoughtful speculation, but speculation nonetheless—as to whether posthumous termination of the privilege would diminish a client's willingness to confide in an attorney. In an area where empirical information would be useful, it is scant and inconclusive.

Rule 501's direction to look to "the principles of the common law as they may be interpreted by the courts of the United States in the light of reason and experience" does not mandate that a rule, once established, should endure for all time. But here the Independent Counsel has simply not made a sufficient showing to overturn the common law rule embodied in the prevailing caselaw. Interpreted in the light of reason and experience, that body of law requires that the attorney client privilege prevent disclosure of the notes at issue in this case. The judgment of the Court of Appeals is

Reversed.

JUSTICE O'CONNOR, with whom JUSTICE SCALIA and JUSTICE THOMAS join, dissenting.

Although the attorney-client privilege ordinarily will survive the death of the client, I do not agree with the Court that it inevitably precludes disclosure of a deceased client's communications in criminal proceedings. In my view, a criminal defendant's right to exculpatory evidence or a compelling law enforcement need for information may, where the testimony is not available from other sources, override a client's posthumous interest in confidentiality.

We have long recognized that "[t]he fundamental basis upon which all rules of evidence must rest—if they are to rest upon reason—is their adaptation to the successful development of the truth." *Funk v. United States* (1933). In light of the heavy burden that they place on the search for truth, see *United States v. Nixon* (1974), "[e]videntiary privileges in litigation are not favored, and even those rooted in the Constitution must give way in proper circumstances," *Herbert v. Lando* (1979). Consequently, we construe the scope of privileges narrowly. We are reluctant to recognize a privilege or read an existing one expansively unless to do so will serve a "public good transcending the normally predominant principle of utilizing all rational means for ascertaining truth." *Trammel v. United States* (1980).

The attorney-client privilege promotes trust in the representational relationship, thereby facilitating the provision of legal services and ultimately the administration of justice. See *Upjohn Co. v. United States* (1981). The systemic benefits of the privilege are commonly understood to outweigh the harm caused by excluding critical evidence. A privilege should operate, however, only where "necessary to achieve its purpose," see *Fisher v. United States* (1976), and an invocation of the attorney-client privilege should not go unexamined "when it is shown that the interests of the administration of justice can only be frustrated by [its] exercise," *Cohen v. Jenkintown Cab Co.* (Pa. Super. (1976)).

I agree that a deceased client may retain a personal, reputational, and economic interest in confidentiality. But, after death, the potential that disclosure will harm the client's interests has been greatly diminished, and the risk that the client will be held criminally liable has abated altogether. Thus, some commentators suggest that terminating the privilege upon the client's death "could not to any substantial degree lessen the encouragement for free disclosure which is [its] purpose." 1 J. Strong, McCormick on Evidence § 94 (4th ed. 1992); see also Restatement (Third) of the Law Governing Lawyers § 127, Comment d (Proposed Final Draft No. 1, Mar. 29, 1996). This diminished risk is coupled with a heightened urgency for discovery of a deceased client's communications in the criminal context. The privilege does not "protect disclosure of the underlying facts by those who communicated with the attorney," *Upjohn*, and were the client living, prosecutors could grant immunity and compel the relevant testimony. After a client's death, however, if the privilege precludes an attorney from testifying in the client's stead, a complete "loss of crucial information" will often result, see 24 C. Wright & K. Graham, Federal Practice and Procedure § 5498 (1986).

As the Court of Appeals observed, the costs of recognizing an absolute posthumous privilege can be inordinately high. See *In re Sealed Case* (CADC 1997). Extreme injustice may occur, for example, where a criminal defendant seeks disclosure of a deceased client's confession to the offense. See *State v. Macumber* (Ariz. 1976); cf. *In the Matter of a John Doe Grand Jury Investigation* (Mass. 1990) (Nolan, J., dissenting). In my view, the paramount value that our criminal justice system places on protecting an innocent defendant should outweigh a deceased client's interest in preserving confidences. Indeed, even petitioner acknowledges that an exception may be appropriate where the constitutional rights of a criminal defendant are at stake. An exception may likewise be warranted in the face of a compelling law enforcement need for the information. . . . Given that the complete exclusion of relevant evidence from a criminal trial or investigation may distort the record, mislead the factfinder, and undermine the central truth-seeking function of the courts, I do not believe that the attorney-client privilege should act as an absolute bar to the disclosure of a deceased client's communications. When the privilege is asserted in the criminal context, and a showing is made that the communications at issue contain necessary factual information not otherwise available, courts should be permitted to assess whether interests in fairness and accuracy outweigh the justifications for the privilege.

A number of exceptions to the privilege already qualify its protections, and an attorney "who tells his client that the expected communications are absolutely and forever privileged is oversimplifying a bit." [Quoting Court of Appeals opinion.] In the situation where the posthumous privilege most frequently arises—a dispute between heirs over the decedent's will—the privilege is widely recognized to give way to the interest in settling the estate. This testamentary exception, moreover, may be invoked in some cases where the decedent would not have chosen to waive the privilege. For example, "a decedent might want to provide for an illegitimate child but at the same time much prefer that the relationship go undisclosed." [Quoting Court of Appeals opinion.] Among the Court's rationales for a broad construction of the posthumous privilege is its assertion that "[m]any attorneys act as counselors on personal and family matters, where, in the course of obtaining the desired advice, confidences about family members or financial problems must be revealed . . . which the client would not wish divulged." That reasoning, however, would apply in the testamentary context with equal force. Nor are other existing exceptions to the privilege—for example, the crime-fraud exception or the exceptions for claims relating to attorney competence or compensation—necessarily consistent with "encouraging full and frank communication" or "protecting the client's interests." Rather, those exceptions reflect the understanding that, in certain circumstances, the privilege " 'ceases to operate' " as a safeguard on "the proper functioning of our adversary system." See *United States v. Zolin* (1989).

Finally, the common law authority for the proposition that the privilege remains absolute after the client's death is not a monolithic body of precedent. Indeed, the Court acknowledges that most cases merely "presume the privilege survives," and it relies on the case law's "implicit acceptance" of a continuous privilege. Opinions squarely addressing the posthumous force of the privilege "are relatively rare." And even in those decisions expressly holding that the privilege continues after the death of the client, courts do not typically engage in detailed reasoning, but rather conclude that the cases construing the testamentary exception imply survival of the privilege. . . . Moreover, as the Court concedes, there is some authority for the proposition that a deceased client's communications may be revealed, even in circumstances outside of the testamentary context. California's Evidence Code, for example, provides that the attorney-client privilege continues only until the deceased client's estate is finally distributed, noting that "there is little reason to preserve secrecy at the expense of excluding relevant evidence after the estate is wound up and the representative is discharged." [Citation omitted.] And a state appellate court has admitted an attorney's testimony concerning a deceased client's communications after "balanc[ing] the necessity for revealing the substance of the [attorney-client conversation] against the unlikelihood of any cognizable injury to the rights, interests, estate or memory of [the client]." See *Cohen.* The American Law Institute, moreover, has recently recommended withholding the privilege when the communication "bears on a litigated issue of pivotal significance" and has suggested that courts "balance the interest in confidentiality against any exceptional need for the communication." Restatement (Third) of the Law Governing Lawyers § 127; see also 2 C. Mueller & L. Kirkpatrick, Federal Evidence, § 199 (2d ed. 1994) ("[I]f a deceased client has confessed to criminal acts that are later charged to another, surely the latter's need for evidence sometimes outweighs the interest in preserving the confidences").

Where the exoneration of an innocent criminal defendant or a compelling law enforcement interest is at stake, the harm of precluding critical evidence that is unavailable by any other means outweighs the potential disincentive to forthright communication. In my view, the cost of silence warrants a narrow exception to the rule that the attorney-client privilege survives the death of the client. Moreover, although I disagree with the Court of Appeals' notion that the context of an initial client interview affects the applicability of the work product doctrine, I do not believe that the doctrine applies where the material concerns a client who is no longer a potential party to adversarial litigation.

Accordingly, I would affirm the judgment of the Court of Appeals. Although the District Court examined the documents *in camera*, it has not had an opportunity to balance these competing considerations and decide whether the privilege should be trumped in the particular circumstances of this case. Thus, I agree with the Court of Appeals' decision to remand for a determination whether any portion of the notes must be disclosed.

With respect, I dissent.

□□□

No. 97-282

Beth Ann Faragher, Petitioner v. City of Boca Raton

On writ of certiorari to the United States Court of Appeals
for the Eleventh Circuit

[June 26, 1998]

JUSTICE SOUTER delivered the opinion of the Court.

This case calls for identification of the circumstances under which an employer may be held liable under Title VII of the Civil Rights Act of 1964 as amended, 42 U. S. C. § 2000e *et seq.*, for the acts of a supervisory employee whose sexual harassment of subordinates has created a hostile work environment amounting to employment discrimination. We hold that an employer is vicariously liable for actionable discrimination caused by a supervisor, but subject to an affirmative defense looking to the reasonableness of the employer's conduct as well as that of a plaintiff victim.

I

Between 1985 and 1990, while attending college, petitioner Beth Ann Faragher worked part time and during the summers as an ocean lifeguard for the Marine Safety Section of the Parks and Recreation Department of respondent, the City of Boca Raton, Florida (City). During this period, Faragher's immediate supervisors were Bill Terry, David Silverman, and Robert Gordon. In June 1990, Faragher resigned.

In 1992, Faragher brought an action against Terry, Silverman, and the City, asserting claims under Title VII, 42 U. S. C. § 1983, and Florida law. So far as it concerns the Title VII claim, the complaint alleged that Terry and Silverman created a "sexually hostile atmosphere" at the beach by repeatedly subjecting Faragher and other female lifeguards to "uninvited and offensive touching," by making lewd remarks, and by speaking of women in offensive terms. The complaint contained specific allegations that Terry once said that he would never promote a woman to the rank of lieutenant, and that Silverman had said to Faragher, "Date me or clean the toilets for a year." Asserting that Terry and Silverman were agents of the City, and that their conduct amounted to discrimination in the "terms, conditions, and privileges" of her employment, 42 U. S. C. § 2000e-2(a)(1), Faragher sought a judgment against the City for nominal damages, costs, and attorney's fees.

Following a bench trial, the United States District Court for the Southern District of Florida found that throughout Faragher's employment with the City, Terry served as Chief of the Marine Safety Division, with authority to hire new lifeguards (subject to the approval of higher management), to supervise all aspects of the lifeguards' work assignments, to engage in counseling, to deliver oral reprimands, and to make a record of any such discipline. (1994). Silverman was a Marine Safety lieutenant from 1985 until June 1989, when he became a captain. Gordon began the employment period as a lieutenant and at some point was promoted to the position of training captain. In these positions, Silverman and Gordon were responsible for making the lifeguards' daily assignments, and for supervising their work and fitness training.

The lifeguards and supervisors were stationed at the city beach and worked out of the Marine Safety Headquarters, a small one-story building containing an office, a meeting room, and a single, unisex locker room with a shower. Their work routine was structured in a "paramilitary configuration," with a clear chain of command. Lifeguards reported to lieutenants and captains, who reported to Terry. He was supervised by the Recreation Superintendent, who in turn reported to a Director of Parks and Recreation, answerable to the City Manager. The lifeguards had no significant contact with higher city officials like the Recreation Superintendent.

In February 1986, the City adopted a sexual harassment policy, which it stated in a memorandum from the City Manager addressed to all employees. In May 1990, the City revised the policy and reissued a statement of it. Although the City may actually have circulated the memos and statements to some employees, it completely failed to disseminate its policy among employees of the Marine Safety Section, with the result that Terry, Silverman, Gordon, and many lifeguards were unaware of it.

From time to time over the course of Faragher's tenure at the Marine Safety Section, between 4 and 6 of the 40 to 50 lifeguards were women. During that 5-year period, Terry repeatedly touched the bodies of female employees without invitation, would put his arm around Faragher, with his hand on her buttocks, and once made contact with another female lifeguard in a motion of sexual simulation. He made crudely demeaning references to women generally, and once commented disparagingly on Faragher's shape. During a job interview with a woman he hired as a lifeguard, Terry said that the female lifeguards had sex with their male counterparts and asked whether she would do the same.

Silverman behaved in similar ways. He once tackled Faragher and remarked that, but for a physical characteristic he found unattractive, he would readily have had sexual relations with her. Another time, he pantomimed an act of oral sex. Within earshot of the female lifeguards, Silverman made frequent, vulgar references to women and sexual matters, commented on the bodies of female lifeguards and beachgoers, and at least twice told female lifeguards that he would like to engage in sex with them.

Faragher did not complain to higher management about Terry or Silverman. Although she spoke of their behavior to Gordon, she did not regard these discussions as formal complaints to a supervisor but as conversations with a person she held in high esteem. Other female lifeguards had similarly informal talks with

Gordon, but because Gordon did not feel that it was his place to do so, he did not report these complaints to Terry, his own supervisor, or to any other city official. Gordon responded to the complaints of one lifeguard by saying that "the City just [doesn't] care."

In April 1990, however, two months before Faragher's resignation, Nancy Ewanchew, a former lifeguard, wrote to Richard Bender, the City's Personnel Director, complaining that Terry and Silverman had harassed her and other female lifeguards. Following investigation of this complaint, the City found that Terry and Silverman had behaved improperly, reprimanded them, and required them to choose between a suspension without pay or the forfeiture of annual leave.

On the basis of these findings, the District Court concluded that the conduct of Terry and Silverman was discriminatory harassment sufficiently serious to alter the conditions of Faragher's employment and constitute an abusive working environment. The District Court then ruled that there were three justifications for holding the City liable for the harassment of its supervisory employees. First, the court noted that the harassment was pervasive enough to support an inference that the City had "knowledge, or constructive knowledge" of it. Next, it ruled that the City was liable under traditional agency principles because Terry and Silverman were acting as its agents when they committed the harassing acts. Finally, the court observed that Gordon's knowledge of the harassment, combined with his inaction, "provides a further basis for imputing liability on [*sic*] the City." The District Court then awarded Faragher one dollar in nominal damages on her Title VII claim.

A panel of the Court of Appeals for the Eleventh Circuit reversed the judgment against the City. (1996). Although the panel had "no trouble concluding that Terry's and Silverman's conduct . . . was severe and pervasive enough to create an objectively abusive work environment," it overturned the District Court's conclusion that the City was liable. The panel ruled that Terry and Silverman were not acting within the scope of their employment when they engaged in the harassment, that they were not aided in their actions by the agency relationship, and that the City had no constructive knowledge of the harassment by virtue of its pervasiveness or Gordon's actual knowledge.

In a 7-to-5 decision, the full Court of Appeals, sitting en banc, adopted the panel's conclusion. (1997). Relying on our decision in *Meritor Savings Bank, FSB v. Vinson* (1986), and on the Restatement (Second) of Agency § 219, the court held that "an employer may be indirectly liable for hostile environment sexual harassment by a superior: (1) if the harassment occurs within the scope of the superior's employment; (2) if the employer assigns performance of a nondelegable duty to a supervisor and an employee is injured because of the supervisor's failure to carry out that duty; or (3) if there is an agency relationship which aids the supervisor's ability or opportunity to harass his subordinate."

Applying these principles, the court rejected Faragher's Title VII claim against the City. First, invoking standard agency language to classify the harassment by each supervisor as a "frolic" unrelated to his authorized tasks, the court found that in harassing Faragher, Terry and Silverman were acting outside of the scope of their employment and solely to further their own personal ends. Next, the court determined that the supervisors' agency relationship with the City did not assist them in perpetrating their harassment. Though noting that "a supervisor is always aided in accomplishing hostile environment sexual harassment by the existence of the agency relationship with his employer because his responsibilities include close proximity to and regular contact with the victim," the court held that traditional agency law does not employ so broad a concept of aid as a predicate of employer liability, but requires something more than a mere combination of agency relationship and improper conduct by the agent. Because neither Terry nor Silverman threatened to fire or demote Faragher, the court concluded that their agency relationship did not facilitate their harassment.

The en banc court also affirmed the panel's ruling that the City lacked constructive knowledge of the supervisors' harassment. The court read the District Court's opinion to rest on an erroneous legal conclusion that any harassment pervasive enough to create a hostile environment must *a fortiori* also suffice to charge the employer with constructive knowledge. Rejecting this approach, the court reviewed the record and found no adequate factual basis to conclude that the harassment was so pervasive that the City should have known of it, relying on the facts that the harassment occurred intermittently, over a long period of time, and at a remote location. In footnotes, the court also rejected the arguments that the City should be deemed to have known of the harassment through Gordon, or charged with constructive knowledge because of its failure to disseminate its sexual harassment policy among the lifeguards.

Since our decision in *Meritor,* Courts of Appeals have struggled to derive manageable standards to govern employer liability for hostile environment harassment perpetrated by supervisory employees. While following our admonition to find guidance in the common law of agency, as embodied in the Restatement, the Courts of Appeals have adopted different approaches. [Citations omitted.] We granted certiorari to address the divergence (1997), and now reverse the judgment of the Eleventh Circuit and remand for entry of judgment in Faragher's favor.

II

A

Under Title VII of the Civil Rights Act of 1964, "[i]t shall be an unlawful employment practice for an employer ... to fail or refuse to hire or to discharge any individual, or otherwise to discriminate against any individual with respect to his compensation, terms, conditions, or privileges of employment, because of such individual's race, color, religion, sex, or national origin." 42 U. S. C. § 2000e-2(a)(1). We have repeatedly made clear that although the statute mentions specific employment decisions with immediate consequences, the scope of the prohibition " 'is not limited to "economic" or "tangible" discrimination,' " *Harris v. Forklift Systems, Inc.* (1993) (quoting *Meritor Savings Bank, FSB v. Vinson*), and that it covers more than " 'terms' and 'conditions' in the narrow contractual sense." *Oncale v. Sundowner Offshore Services, Inc.* (1998). Thus, in *Meritor* we held that sexual harassment so "severe or pervasive" as to " 'alter the conditions of [the victim's] employment and create an abusive working environment' " violates Title VII.

... [I]n *Harris,* we explained that in order to be actionable under the statute, a sexually objectionable environment must be both objectively and subjectively offensive, one that a reasonable person would find hostile or abusive, and one that the victim in fact did perceive to be so. We directed courts to determine whether an environment is sufficiently hostile or abusive by "looking at all the circumstances," including the "frequency of the discriminatory conduct; its severity; whether it is physically threatening or humiliating, or a mere offensive utterance; and whether it unreasonably interferes with an employee's work performance." Most recently, we explained that Title VII does not prohibit "genuine but innocuous differences in the ways men and women routinely interact with members of the same sex and of the opposite sex." *Oncale.* A recurring point in these opinions is that "simple teasing," offhand comments, and isolated incidents (unless extremely serious) will not amount to discriminatory changes in the "terms and conditions of employment."

These standards for judging hostility are sufficiently demanding to ensure that Title VII does not become a "general civility code." Properly applied, they will filter out complaints attacking "the ordinary tribulations of the workplace, such as the sporadic use of abusive language, gender-related jokes, and occasional teasing." . . . We have made it clear that conduct must be extreme to amount to a change in the terms and conditions of employment, and the Courts of Appeals have heeded this view. [Citations omitted.]

While indicating the substantive contours of the hostile environments forbidden by Title VII, our cases have established few definite rules for determining when an employer will be liable for a discriminatory environment that is otherwise actionably abusive. . . .

B

The Court of Appeals identified, and rejected, three possible grounds drawn from agency law for holding the City vicariously liable for the hostile environment created by the supervisors. It considered whether the two supervisors were acting within the scope of their employment when they engaged in the harassing conduct. The court then enquired whether they were significantly aided by the agency relationship in committing the harassment, and also considered the possibility of imputing Gordon's knowledge of the harassment to the City. Finally, the Court of Appeals ruled out liability for negligence in failing to prevent the harassment. Faragher relies principally on the latter three theories of liability.

1

A "master is subject to liability for the torts of his servants committed while acting in the scope of their employment." Restatement § 219(1). This doctrine has traditionally defined the "scope of employment" as including conduct "of the kind [a servant] is employed to perform," occurring "substantially within the authorized time and space limits," and "actuated, at least in part, by a purpose to serve the master," but as excluding an intentional use of force "unexpectable by the master." § 228(1).

Courts of Appeals have typically held, or assumed, that conduct similar to the subject of this complaint falls outside the scope of employment. . . . In so doing, the courts have emphasized that harassment consisting of unwelcome remarks and touching is motivated solely by individual desires and serves no purpose of the employer. For this reason, courts have likened hostile environment sexual harassment to the classic "frolic and detour" for which an employer has no vicarious liability.

These cases ostensibly stand in some tension with others arising outside Title VII, where the scope of employment has been defined broadly enough to hold employers vicariously liable for intentional torts that were in no sense inspired by any purpose to serve the employer. . . . The rationales for these decisions have var-ied, with some courts . . . explaining that the employees' acts were foreseeable and that the employer should in fairness bear the resulting costs of doing business, and others finding that the employee's sexual misconduct arose from or was in some way related to the employee's essential duties. . . .

An assignment to reconcile the run of the Title VII cases with those just cited would be a taxing one. Here it is enough to recognize that their disparate results do not necessarily reflect wildly varying terms of the particular employment contracts involved, but represent differing judgments about the desirability of holding an employer liable for his subordinates' wayward behavior. In the instances in which there is a genuine question about the employer's responsibility for harmful conduct he did not in fact authorize, a holding that the conduct falls within the scope of employment ultimately expresses a conclusion not of fact but of law. . . . Older cases, for example, treated smoking by an employee during working hours as an act out-side the scope of employment, but more recently courts have generally held smok-ing on the job to fall within the scope. It is not that employers formerly did not authorize smoking but have now begun to do so, or that employees previously smoked for their own purposes but now do so to serve the employer. We simply understand smoking differently now and have revised the old judgments about what ought to be done about it.

The proper analysis here, then, calls not for a mechanical application of in-definite and malleable factors set forth in the Restatement, but rather an enquiry into the reasons that would support a conclusion that harassing behavior ought to be held within the scope of a supervisor's employment, and the reasons for the opposite view. . . .

In the case before us, a justification for holding the offensive behavior within the scope of Terry's and Silverman's employment was well put in Judge Barkett's dissent: "[A] pervasively hostile work environment of sexual harassment is never (one would hope) authorized, but the supervisor is clearly charged with maintain-ing a productive, safe work environment. The supervisor directs and controls the conduct of the employees, and the manner of doing so may inure to the employer's benefit or detriment, including subjecting the employer to Title VII liability." It is by now well recognized that hostile environment sexual harassment by supervisors (and, for that matter, co-employees) is a persistent problem in the workplace. . . . An em-ployer can, in a general sense, reasonably anticipate the possibility of such conduct occurring in its workplace, and one might justify the assignment of the burden of the untoward behavior to the employer as one of the costs of doing business, to be charged to the enterprise rather than the victim. . . . [D]evelopments like this occur from time to time in the law of agency.

Two things counsel us to draw the contrary conclusion. First, there is no reason to suppose that Congress wished courts to ignore the traditional distinction between acts falling within the scope and acts amounting to what the older law called frolics or detours from the course of employment. Such a distinction can readily be ap-plied to the spectrum of possible harassing conduct by supervisors. . . .

The second reason goes to an even broader unanimity of views among the holdings of District Courts and Courts of Appeals thus far. Those courts have held not only that the sort of harassment at issue here was outside the scope of supervi-sors' authority, but, by uniformly judging employer liability for co-worker harassment under a negligence standard, they have also implicitly treated such harassment as outside the scope of common employees' duties as well. . . .

2

The Court of Appeals also rejected vicarious liability on the part of the City insofar as it might rest on the concluding principle set forth in § 219(2)(d) of the Restatement, that an employer "is not subject to liability for the torts of his servants acting outside the scope of their employment unless . . . the servant purported to act or speak on behalf of the principal and there was reliance on apparent authority, or he was aided in accomplishing the tort by the existence of the agency relation." Faragher points to several ways in which the agency relationship aided Terry and Silverman in carrying out their harassment. She argues that in general offending supervisors can abuse their authority to keep subordinates in their presence while they make offensive statements, and that they implicitly threaten to misuse their supervisory powers to deter any resistance or complaint. Thus, she maintains that power conferred on Terry and Silverman by the City enabled them to act for so long without provoking defiance or complaint.

The City, however, contends that § 219(2)(d) has no application here. It argues that the second qualification of the subsection, referring to a servant "aided in accomplishing the tort by the existence of the agency relation," merely "refines" the one preceding it, which holds the employer vicariously liable for its servant's abuse of apparent authority. But this narrow reading is untenable; it would render the second qualification of § 219(2)(d) almost entirely superfluous. . . .

We therefore agree with Faragher that in implementing Title VII it makes sense to hold an employer vicariously liable for some tortious conduct of a supervisor made possible by abuse of his supervisory authority, and that the aided-by-agency-relation principle embodied in § 219(2)(d) of the Restatement provides an appropriate starting point for determining liability for the kind of harassment presented here. Several courts, indeed, have noted what Faragher has argued, that there is a sense in which a harassing supervisor is always assisted in his misconduct by the supervisory relationship. . . . The agency relationship affords contact with an employee subjected to a supervisor's sexual harassment, and the victim may well be reluctant to accept the risks of blowing the whistle on a superior. When a person with supervisory authority discriminates in the terms and conditions of subordinates' employment, his actions necessarily draw upon his superior position over the people who report to him, or those under them, whereas an employee generally cannot check a supervisor's abusive conduct the same way that she might deal with abuse from a co-worker. When a fellow employee harasses, the victim can walk away or tell the offender where to go, but it may be difficult to offer such responses to a supervisor. . . . Recognition of employer liability when discriminatory misuse of supervisory authority alters the terms and conditions of a victim's employment is underscored by the fact that the employer has a greater opportunity to guard against misconduct by supervisors than by common workers; employers have greater opportunity and incentive to screen them, train them, and monitor their performance.

In sum, there are good reasons for vicarious liability for misuse of supervisory authority. That rationale must, however, satisfy one more condition. We are not entitled to recognize this theory under Title VII unless we can square it with *Meritor*'s holding that an employer is not "automatically" liable for harassment by a supervisor who creates the requisite degree of discrimination. . . . [W]e think there are two basic alternatives, one being to require proof of some affirmative invocation of that authority by the harassing supervisor, the other to recognize an affirmative defense to liability in some circumstances, even when a supervisor has created the actionable environment.

There is certainly some authority for requiring active or affirmative, as distinct from passive or implicit, misuse of supervisory authority before liability may be imputed. . . .

But neat examples illustrating the line between the affirmative and merely implicit uses of power are not easy to come by in considering management behavior. . . . Judgment calls would often be close, the results would often seem disparate even if not demonstrably contradictory, and the temptation to litigate would be hard to resist. We think plaintiffs and defendants alike would be poorly served by an active-use rule.

The other basic alternative to automatic liability would avoid this particular temptation to litigate, but allow an employer to show as an affirmative defense to liability that the employer had exercised reasonable care to avoid harassment and to eliminate it when it might occur, and that the complaining employee had failed to act with like reasonable care to take advantage of the employer's safeguards and otherwise to prevent harm that could have been avoided. This composite defense would, we think, implement the statute sensibly. . . .

Although Title VII seeks "to make persons whole for injuries suffered on account of unlawful employment discrimination," *Albemarle Paper Co. v. Moody* (1975), its "primary objective," like that of any statute meant to influence primary conduct, is not to provide redress but to avoid harm. As long ago as 1980, the Equal Employment Opportunity Commission (EEOC), charged with the enforcement of Title VII, 42 U. S. C. § 2000e-4, adopted regulations advising employers to "take all steps necessary to prevent sexual harassment from occurring, such as . . . informing employees of their right to raise and how to raise the issue of harassment," and in 1990 the Commission issued a policy statement enjoining employers to establish a complaint procedure "designed to encourage victims of harassment to come forward [without requiring] a victim to complain first to the offending supervisor." EEOC Policy Guidance on Sexual Harassment (Mar. 19, 1990). It would therefore implement clear statutory policy and complement the Government's Title VII enforcement efforts to recognize the employer's affirmative obligation to prevent violations and give credit here to employers who make reasonable efforts to discharge their duty. Indeed, a theory of vicarious liability for misuse of supervisory power would be at odds with the statutory policy if it failed to provide employers with some such incentive.

The requirement to show that the employee has failed in a coordinate duty to avoid or mitigate harm reflects an equally obvious policy imported from the general theory of damages, that a victim has a duty "to use such means as are reasonable under the circumstances to avoid or minimize the damages" that result from violations of the statute. *Ford Motor Co. v. EEOC* (1982). An employer may, for example, have provided a proven, effective mechanism for reporting and resolving complaints of sexual harassment, available to the employee without undue risk or expense. If the plaintiff unreasonably failed to avail herself of the employer's preventive or remedial apparatus, she should not recover damages that could have been avoided if she had done so. If the victim could have avoided harm, no liability should be found against the employer who had taken reasonable care, and if damages could reasonably have been mitigated no award against a liable employer should reward a plaintiff for what her own efforts could have avoided.

In order to accommodate the principle of vicarious liability for harm caused by misuse of supervisory authority, as well as Title VII's equally basic policies of encouraging forethought by employers and saving action by objecting employees, we adopt the following holding in this case and in *Burlington Industries, Inc. v. Ellerth,* also decided today. An employer is subject to vicarious liability to a victimized employee for an actionable hostile environment created by a supervisor with immediate (or successively higher) authority over the employee. When no tangible employment action is taken, a defending employer may raise an affirmative defense to liability or damages, subject to proof by a preponderance of the evidence. The defense comprises two necessary elements: (a) that the employer exercised reasonable care to prevent and correct promptly any sexually harassing behavior, and (b) that the plaintiff employee unreasonably failed to take advantage of any preventive or corrective opportunities provided by the employer or to avoid harm otherwise. While proof that an employer had promulgated an antiharassment policy with complaint procedure is not necessary in every instance as a matter of law, the need for a stated policy suitable to the employment circumstances may appropriately be addressed in any case when litigating the first element of the defense. And while proof that an employee failed to fulfill the corresponding obligation of reasonable care to avoid harm is not limited to showing an unreasonable failure to use any complaint procedure provided by the employer, a demonstration of such failure will normally suffice to satisfy the employer's burden under the second element of the defense. No affirmative defense is available, however, when the supervisor's harassment culminates in a tangible employment action, such as discharge, demotion, or undesirable reassignment. Applying these rules here, we believe that the judgment of the Court of Appeals must be reversed. The District Court found that the degree of hostility in the work environment rose to the actionable level and was attributable to Silverman and Terry. It is undisputed that these supervisors "were granted virtually unchecked authority" over their subordinates, "directly controll[ing] and supervis[ing] all aspects of [Faragher's] day-to-day activities." It is also clear that Faragher and her colleagues were "completely isolated from the City's higher management." The City did not seek review of these findings. While the City would have an opportunity to raise an affirmative defense if there were any serious prospect of its presenting one, it appears from the record that any such avenue is closed. The District Court found that the City had entirely failed to disseminate its policy against sexual harassment among the beach employees and that its officials made no attempt to keep track of the conduct of supervisors like Terry and Silverman. The record also makes clear that the City's policy did not include any assurance that the harassing supervisors could be bypassed in registering complaints. Under such circumstances, we hold as a matter of law that the City could not be found to have exercised reasonable care to prevent the supervisors' harassing conduct. Unlike the employer of a small workforce, who might expect that sufficient care to prevent tortious behavior could be exercised informally, those responsible for city operations could not reasonably have thought that precautions against hostile environments in any one of many departments in far-flung locations could be effective without communicating some formal policy against harassment, with a sensible complaint procedure.

We have drawn this conclusion without overlooking two possible grounds upon which the City might argue for the opportunity to litigate further. There is, first, the Court of Appeals's indulgent gloss on the relevant evidence: "There is some evidence that the City did not effectively disseminate among Marine Safety employees its sexual harassment policy." But, in contrast to the Court of Appeals's characterization, the District Court made an explicit finding of a "complete failure on the part of the City to disseminate said policy among Marine Safety Section employees." The evidence supports the District Court's finding and there is no contrary claim before us.

The second possible ground for pursuing a defense was asserted by the City in its argument addressing the possibility of negligence liability in this case. It said that it should not be held liable for failing to promulgate an antiharassment policy, because there was no apparent duty to do so in the 1985–1990 period. The City purports to rest this argument on the position of the EEOC during the period mentioned, but it turns out that the record on this point is quite against the City's position. Although the EEOC issued regulations dealing with promulgating a statement of policy and providing a complaint mechanism in 1990, ever since 1980 its regulations have called for steps to prevent violations, such as informing employees of their rights and the means to assert them. The City, after all, adopted an antiharassment policy in 1986.

The City points to nothing that might justify a conclusion by the District Court on remand that the City had exercised reasonable care. Nor is there any reason to remand for consideration of Faragher's efforts to mitigate her own damages, since the award to her was solely nominal.

3

The Court of Appeals also rejected the possibility that it could hold the City liable for the reason that it knew of the harassment vicariously through the knowledge of its supervisors. We have no occasion to consider whether this was error, however. We are satisfied that liability on the ground of vicarious knowledge could not be determined without further factfinding on remand, whereas the reversal necessary on the theory of supervisory harassment renders any remand for consideration of imputed knowledge entirely unjustifiable (as would be any consideration of negligence as an alternative to a theory of vicarious liability here).

III

The judgment of the Court of Appeals for the Eleventh Circuit is reversed, and the case is remanded for reinstatement of the judgment of the District Court.

It is so ordered.

JUSTICE THOMAS, with whom JUSTICE SCALIA joins, dissenting.

For the reasons given in my dissenting opinion in *Burlington Industries v. Ellerth,* absent an adverse employment consequence, an employer cannot be held vicariously liable if a supervisor creates a hostile work environment. Petitioner suffered no adverse employment consequence; thus the Court of Appeals was correct to hold that the City is not vicariously liable for the conduct of Chief Terry and Lieutenant Silverman. Because the Court reverses this judgment, I dissent.

As for petitioner's negligence claim, the District Court made no finding as to the City's negligence, and the Court of Appeals did not directly consider the issue. I would therefore remand the case to the District Court for further proceedings on this question alone. I disagree with the Court's conclusion that merely because the City did not disseminate its sexual harassment policy, it should be liable as a matter of law. The City should be allowed to show either that: (1) there was a reasonably available avenue through which petitioner could have complained to a City official who supervised both Chief Terry and Lieutenant Silverman, or (2) it would not have learned of the harassment even if the policy had been distributed. Petitioner, as the plaintiff, would of course bear the burden of proving the City's negligence.

□□□

No. 97-569

Burlington Industries, Inc., Petitioner v. Kimberly B. Ellerth

On writ of certiorari to the United States
Court of Appeals for the Seventh Circuit

[June 26, 1998]

JUSTICE KENNEDY delivered the opinion of the Court.

We decide whether, under Title VII of the Civil Rights Act of 1964 as amended, 42 U. S. C. § 2000e *et seq.*, an employee who refuses the unwelcome and threatening sexual advances of a supervisor, yet suffers no adverse, tangible job consequences, can recover against the employer without showing the employer is negligent or otherwise at fault for the supervisor's actions.

I

Summary judgment was granted for the employer, so we must take the facts alleged by the employee to be true. The employer is Burlington Industries, the petitioner. The employee is Kimberly Ellerth, the respondent. From March 1993 until May 1994, Ellerth worked as a salesperson in one of Burlington's divisions in Chicago, Illinois. During her employment, she alleges, she was subjected to constant sexual harassment by her supervisor, one Ted Slowik.

In the hierarchy of Burlington's management structure, Slowik was a mid-level manager. Burlington has eight divisions, employing more than 22,000 people in some 50 plants around the United States. Slowik was a vice president in one of five business units within one of the divisions. He had authority to make hiring and promotion decisions subject to the approval of his supervisor, who signed the paperwork. According to Slowik's supervisor, his position was "not considered an upper-level management position," and he was "not amongst the decision-making or policy-making hierarchy." Slowik was not Ellerth's immediate supervisor. Ellerth worked in a two-person office in Chicago, and she answered to her office colleague, who in turn answered to Slowik in New York.

Against a background of repeated boorish and offensive remarks and gestures which Slowik allegedly made, Ellerth places particular emphasis on three alleged incidents where Slowik's comments could be construed as threats to deny her tangible job benefits. In the summer of 1993, while on a business trip, Slowik invited Ellerth to the hotel lounge, an invitation Ellerth felt compelled to accept because Slowik was her boss. When Ellerth gave no encouragement to remarks Slowik made about her breasts, he told her to "loosen up" and warned, "[y]ou know, Kim, I could make your life very hard or very easy at Burlington."

In March 1994, when Ellerth was being considered for a promotion, Slowik expressed reservations during the promotion interview because she was not "loose enough." The comment was followed by his reaching over and rubbing her knee. Ellerth did receive the promotion; but when Slowik called to announce it, he told Ellerth, "you're gonna be out there with men who work in factories, and they certainly like women with pretty butts/legs."

In May 1994, Ellerth called Slowik, asking permission to insert a customer's logo into a fabric sample. Slowik responded, "I don't have time for you right now, Kim—unless you want to tell me what you're wearing." Ellerth told Slowik she had to go and ended the call. A day or two later, Ellerth called Slowik to ask permission again. This time he denied her request, but added something along the lines of, "are you wearing shorter skirts yet, Kim, because it would make your job a whole heck of a lot easier."

A short time later, Ellerth's immediate supervisor cautioned her about returning telephone calls to customers in a prompt fashion. In response, Ellerth quit. She faxed a letter giving reasons unrelated to the alleged sexual harassment we have described. About three weeks later, however, she sent a letter explaining she quit because of Slowik's behavior.

During her tenure at Burlington, Ellerth did not inform anyone in authority about Slowik's conduct, despite knowing Burlington had a policy against sexual harassment. In fact, she chose not to inform her immediate supervisor (not Slowik) because " 'it would be his duty as my supervisor to report any incidents of sexual harassment.' " On one occasion, she told Slowik a comment he made was inappropriate.

In October 1994, after receiving a right-to-sue letter from the Equal Employment Opportunity Commission (EEOC), Ellerth filed suit in the United States District Court for the Northern District of Illinois, alleging Burlington engaged in sexual harassment and forced her constructive discharge, in violation of Title VII. The District Court granted summary judgment to Burlington. The Court found Slowik's behavior, as described by Ellerth, severe and pervasive enough to create a hostile work environment, but found Burlington neither knew nor should have known about the conduct. There was no triable issue of fact on the latter point, and the Court noted Ellerth had not used Burlington's internal complaint procedures. Although Ellerth's claim was framed as a hostile work environment complaint, the District Court observed there was a quid pro quo "component" to the hostile environment. Proceeding from the premise that an employer faces vicarious liability for quid pro quo harassment, the District Court thought it necessary to apply a negligence standard because the quid pro quo merely contributed to the hostile work environment. The District Court also dismissed Ellerth's constructive discharge claim.

The Court of Appeals en banc reversed in a decision which produced eight separate opinions and no consensus for a controlling rationale. [Summary of various opinions omitted.]

The disagreement revealed in the careful opinions of the judges of the Court of Appeals reflects the fact that Congress has left it to the courts to determine controlling agency law principles in a new and difficult area of federal law. We granted certiorari to assist in defining the relevant standards of employer liability (1998).

II

At the outset, we assume an important proposition yet to be established before a trier of fact. It is a premise assumed as well, in explicit or implicit terms, in the various opinions by the judges of the Court of Appeals. The premise is: a trier of fact could find in Slowik's remarks numerous threats to retaliate against Ellerth if she denied some sexual liberties. The threats, however, were not carried out or fulfilled. Cases based on threats which are carried out are referred to often as *quid pro quo* cases, as distinct from bothersome attentions or sexual remarks that are sufficiently severe or pervasive to create a hostile work environment. The terms *quid pro quo* and hostile work environment are helpful, perhaps, in making a rough demarcation between cases in which threats are carried out and those where they are not or are absent altogether, but beyond this are of limited utility.

Section 703(a) of Title VII forbids

"an employer—

"(1) to fail or refuse to hire or to discharge any individual, or otherwise to discriminate against any individual with respect to his compensation, terms, conditions or privileges of employment, because of such individual's . . . sex." 42 U. S. C. § 2000e-2(a)(1).

"*Quid pro quo*" and "hostile work environment" do not appear in the statutory text. The terms appeared first in the academic literature; found their way into decisions of the Courts of Appeals; and were mentioned in this Court's decision in *Meritor Savings Bank, FSB v. Vinson* (1986).

In *Meritor,* the terms served a specific and limited purpose. There we considered whether the conduct in question constituted discrimination in the terms or conditions of employment in violation of Title VII. We assumed, and with adequate reason, that if an employer demanded sexual favors from an employee in return for a job benefit, discrimination with respect to terms or conditions of employment was explicit. Less obvious was whether an employer's sexually demeaning behavior altered terms or conditions of employment in violation of Title VII. We distinguished between *quid pro quo* claims and hostile environment claims, and said both were cognizable under Title VII, though the latter requires harassment that is severe or pervasive. The principal significance of the distinction is to instruct that Title VII is violated by either explicit or constructive alterations in the terms or conditions of employment and to explain the latter must be severe or pervasive. The distinction was not discussed for its bearing upon an employer's liability for an employee's discrimination. On this question *Meritor* held, with no further specifics, that agency principles controlled.

Nevertheless, as use of the terms grew in the wake of *Meritor,* they acquired their own significance. The standard of employer responsibility turned on which type of harassment occurred. If the plaintiff established a *quid pro quo* claim, the Courts of Appeals held, the employer was subject to vicarious liability. [Citations omitted.] The rule encouraged Title VII plaintiffs to state their claims as *quid pro quo* claims, which in turn put expansive pressure on the definition. The equivalence of the *quid pro quo* label and vicarious liability is illustrated by this case. The question presented on certiorari is whether Ellerth can state a claim of *quid pro quo* harassment, but the issue of real concern to the parties is whether Burlington has vicarious liability for Slowik's alleged misconduct, rather than liability limited to its own negligence. The question presented for certiorari asks:

> "Whether a claim of *quid pro quo* sexual harassment may be stated under Title VII . . . where the plaintiff employee has neither submitted to the sexual advances of the alleged harasser nor suffered any tangible effects on the compensation, terms, conditions or privileges of employment as a consequence of a refusal to submit to those advances?"

We do not suggest the terms *quid pro quo* and hostile work environment are irrelevant to Title VII litigation. To the extent they illustrate the distinction between cases involving a threat which is carried out and offensive conduct in general, the terms are relevant when there is a threshold question whether a plaintiff can prove discrimination in violation of Title VII. When a plaintiff proves that a tangible employment action resulted from a refusal to submit to a supervisor's sexual demands, he or she establishes that the employment decision itself constitutes a change in the terms and conditions of employment that is actionable under Title VII. For any sexual harassment preceding the employment decision to be actionable, however, the conduct must be severe or pervasive. Because Ellerth's claim involves only unfulfilled threats, it should be categorized as a hostile work environment claim which requires a showing of severe or pervasive conduct. See *Oncale v. Sundowner Offshore Services, Inc.* (1998); *Harris v. Forklift Systems, Inc.* (1993). For purposes of this case, we accept the District Court's finding that the alleged conduct was severe or pervasive. The case before us involves numerous alleged threats, and we express no opinion as to whether a single unfulfilled threat is sufficient to constitute discrimination in the terms or conditions of employment.

When we assume discrimination can be proved, however, the factors we discuss below, and not the categories *quid pro quo* and hostile work environment, will be controlling on the issue of vicarious liability. That is the question we must resolve.

III

We must decide, then, whether an employer has vicarious liability when a supervisor creates a hostile work environment by making explicit threats to alter a subordinate's terms or conditions of employment, based on sex, but does not fulfill the threat. We turn to principles of agency law, for the term "employer" is defined under Title VII to include "agents." 42 U. S. C. § 2000e(b). In express terms, Congress has directed federal courts to interpret Title VII based on agency principles.

Given such an explicit instruction, we conclude a uniform and predictable standard must be established as a matter of federal law. . . .

As *Meritor* acknowledged, the Restatement (Second) of Agency (1957) is a useful beginning point for a discussion of general agency principles. Since our decision in *Meritor*, federal courts have explored agency principles, and we find useful instruction in their decisions, noting that "common-law principles may not be transferable in all their particulars to Title VII." The EEOC has issued Guidelines governing sexual harassment claims under Title VII, but they provide little guidance on the issue of employer liability for supervisor harassment. See 29 CFR § 1604.11(c) (1997) (vicarious liability for supervisor harassment turns on "the particular employment relationship and the job functions performed by the individual").

A

Section 219(1) of the Restatement sets out a central principle of agency law:

"A master is subject to liability for the torts of his servants committed while acting in the scope of their employment."

An employer may be liable for both negligent and intentional torts committed by an employee within the scope of his or her employment. Sexual harassment under Title VII presupposes intentional conduct. While early decisions absolved employers of liability for the intentional torts of their employees, the law now imposes liability where the employee's "purpose, however misguided, is wholly or in part to further the master's business." . . . [Quoting Prosser and Keeton on Torts.]

The general rule is that sexual harassment by a supervisor is not conduct within the scope of employment.

B

Scope of employment does not define the only basis for employer liability under agency principles. In limited circumstances, agency principles impose liability on employers even where employees commit torts outside the scope of employment. The principles are set forth in the much-cited § 219(2) of the Restatement:

"(2) A master is not subject to liability for the torts of his servants acting outside the scope of their employment, unless:

"(a) the master intended the conduct or the consequences, or

"(b) the master was negligent or reckless, or

"(c) the conduct violated a non-delegable duty of the master, or

"(d) the servant purported to act or to speak on behalf of the principal and there was reliance upon apparent authority, or he was aided in accomplishing the tort by the existence of the agency relation."

See also § 219, Comment e (Section 219(2) "enumerates the situations in which a master may be liable for torts of servants acting solely for their own purposes and hence not in the scope of employment").

Subsection (a) addresses direct liability, where the employer acts with tortious intent, and indirect liability, where the agent's high rank in the company makes him or her the employer's alter ego. None of the parties contend Slowik's rank imputes liability under this principle. There is no contention, furthermore, that a nondelegable duty is involved. So, for our purposes here, subsections (a) and (c) can be put aside.

Subsections (b) and (d) are possible grounds for imposing employer liability on account of a supervisor's acts and must be considered. Under subsection (b), an employer is liable when the tort is attributable to the employer's own negligence. Thus, although a supervisor's sexual harassment is outside the scope of employment because the conduct was for personal motives, an employer can be liable, nonetheless, where its own negligence is a cause of the harassment. An employer is negligent with respect to sexual harassment if it knew or should have known about the conduct and failed to stop it. Negligence sets a minimum standard for employer liability under Title VII; but Ellerth seeks to invoke the more stringent standard of vicarious liability.

Subsection 219(2)(d) concerns vicarious liability for intentional torts committed by an employee when the employee uses apparent authority (the apparent authority standard), or when the employee "was aided in accomplishing the tort by the existence of the agency relation" (the aided in the agency relation standard). As other federal decisions have done in discussing vicarious liability for supervisor harassment, we begin with § 219(2)(d).

C

As a general rule, apparent authority is relevant where the agent purports to exercise a power which he or she does not have, as distinct from where the agent threatens to misuse actual power. . . . In the usual case, a supervisor's harassment involves misuse of actual power, not the false impression of its existence. Apparent authority analysis therefore is inappropriate in this context. . . .

D

We turn to the aided in the agency relation standard. In a sense, most workplace tortfeasors are aided in accomplishing their tortious objective by the existence of the agency relation: Proximity and regular contact may afford a captive pool of potential victims. Were this to satisfy the aided in the agency relation standard, an employer would be subject to vicarious liability not only for all supervisor harassment, but also for all co-worker harassment, a result enforced by neither the EEOC nor any court of appeals to have considered the issue. [Citations omitted.] The aided in the agency relation standard, therefore, requires the existence of something more than the employment relation itself.

At the outset, we can identify a class of cases where, beyond question, more than the mere existence of the employment relation aids in commission of the harassment: when a supervisor takes a tangible employment action against the subordinate. Every Federal Court of Appeals to have considered the question has found vicarious liability when a discriminatory act results in a tangible employment action. [Citations omitted.] In *Meritor,* we acknowledged this consensus. . . . Although few courts have elaborated how agency principles support this rule, we think it reflects a correct application of the aided in the agency relation standard.

In the context of this case, a tangible employment action would have taken the form of a denial of a raise or a promotion. The concept of a tangible employment action appears in numerous cases in the Courts of Appeals discussing claims involving race, age, and national origin discrimination, as well as sex discrimination. Without endorsing the specific results of those decisions, we think it prudent to import the concept of a tangible employment action for resolution of the vicarious liability issue we consider here. A tangible employment action constitutes a significant change in employment status, such as hiring, firing, failing to promote, reassignment with significantly different responsibilities, or a decision causing a significant change in benefits. . . .

When a supervisor makes a tangible employment decision, there is assurance the injury could not have been inflicted absent the agency relation. A tangible employment action in most cases inflicts direct economic harm. As a general proposition, only a supervisor, or other person acting with the authority of the company, can cause this sort of injury. A co-worker can break a co-worker's arm as easily as a supervisor, and anyone who has regular contact with an employee can inflict psychological injuries by his or her offensive conduct. . . . But one co-worker (absent some elaborate scheme) cannot dock another's pay, nor can one co-worker demote another. Tangible employment actions fall within the special province of the supervisor. The supervisor has been empowered by the company as a distinct class of agent to make economic decisions affecting other employees under his or her control.

Tangible employment actions are the means by which the supervisor brings the official power of the enterprise to bear on subordinates. A tangible employment decision requires an official act of the enterprise, a company act. The decision in most cases is documented in official company records, and may be subject to review by higher level supervisors. . . . The supervisor often must obtain the imprimatur of the enterprise and use its internal processes. . . .

For these reasons, a tangible employment action taken by the supervisor becomes for Title VII purposes the act of the employer. Whatever the exact contours of the aided in the agency relation standard, its requirements will always be met when a supervisor takes a tangible employment action against a subordinate. In that instance, it would be implausible to interpret agency principles to allow an employer to escape liability, as *Meritor* itself appeared to acknowledge.

Whether the agency relation aids in commission of supervisor harassment which does not culminate in a tangible employment action is less obvious. Application of the standard is made difficult by its malleable terminology, which can be read to either expand or limit liability in the context of supervisor harassment. On the one hand, a supervisor's power and authority invests his or her harassing conduct with a particular threatening character, and in this sense, a supervisor always is aided by the agency relation. . . . On the other hand, there are acts of harassment a supervisor might commit which might be the same acts a co-employee would commit, and there may be some circumstances where the supervisor's status makes little difference.

It is this tension which, we think, has caused so much confusion among the Courts of Appeals which have sought to apply the aided in the agency relation standard to Title VII cases. The aided in the agency relation standard, however, is a developing feature of agency law, and we hesitate to render a definitive explanation of our understanding of the standard in an area where other important considerations must affect our judgment. In particular, we are bound by our holding in *uid pro quo* and hostile work environment are not controlling for purposes of establishing employer liability, Ellerth should have an adequate opportunity to prove she has a claim for which Burlington is liable.

Although Ellerth has not alleged she suffered a tangible employment action at he hands of Slowik, which would deprive Burlington of the availability of the affirmative defense, this is not dispositive. In light of our decision, Burlington is still subject to vicarious liability for Slowik's activity, but Burlington should have an opportunity to assert and prove the affirmative defense to liability.

For these reasons, we will affirm the judgment of the Court of Appeals, reversing the grant of summary judgment against Ellerth. On remand, the District Court will have the opportunity to decide whether it would be appropriate to allow Ellerth to amend her pleading or supplement her discovery.

The judgment of the Court of Appeals is affirmed.

It is so ordered.

JUSTICE GINSBURG, concurring in the judgment.

I agree with the Court's ruling that "the labels *quid pro quo* and hostile work environment are not controlling for purposes of establishing employer liability." I also subscribe to the Court's statement of the rule governing employer liability, which is substantively identical to the rule the Court adopts in *Faragher v. Boca Raton*.

JUSTICE THOMAS, with whom JUSTICE SCALIA joins, dissenting.

The Court today manufactures a rule that employers are vicariously liable if supervisors create a sexually hostile work environment, subject to an affirmative defense that the Court barely attempts to define. This rule applies even if the employer has a policy against sexual harassment, the employee knows about that policy, and the employee never informs anyone in a position of authority about the supervisor's conduct. As a result, employer liability under Title VII is judged by different standards depending upon whether a sexually or racially hostile work environment is alleged. The standard of employer liability should be the same in both instances: An employer should be liable if, and only if, the plaintiff proves that the employer was negligent in permitting the supervisor's conduct to occur.

I

Years before sexual harassment was recognized as "discriminat[ion] . . . because of . . . sex," 42 U. S. C. § 2000e-2(a)(1), the Courts of Appeals considered whether, and when, a racially hostile work environment could violate Title VII. In the landmark case *Rogers v. EEOC* (1971), cert. denied (1972), the Court of Appeals for the Fifth Circuit held that the practice of racially segregating patients in a doctor's office could amount to discrimination in " 'the terms, conditions, or privileges' " of employment, thereby violating Title VII. (Quoting 42 U. S. C. § 2000e-2(a)(1)). The principal opinion in the case concluded that employment discrimination was not limited to the "isolated and distinguishable events" of "hiring, firing, and promoting" (opinion of Goldberg, J.). Rather, Title VII could also be violated by a work environment "heavily polluted with discrimination," because of the deleterious effects of such an atmosphere on an employee's well-being.

Accordingly, after *Rogers*, a plaintiff claiming employment discrimination based upon race could assert a claim for a racially hostile work environment, in addition

Meritor that agency principles constrain the imposition of vicarious liabili
of supervisory harassment. See *Meritor* ("Congress' decision to define 'em
include any 'agent' of an employer, 42 U. S. C. § 2000e(b), surely evinces
to place some limits on the acts of employees for which employers under
are to be held responsible"). Congress has not altered *Meritor*'s rule even t
has made significant amendments to Title VII in the interim. . . .

Although *Meritor* suggested the limitation on employer liability stemm
agency principles, the Court acknowledged other considerations might
evant as well. . . . For example, Title VII is designed to encourage the cre;
antiharassment policies and effective grievance mechanisms. Were empl
ability to depend in part on an employer's effort to create such procedı
would effect Congress' intention to promote conciliation rather than litiga
the Title VII context and the EEOC's policy of encouraging the developm
grievance procedures. To the extent limiting employer liability could encc
employees to report harassing conduct before it becomes severe or pervas
would also serve Title VII's deterrent purpose. As we have observed, Title VI
rows from tort law the avoidable consequences doctrine, and the considerá
which animate that doctrine would also support the limitation of employer l
ity in certain circumstances.

In order to accommodate the agency principles of vicarious liability for I
caused by misuse of supervisory authority, as well as Title VII's equally basic
cies of encouraging forethought by employers and saving action by objecting
ployees, we adopt the following holding in this case and in *Faragher v. Boca Rı*
also decided today. An employer is subject to vicarious liability to a victimı
employee for an actionable hostile environment created by a supervisor with
mediate (or successively higher) authority over the employee. When no tangil
employment action is taken, a defending employer may raise an affirmative ı
fense to liability or damages, subject to proof by a preponderance of the eviden⟨
The defense comprises two necessary elements: (a) that the employer exercis
reasonable care to prevent and correct promptly any sexually harassing behavi
and (b) that the plaintiff employee unreasonably failed to take advantage of a
preventive or corrective opportunities provided by the employer or to avoid har
otherwise. While proof that an employer had promulgated an antiharassment poli
with complaint procedure is not necessary in every instance as a matter of law, tl
need for a stated policy suitable to the employment circumstances may approp
ately be addressed in any case when litigating the first element of the defens
And while proof that an employee failed to fulfill the corresponding obligation
reasonable care to avoid harm is not limited to showing any unreasonable failu
to use any complaint procedure provided by the employer, a demonstration ⟨
such failure will normally suffice to satisfy the employer's burden under the se
ond element of the defense. No affirmative defense is available, however, whe
the supervisor's harassment culminates in a tangible employment action, such ;
discharge, demotion, or undesirable reassignment.

IV

Relying on existing case law which held out the promise of vicarious liabilii
for all *quid pro quo* claims, Ellerth focused all her attention in the Court of Appeal
on proving her claim fit within that category. Given our explanation that the label

to the classic claim of so-called "disparate treatment." A disparate treatment claim required a plaintiff to prove an adverse employment consequence and discriminatory intent by his employer. A hostile environment claim required the plaintiff to show that his work environment was so pervaded by racial harassment as to alter the terms and conditions of his employment. . . . This is the same standard now used when determining whether sexual harassment renders a work environment hostile. See *Harris v. Forklift Systems, Inc.* (1993) (actionable sexual harassment occurs when the workplace is "*permeated* with discriminatory intimidation, ridicule, and insult") (emphasis added).

In race discrimination cases, employer liability has turned on whether the plaintiff has alleged an adverse employment consequence, such as firing or demotion, or a hostile work environment. If a supervisor takes an adverse employment action because of race, causing the employee a tangible job detriment, the employer is vicariously liable for resulting damages. This is because such actions are company acts that can be performed only by the exercise of specific authority granted by the employer, and thus the supervisor acts as the employer. If, on the other hand, the employee alleges a racially hostile work environment, the employer is liable only for negligence: that is, only if the employer knew, or in the exercise of reasonable care should have known, about the harassment and failed to take remedial action. [Citations omitted.] Liability has thus been imposed only if the employer is blameworthy in some way. [Citations omitted.]

This distinction applies with equal force in cases of sexual harassment. When a supervisor inflicts an adverse employment consequence upon an employee who has rebuffed his advances, the supervisor exercises the specific authority granted to him by his company. His acts, therefore, are the company's acts and are properly chargeable to it. . . .

If a supervisor creates a hostile work environment, however, he does not act for the employer. As the Court concedes, a supervisor's creation of a hostile work environment is neither within the scope of his employment, nor part of his apparent authority. Indeed, a hostile work environment is antithetical to the interest of the employer. In such circumstances, an employer should be liable only if it has been negligent. That is, liability should attach only if the employer either knew, or in the exercise of reasonable care should have known, about the hostile work environment and failed to take remedial action.

Sexual harassment is simply not something that employers can wholly prevent without taking extraordinary measures—constant video and audio surveillance, for example—that would revolutionize the workplace in a manner incompatible with a free society. Indeed, such measures could not even detect incidents of harassment such as the comments Slowik allegedly made to respondent in a hotel bar. The most that employers can be charged with, therefore, is a duty to act reasonably under the circumstances. . . .

Under a negligence standard, Burlington cannot be held liable for Slowik's conduct. Although respondent alleged a hostile work environment, she never contended that Burlington had been negligent in permitting the harassment to occur, and there is no question that Burlington acted reasonably under the circumstances. The company had a policy against sexual harassment, and respondent admitted that she was aware of the policy but nonetheless failed to tell anyone with authority over Slowik about his behavior. Burlington therefore cannot be charged with knowledge of Slowik's alleged harassment or with a failure to exercise reasonable care in not knowing about it.

II

Rejecting a negligence standard, the Court instead imposes a rule of vicarious employer liability, subject to a vague affirmative defense, for the acts of supervisors who wield no delegated authority in creating a hostile work environment. This rule is a whole-cloth creation that draws no support from the legal principles on which the Court claims it is based. Compounding its error, the Court fails to explain how employers can rely upon the affirmative defense, thus ensuring a continuing reign of confusion in this important area of the law.

In justifying its holding, the Court refers to our comment in *Meritor Savings Bank, FSB v. Vinson* (1986), that the lower courts should look to "agency principles" for guidance in determining the scope of employer liability. The Court then interprets the term "agency principles" to mean the Restatement (Second) of Agency (1957). The Court finds two portions of the Restatement to be relevant: § 219(2)(b), which provides that a master is liable for his servant's torts if the master is reckless or negligent, and § 219(2)(d), which states that a master is liable for his servant's torts when the servant is "aided in accomplishing the tort by the existence of the agency relation." The Court appears to reason that a supervisor is aided . . . by . . . the agency relation" in creating a hostile work environment because the supervisor's "power and authority invests his or her harassing conduct with a particular threatening character."

Section 219(2)(d) of the Restatement provides no basis whatsoever for imposing vicarious liability for a supervisor's creation of a hostile work environment. Contrary to the Court's suggestions, the principle embodied in § 219(2)(d) has nothing to do with a servant's "power and authority," nor with whether his actions appear "threatening." Rather, as demonstrated by the Restatement's illustrations, liability under § 219(2)(d) depends upon the plaintiff's belief that the agent acted in the ordinary course of business or within the scope of his apparent authority. In this day and age, no sexually harassed employee can reasonably believe that a harassing supervisor is conducting the official business of the company or acting on its behalf. Indeed, the Court admits as much in demonstrating why sexual harassment is not committed within the scope of a supervisor's employment and is not part of his apparent authority.

Thus although the Court implies that it has found guidance in both precedent and statute . . . its holding is a product of willful policymaking, pure and simple. The only agency principle that justifies imposing employer liability in this context is the principle that a master will be liable for a servant's torts if the master was negligent or reckless in permitting them to occur; and as noted, under a negligence standard, Burlington cannot be held liable.

The Court's decision is also in considerable tension with our holding in *Meritor* that employers are not strictly liable for a supervisor's sexual harassment. Although the Court recognizes an affirmative defense . . . it provides shockingly little guidance about how employers can actually avoid vicarious liability. Instead, it issues only Delphic pronouncements and leaves the dirty work to the lower courts:

"While proof that an employer had promulgated an anti-harassment policy with complaint procedure is not necessary in every instance as a matter of law, the need for a stated policy suitable to the employment circumstances may appropriately be addressed in any case when litigating the first element of the defense. And while proof that an employee failed to fulfill the corresponding obligation of reasonable care to avoid harm is not limited to showing any unreasonable failure to use any complaint procedure provided by the employer, a demonstration of such failure will normally suffice to satisfy the employer's burden under the second element of the defense."

What these statements mean for district courts ruling on motions for summary judgment—the critical question for employers now subject to the vicarious liability rule—remains a mystery. Moreover, employers will be liable notwithstanding the affirmative defense, *even though they acted reasonably,* so long as the plaintiff in question fulfilled her duty of reasonable care to avoid harm. In practice, therefore, employer liability very well may be the rule. But as the Court acknowledges, this is the one result that it is clear Congress did not intend.

The Court's holding does guarantee one result: There will be more and more litigation to clarify applicable legal rules in an area in which both practitioners and the courts have long been begging for guidance. It thus truly boggles the mind that the Court can claim that its holding will effect "Congress' intention to promote conciliation rather than litigation in the Title VII context." All in all, today's decision is an ironic result for a case that generated eight separate opinions in the Court of Appeals on a fundamental question, and in which we granted certiorari "to assist in defining the relevant standards of employer liability."

* * *

Popular misconceptions notwithstanding, sexual harassment is not a freestanding federal tort, but a form of employment discrimination. As such, it should be treated no differently (and certainly no better) than the other forms of harassment that are illegal under Title VII. I would restore parallel treatment of employer liability for racial and sexual harassment and hold an employer liable for a hostile work environment only if the employer is truly at fault. I therefore respectfully dissent.

How the Court Works

The Constitution makes the Supreme Court the final arbiter in "cases" and "controversies" arising under the Constitution or the laws of the United States. As the interpreter of the law, the Court often is viewed as the least mutable and most tradition-bound of the three branches of the federal government. But the Court has undergone innumerable changes in its history, some of which have been mandated by law. Some of these changes are embodied in Court rules; others are informal adaptations to needs and circumstances.

The Schedule of the Term

Annual Terms

By law the Supreme Court begins its regular annual term on the first Monday in October, and the term lasts approximately nine months. This session is known as the October term. The summer recess, which is not determined by statute or Court rules, generally begins in late June or early July of the following year. This system—staying in continuous session throughout the year, with periodic recesses—makes it unnecessary to convene a special term to deal with matters arising in the summer.

The justices actually begin work before the official opening of the term. They hold their initial conference during the last week in September. When the justices formally convene on the first Monday in October, oral arguments begin.

Arguments and Conferences

At least four justices must request that a case be argued before it can be accepted. Arguments are heard on Monday, Tuesday, and Wednesday for seven two-week sessions, beginning in the first week in October and ending in mid-April. Recesses of two weeks or longer occur between the sessions of oral arguments so that justices can consider the cases and deal with other Court business.

The schedule for oral arguments is 10:00 a.m. to noon and 1 p.m. to 3 p.m. Because most cases receive one hour apiece for argument, the Court can hear up to twelve cases a week.

The Court holds conferences on the Friday just before the two-week oral argument periods and on Wednesday and Friday during the weeks when oral arguments are scheduled. The conferences are designed for consideration of cases already heard in oral argument.

Before each of the Friday conferences, the chief justice circulates a "discuss" list—a list of cases deemed important enough for discussion and a vote. Appeals are placed on the discuss list almost automatically, but as many as three-quarters of the petitions for certiorari are denied. No case is denied review during conference, however, without an initial examination by the justices and their law clerks. Any justice can have a case placed on the Court's conference agenda for review. Most of the cases scheduled for the discuss list also are denied review in the end but only after discussion by the justices during the conference.

Although the last oral arguments have been heard by mid-April each year, the conferences of the justices continue until the end of the term to consider cases remaining on the Court's agenda. All conferences are held in secret, with no legal assistants or other staff present. The attendance of six justices constitutes a quorum. Conferences begin with handshakes all around. In discussing a case, the chief justice speaks first, followed by each justice in order of seniority.

Decision Days

Opinions are released on Tuesdays and Wednesdays during the weeks that the Court is hearing oral arguments; during other weeks, they are released on Mondays. In addition to opinions, the Court also releases an "orders" list—the summary of the Court's action granting or denying review. The orders list is posted at the beginning of the Monday session. It is not announced orally but can be obtained from the clerk and the public information officer. When urgent or important matters arise, the Court's summary orders may be made available on a day other than Monday.

Unlike its orders, decisions of the Court are announced orally in open Court. The justice who wrote the opinion announces the Court's decision, and justices writing concurring or dissenting opinions may state their views as well. When more than one decision is to be rendered, the justices who wrote the opinion make their announcements in reverse order of seniority. Occasionally, all or a large portion of the opinion is read aloud. More often the author summarizes the opinion or simply announces the result and states that a written opinion has been filed.

Reviewing Cases

In determining whether to accept a case for review, the Court has considerable discretion, subject only to the restraints imposed by the Constitution and Congress. Article III, section 2, of the Constitution provides that "In all

---

Visiting the Supreme Court

The Supreme Court building has six levels, two of which—the ground and main floors—are accessible to the public. The basement contains a parking garage, a printing press, and offices for security guards and maintenance personnel. On the ground floor are the John Marshall statue, the exhibition area, the public information office, and a cafeteria. The main corridor, known as the Great Hall, the courtroom, and justices' offices are on the main floor. The second floor contains dining rooms, the justices' reading room, and other offices; the third floor, the Court library; and the fourth floor, the gym and storage areas.

From October to mid-April, the Court hears oral arguments Monday through Wednesday for about two weeks a month. These sessions begin at 10 a.m. and continue until 3 p.m., with a one-hour recess starting at noon. They are open to the public on a first-come, first-served basis.

Visitors may inspect the Supreme Court chamber any time the Court is not in session. Historical exhibits and a free motion picture on how the Court works also are available throughout the year. The Supreme Court building is open from 9 a.m. to 4:30 p.m. Monday through Friday, except for legal holidays. When the Court is not in session, lectures are given in the courtroom every hour on the half hour between 9:30 a.m. and 3:30 p.m.

Cases affecting Ambassadors, other public Ministers and Consuls, and those in which a State shall be Party, the supreme Court shall have original Jurisdiction. In all the other Cases . . . the supreme Court shall have appellate Jurisdiction, both as to Law and Fact, with such Exceptions, and under such Regulations as the Congress shall make."

Original jurisdiction refers to the right of the Supreme Court to hear a case before any other court does. Appellate jurisdiction is the right to review the decision of a lower court. The vast majority of cases reaching the Supreme Court are appeals from rulings of the lower courts; generally only a handful of original jurisdiction cases are filed each term.

After enactment of the Judiciary Act of 1925, the Supreme Court gained broad discretion to decide for itself what cases it would hear. In 1988 Congress virtually eliminated the Court's mandatory jurisdiction, which obliged it to hear most appeals. Since then that discretion has been nearly unlimited.

Methods of Appeal

Cases come to the Supreme Court in several ways: through petitions for writs of certiorari, appeals, and requests for certification.

In petitioning for a writ of certiorari, a litigant who has lost a case in a lower court sets out the reasons why the Supreme Court should review the case. If a writ is granted, the Court requests a certified record of the case from the lower court.

The main difference between the certiorari and appeal routes is that the Court has complete discretion to grant a request for a writ of certiorari but is under more obligation to accept and decide a case that comes to it on appeal.

Most cases reach the Supreme Court by means of the writ of certiorari. In the relatively few cases to reach the Court by means of appeal, the appellant must file a jurisdictional statement explaining why the case qualifies for review and why the Court should grant it a hearing. Often the justices dispose of these cases by deciding them summarily, without oral argument or formal opinion.

Those whose petitions for certiorari have been granted must pay the Court's standard $300 fee for docketing the case. The U.S. government does not have to pay these fees, nor do persons too poor to afford them. The latter may file in forma pauperis (in the character or manner of a pauper) petitions. Another, seldom used, method of appeal is certification, the request by a lower court—usually a court of appeals—for a final answer to questions of law in a particular case. The Court, after examining the certificate, may order the case argued before it.

Process of Review

In recent terms the Court has been asked to review around 7,000 cases. All petitions are examined by the staff of the clerk of the Court; those found to be in reasonably proper form are placed on the docket and given a number. All cases, except those falling within the Court's original jurisdiction, are placed on a single docket, known simply as "the docket." Only in the numbering of the cases is a distinction made between prepaid and in forma pauperis cases on the docket. The first case filed in the 1996–1997 term, for example, would be designated 96–1. In forma pauperis cases contain the year and begin with the number 5001. The second in forma pauperis case filed in the 1996–1997 term would thus be number 96–5002.

Each justice, aided by law clerks, is responsible for reviewing all cases on the docket. In recent years a number of justices have used a "cert pool" system in this review. Their clerks work together to examine cases, writing a pool memo on several petitions. The memo then is given to the justices who determine if more research is needed. Other justices may prefer to review each petition themselves or have their clerks do it.

Petitions on the docket vary from elegantly printed and bound documents, of which multiple copies are submitted to the Court, to single sheets of prison stationery scribbled in pencil. The decisions to grant or deny review of cases are made in conferences, which are held in the conference room adjacent to the chief justice's chambers. Justices are summoned to the conference room by a buzzer, usually between 9:30 and 10:00 a.m. They shake hands with each other and take their appointed seats, and the chief justice then begins the discussion.

Discuss and Orders Lists

A few days before the conference convenes, the chief justice compiles the discuss list of cases deemed important enough for discussion and a vote. As many as three-quarters of the petitions for certiorari are denied a place on the list and thus rejected without further consideration. Any justice can have a case placed on the discuss list simply by requesting that it be placed there.

Only the justices attend conferences; no legal assistants or staff are present. The junior associate justice acts as doorkeeper and messenger, sending for reference material and receiving messages and data. Unlike with other parts of the federal government, few leaks have occurred about what transpires during the conferences.

At the start of the conference, the chief justice makes a brief statement outlining the facts of each case. Then each justice, beginning with the senior associate justice, comments on the case, usually indicating in the course of the comments how he or she intends to vote. A traditional but unwritten rule is that four affirmative votes puts a case on the schedule for oral argument.

Petitions for certiorari, appeals, and in forma pauperis motions that are approved for review or denied review during conference are placed on a certified orders list to be released the next Monday in open court.

Arguments

Once the Court announces it will hear a case, the clerk of the Court arranges the schedule for oral argument. Cases are argued roughly in the order in which they were granted review, subject to modification if more time is needed to acquire all the necessary documents. Cases generally are heard not sooner than three months after the Court has agreed to review them. Under special circumstances the date scheduled for oral argument can be advanced or postponed.

Well before oral argument takes place, the justices receive the briefs and records from counsel in the case. The measure of attention the brief receives—from a thorough and exhaustive study to a cursory glance—depends both on the nature of the case and the work habits of the justice.

As one of the two public functions of the Court, oral arguments are

Chief Justice William H. Rehnquist, himself a former law clerk for Justice Robert H. Jackson, meets with his clerks to discuss cases before the Court.

viewed by some as very important. Others dispute the significance of oral arguments, contending that by the time a case is heard most of the justices already have made up their minds.

Time Limits

The time allowed each side for oral argument is thirty minutes. Because the time allotted must accommodate any questions the justices may wish to ask, the actual time for presentation may be considerably shorter than thirty minutes. Under the current rules of the Court, one counsel only will be heard for each side, except by special permission.

An exception is made for an amicus curiae, a "friend of the court," a person who volunteers or is invited to take part in matters before a court but is not a party in the case. Counsel for an amicus curiae may participate in oral argument if the party supported by the amicus allows use of part of its argument time or the Court grants a motion permitting argument by this counsel. The motion must show, the rules state, that the amicus's argument "is thought to provide assistance to the Court not otherwise available." The Court is generally unreceptive to such motions.

Court rules provide advice to counsel presenting oral arguments before the Court: "Oral argument should emphasize and clarify the written arguments appearing in the briefs on the merits." That same rule warns—with italicized emphasis—that the Court "looks with disfavor on oral argument read from a prepared text." Most attorneys appearing before the Court use an outline or notes to make sure they cover the important points.

Circulating the Argument

The Supreme Court has tape-recorded oral arguments since 1955. In 1968 the Court, in addition to its own recording, began contracting with private firms to tape and transcribe all oral arguments. The contract stipulates that the transcript "shall include everything spoken in argument, by Court, counsel, or others, and nothing shall be omitted from the transcript unless the Chief Justice or Presiding Justice so directs." But "the names of Justices asking questions shall not be recorded or transcribed; questions shall be indicated by the letter 'Q.'"

The marshal of the Court keeps the tapes during the term, and their use usually is limited to the justices and their law clerks. At the end of the term, the tapes are sent to the National Archives. Persons wishing to listen to the tapes or buy a copy of a transcript can apply to the Archives for permission to do so.

Transcripts made by a private firm can be acquired more quickly. These transcripts usually are available a week after arguments are heard. Transcripts can be read in the Court's library or public information office. Those who purchase the transcripts must agree that they will not be photographically reproduced. In addition, transcripts of oral arguments are available on the Westlaw electronic data retrieval system.

Proposals have been made to tape arguments for television and radio use or to permit live broadcast coverage of arguments. The Court has rejected these proposals.

Use of Briefs

The brief of the petitioner or appellant must be filed within forty-five days of the Court's announced decision to hear the case. Except for in forma pauperis cases, forty copies of the brief must be filed with the Court. For in forma pauperis proceedings, the Court requires only that documents be legible. The opposing brief from the respondent or appellee is to be filed within thirty days of receipt of the brief of the petitioner or appellant. Either party may appeal to the clerk for an extension of time in filing the brief.

Court Rule 24 sets forth the elements that a brief should contain. These are: the questions presented for review; a list of all parties to the proceeding; a table of contents and table of authorities; citations of the opinions and judgments delivered in the lower courts; "a concise statement of the grounds on which the jurisdiction of this Court is invoked"; constitutional provisions, treaties, statutes, ordinances, and regulations involved; "a concise statement of the case containing all that is material to the consideration of the questions presented"; a summary of argument; the argument, which exhibits "clearly the points of fact and of law being presented and citing the authorities and statutes relied upon"; and a conclusion "specifying with particularity the relief which the party seeks."

The form and organization of the brief are covered by rules 33 and 34. The rules limit the number of pages in various types of briefs. The rules also set out a color code for the covers of different kinds of briefs. Petitions are white; motions opposing them are orange. Petitioner's briefs on the merits are light blue, while those of respondents are red. Reply briefs are yellow; amicus curiae, green; and documents filed by the United States, gray.

Questioning

During oral argument the justices may interrupt with questions or remarks as often as they wish. Unless counsel has been granted special permission extending the thirty-minute limit, he or she can continue talking after the time has expired only to complete a sentence.

The frequency of questioning, as well as the manner in which questions are asked, depends on the style of the justices and their interest in a particular case. Of the current justices, all but Clarence Thomas participate, more or less actively, in questioning during oral arguments; Thomas asks questions very, very rarely.

Questions from the justices may upset and unnerve counsel by interrupting a well-rehearsed argument and introducing an unexpected element. Nevertheless, questioning has several advantages. It serves to alert counsel about what aspects of the case need further elaboration or more information. For the Court, questions can bring out weak points in an argument—and sometimes strengthen it.

Conferences

Cases for which oral arguments have been heard are then dealt with in conference. During the Wednesday afternoon conference, the cases that were argued the previous Monday are discussed and decided. At the all-day Friday conference, the cases argued on the preceding Tuesday and Wednesday are discussed and decided. Justices also consider new motions, appeals, and petitions while in conference.

Conferences are conducted in complete secrecy. No secretaries, clerks, stenographers, or messengers are allowed into the room. This practice be-

The Supreme Court's bench, angled at the ends, allows justices to see each other during oral arguments.

gan many years ago when the justices became convinced that decisions were being disclosed prematurely.

The justices meet in an oak-paneled, book-lined conference room adjacent to the chief justice's suite. Nine chairs surround a large rectangular table, each chair bearing the nameplate of the justice who sits there. The chief justice sits at the east end of the table, and the senior associate justice at the west end. The other justices take their places in order of seniority. The junior justice is charged with sending for and receiving documents or other information the Court needs.

On entering the conference room the justices shake hands with each other, a symbol of harmony that began in the 1880s. The chief justice begins the conference by calling the first case to be decided and discussing it. When the chief justice is finished, the senior associate justice speaks, followed by the other justices in order of seniority.

The justices can speak for as long as they wish, but they practice restraint because of the amount of business to be completed. By custom each justice speaks without interruption. Other than these procedural arrangements, little is known about what transpires in conference. Although discussions generally are said to be polite and orderly, occasionally they can be acrimonious. Likewise, consideration of the issues in a particular case may be full and probing, or perfunctory, leaving the real debate on the question until later when the written drafts of opinions are circulated up and down the Court's corridors between chambers.

Generally the discussion of the case clearly indicates how a justice plans to vote on it. A majority vote is needed to decide a case—five votes if all nine justices are participating.

Opinions

After the justices have voted on a case, the writing of the opinion or opinions begins. An opinion is a reasoned argument explaining the legal issues in the case and the precedents on which the opinion is based. Soon after a case is decided in conference, the task of writing the majority opinion is assigned. When in the majority, the chief justice designates the writer. When the chief justice is in the minority, the senior associate justice voting with the majority assigns the job of writing the majority opinion.

Any justice may write a separate opinion. If in agreement with the Court's decision but not with some of the reasoning in the majority opinion, the justice writes a concurring opinion giving his or her reasoning. If in disagreement with the majority, the justice writes a dissenting opinion or simply goes on record as a dissenter without an opinion. More than one justice can sign a concurring opinion or a dissenting opinion.

The amount of time between the vote on a case and the announcement of the decision varies from case to case. In simple cases where few points of law are at issue, the opinion sometimes can be written and cleared by the other justices in a week or less. In more complex cases, especially those with several dissenting or concurring opinions, the process can take six months or more. Some cases may have to be reargued or the initial decision reversed after the drafts of opinions have been circulated.

The assigning justice may consider the points made by majority justices during the conference discussion, the workload of the other justices, the need to avoid the more extreme opinions within the majority, and expertise in the particular area of law involved in a case.

The style of writing a Court opinion—majority, concurring, or dissenting—depends primarily on the individual justice. In some cases, the justice may prefer to write a restricted and limited opinion; in others, he or she may take a broader approach to the subject. The decision likely is to be influenced by the need to satisfy the other justices in the majority.

When a justice is satisfied that the written opinion is conclusive or "unanswerable," it goes into print. Draft opinions are circulated, revised, and printed on a computerized typesetting system. The circulation of the drafts—whether computer-to-computer or on paper—provokes further discussion in many cases. Often the suggestions and criticisms require the writer to juggle opposing views. To retain a majority, the author of the draft opinion frequently feels obliged to make major emendations to satisfy justices who are unhappy with the initial draft. Some opinions have to be rewritten several times.

One reason for the secrecy surrounding the circulation of drafts is that some of the justices who voted with the majority may find the majority draft opinion so unpersuasive—or one or more of the dissenting drafts so convincing—that they change their vote. If enough justices alter their votes, the majority may shift, so that a former dissent becomes the majority opinion. When a new majority emerges from this process, the task of writing, printing, and circulating a new majority draft begins all over again.

When the drafts of an opinion—including dissents and concurring views—have been written, circulated, discussed, and revised, if necessary, the final versions then are printed. Before the opinion is produced the reporter of decisions adds a "headnote" or syllabus summarizing the decision and a "lineup" showing how the justices voted.

Two hundred copies of the "bench opinion" are made. As the decision is announced in Court, the bench opinion is distributed to journalists and others in the public information office. Another copy, with any necessary corrections noted on it, is sent to the U.S. Government Printing Office, which prints 3,397 "slip" opinions, which are distributed to federal and state courts and agencies. The Court receives 400 of these, and they are available to the public free through the Public Information Office as long as supplies last. The Government Printing Office also prints the opinion for inclusion in *United States Reports,* the official record of Supreme Court opinions.

The Court also makes opinions available electronically, through its so-called Hermes system, to a number of large legal publishers, the Government Printing Office, and other information services. These organizations allow redistribution of the opinions to their own subscribers and users. Opinions are available on the Internet through Case Western Reserve University. The Hermes system was established as a pilot project in 1991 and expanded and made permanent in 1993.

In 1996 the Court also established its own electronic bulletin board system (BBS) that provides anyone with a personal computer online access to the Court's opinions, docket, argument calendar, and other information and publications. The telephone number for the Court's BBS is (202) 554-2570.

The public announcement of opinions in Court probably is the Court's most dramatic function. It may also be the most expendable. Depending on who delivers the opinion and how, announcements can take a considerable amount of the Court's time. Opinions are given simultaneously to the public information officer for distribution. Nevertheless, those who are in the courtroom to hear the announcement of a ruling are participating in a very old tradition. The actual delivery may be tedious or exciting, depending on the nature of the case, the eloquence of the opinion, and the style of its oral delivery.

Brief Biographies

William Hubbs Rehnquist

Born: October 1, 1924, Milwaukee, Wisconsin.

Education: Stanford University, B.A., Phi Beta Kappa, and M.A., 1948; Harvard University, M.A., 1949; Stanford University Law School, LL.B., 1952.

Family: Married Natalie Cornell, 1953; died, 1991; two daughters, one son.

Career: Law clerk to Justice Robert H. Jackson, U.S. Supreme Court, 1952–1953; practiced law, 1953–1969; assistant U.S. attorney general, Office of Legal Counsel, 1969–1971.

Supreme Court Service: Nominated as associate justice of the U.S. Supreme Court by President Richard Nixon, October 21, 1971; confirmed, 68–26, December 10, 1971; nominated as chief justice of the United States by President Ronald Reagan, June 17, 1986; confirmed, 65–33, September 17, 1986.

President Reagan's appointment of William H. Rehnquist as chief justice in 1986 was a deliberate effort to shift the Court to the right. Since his

early years as an associate justice in the 1970s, Rehnquist had been the Court's strongest conservative voice. And as chief justice, Rehnquist has helped move the Court to the right in a number of areas, including criminal law, states' rights, civil rights, and church-state issues.

Rehnquist, the fourth associate justice to become chief, argues that the original intent of the Framers of the Constitution and the Bill of Rights is the proper standard for interpreting those documents today. He also takes a literal approach to individual rights. These beliefs have led him to dissent from the Court's rulings protecting a woman's privacy-based right to abortion, to argue that no constitutional barrier exists to school prayer, and to side with police and prosecutors on questions of criminal law. In 1991 he wrote the Court's decision upholding an administration ban on abortion counseling at publicly financed clinics. The next year he vigorously dissented from the Court's affirmation of *Roe v. Wade,* the 1973 opinion that made abortion legal nationwide.

A native of Milwaukee, Rehnquist attended Stanford University, where he earned both a B.A. and an M.A. He received a second M.A. from Harvard before returning to Stanford for law school. His classmates there recalled him as an intelligent student with already well-entrenched conservative views.

After graduating from law school in 1952, Rehnquist came to Washington, D.C., to serve as a law clerk to Supreme Court justice Robert H. Jackson. There he wrote a memorandum that later came back to haunt him during his Senate confirmation hearings. In the memo Rehnquist favored separate but equal schools for blacks and whites. Asked about those views by the Senate Judiciary Committee in 1971, Rehnquist repudiated them, declaring that they were Justice Jackson's, not his own.

Following his clerkship, Rehnquist decided to practice law in the Southwest. He moved to Phoenix and immediately became immersed in Arizona Republican politics. From his earliest days in the state, he was associated with the party's conservative wing. A 1957 speech denouncing the liberalism of the Warren Court typified his views at the time.

During the 1964 presidential race, Rehnquist campaigned ardently for Barry Goldwater. It was then that Rehnquist met and worked with Richard G. Kleindienst, who later, as President Richard Nixon's deputy attorney general, appointed Rehnquist to head the Justice Department's Office of Legal Counsel as an assistant attorney general. In 1971 Nixon nominated him to the Supreme Court.

Rehnquist drew opposition from liberals and civil rights organizations before winning confirmation and again before being approved as chief justice in 1986. The Senate voted to approve his nomination in December 1971 by a vote of 68–26 at the same time that another Nixon nominee, Lewis F. Powell Jr., was winning nearly unanimous confirmation.

In 1986 Rehnquist faced new accusations of having harassed voters as a Republican poll watcher in Phoenix in the 1950s and 1960s. He was also found to have accepted anti-Semitic restrictions in a property deed to a Vermont home. Despite the charges, the Senate approved his appointment as chief justice 65–33. Liberal Democratic senators cast most of the no votes in both confirmations.

Despite his strong views, Rehnquist is popular among his colleagues and staff. When he was nominated for chief justice, Justice William J. Brennan Jr., the leader of the Court's liberal bloc, said Rehnquist would be "a splendid chief justice." After becoming chief justice, Rehnquist was credited with speeding up the Court's conferences, in which the justices decide what cases to hear, vote on cases, and assign opinions.

Rehnquist was married to Natalie Cornell, who died in 1991. They had two daughters and a son.

John Paul Stevens

Born: April 20, 1920, Chicago, Illinois.

Education: University of Chicago, B.A., Phi Beta Kappa, 1941; Northwestern University School of Law, J.D., 1947.

Family: Married Elizabeth Jane Sheeren, 1942; three daughters, one son; divorced 1979; married Maryan Mulholland Simon, 1980.

Career: Law clerk to Justice Wiley B. Rutledge, U.S. Supreme Court, 1947–1948; practiced law, Chicago, 1949–1970; judge, U.S. Court of Appeals for the Seventh Circuit, 1970–1975.

Supreme Court Service: Nominated as associate justice of the U.S. Supreme Court by President Gerald R. Ford, November 28, 1975; confirmed, 98–0, December 17, 1975.

When President Gerald R. Ford nominated federal appeals court judge John Paul Stevens to the Supreme Court seat vacated by veteran liberal William O. Douglas in 1975, Court observers struggled to pin an ideological label on the new nominee. The consensus that finally emerged was that Stevens was neither a doctrinaire liberal nor conservative, but a judicial centrist. His subsequent opinions bear out this description, although in recent years he has moved steadily toward the liberal side.

Stevens is a soft-spoken, mild-mannered man who often sports a bow tie under his judicial robes. A member of a prominent Chicago family, he had a long record of excellence in scholarship, graduating Phi Beta Kappa from the University of Chicago in 1941. He earned the Bronze Star during a wartime stint in the navy and then returned to Chicago to enter Northwestern University Law School, from which he was graduated magna cum laude in 1947. From there Stevens left for Washington, where he served as a law clerk to Supreme Court justice Wiley B. Rutledge. He returned to Chicago to join the prominent law firm of Poppenhusen, Johnston, Thompson & Raymond, which specialized in antitrust law. Stevens developed a reputation as a pre-eminent antitrust lawyer and three years later in 1952 formed his own firm, Rothschild, Stevens, Barry & Myers. He remained there, engaging in private practice and teaching part-time at Northwestern and the University of Chicago law schools, until his appointment by President Richard Nixon in 1970 to the U.S. Court of Appeals for the Seventh Circuit.

Stevens developed a reputation as a political moderate during his undergraduate days at the University of Chicago, then an overwhelmingly liberal campus. Although he is a registered Republican, he has never been active in partisan politics. Nevertheless, Stevens served as Republican counsel in 1951 to the House Judiciary Subcommittee on the Study of Monopoly Power. He also served from 1953 to 1955, during the Eisenhower administration, as a member of the attorney general's committee to study antitrust laws.

In his five years on the federal appeals court, Stevens earned a reputation as an independent-minded judicial craftsman. President Ford, who took office after Nixon's forced resignation, wanted to nominate a moderate of impeccable legal reputation to help restore confidence in government after the Watergate scandals. Stevens was confirmed without dissent, 98–0, on December 17, 1975, and took office two days later.

Stevens has frequently dissented from the most conservative rulings of the Burger and Rehnquist Courts. For example, he dissented from the Burger Court's 1986 decision upholding state antisodomy laws and the Rehnquist Court's 1989 decision permitting states to execute someone for committing a murder at the age of sixteen or seventeen. He has taken liberal positions on abortion rights, civil rights, and church-state issues.

In his second full term on the Court, Stevens wrote the main opinion in a case upholding the right of the Federal Communications Commission to penalize broadcasters for airing indecent material at times when children are in the audience. But in 1997, he led the Court in a major victory for First Amendment interests by striking down a newly enacted law aimed at blocking sexually explicit materials from children on the Internet. In the same year, he wrote the opinion holding that presidents have no immunity while in office from civil suits for private conduct unrelated to their office.

In 1942 Stevens married Elizabeth Jane Sheeren. They have four children. They were divorced in 1979. Stevens subsequently married Maryan Mulholland Simon, a longtime neighbor in Chicago.

Sandra Day O'Connor

Born: March 26, 1930, El Paso, Texas.

Education: Stanford University, B.A., 1950; Stanford University Law School, LL.B., 1952.

Family: Married John J. O'Connor III, 1952; three sons.

Career: Deputy county attorney, San Mateo, California, 1952–1953; assistant attorney general, Arizona, 1965–1969; Arizona state senator, 1969–1975; Arizona Senate majority leader, 1972–1975; judge, Maricopa County Superior Court, 1974–1979; judge, Arizona Court of Appeals, 1979–1981.

Supreme Court Service: Nominated as associate justice of the U.S. Supreme Court by President Ronald Reagan August 19, 1981; confirmed, 99–0, September 21, 1981.

Sandra Day O'Connor, the first woman to serve on the Court, has been a pivotal figure in forming a conservative majority on a range of issues but has also moderated the Rehnquist Court's stance on some questions, including abortion rights and affirmative action.

Pioneering came naturally to O'Connor. Her grandfather left Kansas in 1880 to take up ranching in the desert land that eventually became the state of Arizona. O'Connor, born in El Paso, Texas, where her mother's parents lived, was raised on the Lazy B Ranch, the 198,000-acre spread that her grandfather founded in southeastern Arizona near Duncan. She spent her school years in El Paso, living with her grandmother. She graduated from high school at age sixteen and then entered Stanford University.

Six years later, in 1952, Sandra Day had won degrees with great distinction, both from the university, in economics, and from Stanford Law School. At Stanford she met John J. O'Connor III, her future husband, and William H. Rehnquist, a future colleague on the Supreme Court. While in law school, Sandra Day was an editor of the *Stanford Law Review* and a member of Order of the Coif, the academic honor society.

Despite her record, O'Connor had difficulty finding a job as an attorney in 1952 when relatively few women were practicing law. She applied, among other places, to the firm in which William French Smith—first attorney general in the Reagan administration—was a partner, only to be offered a job as a secretary.

After she completed a short stint as deputy county attorney for San Mateo County (California) while her new husband completed law school at Stanford, the O'Connors moved with the U.S. Army to Frankfurt, Germany. There Sandra O'Connor worked as a civilian attorney for the army, while John O'Connor served his tour of duty. In 1957 they returned to Phoenix, where, during the next eight years, their three sons were born. O'Connor's life was a mix of parenthood, homemaking, volunteer work, and some "miscellaneous legal tasks" on the side.

In 1965 she resumed her legal career on a full-time basis, taking a job as an assistant attorney general for Arizona. After four years in that post she was appointed to fill a vacancy in the state Senate, where she served on the judiciary committee. In 1970 she was elected to the same body and two years later was chosen its majority leader, the first woman in the nation to hold such a post. O'Connor was active in Republican Party politics, serving as co-chair of the Arizona Committee for the Re-election of the President in 1972.

In 1974 she was elected to the Superior Court for Maricopa County, where she served for five years. Then in 1979 Democratic governor Bruce

Babbitt appointed O'Connor to the Arizona Court of Appeals. It was from that post that President Reagan chose her as his first nominee to the Supreme Court, succeeding Potter Stewart, who retired. Reagan described her as "a person for all seasons." The Senate confirmed her on September 21, 1981, by a vote of 99–0.

O'Connor brings to the Court a conservative viewpoint and a cautious, case-by-case decisionmaking style. On criminal law issues, she has generally voted to give broader discretion to police, uphold death penalty cases, and restrict the use of federal habeas corpus to challenge state court convictions. She was a strong supporter of limiting punitive damage awards in state courts and relaxing restrictions on government support for religion.

In two important areas, however, O'Connor's cautious approach has disappointed conservatives. While she voted in many decisions in the 1980s to limit abortion rights, she joined in 1992 with two other Republican-appointed justices, Anthony M. Kennedy and David H. Souter, to form a majority for preserving a modified form of the Court's original abortion rights ruling, *Roe v. Wade*. In a jointly authored opinion the three justices said that *Roe*'s "essential holding"—guaranteeing a woman's right to an abortion during most of her pregnancy—should be reaffirmed. But the joint opinion also said that states could regulate abortion procedures as long as they did not impose "an undue burden" on a woman's choice—a test that O'Connor had advocated in previous opinions.

O'Connor has also voted to limit racial preferences in employment and government contracting and wrote the Court's first opinion restricting the use of race in drawing legislative and congressional districts. But she also joined the majority in a critical 1987 case upholding voluntary affirmative action by government employers to remedy past discrimination against women. And she has refused to limit all consideration of race in redistricting cases.

Antonin Scalia

Born: March 11, 1936, Trenton, New Jersey.

Education: Georgetown University, A.B., 1957; Harvard University Law School, LL.B., 1960.

Family: Married Maureen McCarthy, 1960; five sons, four daughters.

Career: Practiced law, Cleveland, 1960–1967; taught at the University of Virginia, 1967–1971; general counsel, White House Office of Telecommunications Policy, 1971–1972; chairman, Administrative Conference of the United States, 1972–1974; head, Justice Department Office of Legal Counsel, 1974–1977; taught at the University of Chicago Law School, 1977–1982; judge, U.S. Court of Appeals for the District of Columbia Circuit, 1982–1986.

1988. While he adheres to generally conservative views, Kennedy has taken moderate stands on some issues that often make him a pivotal vote between the Court's conservative and liberal blocs.

Before Kennedy's nomination in November 1987, the Senate and the country had agonized through Reagan's two unsuccessful attempts to replace retiring Justice Lewis F. Powell Jr., first with Robert H. Bork and then with Douglas H. Ginsburg. The Senate rejected Bork's nomination after contentious hearings, where opponents depicted the federal appeals court judge as a conservative ideologue. Reagan then turned to Ginsburg, a colleague of Bork's on the federal appeals court in Washington, but he withdrew his name amid controversy about his admitted past use of marijuana.

A quiet sense of relief prevailed when Reagan finally selected a nominee who could be confirmed without another wrenching confrontation. Kennedy spent twelve years as a judge on the U.S. Court of Appeals for the Ninth Circuit. But unlike Bork, who wrote and spoke extensively for twenty years, Kennedy's record was confined mostly to his approximately five hundred judicial opinions, where he generally decided issues narrowly instead of using his opinions as a testing ground for constitutional theories. The Senate voted to confirm him without dissent, 97–0, on February 3, 1988.

A native Californian, Kennedy attended Stanford University from 1954 to 1957 and the London School of Economics from 1957 to 1958. He received an A.B. from Stanford in 1958 and an LL.B. from Harvard Law School in 1961. Admitted to the California bar in 1962, he was in private law practice until 1975, when President Gerald R. Ford appointed him to the appeals court. From 1965 to 1988 he taught constitutional law at McGeorge School of Law, University of the Pacific.

In his first full term on the Court, Kennedy provided a crucial fifth vote for the Court's conservative wing in a number of civil rights cases. He generally favored law enforcement in criminal cases. And in a closely watched abortion-rights case, he voted along with Chief Justice William H. Rehnquist and Justices Byron R. White and Antonin Scalia to overturn the 1973 ruling, *Roe v. Wade*, that first established a constitutional right to abortion.

Many observers viewed Kennedy's arrival as ushering in a new conservative era. But in 1992 he sorely disappointed conservatives in two major cases. In one he provided the critical fifth vote and wrote the majority opinion in a decision barring officially sponsored prayers at public high school graduation ceremonies. In the other he reversed himself on the abortion issue, joining with Justices Sandra Day O'Connor and David H. Souter in an opinion that upheld a modified version of *Roe v. Wade*.

Kennedy has proved to be a strong free speech advocate in First Amendment cases. In 1989 he helped form the 5–4 majority that overturned state laws against burning or desecrating the U.S. flag. The former constitutional law professor has also displayed a special interest in equal protection and federalism issues. He has voted with other conservatives in rulings that limited racially motivated congressional districting and backed states in disputes over federal power. But he was the swing vote in a 1995 decision to bar the states from imposing term limits on members of Congress. And in 1996 he wrote the opinion striking down Colorado's anti–gay rights amendment prohibiting enactment of any laws to bar discrimination against homosexuals.

David Hackett Souter

Born: September 17, 1939, Melrose, Massachusetts.

Education: Harvard College, B.A., 1961; Rhodes scholar, Oxford University, 1961–1963; Harvard University Law School, LL.B., 1966.

Family: Unmarried.

Career: Private law practice, Concord, New Hampshire, 1966–1968; assistant attorney general, New Hampshire, 1968–1971; deputy attorney general, New Hampshire, 1971–1976; attorney general, New Hampshire, 1976–1978; associate justice, New Hampshire Superior Court, 1978–1983; associate justice, New Hampshire Supreme Court, 1983–1990; judge, U.S. Court of Appeals for the First Circuit, 1990.

Supreme Court Service: Nominated as associate justice of the U.S. Supreme Court by President George Bush July 23, 1990; confirmed, 90–9, October 2, 1990.

At first the Senate did not know what to make of David H. Souter, a cerebral, button-down nominee who was President Bush's first appointment

to the Court. Souter was little known outside his home state of New Hampshire, where he had been attorney general, a trial judge, and a state supreme court justice. He had virtually no scholarly writings to dissect and little federal court experience to scrutinize. Only three months earlier Bush had appointed him to the U.S. Court of Appeals for the First Circuit. Souter had yet to write a legal opinion on the appeals court.

During his confirmation hearings, the Harvard graduate and former Rhodes scholar demonstrated intellectual rigor and a masterly approach to constitutional law. His earlier work as state attorney general and New Hampshire Supreme Court justice had a conservative bent, but he came across as more moderate during the hearings.

Under persistent questioning from Democratic senators, Souter refused to say how he would vote on the issue of abortion rights. Abortion rights supporters feared he would provide a fifth vote for overturning the 1973 *Roe v. Wade* decision. Senators in both parties, however, said they were impressed with his legal knowledge. He was confirmed by the Senate 90–9; dissenting senators cited his refusal to take a stand on abortion.

On the bench Souter proved to be a tenacious questioner but reserved in his opinions. He generally voted with the Court's conservative majority in his first term. But in the 1991–1992 term he staked out a middle ground with Justices Sandra Day O'Connor and Anthony M. Kennedy in two crucial cases. In a closely watched abortion case Souter joined with the other two Republican-appointed justices in writing the main opinion reaffirming the "essential holding" of *Roe v. Wade*. The three also joined in forming a 5–4 majority to prohibit school-sponsored prayers at public high school graduation ceremonies.

In the Court's next several terms Souter moved markedly to the left. He joined with liberals in dissenting from cases that restricted racial redistricting. He also voted with the Court's liberal bloc on church-state and some criminal law issues.

Despite his experience in state government, Souter has proved to be a strong supporter of federal power in cases affecting states' rights. He joined the dissenters in a 1995 decision striking down on states' rights grounds a federal law banning the possession of guns near schools. And in 1996 he wrote a massive and scholarly dissent from the Court's decision limiting Congress's power to authorize private citizens to sue states in federal courts to enforce federal law.

Souter is known for his intensely private, ascetic life. He was born September 17, 1939, in Melrose, Massachusetts. An only child, he moved with his parents to Weare, New Hampshire, at age eleven. Except for college, he lived in Weare until 1990.

Graduating from Harvard College in 1961, Souter attended Oxford University on a Rhodes Scholarship from 1961 to 1963, then returned to Cambridge for Harvard Law School. Graduating in 1966, he worked for two years in a Concord law firm. In 1968 he became an assistant attorney general, rose to deputy attorney general in 1971, and in 1976 was appointed attorney general. Souter served as attorney general until 1978, when he was named to the state's trial court. Five years later Gov. John H. Sununu appointed Souter to the state supreme court. Sununu was Bush's chief of staff when Souter was named to the U.S. Supreme Court.

Souter, a bachelor, is a nature enthusiast and avid hiker.

Clarence Thomas

Born: June 23, 1948, Savannah, Georgia.

Education: Immaculate Conception Seminary, 1967–1968; Holy Cross College, B.A., 1971; Yale University Law School, J.D., 1974.

Family: Married Kathy Grace Ambush, 1971; one son; divorced 1984; married Virginia Lamp, 1987.

Career: Assistant attorney general, Missouri, 1974–1977; attorney, Monsanto Co., 1977–1979; legislative assistant to Sen. John C. Danforth, R-Mo., 1979–1981; assistant secretary of education for civil rights, 1981–1982; chairman, Equal Employment Opportunity Commission, 1982–1990; judge, U.S. Court of Appeals for the District of Columbia Circuit, 1990–1991.

Supreme Court Service: Nominated as associate justice of the U.S. Supreme Court by President George Bush July 1, 1991; confirmed, 52–48, October 15, 1991.

Clarence Thomas won a narrow confirmation to the Supreme Court in 1991 after surviving dramatic accusations of sexual harassment. He generated continuing controversy with outspoken conservative views as a justice.

The Senate's 52–48 vote on Thomas was the closest Supreme Court confirmation vote in more than a century. It followed a tumultuous nomination process that included close scrutiny of Thomas's judicial philosophy and sensational charges of sexual harassment brought by a former aide. Thomas denied the charges and accused the Senate Judiciary Committee of conducting a "high-tech lynching."

President George Bush nominated Thomas to succeed Thurgood Marshall, the Court's first black justice and a pioneer of the civil rights movement. Thomas came to prominence as a black conservative while serving as chairman of the Equal Employment Opportunity Commission during the Reagan and Bush administrations. Bush appointed him to the U.S. Court of Appeals for the District of Columbia Circuit in 1990.

Thomas was only forty-three at the time of his nomination to the Court, and senators noted that he likely would be affecting the outcome of major constitutional rulings well into the twenty-first century. Democratic senators closely questioned him on a range of constitutional issues—in particular, abortion. Thomas declined to give his views on abortion, saying he had never discussed the issue.

The committee decided to end its hearings even though it had received an allegation from a University of Oklahoma law professor, Anita Hill, that

Thomas had sexually harassed her while she worked for him at the U.S. Department of Education and the EEOC. When the accusation leaked out, the Judiciary Committee reopened the hearing to take testimony from Hill, Thomas, and other witnesses.

In the end most senators said they could not resolve the conflict between Hill's detailed allegations and Thomas's categorical denials. Instead, senators fell back on their previous positions. Supporters praised his determined character and rise from poverty in rural Georgia. Opponents questioned whether Thomas had been candid with the committee in discussing his judicial philosophy.

After joining the Court, Thomas became one of the Court's most conservative members. He closely aligned himself with fellow conservative Antonin Scalia, voting with Scalia about 90 percent of the time. In 1992 he voted as his opponents had warned to overturn the 1973 abortion rights ruling, *Roe v. Wade*, but the Court reaffirmed the decision by a 5–4 vote.

In later cases Thomas wrote lengthy opinions sharply challenging existing legal doctrines. In 1994 he called for scrapping precedents that allowed courts to order the creation of majority-black districts for legislative or congressional seats. In 1995 he authored opinions that called for restricting the basis for Congress to regulate interstate commerce and for re-examining federal courts' role in desegregating public schools. In a campaign finance case in 1996, he urged the Court to overturn all laws limiting political contributions as an infringement on the First Amendment.

Thomas graduated from Yale Law School in 1974 and became an assistant attorney general of Missouri and, three years later, a staff attorney for Monsanto Company. He worked for Sen. John C. Danforth, R-Mo., as a legislative assistant and served in the Department of Education as assistant secretary for civil rights for one year before being named chairman of the EEOC.

Thomas's wife, the former Virginia Lamp, is a lawyer who served as a legislative official with the U.S. Department of Labor during the Bush administration and since 1993 as a senior policy analyst with the House Republican Conference. They were married in 1987. He has a son from his first marriage, which ended in divorce in 1984.

Ruth Bader Ginsburg

Born: March 15, 1933, Brooklyn, New York.

Education: Cornell University, B.A., 1954; attended Harvard University Law School, 1956–1958; graduated Columbia Law School, J.D., 1959.

Family: Married Martin D. Ginsburg, 1954; one daughter, one son.

Career: Law clerk to U.S. District Court Judge Edmund L. Palmieri, 1959–1961; Columbia Law School Project on International Procedure, 1961–1963; professor, Rutgers University School of Law, 1963–1972; director,

Women's Rights Project, American Civil Liberties Union, 1972–1980; professor, Columbia Law School, 1972–1980; judge, U.S. Court of Appeals for the District of Columbia Circuit, 1980–1993.

Supreme Court Service: Nominated as associate justice of the U.S. Supreme Court by President Bill Clinton, June 22, 1993; confirmed, 96–3, August 3, 1993.

Ruth Bader Ginsburg's path to the U.S. Supreme Court is a classic American story of overcoming obstacles and setbacks through intelligence, persistence, and quiet hard work. Her achievements

as a student, law teacher, advocate, and judge came against a background of personal adversity and institutional discrimination against women. Ginsburg not only surmounted those hurdles for herself but also charted the legal strategy in the 1970s that helped broaden opportunities for women by establishing constitutional principles limiting sex discrimination in the law.

Born into a Jewish family of modest means in Brooklyn, Ruth Bader was greatly influenced by her mother, Celia, who imparted a love of learning and a determination to be independent. Celia Bader died of cancer on the eve of her daughter's high school graduation in 1948.

Ruth Bader attended Cornell University, where she graduated first in her class and met her future husband, Martin Ginsburg, who became a tax lawyer and later a professor at Georgetown University Law Center in Washington.

At Harvard Law School Ruth Bader Ginsburg made law review, cared for an infant daughter, and then helped her husband complete his studies after he was diagnosed with cancer. He recovered, graduated, and got a job in New York, and she transferred to Columbia for her final year of law school.

Although she was tied for first place in her class when she graduated, Ginsburg was unable to land a Supreme Court clerkship or job with a top New York law firm. Instead, she won a two-year clerkship with a federal district court judge. She then accepted a research position at Columbia that took her to Sweden, where she studied civil procedure and began to be stirred by feminist thought.

Ginsburg taught at Rutgers law school in New Jersey from 1963 to 1972. She also worked with the New Jersey affiliate of the American Civil Liberties Union (ACLU), where her caseload included several early sex discrimination complaints. In 1972 Ginsburg became the first woman to be named to a tenured position on the Columbia Law School faculty. As director of the national ACLU's newly established Women's Rights Project, she also handled the cases that over the course of several years led the Supreme Court to require heightened scrutiny of legal classifications based on sex. Ginsburg won five of the six cases she argued before the Court.

President Jimmy Carter named Ginsburg to the U.S. Court of Appeals for the District of Columbia Circuit in 1980. There she earned a reputation as a judicial moderate on a sharply divided court. When Justice Byron R. White announced plans for his retirement in March 1993, Ginsburg was among the large field of candidates President Bill Clinton considered for the vacancy. Clinton considered and passed over two other leading candidates for the position before deciding to interview Ginsburg. White House aides told reporters later that Clinton had been especially impressed with Ginsburg's life story. Reaction to the nomination was overwhelmingly positive.

In three days of confirmation hearings before the Senate Judiciary Committee, Ginsburg depicted herself as an advocate of judicial restraint, but she also said courts sometimes had a role to play in bringing about social change. On specific issues she strongly endorsed abortion rights, equal rights for women, and the constitutional right to privacy. But she declined to give her views on many other issues, including capital punishment. Some senators said that she had been less than forthcoming, but the committee voted unanimously to recommend her for confirmation. The full Senate confirmed her four days later by a vote of 96–3.

Ginsburg was sworn in August 10, 1993, as the Court's second female justice—joining Justice Sandra Day O'Connor—and the first Jewish justice since 1969.

In her first weeks on the bench, Ginsburg startled observers and drew some criticism with her unusually active questioning, but she eased up later. In her voting, she took liberal positions on women's rights, civil rights, church-state, states' rights, and First Amendment issues, but she had a more mixed record in other areas, including criminal law. In 1996 she wrote the Court's opinion in an important sex discrimination case, requiring the all-male Virginia Military Institute to admit women or give up its public funding.

Stephen Gerald Breyer

Born: August 15, 1938, San Francisco, California.

Education: Stanford University, A.B., Phi Beta Kappa, 1959; Oxford University, B.A. (Marshall scholar), 1961; Harvard Law School, LL.B., 1964.

Family: Married Joanna Hare, 1967; two daughters, one son.

Career: Law clerk to Justice Arthur J. Goldberg, U.S. Supreme Court, 1964–1965; assistant to assistant attorney general, antitrust, U.S. Justice Department, 1965–1967; professor, Harvard Law School, 1967–1981; assistant special prosecutor, Watergate Special Prosecution Force, 1973; special counsel, Senate Judiciary Committee, 1974–1975; chief counsel, Senate Judiciary

Committee, 1979–1980; judge, U.S. Court of Appeals for the First Circuit, 1980–1994.

Supreme Court Service: Nominated as associate justice of the U.S. Supreme Court by President Bill Clinton May 17, 1994; confirmed, 87–9, July 29, 1994.

When President Bill Clinton introduced Stephen G. Breyer, his second Supreme Court nominee, at a White House ceremony on May 16, 1994, he

described the federal appeals court judge as a "consensus-builder." The reaction to the nomination proved his point. Senators from both parties quickly endorsed Breyer. The only vocal dissents came from a few liberals and consumer advocates, who said Breyer was too probusiness.

Breyer, chosen to replace the retiring liberal justice Harry A. Blackmun, won a reputation as a centrist in fourteen years on the federal appeals court in Boston and two earlier stints as a staff member for the Senate Judiciary Committee. Breyer's work crossed ideological lines. He played a critical role in enacting airline deregulation in the 1970s and writing federal sentencing guidelines in the 1980s.

Born in 1938 to a politically active family in San Francisco, Breyer earned degrees from Stanford University and Harvard Law School. He clerked for Supreme Court Justice Arthur J. Goldberg and helped draft Goldberg's influential opinion in the 1965 case establishing the right of married couples to use contraceptives. Afterward he served two years in the Justice Department's antitrust division and then took a teaching position at Harvard Law School in 1967.

Breyer took leave from Harvard to serve as an assistant prosecutor in the Watergate investigation in 1973, special counsel to the Judiciary Committee's Administrative Practices Subcommittee from 1974 to 1975, and the full committee's chief counsel from 1979 to 1980. He worked for Sen. Edward Kennedy, D-Mass., but also had good relationships with Republican committee members. His ties to senators paid off when President Jimmy Carter nominated him for the federal appeals court in November 1980. Even though Ronald Reagan had been elected president, GOP senators allowed a vote on Breyer's nomination.

As a judge, Breyer was regarded as scholarly, judicious, and open-minded, with generally conservative views on economic issues and more liberal views on social questions. He wrote two books on regulatory reform that criticized economic regulations as anticompetitive and questioned priorities in some environmental and health rulemaking. He also served as a member of the newly created United States Sentencing Commission from 1985 to 1989. Later he defended the commission's guidelines against criticism from judges and others who viewed them as overly restrictive.

President Clinton interviewed Breyer before his first Supreme Court appointment in 1993 but chose Ruth Bader Ginsburg instead. He picked Breyer in 1994 after Senate Majority Leader George Mitchell took himself out of consideration and problems developed with two other leading candidates.

In his confirmation hearings before the Senate Judiciary Committee, Breyer defused two potential controversies by saying that he accepted Supreme Court precedents upholding abortion rights and capital punishment. The only contentious issue in the confirmation process concerned Breyer's investment in the British insurance syndicate Lloyd's of London. Some senators said Breyer should have recused himself from several environmental pollution cases because of the investment. Breyer told the committee that the cases could not have affected his holdings but also promised to get out of Lloyd's as soon as possible. The panel went on to recommend the nomination unanimously.

One Republican senator, Indiana's Richard Lugar, raised the Lloyd's issue during debate, but Breyer was strongly supported by senators from both parties. The Senate voted to confirm Breyer 87–9. Breyer disposed of his investment in Lloyd's shortly after taking office.

Breyer has compiled a moderately liberal record on the Court. He dissented from several conservative rulings on race and religion and wrote the dissenting opinion for the four liberal justices in a decision that struck down a federal law prohibiting the possession of firearms near schools. But he had a more conservative record on criminal law issues and joined the Court's 1995 opinion permitting random drug testing of high school athletes.

Breyer joined Ginsburg as the Court's second Jewish justice. The Court had two Jewish members only once before, in the 1930s when Louis Brandeis and Benjamin Cardozo served together for six years.

Glossary of Legal Terms

Accessory. In criminal law, a person not present at the commission of an offense who commands, advises, instigates, or conceals the offense.

Acquittal. A person is acquitted when a jury returns a verdict of not guilty. A person also may be acquitted when a judge determines that insufficient evidence exists to convict him or that a violation of due process precludes a fair trial.

Adjudicate. To determine finally by the exercise of judicial authority, to decide a case.

Affidavit. A voluntary written statement of facts or charges affirmed under oath.

A fortiori. With stronger force, with more reason.

Amicus curiae. Friend of the court; a person, not a party to litigation, who volunteers or is invited by the court to give his or her views on a case.

Appeal. A legal proceeding to ask a higher court to review or modify a lower court decision. In a civil case, either the plaintiff or the defendant can appeal an adverse ruling. In criminal cases a defendant can appeal a conviction, but the Double Jeopardy Clause prevents the government from appealing an acquittal. In Supreme Court practice an appeal is a case that falls within the Court's mandatory jurisdiction as opposed to a case that the Court agrees to review under the discretionary writ of certiorari. With the virtual elimination of the Court's mandatory jurisdiction in 1988, the Court now hears very few true appeals, but petitions for certiorari are often referred to imprecisely as appeals.

Appellant. The party who appeals a lower court decision to a higher court.

Appellee. One who has an interest in upholding the decision of a lower court and is compelled to respond when the case is appealed to a higher court by an appellant.

Arraignment. The formal process of charging a person with a crime, reading that person the charge, asking whether he or she pleads guilty or not guilty, and entering the plea.

Attainder, Bill of. A legislative act pronouncing a particular individual guilty of a crime without trial or conviction and imposing a sentence.

Bail. The security, usually money, given as assurance of a prisoner's due appearance at a designated time and place (as in court) to procure in the interim the prisoner's release from jail.

Bailiff. A minor officer of a court, usually serving as an usher or a messenger.

Brief. A document prepared by counsel to serve as the basis for an argument in court, setting out the facts of and the legal arguments in support of the case.

Burden of proof. The need or duty of affirmatively providing a fact or facts that are disputed.

Case law. The law as defined by previously decided cases, distinct from statutes and other sources of law.

Cause. A case, suit, litigation, or action, civil or criminal.

Certiorari, Writ of. A writ issued from the Supreme Court, at its discretion, to order a lower court to prepare the record of a case and send it to the Supreme Court for review.

Civil law. Body of law dealing with the private rights of individuals, as distinguished from criminal law.

Class action. A lawsuit brought by one person or group on behalf of all persons similarly situated.

Code. A collection of laws, arranged systematically.

Comity. Courtesy, respect; usually used in the legal sense to refer to the proper relationship between state and federal courts.

Common law. Collection of principles and rules of action, particularly from unwritten English law, that derive their authority from longstanding usage and custom or from courts recognizing and enforcing these customs. Sometimes used synonymously with case law.

Consent decree. A court-sanctioned agreement settling a legal dispute and entered into by the consent of the parties.

Contempt (civil and criminal). Civil contempt arises from a failure to follow a court order for the benefit of another party. Criminal contempt occurs when a person willfully exhibits disrespect for the court or obstructs the administration of justice.

Conviction. Final judgment or sentence that the defendant is guilty as charged.

Criminal law. The branch of law that deals with the enforcement of laws and the punishment of persons who, by breaking laws, commit crimes.

Declaratory judgment. A court pronouncement declaring a legal right or interpretation but not ordering a specific action.

De facto. In fact, in reality.

Defendant. In a civil action, the party denying or defending itself against charges brought by a plaintiff. In a criminal action, the person indicted for commission of an offense.

De jure. As a result of law or official action.

De novo. Anew; afresh; a second time.

Deposition. Oral testimony from a witness taken out of court in response to written or oral questions, committed to writing, and intended to be used in the preparation of a case.

Dicta. *See* Obiter dictum.

Dismissal. Order disposing of a case without a trial.

Docket. A calendar prepared by the clerks of the court listing the cases set to be tried.

Due process. Fair and regular procedure. The Fifth and Fourteenth amendments guarantee persons that they will not be deprived of life, liberty, or property by the government until fair and usual procedures have been followed.

Error, Writ of. A writ issued from an appeals court to a lower court requiring it to send to the appeals court the record of a case in which it has entered a final judgment and which the appeals court will review for error.

Ex parte. Only from, or on, one side. Application to a court for some ruling or action on behalf of only one party.

Ex post facto. After the fact; an ex post facto law makes an action a crime after it already has been committed, or otherwise changes the legal consequences of some past action.

Ex rel. Upon information from; the term is usually used to describe legal proceedings begun by an official in the name of the state but at the instigation of, and with information from, a private individual interested in the matter.

Grand jury. Group of twelve to twenty-three persons impanelled to hear, in private, evidence presented by the state against an individual or persons accused of a criminal act and to issue indictments when a majority of the jurors find probable cause to believe that the accused has committed a crime. Called a "grand" jury because it comprises a greater number of persons than a "petit" jury.

Grand jury report. A public report, often called "presentments," released by a grand jury after an investigation into activities of public officials that fall short of criminal actions.

Guilty. A word used by a defendant in entering a plea or by a jury in returning a verdict, indicating that the defendant is legally responsible as charged for a crime or other wrongdoing.

Habeas corpus. Literally, "you have the body"; a writ issued to inquire whether a person is lawfully imprisoned or detained. The writ demands that the persons holding the prisoner justify the detention or release the prisoner.

Immunity. A grant of exemption from prosecution in return for evidence or testimony.

In camera. In chambers. Refers to court hearings in private without spectators.

In forma pauperis. In the manner of a pauper, without liability for court costs.

In personam. Done or directed against a particular person.

In re. In the affair of, concerning. Frequent title of judicial proceedings in which there are no adversaries but instead where the matter itself—such as a bankrupt's estate—requires judicial action.

In rem. Done or directed against the thing, not the person.

Indictment. A formal written statement, based on evidence presented by the prosecutor, from a grand jury. Decided by a majority vote, an indictment charges one or more persons with specified offenses.

Information. A written set of accusations, similar to an indictment, but filed directly by a prosecutor.

Injunction. A court order prohibiting the person to whom it is directed from performing a particular act.

Interlocutory decree. A provisional decision of the court before completion of a legal action that temporarily settles an intervening matter.

Judgment. Official decision of a court based on the rights and claims of the parties to a case that was submitted for determination.

Juries. *See* Grand jury; Petit jury.

Jurisdiction. The power of a court to hear a case in question, which exists when the proper parties are present and when the point to be decided is within the issues authorized to be handled by the particular court.

Magistrate. A judicial officer having jurisdiction to try minor criminal cases and conduct preliminary examinations of persons charged with serious crimes.

Majority opinion. An opinion joined by a majority of the justices explaining the legal basis for the Court's decision and regarded as binding precedent for future cases.

Mandamus. "We command." An order issued from a superior court directing a lower court or other authority to perform a particular act.

Moot. Unsettled, undecided. A moot question also is one that no longer is material; a moot case is one that has become hypothetical.

Motion. Written or oral application to a court or a judge to obtain a rule or an order.

Nolo contendere. "I will not contest it." A plea entered by a defendant at the discretion of the judge with the same legal effect as a plea of guilty, but it may not be cited in other proceedings as an admission of guilt.

Obiter dictum. Statements by a judge or justice expressing an opinion and included with, but not essential to, an opinion resolving a case before the court. Dicta are not necessarily binding in future cases.

Parole. A conditional release from imprisonment under conditions that, if the prisoner abides by the law and other restrictions that may be imposed, the prisoner will not have to serve the remainder of the sentence.

Per curiam. "By the court." An unsigned opinion of the court, or an opinion written by the whole court.

Petit jury. A trial jury, originally a panel of twelve persons who tried to reach a unanimous verdict on questions of fact in criminal and civil proceedings. Since 1970 the Supreme Court has upheld the legality of state juries with fewer than twelve persons. Fewer persons serve on a "petit" jury than on a "grand" jury.

Petitioner. One who files a petition with a court seeking action or relief, including a plaintiff or an appellant. But a petitioner also is a person who files for other court action where charges are not necessarily made; for example, a party may petition the court for an order requiring another person or party to produce documents. The opposite party is called the respondent.

   When a writ of certiorari is granted by the Supreme Court, the parties to the case are called petitioner and respondent in contrast to the appellant and appellee terms used in an appeal.

Plaintiff. A party who brings a civil action or sues to obtain a remedy for injury to his or her rights. The party against whom action is brought is termed the defendant.

Plea bargaining. Negotiations between a prosecutor and the defendant aimed at exchanging a plea of guilty from the defendant for concessions by the prosecutor, such as reduction of the charges or a request for leniency.

Pleas. *See* Guilty; Nolo contendere.

Plurality opinion. An opinion supported by the largest number of justices but less than a majority. A plurality opinion typically is not regarded as establishing a binding precedent for future cases.

Precedent. A judicial decision that may be used as a basis for ruling on subsequent similar cases.

Presentment. *See* Grand jury report.

Prima facie. At first sight; referring to a fact or other evidence presumably sufficient to establish a defense or a claim unless otherwise contradicted.

Probation. Process under which a person convicted of an offense, usually a first offense, receives a suspended sentence and is given freedom, usually under the guardianship of a probation officer.

Quash. To overthrow, annul, or vacate; as to quash a subpoena.

Recognizance. An obligation entered into before a court or magistrate requiring the performance of a specified act—usually to appear in court at a later date. It is an alternative to bail for pretrial release.

Remand. To send back. When a decision is remanded, it is sent back by a higher court to the court from which it came for further action.

Respondent. One who is compelled to answer the claims or questions posed in court by a petitioner. A defendant and an appellee may be called respondents, but the term also includes those parties who answer in court during actions where charges are not necessarily brought or where the Supreme Court has granted a writ of certiorari.

Seriatim. Separately, individually, one by one.

Stare decisis. "Let the decision stand." The principle of adherence to settled cases, the doctrine that principles of law established in earlier judicial decisions should be accepted as authoritative in similar subsequent cases.

Statute. A written law enacted by a legislature. A collection of statutes for a particular governmental division is called a code.

Stay. To halt or suspend further judicial proceedings.

Subpoena. An order to present oneself before a grand jury, court, or legislative hearing.

Subpoena duces tecum. An order to produce specified documents or papers.

Tort. An injury or wrong to the person or property of another.

Transactional immunity. Protects a witness from prosecution for any offense mentioned in or related to his or her testimony, regardless of independent evidence against the witness.

Use immunity. Protects a witness from the use of his or her testimony against the witness in prosecution.

Vacate. To make void, annul, or rescind.

Writ. A written court order commanding the designated recipient to perform or not perform specified acts.

United States Constitution

We the People of the United States, in Order to form a more perfect Union, establish Justice, insure domestic Tranquility, provide for the common defence, promote the general Welfare, and secure the Blessings of Liberty to ourselves and our Posterity, do ordain and establish this Constitution for the United States of America.

Article I

Section 1. All legislative Powers herein granted shall be vested in a Congress of the United States, which shall consist of a Senate and House of Representatives.

Section 2. The House of Representatives shall be composed of Members chosen every second Year by the People of the several States, and the Electors in each State shall have the Qualifications requisite for Electors of the most numerous Branch of the State Legislature.

No Person shall be a Representative who shall not have attained to the age of twenty five Years, and been seven Years a Citizen of the United States, and who shall not, when elected, be an Inhabitant of that State in which he shall be chosen.

[Representatives and direct Taxes shall be apportioned among the several States which may be included within this Union, according to their respective Numbers, which shall be determined by adding to the whole Number of free Persons, including those bound to Service for a Term of Years, and excluding Indians not taxed, three fifths of all other Persons.][1] The actual Enumeration shall be made within three Years after the first Meeting of the Congress of the United States, and within every subsequent Term of ten Years, in such Manner as they shall by Law direct. The Number of Representatives shall not exceed one for every thirty Thousand, but each State shall have at Least one Representative; and until such enumeration shall be made, the State of New Hampshire shall be entitled to chuse three, Massachusetts eight, Rhode-Island and Providence Plantations one, Connecticut five, New-York six, New Jersey four, Pennsylvania eight, Delaware one, Maryland six, Virginia ten, North Carolina five, South Carolina five, and Georgia three.

When vacancies happen in the Representation from any State, the Executive Authority thereof shall issue Writs of Election to fill such Vacancies.

The House of Representatives shall chuse their Speaker and other Officers; and shall have the sole Power of Impeachment.

Section 3. The Senate of the United States shall be composed of two Senators from each State, [chosen by the Legislature thereof,][2] for six Years; and each Senator shall have one Vote.

Immediately after they shall be assembled in Consequence of the first Election, they shall be divided as equally as may be into three Classes. The Seats of the Senators of the first Class shall be vacated at the Expiration of the second Year, of the second Class at the Expiration of the fourth Year, and of the third Class at the Expiration of the sixth Year, so that one third may be chosen every second Year; [and if Vacancies happen by Resignation, or otherwise, during the Recess of the Legislature of any State, the Executive thereof may make temporary Appointments until the next Meeting of the Legislature, which shall then fill such Vacancies.][3]

No Person shall be a Senator who shall not have attained to the Age of thirty Years, and been nine Years a Citizen of the United States, and who shall not, when elected, be an Inhabitant of that State for which he shall be chosen.

The Vice President of the United States shall be President of the Senate, but shall have no Vote, unless they be equally divided.

The Senate shall chuse their other Officers, and also a President pro tempore, in the Absence of the Vice President, or when he shall exercise the Office of President of the United States.

The Senate shall have the sole Power to try all Impeachments. When sitting for that Purpose, they shall be on Oath or Affirmation. When the President of the United States is tried, the Chief Justice shall preside: And no Person shall be convicted without the Concurrence of two thirds of the Members present.

Judgment in Cases of Impeachment shall not extend further than to removal from Office, and disqualification to hold and enjoy any Office of honor, Trust or Profit under the United States: but the Party convicted shall nevertheless be liable and subject to Indictment, Trial, Judgment and Punishment, according to Law.

Section 4. The Times, Places and Manner of holding Elections for Senators and Representatives, shall be prescribed in each State by the Legislature thereof; but the Congress may at any time by Law make or alter such Regulations, except as to the Places of chusing Senators.

The Congress shall assemble at least once in every Year, and such Meeting shall [be on the first Monday in December],[4] unless they shall by Law appoint a different Day.

Section 5. Each House shall be the Judge of the Elections, Returns and Qualifications of its own Members, and a Majority of each shall constitute a Quorum to do Business; but a smaller Number may adjourn from day to day, and may be authorized to compel the Attendance of absent Members, in such Manner, and under such Penalties as each House may provide.

Each House may determine the Rules of its Proceedings, punish its Members for disorderly Behaviour, and, with the Concurrence of two thirds, expel a Member.

Each House shall keep a Journal of its Proceedings, and from time to time publish the same, excepting such Parts as may in their Judgment require Secrecy; and the Yeas and Nays of the Members of either House on any question shall, at the Desire of one fifth of those Present, be entered on the Journal.

Neither House, during the Session of Congress, shall, without the Consent of the other, adjourn for more than three days, nor to any other Place than that in which the two Houses shall be sitting.

Section 6. The Senators and Representatives shall receive a Compensation for their Services, to be ascertained by Law, and paid out of the Treasury of the United States. They shall in all Cases, except Treason, Felony and Breach of the Peace, be privileged from Arrest during their Attendance at the Session of their respective

Houses, and in going to and returning from the same; and for any Speech or Debate in either House, they shall not be questioned in any other Place.

No Senator or Representative shall, during the Time for which he was elected, be appointed to any civil Office under the Authority of the United States, which shall have been created, or the Emoluments whereof shall have been encreased during such time; and no Person holding any Office under the United States, shall be a Member of either House during his Continuance in Office.

Section 7. All Bills for raising Revenue shall originate in the House of Representatives; but the Senate may propose or concur with Amendments as on other Bills.

Every Bill which shall have passed the House of Representatives and the Senate, shall, before it become a Law, be presented to the President of the United States; If he approve he shall sign it, but if not he shall return it, with his Objections to that House in which it shall have originated, who shall enter the Objections at large on their Journal, and proceed to reconsider it. If after such Reconsideration two thirds of that House shall agree to pass the Bill, it shall be sent, together with the Objections, to the other House, by which it shall likewise be reconsidered, and if approved by two thirds of that House, it shall become a Law. But in all such Cases the Votes of both Houses shall be determined by yeas and Nays, and the Names of the Persons voting for and against the Bill shall be entered on the Journal of each House respectively. If any Bill shall not be returned by the President within ten Days (Sundays excepted) after it shall have been presented to him, the Same shall be a Law, in like Manner as if he had signed it, unless the Congress by their Adjournment prevent its Return, in which Case it shall not be a Law.

Every Order, Resolution, or Vote to which the Concurrence of the Senate and House of Representatives may be necessary (except on a question of Adjournment) shall be presented to the President of the United States; and before the Same shall take Effect, shall be approved by him, or being disapproved by him, shall be repassed by two thirds of the Senate and House of Representatives, according to the Rules and Limitations prescribed in the Case of a Bill.

Section 8. The Congress shall have Power To lay and collect Taxes, Duties, Imposts and Excises, to pay the Debts and provide for the common Defence and general Welfare of the United States; but all Duties, Imposts and Excises shall be uniform throughout the United States;

To borrow Money on the credit of the United States;

To regulate Commerce with foreign Nations, and among the several States, and with the Indian Tribes;

To establish an uniform Rule of Naturalization, and uniform Laws on the subject of Bankruptcies throughout the United States;

To coin Money, regulate the Value thereof, and of foreign Coin, and fix the Standard of Weights and Measures;

To provide for the Punishment of counterfeiting the Securities and current Coin of the United States;

To establish Post Offices and post Roads;

To promote the Progress of Science and useful Arts, by securing for limited Times to Authors and Inventors the exclusive Right to their respective Writings and Discoveries;

To constitute Tribunals inferior to the supreme Court;

To define and punish Piracies and Felonies committed on the high Seas, and Offences against the Law of Nations;

To declare War, grant Letters of Marque and Reprisal, and make Rules concerning Captures on Land and Water;

To raise and support Armies, but no Appropriation of Money to that Use shall be for a longer Term than two Years;

To provide and maintain a Navy;

To make Rules for the Government and Regulation of the land and naval Forces;

To provide for calling forth the Militia to execute the Laws of the Union, suppress Insurrections and repel Invasions;

To provide for organizing, arming, and disciplining, the Militia, and for governing such Part of them as may be employed in the Service of the United States, reserving to the States respectively, the Appointment of the Officers, and the Authority of training the Militia according to the discipline prescribed by Congress;

To exercise exclusive Legislation in all Cases whatsoever, over such District (not exceeding ten Miles square) as may, by Cession of particular States, and the Acceptance of Congress, become the Seat of the Government of the United States, and to exercise like Authority over all Places purchased by the Consent of the Legislature of the State in which the Same shall be, for the Erection of Forts, Magazines, Arsenals, dock-Yards, and other needful Buildings; — And

To make all Laws which shall be necessary and proper for carrying into Execution the foregoing Powers, and all other Powers vested by this Constitution in the Government of the United States, or in any Department or Officer thereof.

Section 9. The Migration or Importation of such Persons as any of the States now existing shall think proper to admit, shall not be prohibited by the Congress prior to the Year one thousand eight hundred and eight, but a Tax or duty may be imposed on such Importation, not exceeding ten dollars for each Person.

The Privilege of the Writ of Habeas Corpus shall not be suspended, unless when in Cases of Rebellion or Invasion the public Safety may require it.

No Bill of Attainder or ex post facto Law shall be passed.

No Capitation, or other direct, Tax shall be laid, unless in Proportion to the Census or Enumeration herein before directed to be taken.[5]

No Tax or Duty shall be laid on Articles exported from any State.

No Preference shall be given by any Regulation of Commerce or Revenue to the Ports of one State over those of another; nor shall Vessels bound to, or from, one State, be obliged to enter, clear, or pay Duties in another.

No Money shall be drawn from the Treasury, but in Consequence of Appropriations made by Law; and a regular Statement and Account of the Receipts and Expenditures of all public Money shall be published from time to time.

No Title of Nobility shall be granted by the United States: And no Person holding any Office of Profit or Trust under them, shall, without the Consent of the Congress, accept of any present, Emolument, Office, or Title, of any kind whatever, from any King, Prince, or foreign State.

Section 10. No State shall enter into any Treaty, Alliance, or Confederation; grant Letters of Marque and Reprisal; coin Money; emit Bills of Credit; make any

Thing but gold and silver Coin a Tender in Payment of Debts; pass any Bill of Attainder, ex post facto Law, or Law impairing the Obligation of Contracts, or grant any Title of Nobility.

No State shall, without the Consent of the Congress, lay any Imposts or Duties on Imports or Exports, except what may be absolutely necessary for executing it's inspection Laws: and the net Produce of all Duties and Imposts, laid by any State on Imports or Exports, shall be for the Use of the Treasury of the United States; and all such Laws shall be subject to the Revision and Controul of the Congress.

No State shall, without the Consent of Congress, lay any Duty of Tonnage, keep Troops, or Ships of War in time of Peace, enter into any Agreement or Compact with another State, or with a foreign Power, or engage in War, unless actually invaded, or in such imminent Danger as will not admit of delay.

Article II

Section 1. The executive Power shall be vested in a President of the United States of America. He shall hold his Office during the Term of four Years, and, together with the Vice President, chosen for the same Term, be elected, as follows

Each State shall appoint, in such Manner as the Legislature thereof may direct, a Number of Electors, equal to the whole Number of Senators and Representatives to which the State may be entitled in the Congress: but no Senator or Representative, or Person holding an Office of Trust or Profit under the United States, shall be appointed an Elector.

[The Electors shall meet in their respective States, and vote by Ballot for two Persons, of whom one at least shall not be an Inhabitant of the same State with themselves. And they shall make a List of all the Persons voted for, and of the Number of Votes for each; which List they shall sign and certify, and transmit sealed to the Seat of the Government of the United States, directed to the President of the Senate. The President of the Senate shall, in the Presence of the Senate and House of Representatives, open all the Certificates, and the Votes shall then be counted. The Person having the greatest Number of Votes shall be the President, if such Number be a Majority of the whole Number of Electors appointed; and if there be more than one who have such Majority, and have an equal Number of Votes, then the House of Representatives shall immediately chuse by Ballot one of them for President; and if no Person have a Majority, then from the five highest on the list the said House shall in like Manner chuse the President. But in chusing the President, the Votes shall be taken by States, the Representation from each State having one Vote; A quorum for this Purpose shall consist of a Member or Members from two thirds of the States, and a Majority of all the States shall be necessary to a Choice. In every Case, after the Choice of the President, the Person having the greatest Number of Votes of the Electors shall be the Vice President. But if there should remain two or more who have equal Votes, the Senate shall chuse from them by Ballot the Vice President.][6]

The Congress may determine the Time of chusing the Electors, and the Day on which they shall give their Votes; which Day shall be the same throughout the United States.

No Person except a natural born Citizen, or a Citizen of the United States, at the time of the Adoption of this Constitution, shall be eligible to the Office of President; neither shall any Person be eligible to that Office who shall not have attained to the Age of thirty five Years, and been fourteen Years a Resident within the United States.

In Case of the Removal of the President from Office, or of his Death, Resignation, or Inability to discharge the Powers and Duties of the said Office,[7] the Same shall devolve on the Vice President, and the Congress may by Law provide for the Case of Removal, Death, Resignation or Inability, both of the President and Vice President, declaring what Officer shall then act as President, and such Officer shall act accordingly, until the Disability be removed, or a President shall be elected.

The President shall, at stated Times, receive for his Services, a Compensation, which shall neither be encreased nor diminished during the Period for which he shall have been elected, and he shall not receive within that Period any other Emolument from the United States, or any of them.

Before he enter on the Execution of his Office, he shall take the following Oath or Affirmation:—"I do solemnly swear (or affirm) that I will faithfully execute the Office of President of the United States, and will to the best of my Ability, preserve, protect and defend the Constitution of the United States."

Section 2. The President shall be Commander in Chief of the Army and Navy of the United States, and of the Militia of the several States, when called into the actual Service of the United States; he may require the Opinion, in writing, of the principal Officer in each of the executive Departments, upon any Subject relating to the Duties of their respective Offices, and he shall have Power to grant Reprieves and Pardons for Offences against the United States, except in Cases of Impeachment.

He shall have Power, by and with the Advice and Consent of the Senate, to make Treaties, provided two thirds of the Senators present concur; and he shall nominate, and by and with the Advice and Consent of the Senate, shall appoint Ambassadors, other public Ministers and Consuls, Judges of the supreme Court, and all other Officers of the United States, whose Appointments are not herein otherwise provided for, and which shall be established by Law: but the Congress may by Law vest the Appointment of such inferior Officers, as they think proper, in the President alone, in the Courts of Law, or in the Heads of Departments.

The President shall have Power to fill up all Vacancies that may happen during the Recess of the Senate, by granting Commissions which shall expire at the End of their next Session.

Section 3. He shall from time to time give to the Congress Information of the State of the Union, and recommend to their Consideration such Measures as he shall judge necessary and expedient; he may, on extraordinary Occasions, convene both Houses, or either of them, and in Case of Disagreement between them, with Respect to the Time of Adjournment, he may adjourn them to such Time as he shall think proper; he shall receive Ambassadors and other public Ministers; he shall take Care that the Laws be faithfully executed, and shall Commission all the Officers of the United States.

Section 4. The President, Vice President and all civil Officers of the United States, shall be removed from Office on Impeachment for, and Conviction of, Treason, Bribery, or other high Crimes and Misdemeanors.

Article III

Section 1. The judicial Power of the United States, shall be vested in one supreme Court, and in such inferior Courts as the Congress may from time to time ordain and establish. The Judges, both of the supreme and inferior Courts, shall hold their Offices during good Behaviour, and shall, at stated Times, receive for their Services, a Compensation, which shall not be diminished during their Continuance in Office.

Section 2. The judicial Power shall extend to all Cases, in Law and Equity, arising under this Constitution, the Laws of the United States, and Treaties made, or which shall be made, under their Authority; — to all Cases affecting Ambassadors, other public Ministers and Consuls; — to all Cases of admiralty and maritime Jurisdiction; — to Controversies to which the United States shall be a Party; — to Controversies between two or more States; — between a State and Citizens of another State;[8] — between Citizens of different States; — between Citizens of the same State claiming Lands under Grants of different States, and between a State, or the Citizens thereof, and foreign States, Citizens or Subjects.[8]

In all Cases affecting Ambassadors, other public Ministers and Consuls, and those in which a State shall be Party, the supreme Court shall have original Jurisdiction. In all the other Cases before mentioned, the supreme Court shall have appellate Jurisdiction, both as to Law and Fact, with such Exceptions, and under such Regulations as the Congress shall make.

The Trial of all Crimes, except in Cases of Impeachment, shall be by Jury; and such Trial shall be held in the State where the said Crimes shall have been committed; but when not committed within any State, the Trial shall be at such Place or Places as the Congress may by Law have directed.

Section 3. Treason against the United States, shall consist only in levying War against them, or in adhering to their Enemies, giving them Aid and Comfort. No Person shall be convicted of Treason unless on the Testimony of two Witnesses to the same overt Act, or on Confession in open Court.

The Congress shall have Power to declare the Punishment of Treason, but no Attainder of Treason shall work Corruption of Blood, or Forfeiture except during the Life of the Person attainted.

Article IV

Section 1. Full Faith and Credit shall be given in each State to the public Acts, Records, and judicial Proceedings of every other State. And the Congress may by general Laws prescribe the Manner in which such Acts, Records and Proceedings shall be proved, and the Effect thereof.

Section 2. The Citizens of each State shall be entitled to all Privileges and Immunities of Citizens in the several States.

A Person charged in any State with Treason, Felony, or other Crime, who shall flee from Justice, and be found in another State, shall on Demand of the executive Authority of the State from which he fled, be delivered up, to be removed to the State having Jurisdiction of the Crime.

[No Person held to Service or Labour in one State, under the Laws thereof, escaping into another, shall, in Consequence of any Law or Regulation therein, be discharged from such Service or Labour, but shall be delivered up on Claim of the Party to whom such Service or Labour may be due.][9]

Section 3. New States may be admitted by the Congress into this Union; but no new State shall be formed or erected within the Jurisdiction of any other State; nor any State be formed by the Junction of two or more States, or Parts of States, without the Consent of the Legislatures of the States concerned as well as of the Congress.

The Congress shall have Power to dispose of and make all needful Rules and Regulations respecting the Territory or other Property belonging to the United States; and nothing in this Constitution shall be so construed as to Prejudice any Claims of the United States, or of any particular State.

Section 4. The United States shall guarantee to every State in this Union a Republican Form of Government, and shall protect each of them against Invasion; and on Application of the Legislature, or of the Executive (when the Legislature cannot be convened) against domestic Violence.

Article V

The Congress, whenever two thirds of both Houses shall deem it necessary, shall propose Amendments to this Constitution, or, on the Application of the Legislatures of two thirds of the several States, shall call a Convention for proposing Amendments, which, in either Case, shall be valid to all Intents and Purposes, as Part of this Constitution, when ratified by the Legislatures of three fourths of the several States, or by Conventions in three fourths thereof, as the one or the other Mode of Ratification may be proposed by the Congress; Provided [that no Amendment which may be made prior to the Year One thousand eight hundred and eight shall in any Manner affect the first and fourth Clauses in the Ninth Section of the first Article; and][10] that no State, without its Consent, shall be deprived of its equal Suffrage in the Senate.

Article VI

All Debts contracted and Engagements entered into, before the Adoption of this Constitution, shall be as valid against the United States under this Constitution, as under the Confederation.

This Constitution, and the Laws of the United States which shall be made in Pursuance thereof; and all Treaties made, or which shall be made, under the Authority of the United States, shall be the supreme Law of the Land; and the Judges in every State shall be bound thereby, any Thing in the Constitution or Laws of any State to the Contrary notwithstanding.

The Senators and Representatives before mentioned, and the Members of the several State Legislatures, and all executive and judicial Officers, both of the United States and of the several States, shall be bound by Oath or Affirmation, to support this Constitution; but no religious Test shall ever be required as a Qualification to any Office or public Trust under the United States.

Article VII

The Ratification of the Conventions of nine States, shall be sufficient for the Establishment of this Constitution between the States so ratifying the Same.

Done in Convention by the Unanimous Consent of the States present the Seventeenth Day of September in the Year of our Lord one thousand seven hundred and Eighty seven and of the Independence of the United States of America the Twelfth. IN WITNESS whereof We have hereunto subscribed our Names,

George Washington,
President and
deputy from Virginia.

New Hampshire: John Langdon,
Nicholas Gilman.

Massachusetts: Nathaniel Gorham,
Rufus King.

Connecticut: William Samuel Johnson,
Roger Sherman.

New York: Alexander Hamilton.

New Jersey: William Livingston,
David Brearley,
William Paterson,
Jonathan Dayton.

Pennsylvania: Benjamin Franklin,
Thomas Mifflin,
Robert Morris,
George Clymer,
Thomas FitzSimons,
Jared Ingersoll,
James Wilson,
Gouverneur Morris.

Delaware: George Read,
Gunning Bedford Jr.,
John Dickinson,
Richard Bassett,
Jacob Broom.

Maryland: James McHenry,
Daniel of St. Thomas Jenifer,
Daniel Carroll.

Virginia:	John Blair, James Madison Jr.
North Carolina:	William Blount, Richard Dobbs Spaight, Hugh Williamson.
South Carolina:	John Rutledge, Charles Cotesworth Pinckney, Charles Pinckney, Pierce Butler.
Georgia:	William Few, Abraham Baldwin.

[The language of the original Constitution, not including the Amendments, was adopted by a convention of the states on September 17, 1787, and was subsequently ratified by the states on the following dates: Delaware, December 7, 1787; Pennsylvania, December 12, 1787; New Jersey, December 18, 1787; Georgia, January 2, 1788; Connecticut, January 9, 1788; Massachusetts, February 6, 1788; Maryland, April 28, 1788; South Carolina, May 23, 1788; New Hampshire, June 21, 1788.

Ratification was completed on June 21, 1788.

The Constitution subsequently was ratified by Virginia, June 25, 1788; New York, July 26, 1788; North Carolina, November 21, 1789; Rhode Island, May 29, 1790; and Vermont, January 10, 1791.]

Amendments

Amendment I

(First ten amendments ratified December 15, 1791.)

Congress shall make no law respecting an establishment of religion, or prohibiting the free exercise thereof; or abridging the freedom of speech, or of the press; or the right of the people peaceably to assemble, and to petition the Government for a redress of grievances.

Amendment II

A well regulated Militia, being necessary to the security of a free State, the right of the people to keep and bear Arms, shall not be infringed.

Amendment III

No Soldier shall, in time of peace be quartered in any house, without the consent of the Owner, nor in time of war, but in a manner to be prescribed by law.

Amendment IV

The right of the people to be secure in their persons, houses, papers, and effects, against unreasonable searches and seizures, shall not be violated, and no Warrants shall issue, but upon probable cause, supported by Oath or affirmation, and particularly describing the place to be searched, and the persons or things to be seized.

Amendment V

No person shall be held to answer for a capital, or otherwise infamous crime, unless on a presentment or indictment of a Grand Jury, except in cases arising in the land or naval forces, or in the Militia, when in actual service in time of War or public danger; nor shall any person be subject for the same offence to be twice put in jeopardy of life or limb; nor shall be compelled in any criminal case to be a witness against himself, nor be deprived of life, liberty, or property, without due process of law; nor shall private property be taken for public use, without just compensation.

Amendment VI

In all criminal prosecutions, the accused shall enjoy the right to a speedy and public trial, by an impartial jury of the State and district wherein the crime shall have been committed, which district shall have been previously ascertained by law, and to be informed of the nature and cause of the accusation; to be confronted with the witnesses against him; to have compulsory process for obtaining witnesses in his favor, and to have the Assistance of Counsel for his defence.

Amendment VII

In Suits at common law, where the value in controversy shall exceed twenty dollars, the right of trial by jury shall be preserved, and no fact tried by a jury, shall be otherwise re-examined in any Court of the United States, than according to the rules of the common law.

Amendment VIII

Excessive bail shall not be required, nor excessive fines imposed, nor cruel and unusual punishments inflicted.

Amendment IX

The enumeration in the Constitution, of certain rights, shall not be construed to deny or disparage others retained by the people.

Amendment X

The powers not delegated to the United States by the Constitution, nor prohibited by it to the States, are reserved to the States respectively, or to the people.

Amendment XI

(Ratified February 7, 1795)

The Judicial power of the United States shall not be construed to extend to any suit in law or equity, commenced or prosecuted against one of the United States by Citizens of another State, or by Citizens or Subjects of any Foreign State.

Amendment XII

(Ratified June 15, 1804)

The Electors shall meet in their respective states and vote by ballot for President and Vice-President, one of whom, at least, shall not be an inhabitant of the same state with themselves; they shall name in their ballots the person voted for as President, and in distinct ballots the person voted for as Vice-President, and they shall make distinct lists of all persons voted for as President, and of all persons voted for as Vice-President, and of the number of votes for each, which lists they shall sign and certify, and transmit sealed to the seat of the government of the United States, directed to the President of the Senate; — The President of the Senate shall, in the presence of the Senate and House of Representatives, open all the certificates and the votes shall then be counted; — The person having the greatest number of votes for President, shall be the President, if such number be a majority of the whole number of Electors appointed; and if no person have such majority, then from the persons having the highest numbers not exceeding three on the list of those voted for as President, the House of Representatives shall choose immediately, by ballot, the President. But in choosing the President, the votes shall be taken by states, the representation from each state having one vote; a quorum for this purpose shall consist of a member or members from two-thirds of the states, and a majority of all the states shall be necessary to a choice. [And if the House of Representatives shall not choose a President whenever the right of choice shall devolve upon them, before the fourth day of March next following, then the Vice-President shall act as President, as in the case of the death or other constitutional disability of the President. —][11] The person having the greatest number of votes as Vice-President, shall be the Vice-President, if such number be a majority of the whole number of Electors appointed, and if no person have a majority, then from the two highest numbers on the list, the Senate shall choose the Vice-President; a quorum for the purpose shall consist of two-thirds of the whole number of Senators, and a majority of the whole number shall be necessary to a choice. But no person constitutionally ineligible to the office of President shall be eligible to that of Vice-President of the United States.

Amendment XIII

(Ratified December 6, 1865)

Section 1. Neither slavery nor involuntary servitude, except as a punishment for crime whereof the party shall have been duly convicted, shall exist within the United States, or any place subject to their jurisdiction.

Section 2. Congress shall have power to enforce this article by appropriate legislation.

Amendment XIV

(Ratified July 9, 1868)

Section 1. All persons born or naturalized in the United States, and subject to the jurisdiction thereof, are citizens of the United States and of the State wherein they reside. No State shall make or enforce any law which shall abridge the privileges or immunities of citizens of the United States; nor shall any State deprive any person of life, liberty, or property, without due process of law; nor deny to any person within its jurisdiction the equal protection of the laws.

Section 2. Representatives shall be apportioned among the several States according to their respective numbers, counting the whole number of persons in each State, excluding Indians not taxed. But when the right to vote at any election for the choice of electors for President and Vice President of the United States, Representatives in Congress, the Executive and Judicial officers of a State, or the members of the Legislature thereof, is denied to any of the male inhabitants of such State, being twenty-one years of age,[12] and citizens of the United States, or in any way abridged, except for participation in rebellion, or other crime, the basis of representation therein shall be reduced in the proportion which the number of such male citizens shall bear to the whole number of male citizens twenty-one years of age in such State.

Section 3. No person shall be a Senator or Representative in Congress, or elector of President and Vice President, or hold any office, civil or military, under the United States, or under any State, who, having previously taken an oath, as a member of Congress, or as an officer of the United States, or as a member of any State legislature, or as an executive or judicial officer of any State, to support the Constitution of the United States, shall have engaged in insurrection or rebellion against the same, or given aid or comfort to the enemies thereof. But Congress may by a vote of two-thirds of each House, remove such disability.

Section 4. The validity of the public debt of the United States, authorized by law, including debts incurred for payment of pensions and bounties for services in suppressing insurrection or rebellion, shall not be questioned. But neither the United States nor any State shall assume or pay any debt or obligation incurred in aid of insurrection or rebellion against the United States, or any claim for the loss or emancipation of any slave; but all such debts, obligations and claims shall be held illegal and void.

Section 5. The Congress shall have power to enforce, by appropriate legislation, the provisions of this article.

Amendment XV

(Ratified February 3, 1870)

Section 1. The right of citizens of the United States to vote shall not be denied or abridged by the United States or by any State on account of race, color, or previous condition of servitude.

Section 2. The Congress shall have power to enforce this article by appropriate legislation.

Amendment XVI

(Ratified February 3, 1913)

The Congress shall have power to lay and collect taxes on incomes, from whatever source derived, without apportionment among the several States, and without regard to any census or enumeration.

Amendment XVII

(Ratified April 8, 1913)

The Senate of the United States shall be composed of two Senators from each State, elected by the people thereof, for six years; and each Senator shall have one vote. The electors in each State shall have the qualifications requisite for electors of the most numerous branch of the State legislatures.

When vacancies happen in the representation of any State in the Senate, the executive authority of such State shall issue writs of election to fill such vacancies: *Provided,* That the legislature of any State may empower the executive thereof to make temporary appointments until the people fill the vacancies by election as the legislature may direct.

This amendment shall not be so construed as to affect the election or term of any Senator chosen before it becomes valid as part of the Constitution.

Amendment XVIII

(Ratified January 16, 1919)[13]

Section 1. After one year from the ratification of this article the manufacture, sale, or transportation of intoxicating liquors within, the importation thereof into, or the exportation thereof from the United States and all territory subject to the jurisdiction thereof for beverage purposes is hereby prohibited.

Section 2. The Congress and the several States shall have concurrent power to enforce this article by appropriate legislation.

Section 3. This article shall be inoperative unless it shall have been ratified as an amendment to the Constitution by the legislatures of the several States, as provided in the Constitution, within seven years from the date of the submission hereof to the States by the Congress.

Amendment XIX

(Ratified August 18, 1920)

The right of citizens of the United States to vote shall not be denied or abridged by the United States or by any State on account of sex.

Congress shall have power to enforce this article by appropriate legislation.

Amendment XX

(Ratified January 23, 1933)

Section 1. The terms of the President and Vice President shall end at noon on the 20th day of January, and the terms of Senators and Representatives at noon on the 3d day of January, of the years in which such terms would have ended if this article had not been ratified; and the terms of their successors shall then begin.

Section 2. The Congress shall assemble at least once in every year, and such meeting shall begin at noon on the 3d day of January, unless they shall by law appoint a different day.

Section 3.[14] If, at the time fixed for the beginning of the term of the President, the President elect shall have died, the Vice President elect shall become President. If a President shall not have been chosen before the time fixed for the beginning of his term, or if the President elect shall have failed to qualify, then the Vice President elect shall act as President until a President shall have qualified; and the Congress may by law provide for the case wherein neither a President elect nor a Vice President elect shall have qualified, declaring who shall then act as President, or the manner in which one who is to act shall be selected, and such person shall act accordingly until a President or Vice President shall have qualified.

Section 4. The Congress may by law provide for the case of the death of any of the persons from whom the House of Representatives may choose a President whenever the right of choice shall have devolved upon them, and for the case of the death of any of the persons from whom the Senate may choose a Vice President whenever the right of choice shall have devolved upon them.

Section 5. Sections 1 and 2 shall take effect on the 15th day of October following the ratification of this article.

Section 6. This article shall be inoperative unless it shall have been ratified as an amendment to the Constitution by the legislatures of three-fourths of the several States within seven years from the date of its submission.

Amendment XXI

(Ratified December 5, 1933)

Section 1. The eighteenth article of amendment to the Constitution of the United States is hereby repealed.

Section 2. The transportation or importation into any State, Territory, or possession of the United States for delivery or use therein of intoxicating liquors, in violation of the laws thereof, is hereby prohibited.

Section 3. This article shall be inoperative unless it shall have been ratified as an amendment to the Constitution by conventions in the several States, as provided in the Constitution, within seven years from the date of the submission hereof to the States by the Congress.

Amendment XXII

(Ratified February 27, 1951)

Section 1. No person shall be elected to the office of the President more than twice, and no person who has held the office of President, or acted as President, for more than two years of a term to which some other person was elected President shall be elected to the office of the President more than once. But this Article shall not apply to any person holding the office of President when this Article was proposed by the Congress, and shall not prevent any person who may be holding the office of President, or acting as President, during the term within which this Article become operative from holding the office of President or acting as President during the remainder of such term.

Section 2. This article shall be inoperative unless it shall have been ratified as an amendment to the Constitution by the legislatures of three-fourths of the several States within seven years from the date of its submission to the States by the Congress.

Amendment XXIII

(Ratified March 29, 1961)

Section 1. The District constituting the seat of Government of the United States shall appoint in such manner as the Congress may direct:
A number of electors of President and Vice President equal to the whole number of Senators and Representatives in Congress to which the District would be entitled if it were a State, but in no event more than the least populous State; they shall be in addition to those appointed by the States, but they shall be considered, for the purposes of the election of President and Vice President, to be electors appointed by a State; and they shall meet in the District and perform such duties as provided by the twelfth article of amendment.

Section 2. The Congress shall have power to enforce this article by appropriate legislation.

Amendment XXIV

(Ratified January 23, 1964)

Section 1. The right of citizens of the United States to vote in any primary or other election for President or Vice President, for electors for President or Vice President, or for Senator or Representative in Congress, shall not be denied or abridged by the United States or any State by reason of failure to pay any poll tax or other tax.

Section 2. The Congress shall have power to enforce this article by appropriate legislation.

Amendment XXV

(Ratified February 10, 1967)

Section 1. In case of the removal of the President from office or of his death or resignation, the Vice President shall become President.

Section 2. Whenever there is a vacancy in the office of the Vice President, the President shall nominate a Vice President who shall take office upon confirmation by a majority vote of both Houses of Congress.

Section 3. Whenever the President transmits to the President pro tempore of the Senate and the Speaker of the House of Representatives his written declaration that he is unable to discharge the powers and duties of his office, and until he transmits to them a written declaration to the contrary, such powers and duties shall be discharged by the Vice President as Acting President.

Section 4. Whenever the Vice President and a majority of either the principal officers of the executive departments or of such other body as Congress may by law provide, transmit to the President pro tempore of the Senate and the Speaker of the House of Representatives their written declaration that the President is unable to discharge the powers and duties of his office, the Vice President shall immediately assume the powers and duties of the office as Acting President.

Thereafter, when the President transmits to the President pro tempore of the Senate and the Speaker of the House of Representatives his written declaration that no inability exists, he shall resume the powers and duties of his office unless the Vice President and a majority of either the principal officers of the executive department or of such other body as Congress may by law provide, transmit within four days to the President pro tempore of the Senate and the Speaker of the House of Representatives their written declaration that the President is unable to discharge the powers and duties of his office. Thereupon Congress shall decide the issue, assembling within forty-eight hours for that purpose if not in session. If the Congress, within twenty-one days after receipt of the latter written declaration, or, if Congress is not in session, within twenty-one days after Congress is required to assemble, determines by two-thirds vote of both Houses that the President is unable to discharge the powers and duties of his office, the Vice President shall continue to discharge the same as Acting President; otherwise, the President shall resume the powers and duties of his office.

Amendment XXVI

(Ratified July 1, 1971)

Section 1. The right of citizens of the United States, who are eighteen years of age or older, to vote shall not be denied or abridged by the United States or by any State on account of age.

Section 2. The Congress shall have power to enforce this article by appropriate legislation.

Amendment XXVII

(Ratified May 7, 1992)

No law varying the compensation for the services of the Senators and Representatives shall take effect, until an election of Representatives shall have intervened.

Notes

1. The part in brackets was by section 2 of the Fourteenth Amendment.
2. The part in brackets was changed by the first paragraph of the Seventeenth Amendment.
3. The part in brackets was changed by the second paragraph of the Seventeenth Amendment.
4. The part in brackets was changed by section 2 of the Twentieth Amendment.
5. The Sixteenth Amendment gave Congress the power to tax incomes.
6. The material in brackets has been superseded by the Twelfth Amendment.
7. This provision has been affected by the Twenty-fifth Amendment.
8. These clauses were affected by the Eleventh Amendment.
9. This paragraph has been superseded by the Thirteenth Amendment.
10. Obsolete.
11. The part in brackets has been superseded by section 3 of the Twentieth Amendment.
12. See the Nineteenth and Twenty-sixth Amendments.
13. This Amendment was repealed by section 1 of the Twenty-first Amendment.
14. See the Twenty-fifth Amendment.

Source: U.S. Congress, House, Committee on the Judiciary, *The Constitution of the United States of America, as Amended,* 100th Cong., 1st sess., 1987, H Doc 100-94.

Index